History of the Italian People

PROCACCI, Giuliano. **History of the Italian people, tr. by A. Paul.** Harper & Row, 1971 (c1970). 394p 78-127832. 10.00

CHOICE JUL./AUG. '71

History, Geography & Travel

Europe

The English title of this book is very misleading, for it is not a history of the Italian people but rather a brief survey, though entertaining and informative, of Italian political history from medieval times to the present. Though recent revisionist political materials are skillfully woven into the text, there is little attention to social structure or to the quantitative analyses of socioeconomic problems which now grace Italian historical journals. This is not a scholarly monograph. It lacks footnotes and bibliography, and the limited index contains only proper names. Except for its more recent date, there is little to distinguish it from J. Trevelyan's *Short history of the Italian people* (4th ed., 1956) or that of H. Hearder and D. Waley's *Short history of Italy from classical times to the present day* (1963). A general college library and public library may find it useful.

History of the Italian People

GIULIANO PROCACCI

PROFESSOR OF MODERN HISTORY
UNIVERSITY OF FLORENCE

TRANSLATED FROM THE ITALIAN BY
ANTHONY PAUL

HARPER & ROW, PUBLISHERS
New York and Evanston

To Sereulla

First Published in France under the title *Histoire d'Italie*

HISTORY OF THE ITALIAN PEOPLE
© 1968 by Librairie Arthème Fayard.
English translation copyright © 1970 by George Weidenfeld
and Nicolson, Ltd. All rights reserved. No part of this
book may be used or reproduced in any manner
whatsoever without written permission except in the case of
brief quotations embodied in critical articles and reviews.
Printed in Great Britain for Harper & Row, Publishers.
For information address Harper & Row, Publishers,
Inc., 49 East 33rd Street, New York, N.Y. 10016.

FIRST U.S. EDITION

LIBRARY OF CONGRESS CATALOG CARD
NUMBER: 78-127832

CONTENTS

CHAPTER

1	The years around 1000	1
2	Commune civilization	26
3	The crises and the vitality of an age of transition	43
4	1450–1550: Greatness and decadence	74
5	1550–1600: Decadence and greatness	115
6	A century of stagnation	152
7	Italy and the Enlightenment	171
8	The age of reform	184
9	The French Revolution and Italy	205
10	Restoration and Romanticism	219
11	The defeats of the Risorgimento	233
12	The victories of the Risorgimento	249
13	A difficult take-off	265
14	Origins and character of Italian capitalism	280
15	The end of century crisis	294
16	The fifteen-year 'Belle Epoque'	308
17	From the war to fascism	330
18	From fascism to the war	347
19	The last decades	365

'Professore,' exclaimed Nando, lowering his head,
'do you love Italy?'

Once again all their faces were around me: Tono,
the old woman, the girls, Cate. Fonso smiled.

'No,' I said quietly, 'not Italy. The Italians.'
(Pavese, *La casa in collina*)

The years around 1000

ITALY'S PLACE IN THE *RESPUBLICA CHRISTIANORUM*

The Papacy and the Empire are the two great back-drops to mediaeval European history. If one becomes over-involved in the drama one's view may be blocked by the greater and lesser characters taking part in it, and one may lose sight of them; but if one looks from a distance and remains aware of the whole action, one is bound to realize that every movement is conditioned by their looming presence. It is impossible to trace the history of any country of Western Christendom in the Middle Ages without having continually to refer to these universal organizations.

This is particularly true of Italy, which was not only, like the other nations, a member of the community of Christian peoples, but also its centre of gravity and its heart. Without Rome, without Italy, the *respublica christianorum* would in fact have ceased to exist.

Gregory the Great, the Pope who launched the conversion of the barbarian West, and the liturgical and organizational reform of the mediaeval Church, was a Roman nobleman who brought into the government of the Church the colonizing, imperialist spirit of the city and class whose son he was; and most of his successors were also Romans. At Rome, on that fateful Christmas night of the year 800, Charlemagne had received the Imperial diadem from the hands of Pope Leo III; from that moment the image of Christian Rome, the city of Peter, fused with that of Imperial Rome, the city of Caesar, to give life to the myth of the Holy Roman Republic. It is true that the Carolingian Empire did not long stay unified, nor did the Papacy retain the prestige it had acquired by its alliance with the undefeated Charlemagne: during the century between the partition of Verdun (843) and the invasion of Italy by Otto I (951), Christian Europe was penned in and ravaged from different directions by the Arabs and the Normans and the raids of the Hungarians. It is a dark period in the histories of both Empire and Papacy. While the Imperial crown was the brief prize of this or that powerful man of the moment, in Rome the various factions of the aristocracy fought ruthlessly among themselves for the Papacy: to this period belongs the macabre episode of the trial of Pope Formosus's corpse.

Even so, the sense of belonging to a single Christian republic, with Rome as its centre and the Emperor, crowned by the Pope, as its temporal head, was always present in the minds of men of learning and power: it provided a stable point of reference in the intellectual Christian universe. In a world where there was no half-way stage between the humble man's love for his birthplace and the universal cosmopolitanism of the clergy and the intellectuals, the myth of Rome, a city doubly universal, still had powerful roots. When the storm of Hungarian invasion and Moslem raids, and the dark times of the most unbridled feudal anarchy, were past, it re-emerged and flourished at the court of Otto III (996–1002), the Saxon Emperor who surrounded himself with learned and pious men, made Rome his own dwelling-place, and during his brief reign pursued the mirage of a renewed Empire.

The ideal of a Church that would perform her pastoral mission on a universal scale was however central to the reforming activity of the eleventh-century Popes. They considerably extended and strengthened the Papacy's international prestige. It was with the benediction of Rome and under the banner of the reformed Church's new Imperialism that the Norman conquest of England and of southern Italy, the 'reconquest' of Spain, not to mention the great collective enterprise of the Crusades, all took place. Yet as the Church became universal, it did not cease to be Roman. It is true that with reform the Papacy was no longer the almost exclusive prerogative of the great Roman families: during the eleventh and twelfth centuries the throne was occupied by Germans, Burgundians, Italians from the various provinces, and even an Englishman. However, though by the Lateran Synod of 1059 the election of the Pope was entrusted to the cardinals and thus taken away from the Roman clergy and people and from the pressures usually exerted on them by the lay and Imperial powers, the cardinals were the incumbents of the churches of Rome and the suburbicarian dioceses, and were therefore predominantly not only Italian but also Roman. Above all it is important to remember that the new reformed Church was an intensely unitary and centralized body, ruled by a truly theo-cratic monarchy whose control, in the centuries that followed, was not altered save in the sense that it became more efficient. All the Councils, from the first Lateran Council (1123) to the fourth (1215), under the great Pope Innocent III, on the eve after the battle of Bouvines – the

Council that seemed to seal the Church's triumph as adjudicator of international controversies – were held at Rome.

The Empire too, though it might find German feudal princes at its head, remained Roman. The long struggle sustained by the Franconian Emperors against the Papacy during the eleventh century, over the question of investitures, was animated by their conviction and that of their followers as to the universal character of their own power and mission. More than any other, Frederick I Barbarossa (1152–90) was deeply convinced that he was the successor of Caesar and Trajan, and to vindicate this right he did not hesitate, as his predecessors had, to lead his armies into Italy seven times, neglecting and delegating to others the affairs of Germany. Without the possession of Italy and a Roman coronation, the Imperial title had no value or prestige.

But if Rome, and with her Italy, was politically and spiritually the centre of gravity of the *respublica christianorum*, geographically they were on its fringe: Italy had for a long time been a frontier, and to some extent was to continue being one. For hundreds of years the border between Charlemagne's continental Europe and the maritime Empire of the Arabs and Byzantium had passed through Italy.

Rome herself, or rather what remained of Imperial Rome, had until the beginning of the eighth century been under the temporal power of a Byzantine duke, and the Greek language had for a long time been current there. Byzantine influences are many: they can be traced in the Roman monuments of the age, and in the ceremonial and ritual of the early mediaeval Church. One thinks first of the gold-ground mosaics of the churches of Sant'Agnese, Santa Maria Antiqua and Santa Prassede, next of Pope Leo III, prostrate as if before an Eastern Emperor in the rite of the *adoratio* at the feet of Charlemagne. It was only in 1054, at the high point of the reform movement, that the Roman Church finally broke away from the Eastern one.

Not only Rome, but also Amalfi, Naples, Gaeta and the Adriatic cities of the Pentapolis had for centuries been under the authority of the Byzantine dukes; not to mention Ravenna, capital of the Exarchate, with its churches and mosaics rivalling those of Santa Sophia, which celebrate the glories of the court of Constantinople. As for Venice, her Doge was a Byzantine duke who had gradually become independent of Byzantium, her bishop a patriarch, her holy patron Mark came from the East, and the church that had been built to guard his relics probably had in its original form the structure of a Greek basilica.

But the Italian provinces in which Byzantine domination kept its hold longest were the southern ones: Apulia and Calabria. They continued to be subject to Constantinople until the mid-tenth century – long enough to profit from the political and artistic rebirth encouraged by the Macedonian dynasty. Evidence of this is offered by the many Greek churches and other buildings in Calabria. Sicily, on the other hand, was taken away from Byzantium in the ninth century by the Arabs, who held it for two centuries until the Norman conquest. Palermo, we can see from descriptions by Arab geographers and travellers, had time to acquire the characteristics of an Eastern Mediterranean metropolis, crowded with cloth-merchants and stalls, and swarming with life, characteristics which the city still partly retains. The most fertile parts of Sicily were ably irrigated and taken over by the new cultivation of citrus-fruits, mulberries, cotton and sugar-cane. Confronted with this exotic oriental vegetation, the Norman conquerors, though they were great travellers, could not get over their amazement, or escape the sensation of having landed in another world.

By the mid-eleventh century the political map of Italy was radically different from that of the early Middle Ages. In the North the Lombard conquest of Ravenna in 751 had practically put an end to Byzantine domination of the coastal zone of northern Italy. In the South the Norman re-conquest was in full swing, and its victorious outcome could already be foreseen. Rome, formerly a Byzantine dukedom, had become the patrimony of St Peter, and Venice had for some time ruled herself autonomously, and dealt on equal terms with the Eastern Empire. In a word, Italy was no longer a political frontier. She continued to be a frontier in a broader and more significant sense, however: of the Western Christian countries she remained the most exposed and receptive in relation to the Eastern world. Venice, Amalfi, Bari, once they had gained their independence, had certainly not ceased to keep up regular commercial relations with Byzantium and the Arabs; in fact, they extended and intensified them. Now the frontier was the sea, eternal vehicle of human contact.

This fact of being a frontier had no less influence on Italy's future history than her privileged position as the ideal centre of the *respublica christianorum*. To neglect either of these elements, or emphasize one at the expense of the other, would be to close the way to an effective understanding of Italian history in its variety and contradiction, in its singular grandeur. To take the great collective experience of the Crusades, which made the Christian West aware of itself and its renewed vitality: the fervent exhortations of the Roman pontiffs and the piety of the faithful played no greater part in their success than did the adventurous frontier spirit and open-mindedness of the shipowners and merchants of the Italian sea-ports. Indeed, one could well start from here: Italy's history begins with the ports and the sea.

THE PORTS

The rise of the Italian sea-towns, as has already been suggested, took place well before the First Crusade; and for some of them, before the great watershed of the year 1000.

On the Tyrrhenian coast, Amalfi was already well-established at the beginning of the eleventh century. She had regular commercial relations with Byzantium and with Syria, had colonies at Constantinople and Antioch, and her ships frequented the ports of Egypt, Tunisia and Spain. The presence of merchants from Amalfi is recorded at Pisa, Genoa, Ravenna, Pavia, the ancient capital of the Italic kingdom, at Durazzo and perhaps also in Provence. At Rome they acted as suppliers to the Curia, a big consumer of prized Eastern products, and one of them, Mauro Pantaleoni, a great builder and benefactor of the Church, was one of Gregory vii's main colleagues in the negotiating and scheming of international politics. But the Norman conquest of the South deprived Amalfi of her role as supplier to the hinterland and marked the beginning of her decline. The final blow was the storming and sack of the city in 1135, by the new rising star among Italian ports, Pisa.

Unlike Amalfi, whose fortunes had been founded on a policy of appeasement with the Arab world, Pisa chose from the start the way of combat and Crusade. When she had obtained control of Corsica and the northern part of Sardinia, Pisa, allied to the Normans, confronted and defeated the Moslem fleet off Palermo in 1062. In 1087 she was bold enough to launch a successful raid against Mahdia in North Africa, and later against the Balearics. With these expeditions, in which all the citizens wholeheartedly took part, with the consuls and bishops at their head, Pisa made sure of the mastery of the Western Mediterranean. Her chroniclers, magnifying the exploits, did not hesitate to compare them with those of Rome against Carthage. In the city, meanwhile, work on the cathedral was in full swing; it was begun in 1062, and consecrated in 1118.

The rise of Genoa, which an Imperial envoy of the early tenth century had described as still a predominantly agricultural community, was more difficult. It is necessary to remember the geographical position of the city, cut off from the *via francigena*, the most commonly used means of communication in early mediaeval Italy; and the fact that Genoa had never entirely recovered after the Lombard occupation of 642. So to begin with, Genoa operated in the shadow and in the wake of Pisa, but soon, as we shall see, acquired independent power and prosperity. The first extension of the city wall was in 1151.

Since Ravenna had ceased to be the illustrious capital of the Byzantine Exarchate in the eighth century, Venice had had no rivals in the Adriatic. Neither the cities of the Pentapolis, nor Bari and the other minor ports of Apulia, could begin to compete with her. Yet her origins had been humble: a people of boatmen, salters and fishermen, and an aristocracy of landowners who had fled to the islands of the lagoon in successive waves, to escape the barbarian invasions. But from small beginnings her rise was dizzy.

In the mid-ninth century, Venice already controlled the river-mouths of the Po Valley and the traffic which passed along them, and also the hinterland. At the end of the tenth century she had made herself ruler of navigation in the Adriatic, and her Doge decorated himself with the title *Dux Dalmaticorum*. To this period belong the consecration of the new building of St Mark's (1094) and the origin of the ceremony of marriage with the sea. Venice's maritime vocation was by now finally decided, and Venetian ships left in increasingly large convoys for the East, loaded with wood, metal, slaves captured along the Dalmatian coast, and pilgrims, and returned with silk, oil, spices, perfumes, dyes: all the things that could provide luxury for the élite of feudal Europe. Before long the number of Venetians in the territories of the Byzantine Empire became considerable: towards the middle of the twelfth century there were thousands of them, and the chroniclers speak of ten thousand being arrested at the time of the xenophobic revolt of 1171. In 1082 Venice obtained from the Emperor Alexius the guarantee of absolute freedom of trade throughout the Empire, exemption from all duties, and permission to maintain her own trade centres on Byzantine soil.

So the First Crusade found the Italian ports already well along the way of commercial penetration within the Arab and Byzantine world, and well prepared to take the historical opportunity offered them. Genoa and Pisa were the first to take advantage of it: Pisa took part in the siege of Jerusalem with 120 ships commanded by her Archbishop, while Genoa gave strong support to the Norman Prince Bohemond of Taranto in the siege of Antioch. Naturally, when victory was achieved, neither was slow to demand rewards for its help. The Pisans were able to establish a colony at Jaffa, while the Genoese installed themselves at Antioch. Other colonies followed, and by the mid-twelfth century there was practically no Mediterranean town or market from the coast of Algeria to that of Syria that did not have its Pisan or Genoese 'nation' with its church, its trade centres, and its consuls.

Venice on the other hand did not take part in the First Crusade: her relations with the Eastern Empire were harmonious and profitable, and she did not want any change in the Eastern Mediterranean status quo. On the contrary, she regarded her Norman rivals' attempts with suspicion. But when the enterprise ended in victory she was quick to recognize the new possibilities for Christian and Western supremacy that it had opened up: as early as 1100 a Venetian fleet of two hundred ships dropped anchor before Jaffa and demanded substantial commercial concessions from Godfrey of Bouillon. The xenophobic anti-Venetian revolts at Constantinople in 1171 and 1182 subsequently offered Venice a pretext for revising or rather reversing her policy of appeasement towards the Eastern Empire. This new political course was sealed in 1202, when Venice's able diplomacy and generous gifts managed to divert towards Constantinople the armies on their way to the Fourth Crusade. The capital of the Eastern Empire was stormed on 12 April 1204, and the Doge of Venice proclaimed lord of three-eighths of the new Latin Empire of the East. This turned out to be a feeble political organism that did not survive long; but the commercial privileges and ports of call Venice had assured herself on the coasts and islands of the Greek archipelago and at Constantinople were to remain in her hands through various vicissitudes, and would constitute the solid foundation of her later fortune.

But the importance and the historical rôle of the Italian ports were not due only to their warlike enterprises and their contribution to the assertion of Christian political and commercial supremacy in the Mediterranean. Amalfi, Pisa, Genoa and Venice were also the first doors and windows through which an isolated world, closed in on itself, established a permanent contact with the East, and began to benefit from its civilization. The sea-towns were a means of cultural communication. Arabic numerals, which were to simplify and revolutionize the accounting of merchants, were introduced to the West by the Pisan Leonardo Fibonacci, author of a *Liber abbaci*, who lived in the late twelfth and early thirteenth centuries. The compass, already known to the Arabs, was adopted by the Amalfitani, and the Latin sail of the crusader galleys was in fact a Byzantine or Syrian sail.

Besides, in an ill-equipped world, at a low level of technical knowledge and ability, the Italian ports represented so many islands of technical progress; they were almost experimental laboratories. In a society where technology was at such a low stage of development, the professions of sailor and ship-builder were among the few skilled trades that required a considerable range of technical knowledge and qualifications. Once manual ability and technical knowledge had been acquired they could relatively easily be applied to other activities and trades; anyone who can work in wood eventually learns how to work in stone. And what stone-workers showed greater mastery and taste for virtuosity than the builders of the Pisa Cathedral or the mosaicists of St Mark's in Venice?

The intellectually and technically advanced Italian sea-towns were also the places where the forms of communal self-government by the citizens most rapidly took shape. At Venice the transformation of the Doge from a functionary of the Eastern Empire to an electoral magistrate had already begun in the eighth century. During the twelfth century the form of his election and the limits of his power were strictly defined. By this time, the town's merchant aristocracy, represented by the *Maggior Consiglio* or Great Council, was already the city's unquestioned arbiter. At Pisa the first mention of the magistracy of the consuls is in 1080, and its advent marks the decline of the bishop's authority and that of the feudal nobility. At Genoa, however, progress towards forms of self-government by the citizens was hindered and delayed by the power of attraction and organization long retained by the city patricians. The trend towards association showed itself in the form of 'companies' of a private nature among individual groups of citizens. Later Genoa too was to evolve towards more highly-developed and more collective forms of political rule, but as we shall see a certain amount of individualism and clique-spirit survived in the life of the city for a long time.

In late eleventh-century Europe the Italian ports were thus in many ways an exception: one may understand the wonder of the pious bishop Donizone at the sight of the exotic crowds in the streets of Pisa, and of the chronicler from Pavia who found himself in Venice and could not believe that the world contained a city whose inhabitants did not sow, or plough, or reap; or the astonishment of the rough Norman and Burgundian warriors, on their way to the Fourth Crusade, among the churches and canals of Venice. But they were not to remain an exception for long: the impetuous wind of the year 1000 was also blowing inland.

CITY AND COUNTRYSIDE AFTER THE YEAR 1000

In Italy as in all Europe the year 1000 ushered in an age of bewildering economic development and profound social change. First to be affected was the countryside: the very base and foundation of mediaeval society. Italy too, or at least a great part of Italy, had her newly cultivated areas; countless place-names record the process of clearing or draining the land (Ronchi, Fratta, Frassineto, Carpineto, Selva, Palù)* and others derive from a history of settlement in the age of the

* These names refer respectively to billhooks, rough scrubland, ash-trees, hornbeams, a forest, a marsh (Trans.).

communes (Castelfranco, Villafranca, Francavilla). Near the big rivers
of the Po valley, particularly, wide uncultivated areas were reclaimed,
often by means of impressive hydraulic works: the digging of canals,
diversion of rivers, and works of irrigation and land-improvement. But
new settlements also sprang up in the hilly and mountainous parts of
the country: at Garfagnana, at Casentino, in the Alpine and Appenine
valleys. The registers for the collection of tithes, which were first drawn
up early in the thirteenth century, follow the spread of colonization,
and give the picture of a land densely populated in every corner. In
fact, as available land ran out, the powerful thrust of the growing
population drove men to less inviting areas – later, saturation point
would inevitably be reached, though for the moment wide margins of
development remained.

Though they survived elsewhere, feudal structures and the feudal
system of social relations were unable to contain this radical transformation of agriculture and of the agricultural landscape itself. By the
mid-eleventh century the feudal seigniory was in an advanced state of
decline in the central and northern parts of Italy that had been most
affected by the wave of exuberant economic growth, and still-flourish-
ing fiefs could only be found in the more remote regions, in certain parts
of Piedmont, in Friuli, in the valleys of the Alps and Appenines. At the
same time, documents contain fewer references to unpaid or forced
labour (*corvée*).

The dawning of the year 1000 meant a renewal of vitality not only
for the countryside but also for the other great protagonist of Italian
history, the town. Yet even during the early Middle Ages various
Italian towns had continued to sustain within their walls a fairly substantial economic life, sometimes including crafts: Lucca and Piacenza
for example, both on the main trade-route, and Pavia, the Lombard
capital on the confluence of the Tricino and the Po, which was the site
of annual fairs. Many factors helped to keep up the quality of urban life:
the deep impression of Roman colonization, the stimulus of the nearby
Byzantine ports, the frontier-position that Italy had occupied during
the early Middle Ages. But most important had been the fact that the
Lombard dukes and their administrative officials (*Gastaldi*), the
Imperial Courts, and the bishops, with all their followers and households, had settled in the towns and not in castles. As centres of dioceses
and seats of judicial and administrative bodies, the modest urban
agglomerations of the early Middle Ages had continued to be, to a lesser
extent, the cohesive force they had been in the Roman municipality. So
the year 1000 does not, properly speaking, signal a rebirth of town life,
but merely a recrudescence, though one on a grand scale.

In a society that was beginning to free itself from the iron necessity of a subsistence economy to which it had been condemned for centuries, the town gradually began to resume its function as a centre of exchange and market-place, a consumer of agricultural produce and provider of services and manufactured goods. Little by little, as there were more opportunities for work, exchange and human contact, the open spaces, whether bare or cultivated, that characterized the early mediaeval town – there is no need to fall back on an old-fashioned evocation of Rome reduced to pasturage for flocks of sheep – were filled with men and houses. The steep rise in the price of land within or near the city walls is documented; it indicates how rapid the growth-rate was. The massive bulk of the church dominated the new urban panorama: the great romanesque cathedrals of the Italian towns were built in the early years of the communes. S. Ambrogio in Milan, the most austere and beautiful, was built around 1100; S. Zeno in Verona between 1120 and 1138; the cathedral of Modena was begun in 1099 and completed in 1184. Their bell-towers surveyed a continually expanding town. Building-fever reached a point where the town literally exploded, and a new outer wall had to be built. Between 1050 and 1100 almost all the major towns of Italy – for example Florence, Genoa, Milan – had to replace the old city wall with a new, larger one. From twenty-four hectares the area of Florence thus became seventy-five. Parma grew from twenty-three to seventy-six hectares and Milan reached two hundred. Within a century this space also became insufficient, and in the second half of the eleventh century almost all the main towns had to put up a third wall.

Towns like this, which had grown so much and become so complex, could not be ruled by the traditional authority of the bishop or the count, but only by bodies that were representative of the various social groups and interests that the town brought together. In towns as in the country, economic development and changes in the way people lived brought about a crisis in the existing type of social organization and generated a thrust towards citizen self-government that was difficult to withstand. The consular system first appears, as we have seen, in documents belonging to the second half of the eleventh century.

It goes without saying that in Italy, as in the rest of Europe, agricultural and urban development were correlated and interdependent: they were manifestations of a single process of expansion and social improvement. What is less obvious, and represents a new trait in the evolution of Italian society, is the fact that in much of Italy this economic interdependence allowed a fusion of city and country also on the territorial, political and human level. This is what makes the Italian commune new and what gives it its character; and this is one of the key points of Italian history.

THE COMMUNE

The process of the formation and consolidation of the commune is a complex phenomenon made up of various component factors. It must first be seen as a conquest of the country by the city, both by means of economic penetration on the part of townsmen who bought land in the surrounding countryside, and by armed force and the submission of country people to the town. In this way Florence took Fiesole and attacked the feudal Alberti and Guidi families; Milan took over the surrounding countryside by fighting Lodo, Como, and other neighbouring towns; Asti forced the proud Tommaso di Savoia to become a vassal. So, with these forces, the townsman's economic presence in the countryside was transformed into political control of the country by the town.

Once the city had completed the subjugation of its territory it imposed its laws: the fortresses and castles were pulled down, the most savage and riotous feudal lords were compelled to live in the town for at least part of the year. The laws went further: in the conquered countryside the commune in many cases went on to pursue a policy of territorial reorganization, promoting 'free towns' and organizing great schemes for land-improvement and water-regulation. The commune of Milan had the *Naviglio Grande* (great canal) built, and the Padua commune financed the construction of drainage canals, carrying water into the Venetian lagoon. The communes of Mantua and Verona promoted impressive improvement schemes, and a whole book could be written on the hydraulic achievements of the other Po communes. In some cases the serfs were freed from crippling feudal taxes; the most famous but not the only act of general emancipation was that of the commune of Bologna in 1257, when it conferred on six thousand of its serfs a condition of 'perfect and perpetual freedom'. In this way land-workers ceased to be defined, according to their greater or lesser degree of freedom, as husbandmen, farmers, serfs, and by the many other names provided by complex feudal nomenclature, to become simply villeins or peasants (*contadini*), that is to say people of the county (*contado*). Landowners living in the town established new relations with these peasants, no longer based on personal dependence but on the principle of a contractual association and sharing of the risks and earnings of the business. These contracts were founded on the idea of *métayage*, which still remains dominant in wide areas of Italy where the old communes survive; its spread dates from the twelfth and thirteenth centuries.

So the town conquered the surrounding land. But the inverse process has been mentioned; and with reason. During the first centuries of our millennium there was continuous migration from the country to the towns. The migrants were not only serfs who had fled from their masters, or *déracinés* looking for fortune, but also landowners and feudal lords—to such an extent that some Italian communes could speak of their seigniorial origin. Once they had settled in the town, however, these new citizens did not give up the way of life they were used to: they went about the narrow streets surrounded by their gangs, and when they decided to build a house they often put up a tower beside it as a symbol of their power and 'magnate' status. Many Italian communes, including Florence, must in their early days have looked much as the small Tuscan town of San Gimignano still does. Besides, many of the landowners and feudal lords who had moved to the towns, of their own will or because they were forced to, retained their links with the countryside, and even if they had had to give up all or almost all their seigniorial rights, they still remained *rentiers*, and as such shared in the income of the countryside, even though not in the new ways and not to the same extent as the new bourgeois landowners.

The merging of the various component parts and strata of the new commune-society was not easy or immediate. This is shown, for example, by the history of the beginnings of the Milan commune, which is all a succession of alliances and conflicts between the great feudal lords led by the Archbishop, the lesser feudal lords (the vavasours) and the city's merchant and professional classes. Other Italian communes experienced similar friction, though we should guard against the temptation of always finding class-struggles everywhere, for there were often only conflicts between clans and cliques or between generations: between old inhabitants and 'new people'. In fact, in spite of the factions that went on troubling town life for a long time, the basic tendency was towards a gradual homogenization. On the one hand, the scions of magnate families did not disdain to marry into bourgeois families and to carry on their trades or crafts; on the other, by buying land in the *contado* the bourgeois tended to acquire that respectability that only land ownership could confer in the society of the time.

In many communes, though they had flourishing trades and crafts, landownership came to be considered a prerequisite for the true citizen, and some statutes even made it a necessary condition for citizenship. But even without this clause, many communes became in effect associations of landowners within and beyond the town. At Chieri in 1253, for example, two-thirds of the citizens owned land, and around the same date we find the same proportion at Moncalieri, at Perugia, at Macerata and at Orvieto, while in the territory of San Gimignano in 1314, 84 per cent of the land was owned by the citizens. Similar statistics are not available for the larger communes, but there is no reason to believe that their situation was very different. At this point there is no need to underline the fact that this shared ownership was a new source of social cohesion.

Unlike the cities beyond the Alps, whose privileges and freedom remained confined within the walls, and to the narrow strip of orchards and mean houses that constituted the suburb, the Italian communes were one with their *contado*, and had the character of a territorial organism. This was a substantial difference, rich in consequences, and it was noticed by the more acute observers of the age. One of these was the German Bishop Otto of Frisinga, who came down into Italy in Barbarossa's retinue. His words serve as a recapitulation of what has so far been said.

The inhabitants of Italy still imitate the perspicacity of the ancient Romans in the ordering of towns and public matters. Indeed, they so much love liberty that to escape the arrogance of rulers they put themselves under the rule of consuls rather than of sovereigns. Since they know that there are three social classes among them: that is, the lords, the vavasours and the common people, to keep down pride they choose those consuls not from one but from each of the three social classes, and so that they shall not be carried away by the lust for power they change them almost year by year. So, since that land is almost entirely divided into cities, each of these cities has forced the inhabitants of the diocese to stay with her, and one may hardly find any noble or great man so powerful that he does not obey the rule of his city. . . . And so as not to lack the means by which they can hold down their neighbours, they do not disdain to raise to knighthood and the honours of office young men of base birth, or any man practising low manual work, whom other peoples keep as far as the plague from higher and freer activities: for this reason they greatly exceed the other cities of the world in wealth and power.

Allowing for simplifications and exaggerations, the essential points of the question are neatly gathered together, even if they remain disconnected: according to the German bishop the power and wealth of the Italian cities was based on their rule over the *contadi* ('since that land is almost entirely divided into cities') and this rule was in turn the result of the intermingling that went on between the classes of feudal and country origin and those of the town.

The Italian commune was a composite, dual organism that had from its beginnings two spirits and two vocations: the one bourgeois and enterprising, the other landowning and deriving profit from the land. For the moment, in the general exuberance of an expanding and transforming society, the first clearly prevailed. Those cities whose merchants travelled the world and whose bankers lent money to the great, were also the ones who promoted, in the countryside of their counties, impressive schemes of improvement, who freed the serfs and destroyed the castles. But the time was to come when the other spirit – that of the landowner and *rentier* – would reappear and give its stamp to a later, less inspiring phase in the long history of Italian towns.

But though there were two spirits the body was and would remain one, and the attachment to one's town, one's own small nation, was the banner under which Italian commune-life developed. In a world where a man was defined more by the town he belonged to than by his class of social level identification with one's town reached a pitch unknown elsewhere, and no condition seemed worse than that of the bandit and the exile, the man who had no homeland and no roots.

The greatest centuries were economically and culturally exuberant, the age of decadence more timid and conservative; but there was always the sense of identification with the town: all Italian history seems to be anticipated and condensed in the microcosm of the commune.

THE NORMAN KINGDOM OF THE SOUTH

On the eve of the year 1000 the political map of southern Italy was more fragmented than that of central and northern Italy. Central Italy was united, at least nominally, in the form of the Kingdom of Italy, whereas the South and the islands were divided between the Arabs who ruled Sicily, the Byzantines in Apulia and Calabria, the Lombards in the inland and more mountainous regions, and the various virtually independent coastal towns. One may go further and say that the contrast between southern and northern Italy was also a contrast between two different types of social structure. Whereas in the Kingdom of Italy feudal institutions had arrived and become acclimatized some time ago, there had in the South been no such modification of the older forms of social relationship. But by the end of the eleventh century the situation was dramatically reversed: in northern and central Italy the communes had begun to flourish, and the feudal system was clearly in decline, while the South and Sicily obeyed a single king, and feudal institutions and the feudal hierarchy had recently been introduced.

The most extraordinary thing about this reversal is that it was brought about not by the Arabs, nor by the Byzantines, nor by the Lombards, but by a small band of adventurers and conquerors who had come a great distance: the Normans. The first group came from Normandy to the South at the beginning of the eleventh century;

specialists in feudal war, they were immediately taken on as mercenaries, first by the Lombards, then by the Byzantines. Soon they began to ask not money but lands for their services; in 1027 one of them, Rainulf Drengot, was presented with the estate of Aversa, and in 1046 William of Hauteville received that of Melfi, on the threshold of Apulia. From then on, as the successes of the first arrivals gradually attracted new waves of immigrants, their fortunes continued to rise. This was due not only to their military skill and their ferocity, of which chronicles of the time are full, but also to the friendly relations they were shrewd enough to form with the Papacy. At first the Popes had opposed them, but later realized the usefulness of Norman support; the Normans became Gregory VII's most powerful allies in his struggle against the Franconian Emperors. Strong in this most authoritative protection, the Normans were able to turn their war against the infidels of Sicily and the schismatic Byzantines of southern Italy into a crusade *ante litteram*. At the end of the eleventh century this war was almost over, and they found themselves in control of the whole southern part of Italy, at the moment when Western Christendom was hurrying to the Crusades, and preparing to conquer the Mediterranean. The Normans took advantage of this lucky coincidence by plunging into international Mediterranean and Eastern affairs. Already before this, Robert Guiscard had put forward his own claims to the Imperial throne of Constantinople: he had landed at Durazzo and set off towards the East; he had got as far as Salonika when the news of Henry IV's entry into Rome forced him to retrace his steps. Now the Normans directed their expansionist ambitions towards the Arab world, and managed to win Malta and, for a time, Tunis and Tripoli. Moreover, leaving aside the conspicuous contribution made by the Norman barons to the expeditions to the Holy Land, the great exploit of the Crusades would hardly have been possible without the aid of Norman ships, and the fact that the Crusaders could safely use the important route through the Straits of Messina.

We may well wonder how this small group of conquerors was so unusually fortunate as to be able, within a hundred years, to found and rule one of the most powerful kingdoms in Christian Europe. In this connection we must remember that while the Normans were completing the conquest of southern Italy, another expedition left from the coast of Normandy, landed on the English coast and remained as conquerors. The adventurers who had come to southern Italy belonged to the same breed, and even to the same families, as the followers of William the Conqueror. Of the two sons of Hugh Grandmesnil, who fought at Hastings and was made Duke of Westminster, one, William, married a daughter of Robert Guiscard and fought at his side at Durazzo; the other, Robert, became Abbot of the Calabrian monastery of Santa Eufemia. Like the victors of Hastings, the Normans of southern Italy were above all warriors. They had not only the valour and fierceness of soldiers, but also a military sense of hierarchic order, which was, in the social context of the age, one of the few links able to hold a political community together. The feudal structures of the state in fact imitated the knightly ones of the Army, and the king derived his authority essentially from his role as commander.

The Norman monarchy in southern Italy, like that in England, was feudal. The conquered lands were split up and assigned as fiefs to the conquering warriors who, once they had become barons, were kept in fealty to their king, and paid him an annual tribute as a sign of their vassalage. When they had fulfilled these obligations they could claim their rights as partners of the monarchy, above all the right of ratifying the succession to the throne. Like that of England, the Sicilian Norman kingdom had its parliament and its baronage, who more than once, especially under the successors of Roger II in the later twelfth century, fomented sedition and feudal anarchy. In this respect the history of the Norman kingdom is no different from that of the other feudal kingdoms of the age, such as France under the first Capets, or England under Henry I.

But the oriental Arab and Byzantine political traditions which had been preserved in Sicily provided the Normans with a means of re-affirming and consolidating their rule. These traditions identified the figure of the king with that of the *dominus*, supreme political and religious authority, to whom was owed not only the fealty of his vassals but also the obedience of his subjects. With a nomadic people's opportunism and capacity for assimilation, they did not hesitate to avail themselves of this instrument, and use Arab and Byzantine men and institutions for their own ends. George of Antioch, one of the most able organizers of the Norman fleet, was a Byzantine, and the title he boasted – that of Admiral – derived from the Arabic. The collaboration of Arab and Byzantine staff and experts in the field of financial and tax administration was particularly sought, as this alone could provide the central power with effective control. Two customs ('*dogane*', another word from Arabic) were evolved: the '*dohana baronum*' and the '*dohana de secretis*' – the first to keep control of feudal income, the second to look after Crown properties.

The Norman monarchy's tendency to assimilate Eastern elements and traditions is illustrated most clearly by the decision of Roger II, the conqueror of Sicily, to fix the seat of his court and the centre of his kingdom at Palermo, magnificent capital of the Arab emirate. Under him it continued to be the great market it had been in the past, and the

Arab chronicler Ibn Jbair, who travelled in Norman Sicily, describes it as a populous and flourishing capital in whose sky the church towers rose beside the domes of the mosques. His account is borne out by the churches of the Martorana and the Eremitani, the Zisa and Cuba palaces, and the thousand-and-one-nights artifice of the Palatine chapel, all buildings of the twelfth century. At Roger's court between 1139 and 1154 the great Arab traveller Idris dictated his famous work of geography, which was to be so important to mediaeval cartographers; in the reign of William II the Cathedral of Monreale was built – a monumental complex that, with its sober façade and Romanesque stamp, its Arabic cloister and its mosaics of the Byzantine school and Byzantine taste, provides the most eloquent testimony to the intellectual eclecticism that thrived under the Norman monarchy. Also during this period another eclectic institution, the medical school of Salerno, was acquiring authority and fame. The legend that claims it was founded by four masters, a Greek, an Arab, a Jew and a Latin, contains a grain of truth. We know in fact that its success was made possible by the translation of Arabic and Greek medical texts by scholars who lived in the second half of the eleventh century. One of these, Constantine the African, was secretary to Robert Guiscard.

On the political level and on the level of relations between men, the assimilation of the various races and cultures that history had capriciously juxtaposed in southern Italy turned out to be much more difficult than on the level of the court and of relations between the learned. In the second half of the twelfth century the tendency of the feudal baronage to split up the state and form separate centres often emerged, and there were moments when it gained the ascendency. There were also demonstrations of intolerance, amounting to pogroms against the Arab population. Even so, within the limits allowed by history, the Norman kingdom of Sicily, a feudal monarchy with an Eastern capital, represented something exceptional in the Europe of the time. This would be seen clearly when Frederick II of Hohenstaufen assumed its crown.

THE COMMUNES AND THE EMPIRE

In 1152 Frederick I, called Barbarossa, was elected Emperor. Deeply aware of his dignity and power, he considered that his main mission was to restore in its entirety the absolute sovereignty and the majesty of the Empire. So his attention naturally turned to Italy, and in fact in the course of his reign he invaded Italy no less than seven times, and made her the principal objective of his policies. In one of his first invasions he called together in the plains of Roncaglia an assembly of prominent men, conspicuous among whom were the masters of Roman law of the Bologna school; this assembly was made to proclaim the principle that all sovereign rights – the ports, the rivers, the taxes, the appointing of magistrates – could belong only to the Emperor. It was a challenge flung at the independent power of the towns and communes, and it was taken up. The struggle between Barbarossa and the communes of northern Italy, drawn together in a league, lasted more than twenty years, with dramatic vicissitudes. All the powers and nobility of Italy were drawn into it: in first place the Pope, who at one point took on the rôle of patron and leader of the anti-Imperial forces. In the end it was papal mediation that imposed a compromise solution on the contenders; the communes recognized the overall sovereignty of the Emperor, but kept the sovereign rights they held (the Treaty of Costanza, 1183). A few years later Barbarossa left for the Crusade, and did not return.

Before he went he fired his Parthian shot by arranging the marriage between his son Henry and the much older Constance of Hauteville, heiress to the Norman throne. So at his father's death, Henry found himself with both the Imperial and the Sicilian crowns. Though he made a brilliant beginning, he was prevented from developing the restoration of the Empire in Italy by his own premature death in 1197; and the next twenty years were dominated by the great personality and great Guelf policy of Innocent III. These were the years of the Fourth Crusade and of the Ecumenical Council of 1215. When Innocent died in 1216, Henry's son Frederick had come of age and was ready to step on to the stage. He won the battle of Bouvines, and managed to get himself crowned Emperor by Pope Honorius III in 1220: once again the dignity of the Empire was united with that of the Kingdom of Sicily. The return of Imperial and Ghibelline forces to the offensive against the Papacy and the northern Italian communes could now only be a question of time, however uncertain its outcome seemed: for it was a struggle between two sides whose resources and forces were more or less equal.

Frederick II and the Ghibellines undoubtedly had the advantage of greater political cohesion. Unlike Frederick Barbarossa, whose descents on Italy had depended on the agreement of the feudal nobles to follow him and to provide him with troops, Frederick had in his Kingdom of Sicily a firm base in the very territory of the peninsula, and a notably efficient and flexible political organization. As King of Sicily his work had essentially been to strengthen the political structure inherited from the Norman kings, and to consolidate the monarchy's prestige and power, making it once and for all safe from the baronial turbulence and sedition of the later days of Norman rule. Many of the feudal fortresses that had been built in the previous thirty years were demolished, and in their place, as sentinels of the Kingdom and its internal peace, rose many royal castles. The most famous of these and the most splendid is Castel del Monte at Andria, a noble building on an octagonal plan, and a fascinating marriage of Gothic and Arabic styles of architecture. Farther north was the castle of Lucera, where Frederick had installed 10,000 Saracens deported from Sicily; he formed them into an autonomous community, from which he drew his most loyal soldiers.

Frederick was a stern controller both of baronial restlessness and of the cities' aspirations to independence. He put them under the control of officials appointed by himself, and those cities that, like Messina or Gaeta, tried to rebel, were made to feel all the severity of the Emperor's revenge. Unlike the northern citizen communes, the southern cities had the character of 'villes du roi'. One such, whose name even evokes the Ghibelline symbol, was Aquila, founded in 1254, in compliance with a previous decision of Frederick's.

A state organized on such a basis could not have existed and worked without an adequate team of able, highly-qualified specialists and functionaries. But Frederick II knew how to find such men, and his court and chancellery, as we shall see later, occupy a prominent place in the history of Italian culture in the thirteenth century. The Emperor himself, a cultured man and friend of culture, fully realized how important trained ability could and should be in the running of the state. One of his achievements was the founding of the University of Naples in 1224, with the precise idea of assuring the Kingdom a regular flow of administrators.

The centralized edifice of the Sicilian monarchy was crowned in 1231 with the publication of its fundamental law, the *Constitutiones Melphitane*. Its inspiration, which it openly propounded, was the half-Roman, half-Byzantine idea of the *imperium* as fulness of power and the Emperor as the executor of God's will on earth and the living personification of the law and of justice, *lex animata in terris*.

The ruler of such a firmly-founded kingdom, and an Emperor of such fame, found allies easily. By able diplomacy, Frederick II managed to construct a network of alliance and friendship across the whole of Italy. The great northern feudal lords of Piedmont and Savoy naturally marched under the Ghibelline banner, since they were sworn enemies of the communes, and so did the marquises of Monferrato, who had been among Barbarossa's main supporters. So did Ezelino da Romano, in the Veneto, who controlled, among other things, the vital route across the borders of Verona, which ensured contact with Germany. But among Frederick's allies there were also some communes and towns which were worried by the intrusiveness and expansionist ambitions of their Guelf neighbours: Siena and Pisa in Tuscany; Cremona, Parma and Modena in the Po plain. The prestige and personality of its leader helped to hold together this heterogeneous gathering of forces. Warrior and man of letters, legislator and student of philosophy and magic, Crusader and deep admirer of Arab culture, persecutor of heretics and enemy of popes, Frederick II was an enigma and a legend in his own lifetime: he was *stupor mundi*. Some saw him as Caesar, others as Antichrist, but enemies and followers alike felt the fascination of his intellectual superiority, and acknowledged his power and magnificence.

In comparison with the Ghibelline camp, the Guelf seemed less united, more vulnerable. As in the days of Barbarossa, its political organization was based on a league of communes that, though drawn together against the common enemy, continued to be divided by a succession of clashes of interest, and by frictions of a local nature. Besides, within many of them lurked the seeds of discord, and civil war between the Guelf and Ghibelline factions was often superimposed on that between classes and families: that is to say, those who got the worst of such rivalries, or were actually forced into exile, often had no other choice than a complete political reversal if they wished to continue the struggle – they had to join the ranks of those hostile to the city's masters. Finally it must be added that the Guelfs lacked a leader of Frederick's stature. Of the popes who took office between 1220 and 1250, only Gregory IX could match his great antagonist's fighting spirit; but no one had his magnetism or his style.

Though they were less united and slower to move into action, the communes and towns of central and northern Italy had access to far greater financial resources than those of their adversary, particularly when they were joined by Genoa and Venice, with their fleets and their money. Of the towns of Sicily there was none that could remotely rival the prosperous centres of Guelf Italy; and the policy practised first by the Normans, then by Frederick, of repressing local independence, certainly did not favour the development and spread of trade. By the thirteenth century the glory of Amalfi was no more than a memory, and most of the trade of the southern ports had got into the hands of the Pisans, the Genoese and the Venetians. The only solid resource the Kingdom of Sicily had was her agriculture, and the considerable flow of exports to the North, which she supplied with food. But this was not because the southern countryside was richer or more highly developed, but simply because the South was less densely populated, and the drift to the towns less marked. It has been calculated that the Kingdom of Sicily's population was about half that of northern Italy, and that of the twenty-six Italian towns whose population in the thirteenth century was higher than 20,000, only three were in the South. In the last analysis then, the Kingdom's only resource was yet another symptom of her backwardness.

Frederick II tried to get round this economic inferiority, first by monopolizing exports, then by trying to attract trade from the cities that supported him, by instituting fairs there and bestowing privileges on them, and finally by falling back, like all the kings of that age, on monetary tricks and manipulations. But these were double-edged weapons, and did not succeed in preventing the Kingdom from being plunged into considerable financial and economic difficulties several times during the long, hard struggle against the Papacy and the communes.

This struggle had its alternating phases, its dramatic moments and spectacular incidents, such as the occasion in 1241 when the Sicilian fleet scattered the Genoese ships on which Spanish and French prelates were travelling to Rome, to take part in a council at which Frederick was to have been solemnly excommunicated. But the most unexpected twist was the sudden death of Frederick himself in 1250, when even though the Emperor had just suffered a severe defeat at the hands of the communes, the fight was still far from being decided. In fact, once he had got over the first inevitable disarray and confusion, and although he did not hold the impressive title of Emperor, Frederick's son Manfred managed to gain control of the situation, reorganize the Ghibelline forces and win back many of the positions that had been lost in the mean time. The Ghibellines were not finally defeated until 1266, when Charles d'Anjou, the brother of Louis IX and lord of Provence, was called into Italy by Clement IV and financed by the great Florentine and Genoese bankers. He won the Kingdom of Sicily by defeating Manfred on the battlefield and successfully resisting the counter-offensive of Frederick II's second son, the young Conradin.

From that moment the ambitions of Frederick I and Frederick II to restore the Empire and its universal power had to be abandoned for ever and the independence of the Italian communes was no longer threatened. It is true that during the first half of the fourteenth century other Emperors marched into Italy: Henry VII of Luxembourg in 1312 and Ludwig the Bavarian in 1327–8. But the first invasion became a pointless and humiliating pilgrimage through the cities of Italy, and the second resulted in a ceremony which, by its circumstances and the way in which it was performed, marked the end of the Imperial myth that had been initiated by a similar ceremony on Christmas night in the year 800. This coronation, unlike its predecessors, was not performed in a sacred place, but on the Campidoglio, in the name not of the Pope but of the Roman people. This greatly pleased the intellectuals and scholars who followed Ludwig, but it had no political consequence.

THE VICTORY OF LOCAL CENTRES IN ITALIAN LIFE

Once Charles d'Anjou, the vanquisher of Manfred, had installed himself on the throne that had belonged to the great Frederick II, his position and titles seemed to make him the political master of Italy. He was the brother of one of the most illustrious and most pious kings of Western Christendom, and was associated with him in the glories and profits of the Crusade and of Mediterranean politics; he was a candidate for the vacant Imperial throne in the West, and aspired to that of the East; he was the recognized leader of the Guelf party; he enjoyed the spiritual support of the reigning Pope and the financial support of the Florentine bankers. His arrival seemed to herald an era of stability under the Guelf banner. And for some years he did successfully play the part he had been assigned, of judge and moderator. But once again it was a precarious balance: the communes and Italian towns had not fought against Frederick II and against Manfred only to put themselves under the tutelage of Charles, but to be free to develop their own political initiatives, and to follow their own interests. For them a *pax guelfa* was no more acceptable than a *pax ghibellina*. The urge towards local independence was by now too deeply rooted in Italian history, and only awaited the right moment to spread victoriously everywhere; this moment soon arrived.

On 30 March 1282, the day of the uprising known as the Sicilian Vespers, the city of Palermo, which Charles, by moving his court to Naples, had humiliated and demoted from capital status, rose up against its Angevin masters. This example was swiftly followed throughout the island, and on 4 September the nobility of Sicily offered the crown to Peter III of Aragon, who had married one of Manfred's daughters, and at whose court the partisans of the deposed dynasty had found refuge. He accepted, and so the long war of the Sicilian Vespers began, which was to end after twenty years with Sicily being separated from the Kingdom and assigned to the house of Aragon. All the Italian states were directly or indirectly involved in the conflict: for most of them it represented the chance they had been waiting for to shake off all Angevin control, and to be free to follow their own policies independently. Besides, how could a king claim to lay down the law to others if he could not put down rebellion among his own subjects?

The war of the Vespers thus aroused a chain of reactions across the whole Guelf-Ghibelline battlefield. Genoa, an ally of the Aragonese, took the opportunity of settling her score with Pisa by crushing her rival at the sea-battle of Meloria in 1284. She also struck at Venice with the battle of the Curzolani islands in 1298, following up the attack of 1261, when with the help of Manfred she had defeated the Latin Empire of the East, and confined Venetian activity to Constantinople. Florence, having defeated Arezzo, Prato and Pistoia, became a threat to Lucca and Pisa. In Piedmont the struggle raged between the feudal houses of Monferrato and Savoy, while in the eastern part of the Po plain, Estensi of Ferrara, Scaligeri of Verona and other feudal powers were still committed to cutting out for themselves the biggest possible portion of the territories that had formerly belonged to the da Romano domain.

The Aragonese in Sicily fought the Angevins in Naples, Genoa fought Pisa and Venice, Florence fought Pisa, the Torriani and Visconti families battled for supremacy at Milan, and at Rome the eternal duel between the Orsini and Colonna houses went on: the spectacle Italy presents in the last quarter of the thirteenth century is really one of *bellum omnium contra omnes*. The chronicles of this age of steel are full of episodes in which the spirit of faction reaches extremes of ferocious cruelty; the story told by Dante of the Pisan Count Ugolino, who was shut in a tower and left to die with his two sons because he was suspected of having wanted to betray the city to the Florentines, is only the best-known of many.

In this 'great tempest', to use a phrase of Dante's, which afflicted the whole of Italy, even the Church was unable to find its way. Under Clement IV it supported the Angevins, but with Gregory X and Nicholas III it strove to limit Charles's power; it was pro-Angevin and pro-French again with Martin IV and Nicholas IV: contemporaries did not see the Papacy in the position of a judge, above political struggles. On the contrary, it was obviously a deeply involved participant. This widespread sense, and the lack of direction it aroused in the faithful and in the Church itself, in this fin-de-siècle of millennial prophecies and the anticipation of great events, added to an atmosphere heavy with expectation, with hopes and fears. In these circumstances the election of a pious and poor Abbruzzese monk, Celestine V, in 1294, seemed to many people the advent of the 'angelic Pope' spoken of in the prophecies of Gioacchino da Fiore. His sudden and probably forced abdication – an event without precedent in Church history – and his subsequent death in the isolation in which he was confined by his successor, Boniface VIII, cast further shadows on Boniface's already dubious character. Some went so far as to see the new Pope as the Antichrist, which obviously did not help in restoring the Church's compromised prestige. When Boniface's ambitious and anachronistic theocratic policy brought him into conflict with Philippe Le Bel and his monarchic absolutism, Philippe was able to launch a highly effective propaganda campaign and political offensive against the Pope, culminating in the famous humiliation at Anagni. Boniface did not long survive this outrage, and his successor, the French Clement v, transferred the papal seat to Avignon, where it was to remain for more than seventy years.

It was some time since the Empire had gravitated towards Italy, and now the Papacy too abandoned her: she suddenly found that she was no longer the centre and heart of the Christian *respublica*. One may easily sympathize with the confusion and disorientation of Italians of the time, who were accustomed by long tradition to regard the two supreme institutions of the mediaeval political universe as the pillars of every form of order. Without Emperor, without Pope, Italian political reality seemed empty and vain. These feelings find expression in Dante's invective against the Emperors, who had abandoned Rome 'a widow and alone', against the Popes, who from shepherds of the Christian flock had transformed themselves into 'rapacious wolves', and against the factions devoid of any firm ideal, which tore Italy apart. Guelfism and Ghibellinism had by now become, in Dante's words, mere 'marks on a flag'; a flag in whose shadow each man pursued his own mean interests. But one should be careful not to see such states of mind and such judgements as historically reliable, as Italian historians of the Risorgimento period were inclined to do: nostalgia for lost Imperial unity should not be seen as a foreshadowing of national consciousness.

But if the age of Italian history that has so far been summarized is examined, as it must be, from the point of view of the emerging forces and not those in decline, in terms of its real, living multiplicity and not of an imagined unity, it seems neither empty nor confused. On the contrary no age is as full, abundant and vital, nor as coherent, either, as that of Giotto, Dante and Marco Polo. The end of the thirteenth century saw the complete spread of commune civilization. After the collapse of those two great back-drops that had conditioned the movements of every human group, the Italian communes and towns stepped forward on to the front of the stage; they occupied the stage, and became aware of their strength and their freedom. The signs of this awakening are everywhere. This was the moment when, as we have seen, the city walls of most Italian towns were extended, the first town chronicles were written, the massive communal palaces were built. Those of Florence, Siena, Perugia, Todi, to take the most splendid examples, all belong to the last decade of the thirteenth century. And soon the towns were to be reinforced by political theory: in the first years of the fourteenth century Marsillio of Padua argued in his *Defensor Pacis* that sovereignty did not derive from God or the Emperor, but was the expression and result of a bond of association and an organized human community.

But the Italy of the towns and communes was obviously a many-centred universe, and as such divided by deep rivalries and bitter conflicts. It is not surprising: Venice, Genoa and Florence were great powers, and in every age the relations between great powers have been difficult. But those wars against which Dante hurled his invective were certainly not the only result of there being many centres: the situation also allowed all the aspects of Italian city-civilization to develop, including the most creative and long-lasting. Italian art itself received the city-stamp: it does not take a highly-trained eye to tell a painting of the Florentine school from one of the Sienese school, or a grave figure from the Po region by Antelami from a lively Ghibelline by Nicola Pisano. Without its past of local loyalty and fragmentation, Italy would not be the country we all love. No-one, perhaps, understood this sooner or better than the humanist Leonardo Bruni, whose words may provide a conclusion to what has so far been said:

Just as great trees prevent little plants from growing, when they are near, so the great might of Rome overshadowed her (Florence) and all the other towns of Italy . . . That was where the crowds were, where things could be sold and trade arranged, theirs were the ports and the islands and the places suited to many activities. And so if anyone of talent was born in the neighbouring towns, having the chance of so many advantages, he would very likely go to Rome. And in this way Rome came to flourish, and the other towns of Italy came to lack any of the talents of accomplished men. One may understand this effect from the experience of the towns that were repudiated when they stood before the greatness of the Roman Empire, and similarly (from their experience) after the Empire's decline, in such a way that it seems that what the growth of Rome had taken away from the other towns, her shrinking later gave them.

Now that the broad outlines of Italian history have been traced, up to the threshold of the fourteenth century, it is time to examine the many 'histories' woven into it, and of which it is comprised: the histories of Venice, Genoa, Florence, Milan and Rome.

Commune civilization

THE CITY-STATES OF ITALY

The Mediterranean had perhaps never been the centre of the world to the extent it was in the thirteenth century, which opened with the victorious enterprise of the Fourth Crusade. Across the Mediterranean the mighty empires and great civilizations of Western Christendom, Islam and Byzantium faced one another, and into it and its dependency the Black Sea flowed the trade-routes that brought the valuable and eagerly sought products of Africa – ivory, gold from Senegal – and the rare goods of the East. These had been arriving more steadily ever since the Mongol peace over all the vast area between Baghdad and Peking had made caravan routes safer – the routes followed by Marco Polo and the Florentine Francesco Pegoletti. Besides being a basin that collected the widest possible variety of goods, from many sources, the Mediterranean was a centre of distribution. By way of the Italian Alpine passes or the Aragonese ports and those of Southern France, Eastern goods reached the fairs of Champagne and the markets of Northern and Baltic Europe. Later, after a Genoese galley had opened up the Atlantic routes to Northern Europe in 1277, it was the turn of Bruges to be the port most frequented by the merchants of the Italian cities.

The cities profited most from Mediterranean prosperity, and the one which profited most of all was Venice, which controlled Crete and the main islands and ports of the Aegean, and had a firmly established, prospering colony at Constantinople. In spite of Genoese competition and the loss of that position of absolute privilege that the Fourth Crusade had assured her up to mid-century, Venice was still the first of Italian sea-powers. Above all she was the best organized and most united: the trade expeditions that left every year for Constantinople, Beirut and Alexandria were organized by the state, which also supervised the depositing of goods in the warehouses and the distribution of imported goods. In addition, the state controlled the immense arsenal.

Since the city was well armed with ships and since free navigation was firmly established, Venetian merchants felt that they were all partners in a great, planned, collective enterprise. This contributed to the strong corporate sense of the Venetian merchant aristocracy and helped to make Venice's political institutions a model of stability and efficiency. The city's leader was the Doge, elected by the Grand Council, who ruled with the help of a more limited council; in addition, his activities were subject to the inspection of a whole series of controlling bodies: the *Consiglio dei Pregadi*, which took the name of Senate in 1250, the *Tribunale della Quarantia*, and later, after the failed conspiracy of Baiamonte Tiepolo in 1310, the famous Council of Ten. The existence of these several bodies brought about a system of counterbalances, of reciprocal checks. But this division of power was balanced by the extreme unity and homogeneity of the ruling class, qualities that were reinforced in 1297 by the so-called *serrata* (closing) of the Great Council, by which membership was forbidden to those families who had not provided members in the past. So already at the end of the thirteenth century the Venetian ruling body had taken the shape of a merchant aristocracy, which it was to maintain for centuries; classes were rigidly delimited but the internal mechanisms of the system were sufficiently elastic to permit a fertile alternation of men and of political attitudes.

For Genoa too the thirteenth century was a triumphal progress of successes and victories. The dissolution of the Latin Empire of the East in 1261 and the victory over Venice at the Curzolani islands in 1298 had strengthened Genoa's position in the Eastern Mediterranean and the Black Sea. In the Black Sea the Genoese had established themselves in the colonies of Caffa and Tana, and so controlled the trade of the Russian plains and the caravan routes that ended in these places. After their victory over the Pisans in 1284 the Genoese were more or less the masters of the Western Mediterranean; the rising power of the Aragonese was not yet strong enough to present any real challenge to their supremacy. In the wake of these political and military successes the economic importance of the city and the volume of its trade naturally grew. It has been calculated that in 1274 the value of the goods coming into and leaving the port of Genoa was 936,000 Genoese lire, and in 1292 had risen to 3,822,000. Genoa, with her houses of several storeys that earned her the name of 'superba', was probably the most densely populated city of Western Europe in the early fourteenth century. Later, with the construction of the new city wall in 1320, the density diminished, and only in the eighteenth century returned to what it had been.

The foundations of Genoa's fortunes were quite different from those of Venice. The city was armed privately, for the most part; her merchant convoys, and occasionally even her military sea expeditions, were privately organized. The warehouses were individually owned, and Genoese travellers were adventurers who did not hesitate to put themselves at the service of anyone who was ready to pay them. Marco Polo, in the presence of the Khan of the Tartars, or in prison, never forgot that he was a citizen of Venice; he fought for Venice, he was married and he died at Venice. But already early in the fourteenth century we find a Genoese, Manuele Pessagno, as admiral of the King of Portugal, and another, Enrico Marchese, building ships on the Seine for Philippe Le Bel. They were the forbears of a Genoese progeny that includes Christopher Columbus, who discovered America for the King of Spain.

This Genoese 'individualism' has been mentioned several times, and one cannot help continuing to speak of it: it was reflected in the very structure of the city, which was a patchwork of neighbourhoods, of noble *consorterie*, of religious and popular confraternities. It shaped the townscape, which was more an agglomeration of quarters – rich, poor, noble and plebeian – than a unity. Genoa is one of the few Italian cities of Roman origin that retains hardly any trace of its original lay-out, and where we do not find, as we do in the mediaeval quarters of other Italian towns, streets named after the craft or trade that was concentrated in them: both symptoms of a fragmentation of communal life, and of a town divided into watertight compartments. We shall often see what effect this had on Genoa's proverbial political instability, and on her history.

Among the communes of the Po valley, Milan, which had been the standard-bearer of the struggle against Barbarossa, emerged at the end of the thirteenth century as the most powerful and prosperous. The city was the natural junction of Genoese and Venetian traffic, and was provisioned by a countryside that was already among the most fertile of Italy; she took full advantage of the opening of the new St Gothard pass in about 1270: it brought her a considerable part of the trade with Germany. Milan was portrayed in 1288 by the chronicler Bonvesin de la Riva in his *De Magnalibus urbis Mediolani*; the picture he gives is one of a true metropolis: 200,000 inhabitants, 11,500 houses, 200 churches, 150 'villas with castles in the *contado*', 10 hospitals, 300 bakeries, more than 1,000 workshops and a great number of merchants and craftsmen. These are of course unreliable if not fantastic figures; but the sensation the chronicler conveys of a diversified and diffused town-economy is reliable. Unlike Florence, Milan was a city whose manufacturing activities were increasingly diversified, and whose craftsmen increasingly versatile; but this resulted in a dissipation of energy. Besides the weaving of woollen cloth, developed mainly by the religious order of the Umiliati, and other activities belonging to the textile industry – the heavy industry of the age – Milan was the scene of many other crafts: above all, armour-manufacture, using the iron of the Val Trompia and of Brescia. The armourers of Milan soon acquired very wide fame. But the firms active in all those trades remained on the scale of small work-shops, just as Milan's flourishing trade was mostly retail. In this period there is no mention of Milanese companies and trade dynasties whose business activities are comparable in breadth or continuity with those of Florence, or even of lesser towns. These narrower horizons, and this less-developed power of organization perhaps explain (though it is only a hypothesis) why the Milanese merchant and craftsman classes and their co-operative organizations – the *Consolato dei Mercanti* and the *Credenza di S. Ambrogio* respectively – did not manage to produce a political class of their own (the point of comparison is still Florence) and why in the end the rule of the city and arbitration between the factions was entrusted to representatives of the families of the old chivalric nobility within the city. Such were the Torriani, Guelf feudal lords originally from the Val Sassina, who were supported by the *Credenza di S. Ambrogio* and ruled the city from 1247 to 1277; and such were the Visconti, whose name alone is proof of their noble descent, who seized power from the Torriani, obtained the title of Imperial deputies in 1294, and remained '*signori*' of Milan until the mid-fifteenth century. So at the beginning of the fourteenth century Milan had already ceased to be a commune and had become a seigniory, a term that normally defines that type of town government in which by force or agreement the authority of a 'signore' and his family is substituted for or superimposed on that of the pre-existing communal bodies.

Milan was not the only city to follow this evolution. At about the same time most of the communes of the Po valley were transformed into seigniories, to the advantage of this or that noble family. The Scaligeri family were lords of Verona, the Este family of Ferrara, the Da Camino family of Treviso, the Carraresi family of Padua, the Montefeltro family of Urbino – all houses distinguished by their long history and chiv-alrous traditions. They had lived in the towns for a long time, and now offered the towns and their burghers and businesses a capacity for leadership that would otherwise have found no expression in such a non-feudal society.

In the light of this process of transformation that took place in most of the Italian communes at the end of the thirteenth and beginning of the fourteenth centuries, the case of Florence is all the more notable. This was the only major city of Italy save Venice which succeeded in evolving institutions that wholly corresponded to its economic organiza-tion and social stratification. Compared with the communes of northern Italy, Florence was a newcomer. At the time when Milan was winning the fight against Barbarossa, she was hardly able to impose her law on the feudal lords of the neighbouring countryside, and her role in the struggle against Frederick II was far smaller than that of the larger northern communes. But as often happens with late arrivals, once she had got going she made her choices wholesale, benefiting from the experience of those who had preceded her. In 1252, Florence was the first city to coin a gold piece – the florin – thus providing her own merchants and financiers, operating in all the market-squares of Europe, with a monetary instrument of the highest value and prestige, and allowing them to gain a leading position in the international market of goods and capital. As we have seen, only a little after the mid-thirteenth century, the Florentine bankers were able to collaborate in financing Charles d'Anjou's expedition; and they lent money to many other great men. The only city that could compete with Florence in great financial operations was her neighbour, Siena, where the bankers made huge profits out of their posts as leaseholders and debt-collectors for the Roman Curia. But the defeat inflicted on them by Florence in 1269, at Colle Val d'Elsa, and the resounding collapse of the leading Sienese banking house, the Tavola dei Bonsignori, in 1298, assured Florence a position of absolute pre-eminence in the money market.

It was not only in commerce and banking that Florence acted on a big scale: in industry too she pursued a policy of concentrating her energies firmly on textiles, and particularly woollen cloth. Also in Florence the concerns were on the scale of craftsmen's workshops, but the supplying of raw materials and the distribution of the finished products was quite often managed by a single wool merchant, who thus assumed the appearance and function of an entrepreneur, and regulated production according to the needs of the market. From this, it was not a great step to concentrate and rationalize production one stage further and assign certain stages of the work to townsmen in their homes, to people in the *contado*, or even to wage-earning workers gathered together in large ateliers; and this was soon done.

By means of their journeys, their contacts with the great, and their experience as managers of complex commercial and financial operations, the Florentine burghers and merchants not only accumulated enormous wealth, but gradually acquired knowledge of the world and of men, broad horizons, ability to command, and above all an awareness of their own resources and of opportunities, which could not have existed in that age save in exceptional circumstances. This explains why, unlike those in most Italian cities, the merchants of Florence were not content with giving themselves a corporate trade organization, but demanded for themselves, and won the right to control the affairs of the city. They did so in 1282 with the reform of the commune-system, by which the rule of the city was entrusted to the *Priori* of the larger and medium guilds, who in practice became the masters of the city's life. Some years later, in 1293, the *ordinamenti di giustizia* excluded from public posts those magnates who were not members of the guilds, and created the new magistracy of the *Gonfalonieri di Giustizia*; thus the victory of the citizen order was confirmed. It is not in fact very significant that men belonging to families of chivalrous or feudal traditions or origins often appear in the city's ruling bodies; what counts is that these men ruled the city on behalf of the guilds and in their interest. At the end of the thirteenth century there was no other Italian city where self-government had been achieved with such completeness and breadth, or made to fit the social texture of an industrious community so closely. And in no other city did commune civilization achieve as much as in Florence.

Venice, Genoa, Milan and Florence were the four great Italian communes, each the possessor of its own unmistakable personality. But when we have looked at them, much of the picture still remains: around the great capitals there was a whole series of 'little capitals', each of which also had its own appearance and character. Siena had its bankers, Lucca its silk, Cremona its fustian, Piacenza its fairs, Asti its 'Lombards', and each one its own town hall and pride in its freedom.

But however much they were divided by economic and political rivalries, and even though they were ruled by different laws and institutions, the cities of Italy were still unalterably, all of them, cities. So the Italy of the communes as a whole, in spite of its many-centredness and its particularism, acquired a certain homogeneity: that of an intensely urbanized area, the most intensely urbanized of all Europe. In the long run this was bound to favour the formation of a sort of national Italian consciousness, above and beyond the divisions of local patriotism; and this slowly took shape from the thirteenth century on. To follow the development of this formative process we must first consider the religious and intellectual history of the thirteenth century.

THE FRANCISCAN REVIVAL

The religious history of Italy in the eleventh and twelfth centuries is not substantially different from that of the other countries of Christian Europe. The first heretical ferments broke out in Italy too, in the restless and receptive atmosphere of cities that were developing and changing. Milan in particular, which later earned the name of 'ditch of the heretics', had her 'patari' and heretics from the eleventh century on. But in Italy as elsewhere the Church's reform movement was for the moment able to satisfy most of the demands for religious and social change that had been expressed through heretical and reformist unrest. During the twelfth century however there was a new wave of this unrest. A popular uprising temporarily drove the Pope out of Rome, and from 1145 to 1154 Arnaldo da Brescia, a tempestuous pupil of the tempestuous Abelard, preached there. The main theme of his preaching was that of all mediaeval heretical movements: he railed against the degeneration and corruption of the Church, which he aimed to restore to its primitive purity. Arnaldo was captured by Barbarossa, who handed him over to the Pope; he died bravely at the stake – but this did not check the spread of heresy and of reformist movements. In the advanced urban society of the late twelfth and early thirteenth centuries these sprang up everywhere. Widespread in northern Italy, under various names and in various forms, were the Waldensians and the more intransigently Manichaean Catharists; while from Calabria came the millenarianist predictions of the Abbot Joachim of Fiore, a Cistercian who had broken away from his order to form a monastery of his own; he was the author of prophetic writings that were to exert a wide influence over entire generations of believers. From the doctrinal point of view there were certainly great differences among these movements, and it is extremely hard to fix the borderline between orthodoxy and heresy. Yet they were all evidence of general unrest, of the unease of a new society, or one undergoing rapid change, dissatisfied with a faith and a liturgy that could hardly keep up with the times.

The Church, as is well known, reacted also on this occasion, under Innocent III; its reaction was designed on the one hand to crush the agitation of the heretical movement, and its demands for reform, and on the other to absorb them and canalize them towards orthodoxy. So on the one hand there was the Crusade against the Albigensians in 1209, and the founding of the Inquisition, on the other the approving of new mendicant orders and of the new forms of devotion they introduced.

But the methods and the efficacy of this double reaction of reform and counter-reform were not the same everywhere, and it is from this point that the religious history of Italy begins to diverge from that of the other countries of Western Europe. Outside Italy the Papacy's action against heretics succeeded neither in suppressing them nor in completely absorbing the heretical potentialities of popular religious feeling, which survived underground and were to burst out occasionally during the centuries to come, in one form or another, eventually flowing together in the great upsurge of the Reformation. In Italy, on the other hand, the operation could be said to have succeeded. The reasons for this divergence are many and complex, and involve a span of time that goes well beyond the thirteenth century. For one thing, Italy was and continued to be, apart from the Avignon interlude, the seat and see of the Papacy. But Italy was also – which takes us into the heart of the thirteenth century – the cradle of the Franciscan movement, whose following and profound influence can hardly be over-estimated. It is in this that we shall find the reasons for the particular character of Italy's religious history – and not only her religious history – from the thirteenth century onwards.

Francis of Assisi (born 1182) had something in common both with Peter Waldo of Lyons and with Domingo de Guzman. Like the first he was a rich merchant's son who spent a self-indulgent youth and then turned his back on the world's goods and made a vow of poverty; like the second he was above all an itinerant preacher gifted with an exceptional power to communicate with the mass of the faithful, whom he addressed in their 'vulgar' tongue. Unlike the followers of Waldo, Francis did not attack the corruption of the clergy and the Church, and unlike the Dominicans, he did not preach the necessity and the holiness of the struggle against heresy. His words lacked any trace of a doctrinal or polemical view of religious action. The ideal he preached, and of which his own wandering, picturesque life seemed a living incarnation, was of a natural, spontaneous religion, to be lived more than believed or meditated. For him Christianity was essentially the religion of Christ; that is to say, of a man who had lived among men, sharing human suffering and death, who had expressed eternal truths in the form of clear, intelligible parables, who had loved children and admired the beauty of the lilies of the field. The Imitation of Christ is most perfectly exemplified by St Francis's life as it is represented in Franciscan legend and iconography, for he succeeded to the point of sharing with Christ the martyrdom of the stigmata. This imitation involves the love of all that is human, because all human life in some way shares the Divine nature – sinners as well as saints, the wolf as well as the lamb, death as well as life.

Thus a new form of religious feeling was born, less intimidating and more familiar, suited to an industrious, extrovert society: a popular religion that gave the merchants and craftsmen of Italian towns the chance to remain Christian without being either heretics or clergymen. Besides, however paradoxical it may seem to say so of one of the greatest saints of Christianity, there was in Francis's religious realism something that reached down to an ancient pagan substratum in the minds of the Italian people: a traditional, instinctive, rustic idea of God as the daily companion of man's life, of his joy, his sorrow and his work. The famous *Canticle of All Created Things* conveys this feeling: in it the chorus of created things – water, fire, the stars – unite to give praise to the Lord, evoking the image of a universe in which everything and every element is a manifestation of God. Perhaps this contact with a deep layer of popular consciousness gave St Francis's teaching its popularity.

His teaching was in any case enormously successful, and made a decisive contribution to those episodes of genuine religious revival of which Italian history in the thirteenth century is full. The first was in 1233, when, under the impact of the preaching of the Dominican Giovianni di Vicenza and the Franciscan Anthony of Padua, the cities and countryside of northern Italy were swept by the 'Hallellujah' movement, and such a climate of general religious fervour was aroused that many cities committed themselves to a short-lived 'pacification'. This was not an isolated episode: 'general devotions', accompanied by a mass abstention from work and from arms, for days and sometimes for weeks, took place in various Italian cities at various times. But the culmination was reached in 1260, a year singled out by the prophecies of Joachim, when processions of flagellants spread out from Perugia across all central Italy.

To have some idea of the relevance and impact of the Franciscan phenomenon on thirteenth-century Italy, one must look above all at art and literature. There is of course a Franciscan literature, of which the famous *Fioretti* are the last and most stylized example. Before them had come the burning poetry of Jacopone da Todi, and before that the '*Laudi*' (a type of poetic composition derived from love-poetry), and sacred representations by anonymous writers of Umbria, the Marche and Tuscany. It would on the other hand be a facile sociological simplification to speak of a Franciscan school of painting. The great work of thirteenth-century Italian masters cannot be summed up by such a formula; as far as the supreme Giotto is concerned, we must remember that before he went to work at Assisi he had travelled to Rome and had learned from Cavallini. At the same time it is true that Giotto played a very considerable part in the formation of a Franciscan legend and iconography, and that the Franciscans were his principal clients: the Basilica of Assisi and Santa Croce in Florence, in which he left his principal series of frescoes, are both Franciscan churches. The aesthetic pleasure that the masterpieces of thirteenth-century painting give us today must not allow us to overlook their essentially pedagogic, illustrative function in a world of illiterates, for whom the depiction of a miracle almost constituted its proof.

Faced with such an original and impressive revival, the Church soon realized that it represented an opportunity, and a unique means of saving itself from being isolated from a fast changing world, and even of putting down deeper roots into the world. To do this however the Church had to keep the Franciscan movement within the orthodox fold and, while respecting its original character, give it an official stamp. While Francis was alive, this attempt went slowly—he was rather bewildered when he yielded to the pressure put on him by Cardinal Ugolino da Ostia (the future Gregory IX) and agreed to transform his community of 'brothers' into the order of minors.

But after Francis's death in 1226 his followers, particularly the first General of the order, Elia de Cortona, speeded things up. In his will, Francis had confirmed that the minors were not allowed to own houses 'except those meet for holy poverty', but once he had been proclaimed a saint in 1228, work was immediately begun on the construction of the Basilica of Assisi, the mother of a whole series of Franciscan churches that sprang up during the century, throughout Italy. Some of them, such as Santa Croce in Florence, are notable examples of the new Gothic style. Another 'novelty' of the century was the university; and here too Franciscans were soon prominent; one only has to think of Bonaventura of Bagnorea, for many years General of the order, and of William of Ockham. This process of institutionalization and assimilation into the Catholic hierarchy aroused resistance and bewilderment – many thought it represented a deviation and degeneration of the primitive Franciscan rule and its precept of absolute poverty. During the whole thirteenth century and afterwards there was dispute between the 'conventuals', partisans of a wider interpretation of the rule, and the 'spirituals', who were more rigorous and intransigent. Jacopone da Todi belonged to the second group. The dissidence between them was most extreme during the papacy of Celestine V, but its consequences lasted much longer.

Yet these internal quarrels only partially and marginally damaged the hold that the Franciscan message had on the mass of the faithful. The mark it had left on them was too deep to be erased: Francis had been the first to break the barrier between the religion of the clergy and that of the people; he had sensed and satisfied an ancient, unexpressed need for a more solid everyday faith, more modern and at the same time older, that was for the rich and for the poor, that was both Christian and pagan. With Francis, Christianity became the religion of the Madonna and Child, of Christ suffering on the Cross, and also of St Francis himself and his humble, miraculous life. The symbols and summary of the life in its essence – love, death, faith – were portrayed in the canvases of the thirteenth-century masters, and comforted man at all times of the day and every stage of his life: they helped man to live. This substratum of vitality and resignation was from this time on to be a dominant and familiar part of Italian religion.

INTELLECTUALS AND THE VERNACULAR

A rich, articulate, highly evolved society like the Italy of the communes needed a large and highly qualified intellectual class if it was to function. It needed jurists and administrative experts to whom the business of chancelleries and the government of public matters could be entrusted, it needed orators to act as ambassadors, notaries to draw up the various types of contract demanded by the citizens, teachers of reading, writing and arithmetic for the sons of merchants, burgesses and doctors. The universities provided these experts, and their history and development runs parallel with that of commune civilization. The first and most famous of Italian universities was that of Bologna, the origin of which goes back to the beginning of the eleventh century. It soon acquired fame in the field of the study and teaching of law. During the late twelfth and early thirteenth centuries, at the moment when Italian town civilization burst into life, other universities followed in quick succession: in 1222 the University of Padua was instituted, which was to become a fortress of Aristotelianism and Averroism, thus inaugurating a tradition of naturalistic objectivity that leads, by way of Marsilio and Pomponazzi, to Galileo. In 1224, as we have seen, Frederick II founded the University of Naples, and at about the same time, universities opened at Vercelli, Modena, Siena and numerous other cities. Rome too had hers: the Curia Romana, founded in 1244.

The university was in every way a new kind of school. It was new because it was in a town, which broke with the traditions of isolation and segregation of the monastic schools, and put teachers and students in contact with a richly fermenting town life responsive to all modern developments. It was new in its organization, on the model of the trade corporations, which made it a free community in which the necessary hierarchy of relations between teachers and students was tempered with a common *esprit de corps*; there was less hostility and more communication. The universities, particularly those in Italy, were above all a novelty for the aims and content of their teachings. Unlike the Sorbonne and other famous universities beyond the Alps, the major Italian schools, especially that of Bologna, managed for some time to stay independent of the Church's authority; and the study of science and the humanities – law and medicine – either prevailed over that of theology or was at any rate independent of it. In speaking of law one is naturally speaking of Roman Law, of which Bologna University was the school par excellence, and which the Church had forbidden at the Sorbonne: it was the true 'new science' of town and commune society,

anxious to find its own legitimacy. As for medicine, the lesson of
Greek and Arab naturalism had already been known to the doctors of
Salerno, and spread throughout the thirteenth century, as the schools
of Toledo and Palermo produced their translations of Arab comments
on Aristotle, so that it became assimilated into the culture of the age. Up
to the Renaissance and beyond, doctors were probably the most
advanced of all intellectuals, and the most representative of a spirit of
research and inquiry that tended to set aside established authority. The
study of medicine was closely linked to that of philosophy: Taddeo
Alderotti, the greatest doctor of the thirteenth century, and professor at
Bologna, was also one of the first translators of Aristotle.

These universities produced the major personalities of cultural and
intellectual life in the thirteenth century. Pier delle Vigne, Frederick
II's chief notary and the century's undisputed master of rhetoric and
the *ars dictandi*, had been educated at Bologna, where he had learned to
infuse his chancellery documents with the phrasing and the cadences of
great classical prose. Guido Guinizelli and Cino da Pistoia, two of
the greatest poets of the century, were students of Bologna and experts
in law. It seems that Dante too studied there for some time. Besides
these illustrious names there were a whole host of lesser people, from
whom the communes drew the 'cadres' and skills they urgently needed.
So a new body of intellectuals was created, profoundly different from
the clerics of feudal communities, professionally trained and ready to
take its place in the new political and social order, intellectually more
open, and closer to the business and political struggles of a turbulent
and vital society.

However integrated the new intellectuals were within the society of
their time, they could not wholly share in town life and municipal
pride. They remained an élite, set apart by their training, with their
own mental habits and their own characteristics. In many cases
they were not fixed in any one town: so in thirteenth-century Italian
towns there developed what may be called a market of talents and
qualifications; and the most prominent cities and courts, with the jobs
and professional opportunities they provided, were powerfully attractive. The custom of inviting a man from another city to be the leader of
a commune, which became widespread during this century, is an
example of the kind of practice that contributed to a freer circulation of
men, ideas and experience.

Thus the Italian intellectual of the commune era had a double
nature and function. On the one hand he was an organic part of
commune civilization, on the other the member of a caste that
gradually came to constitute something like a new aristocracy, beyond
the sphere of city life. He was at the intersection of two circuits: the one

that went over all frontiers and joined the learned, the chosen spirits, and the other one that joined together all the components of a certain community.

So the first task facing the intellectuals was that of linking these two circuits, and creating a literature that would be accessible both to the traditional learned public and to the wider and more varied one that the growth of commune society had created: a public that included burgesses, merchants, the people; not only men but also women who had, like Dante's Francesca, learned to read, and were delighted by the love-romances that came from France. These people had to be addressed in the 'vulgar' language of every day. But there were many 'vulgar' Italian tongues, all vaguely defined, unformed idioms; so a literature in the vernacular ran the risk of being confined to the narrow sphere of its birth, while Latin continued to act as the literary language of the educated classes. A happy medium had to be found between dialect and a sort of Esperanto: an ennobled vulgar tongue, which would unite the advantages of communication in depth with those of the clarity of the learned language, and would be able to pass from the low, familiar style of comedy to the sublime style of tragedy. Naturally the formation of a literary Italian language was bound to be slow and gradual; and what has been said of the political history of Italy can also be applied here: one should be on one's guard against seeing its unity as a condition present from the beginning rather than as the end of a laborious process.

But there is no doubt that the beginnings of the Italian literary language must be sought in the thirteenth century. It was launched by a group of poets that gathered in the first half of the century around the splendid court of Frederick II at Palermo: in this group were the Chancellor Pier delle Vigne, the 'notary' Iacopo da Lentini, Frederick himself with his son Enzo, and others. The almost exclusive theme of their compositions was courtly love, dear to Provençal and Troubadour poetry, and their language a Sicilian dialect purified and refined, with Provençal and Latin borrowings. In the second half of the century, after Frederick's death and the final defeat of his son Manfred, literary activity centred in certain of the great communes of northern Italy, such as Bologna and, even more, Florence. In these two cities, with Guido Guinizelli, Guido Cavalcanti, Cino da Pistoia and Dante Alighieri, flourished the poetic school of the '*dolce stil novo*'. The 'newness' of these poets, compared with the Sicilians, consisted in their refining of the linguistic medium, and their enriching of the poetic content, which still remained closely linked to the theme of love and woman, but also embraced philosophical and moral debate, tinged with the philosophic culture of the age. The '*dolce stil novo*' was in short a clear step ahead on the way to a richer, more flexible and more authoritative vernacular. The manifesto of the new language and the new literature was provided by Dante. In the *Convivium* and the *De Vulgari Eloquentia*, composed between 1304 and 1307, he vindicated the 'noble vulgar' that, with the experiments and attempts of a century, from the Sicilians to the *stil novo*, to himself, had gradually formed the right to handle 'the highest themes: love, arms and virtue' (Sapegno).

Destined to satisfy the thirst for knowledge of the unlearned and of those who had not been able to go to the schools, and at the same time purified as it is of elements of dialect, and endowed with a firm grammatical and syntactical structure, Dante's noble vernacular is an eminently literary language. It precisely demonstrates the rôle in which Italian intellectuals were beginning to see themselves – a national, Italian rôle, which they began to fill from the time of Dante onwards. This language – he noted – was the language that would have been spoken by the learned and the prominent people of an Italian *curia regis*, if there had been such a thing, as there was in Germany. Anticipating the objection that such a court did not exist, Dante went on to emphasize that even if there was no one prince of Italy, there was a *curia* all the same, 'because we have a court, however scattered it may seem' – and who were the members and dignitaries of this scattered, ideal Italian court, if not the intellectuals and men of letters, dispersed about the cities and courts of Italy?

The formation of an Italian, if not national, awareness thus originated on the literary level, among intellectuals. And as little by little they grew conscious of themselves and the links that bound them, and of the ideal community they represented, they also began to discover that their rôle belonged to a certain kind of society – the whole Italian community, with its lively civil and economic interchange, its Guelf and Ghibelline factions, its cities, its Roman law, its culture. This Italian awareness was soon to appear fully-formed in Petrarch: for him, Italy was the country bounded by the sea and by the Alps, and the Italians were the most legitimate heirs of the Roman tradition: *sumus non graeci, non barbari, sed itali et latini*. In the attempt to reduce this complicated process into a formula, we may say that in such a complex, varied and scattered society as Italy in the era of the communes, the intellectuals were the only social group to possess any vision of the whole, any germ of national feeling. So the first embryo of Italian consciousness was conceived with the emergence of a new intellectual class and its awareness of its own position. We have only to consider the part played by Dante's language in the history not only of Italian literature but also of Italian society.

DANTE ALIGHIERI

Dante Alighieri was born in Florence in 1265, and lived there until the age of thirty-five, taking an active part in the political life of the city, and holding public offices. In his youth and early manhood at Florence he produced his first work, the *Vita Nuova*, a diary in prose and verse, half real, half imaginary, about his love for the gentlewoman Beatrice Portinari. In 1301, when the 'Black' party, helped by Pope Boniface VIII and the intermediary sent by him to Florence, triumphed over the 'Whites', to whom Dante belonged, he was banished from the town and forced to take the road of exile. For twenty years – he died in 1321 – he wandered from one Italian court to another. He was at Verona with the Della Scala family, at Lunigiana with the Malaspina family, and at Ravenna, where he died, with the Da Polenta family. Between these wanderings, and out of them, he conceived and wrote the *Commedia*, which posterity has called 'Divine'.

Almost all countries have a national poet, but perhaps none of them occupies a place in their national culture and history equal to Dante's in the literary and social history of Italy. Whole generations, especially in the last century, have looked on him as the father and prophet of a yet unborn Italy, and his poetry and his person have been the objects of a cult. There is hardly a town in Italy that has not named one of its main streets or piazzas after Dante, or has not put up a monument to him. The first Italian ironclad was named the *Dante Alighieri*. This myth, at least in its more rhetorical and pompous form, is of fairly recent origin and is, on the whole, rather inconsistent. A simple school reading of the *Divine Comedy* is enough to show clearly that the pacification of Italy Dante invokes belongs only in the context of his ideal of a restoration of the Empire's universal monarchy, and that his condemnation of Italian sects and factions leads him to condemn Italian society in general, and the fermentation of new forces that agitated it and drove it forward. Does Dante not inveigh against 'new people and quick gains', and exalt the 'sober and modest' Florence of the days of the commune with 'towers,' contrasting it with the rich and triumphant one of the century's end?

Yet, in spite of these firmly-founded considerations, it remains true that Dante's place and position in the literary and social history of Italy, though not in the rhetorical, patriotic nineteenth-century sense, remains that of a 'father', as he already was for Machiavelli. In what sense, therefore? To go back to what was said in the previous section: it was through Dante that the particular pedagogic and civil rôle of the intellectuals in forming an Italian community was expressed and exalted; it was by reading the *Divine Comedy* that the educated Italian public had for the first time the clear sensation of belonging to a civiliz-ation that, even with its variety and its many centres, had common foundations.

The *Divine Comedy* is one of the few works of world literature, like Tolstoy's *War and Peace* or Joyce's *Ulysses*, that can be said to contain everything, the whole sense of an age, with all its contradictions and doubts.

The poem deals with the journey that the poet makes, accompanied first by Virgil then by Beatrice, through the three kingdoms of the extramundane world, from the cone of Hell, which penetrates to the centre of the earth, to the mountain of Purgatory and then to the seven heavens of Paradise, to end gazing at the glory of God in the Empy-rean. During his journey, Dante meets a crowd of spirits, damned or blessed souls or those undergoing purgation, from famous ancient figures like Ulysses, Cato and Justinian, to those of the contemporary world, like Pier delle Vigne, Manfred and St Francis. He also meets the protagonists of events that had most struck the imagination of men of that time: Piero and Francesca, the unfortunate lovers who were betrayed and killed; Pia de' Tolomei, killed by her jealous husband in a castle of Maremma. He meets many of his fellow citizens: Farinata degli Uberti, the 'magnanimous' Ghibelline leader; his own master Brunetto Latini; his friend Forese Donati; Filippo Argenti, 'fierce Florentine spirit'. Some of these dead people realize that the chance of speaking with a living man who will return to the world is a chance to send a message to their dear ones; the story of their lives, the picture they give of themselves, their explanations of their own fate of dam-nation or salvation, are bound to be absolutely sincere and quintessential. An authoritative critic, Auerbach, writes: 'The passion that during earthly existence may easily be hidden by shame or the lack of oppor-tunity for its expression, here breaks out in its totality, if only because of the knowledge that it may be expressed only this once.' The general plan and structure of the poem are not depressing, but exalt the power of poetic representation. From the whole, one takes away a staggeringly varied and sincere picture of man's condition in Dante's time, a match-less panorama of the loves and hates, contradictions and uncertainties of that period.

Then there is the incomparable language of the *Divine Comedy*: with this poem Dante showed that the language of Florentine merchants and chroniclers, the language in which Franciscan friars sang God's praise, could be very effectively employed in the most difficult of literary genres. He had written in the language of comedy (whence the title of the work), he had adopted the most popular of the metres in use, the three-line verse of the *sirventes*, and yet he had succeeded in describing the horrors of Hell and the stellar rarefaction of Paradise. By means of his similes, monstrous and sublime spectacles were translated into the familiar household images of everyday life. So the boiling pitch in which the swindlers are plunged calls to his mind the arsenal of Venice, with its hubbub of men and work; the sight of the evanescent masks of the blessed in Heaven, that of human faces reflected in 'clear, calm water'. Elsewhere, the groan of one of the damned, transmuted into a tree-trunk, calls to the poet's mind the homely image of a firebrand burning from one end while sap oozes from the other, 'sizzling as the air escapes', and the glorious surge of the blessed towards the Empyrean, the movement of 'a baby, reaching towards its mother to take milk'.

With this language, for which there seem to exist no difficulties of expression or of representation, Dante gave Italian culture a model that it has been impossible to neglect from that time on. This alone must explain to us why a poet and scholar, and not a legislator or warrior, passed into history as the father of the Italian nation.

3

The crises and the vitality of an age of transition

ITALY AND THE CRISIS OF THE FOURTEENTH CENTURY

The dynamic of the general crisis that struck European society in the fourteenth century is well known, at least in its outlines. It too, like all the deep currents that convulsed the mediaeval economy and mediaeval society, originated in the countryside. During the late thirteenth and early fourteenth centuries, the phase of expansion that had begun around the year 1000 went as far as it could, and reached breaking-point. Up to that time it had been possible for the pressure of a constantly increasing population to be offset by the cultivation of new areas, and the continual extension of the bounds of human settlement. But with the passing of time, the margins of such possibilities became ever narrower, and by the beginning of the fourteenth century the limit of what may be called 'marginal' lands had been reached, or even passed, in many parts of Europe. Besides, the land had often been stupidly cultivated: agriculture often amounted to little more than rape of the land. These chickens now came home to roost: the food-balance of the age, which in spite of everything remained its chief problem, was upset. Famine had always been a threat to mediaeval society, but from the beginning of the fourteenth century it became more frequent, and affected wider areas. The famine that reached its peak in the years 1315–17, for example, was appalling.

So the world of the fourteenth century was overcrowded, and its unfortunate generations underfed and thus more vulnerable to the pestilence they were periodically exposed to. This explains the virulence with which the great plague of 1348, the terrible 'Black Death', spread across all Europe, from Italy to Scandinavia. It has been calculated – as far as precise estimates can be made – that this plague killed about one-third of the population of Italy, France and England. Such drastic reductions of the number of men and mouths could not at first greatly alleviate the food shortage of the surviving population, for with the plague many cultivated areas were abandoned. The agricultural landscape and the pattern of human settlement were disrupted – in many places cultivated land fell back before woods and marshes. For decades, the people of the fourteenth century continued to live in the terrible, vicious circle of famine and epidemic – the plague returned at intervals to one region or another.

The new balance of food and the social and political equilibrium that was in the end laboriously and gradually reached had to be paid for by violent upheavals and crises. In no other period of European history are the signs of social instability so endemic – citizen revolts, peasant revolts and guerrilla movements in the countryside, the banditry of nobles who had been reduced to adventurers and of demobilized armies who lived by pillage. As in no other period, war became a more or less permanent condition. It was the frame around all the contradictions of a disintegrating society in the desperate search for a new order of things. What is the Hundred Years War if not the outward and visible form of the inner conflicts and crises that tormented English and French society for a century?

This is the outline of the crisis of the fourteenth and fifteenth centuries. What is Italy's place in it? What actions and circumstances involved her in it? There has not been enough research in this field for these questions to be answered easily. But it is useful to reconsider the broad outlines of Italy's history during the period, in terms of the pattern that has just been traced.

Italy at the end of the thirteenth century was once again a densely populated country: this is the picture we get from, for instance, the *rationes decimarum*, the registers for the collection of tithes, which were first drawn up during the thirteenth century. The total population of the peninsula can roughly be estimated at between seven and nine million. In the north and central part of the country a considerable proportion of the people lived in towns. At Bologna for example there were 17,000 people in the surrounding country and 12,000 within the city walls: a ratio of seven townsmen to ten countrymen. At Padua the ratio was two to five, at Perugia five to eight, at Pistoia one to three, and in certain areas the relative positions of town and country were actually reversed, so that at San Gimignano there were three townsmen to every two countrymen, and at Prato thirteen to ten.

This density of population, particularly urban population, naturally meant that a heavy pressure was placed on agriculture and on the land. Florence could only be fed by the produce of its territory for five

months in the year, and cities like Venice and Genoa had to be provisioned entirely from outside and by sea; and farmers often tried to
grow more than their land could produce. As we have seen, there had
been instances of agrarian progress and rationalization in the era of the
communes; and it is certainly no coincidence that the region in which
works of land-improvement and irrigation had been most intense and
most efficiently organized – Lombardy – should have been the one
region to emerge from the crisis of the fourteenth and fifteenth centuries not just unharmed but more prosperous than before. However,
Italian agriculture of the commune-period had remained on the whole
an agriculture of subsistence, characterized by widespread mixed
cultivation, low-quality livestock and thus also manure: the techniques used, except in certain parts of the Po plain, were at the same
level as those described in ancient Roman accounts. The climate was
the source of further difficulties: Italy's dry summers made spring
sowing difficult and affected the rhythm of crop-rotation, while the
fields were laid waste by the floods of the autumn and the spring. Men
themselves shared the responsibility for these floods, for indiscriminate
deforestation was already a problem. Italian towns devoured not only
cereals but also wood: at the end of the thirteenth century Milan
annually consumed 150,000 '*some*' of wood for fuel, and quite early on
Pisa and Genoa had to import wood for their ships, having exhausted
the resources of the nearby mountains.

Italy was a land overloaded with people and exploited down to the
last calorie, the last clod: here as much as anywhere was a situation
where the plague could make wide gaps and cause violent upheavals.

Overall calculations are, as we have seen, difficult to make. The only
reliable evidence is local. So for example at San Gimignano the
successive plague censuses show that two-thirds of the people died;
at Pistoia the 36,000 inhabitants of the town and *contado* of 1300–10
were reduced to 19,000 by the last decade of the century; Orrieto's
2,816 households of 1290 were reduced to 1,381 in 1402; at Florence,
one of the great metropolises of the age, the chroniclers record that the
plague left the population a quarter of what it had been. It is reasonable
to suppose that in an urbanized society like Italy the gaps made by the
disease would be more severe than elsewhere.

Not that the countryside escaped unscathed. Matteo Villani's
account, confirmed by the most recent studies of Florence's *contado*,
tells us that the peasants wished to cultivate the best land and abandon
the rest. The consequences of this tendency were felt throughout Italy,
to varying degrees, most acutely in the South and the islands. So Italy
too had her deserted villages; a steady procession of desertion in fact,
from the fourteenth century on, reducing entire regions that had been

inhabited and cultivated to malarial swamps. This was the fate of the
Roman marshes and campagna and of the Sienese marshes, which lost
80 per cent of their population during the last decades of the fourteenth
century. Later, to satisfy the wool industry's demands for raw material,
many of these abandoned areas were turned into winter pasturage for
sheep. We find various sheep taxes imposed during the fifteenth century: at Foggia, at Siena in about 1402, and at Rome in about 1419.
Broad stretches of the country around Pisa were transformed into pasture-land in the late thirteenth and early fourteenth centuries, with the
result that drainage and other hydraulic systems began to deteriorate –
in the fifteenth century Pisa was surrounded by marshes and by malaria,
and continually exposed to the dangers of flooding. At the same time,
the port was steadily silted up by the alluvial detritus that the Arno
brought down when it was in flood. The case of Pisa is one example of
how the social crisis could work away, to the point of reducing a once-
prosperous human *milieu* to decadence. Almost all parts of Italy were
hit to a greater or lesser extent, and many decades were to pass before
the wounds could heal. After the terrible plague of 1348 there were
other waves of pestilence that afflicted now one region, now another.
And for a long time famine remained the nightmare of Italian cities,
and food their main concern.

An earthquake like that which shook Italian society in the mid-
fourteenth century was bound to have a profound effect not only on the
balance of the economy and food, but also on social and political
structures. From this point of view too, the history of Italy runs parallel
with that of the rest of Europe. Like the cities of Flanders and the
Paris of Etienne Marcel, the Italian cities were stages for popular
risings and revolts. The uprising of the Florentine artisans (the *Ciompi*)
in 1378, which we shall return to, is the best-known of many. Seven
years before, in 1371, there had been similar events at Perugia and
Siena, and there were also – though on a smaller scale than the French
Jacquerie or John Ball's revolt in England – outbreaks of peasant
rebellion and warfare. The most serious instance was the bloody uprising in the countryside of Calabria during the reign of Alfonso of
Aragon. But the country around Parma, in 1385, and that of Pistoia in
about 1455, also had moments of unrest.

The crisis affected not only the lower levels of society: the discontent
that stirred the people into revolt was matched by the difficulties faced
by the privileged classes. Where, as in the South, a feudal nobility still
existed, anger at the impoverishment and loss of status that had come
with the reduction of its rents found vent in anarchy. In the rest of the
country the crisis of the ruling classes took forms that were less clamorous but just as heavy in consequences. To sum up, and go back to a

previous point: the difficult times of the fourteenth and fifteenth centuries reawakened and revived in Italian merchants and burgesses that *rentier* spirit that had always existed in them, from their beginnings. Every day it seemed clearer to them that property investment, whether in lands or houses or in public bonds, was the only way to protect from the blows of circumstance the wealth they had accumulated by trade and speculation. So the first noble palaces rose in the towns, and the first villas in the country. To our eyes these villas and palaces represent, above all, the fruit of a civilization and taste that had reached full maturity; but for those who built them they were first of all an investment – a conspicuous investment. This trend towards property did not always or necessarily go with a corresponding drift away from trade and production. Indeed, the reverse was often the case: the more frenzied and hazardous the business and the speculations, the more desirable and reassuring appeared the safety of property. No family built as much, or had such a passion for building, as the Medici, the most enterprising bankers of Italian history. Speculation and the freezing of money in property are phenomena that run parallel all through Italian history from the communes up to our own time.

At this point – the point where wealth became opulence – the merchants of various Italian cities became an aristocracy: that is, they became aware of their privileged position and their rank. This was the moment when they naturally began to transform their wealth into power, and to use that power as the natural right of their wealth. In various ways and to differing extents oligarchic régimes developed in all the major Italian towns.

In short, the great continuing crisis affected the whole web of social relations: the cumulative effect was of widespread unease and instability. In the age of the Hundred Years War and the Great Schism, war became an almost permanent state of affairs, representing the expression of all the frictions and conflicts of a society that had fallen in pieces and was desperately looking for a new equilibrium; war was rather like fever in the human body: both a sign of illness and a reaction against it.

In war, all the bitterness and vindictiveness of the minor nobility, for whom the trade of arms had now become the only possible source of income, flowed together with the adventurous spirit of exiles and *déracinés*, the ambition of new men, and, last but not least, the inveterate local patriotism of citizens.

In this respect too the history of Italy between 1350 and 1450 is basically that of all Europe: a history of almost uninterrupted wars. To enumerate them without risking some omission would be practically impossible. Most of them were 'local'; only after the rise of Gian

Galeazzo Visconti and, even more, in the first half of the fifteenth century, did these 'local' wars fuse together into general ones involving all the states of the peninsula. When war was continuous the exercise of arms naturally tended to become a profession, and it was during this period that the 'companies of adventure' were formed. The first were remnants of the armies that had fought in the battles of the Hundred Years War and the Flanders war, like the band led by the Englishman, Sir John Hawkwood, who served Florence in the War of the Eight Saints. In recognition of his services the city dedicated a funeral monument to him in Santa Maria del Fiore. Other companies were that of the Breton Jean de Montreal (Fra Moriale), who accompanied Cola di Rienzo on his return to Rome, and was put to death by him, and that of the German Walter of Urselingen, 'enemy of God, piety and compassion'. But the example of these transalpine adventurers was soon followed, and Italy became the chosen land of the *condottieri*, true 'gentlemen of war', who came for the most part from the central Appenine region and the Romagna, formed bands among the tough people of the mountain valleys, swelling their numbers with any wanderers they met on the road, until they had a *condotta*, which they put at the service of the rich but unarmed cities of the plain. The rise of these companies and of military professionalism helped to introduce to Italy new forms of war; it was now based not on battles in the open field but on tactics of attrition, skirmishing, sieges in which the first firearms and the first field fortifications made their appearance: a kind of total war, which was exhausting and very expensive. To take an example at random, the War of the Eight Saints alone cost Florence two and a half million gold florins, a considerable sum even for that rich city.

If one considers the expense of war, its new forms, its long duration, and most important of all, the fact that it was the expression of a broader social crisis, one sees how it could contribute to a profound modification of the very political basis of Italy. Independence became more expensive every day: even illustrious cities like Pisa, Padua and Bologna had to give it up for ever. 'Proud Genoa' was several times forced to ask first the Visconti and later France for protection. Other states on the contrary emerged politically strengthened and with territorial gains from the long series of wars in the later fourteenth century. At the date of the Peace of Lodi (1454) the map of Italy was considerably simpler than in the early fourteenth century: Italian political life was now dominated by a system of states of regional dimensions. Only then, after a century of disturbance and war, was Italy able to reach a new, provisional equilibrium.

VENICE, BETWEEN THE SEA AND THE LAND

In 1421, Doge Tomaso Mocenigo addressed to his fellow-citizens a testamentary letter in which he traced an impressive picture of the wealth and power the city had achieved. According to Mocenigo, Venice had 195,000 inhabitants, who annually consumed 355,000 *staia* of corn. The value of their houses, all built in stone, had reached 7,050,000 ducats, and the sums engaged in commerce 10,000,000, with an annual profit of four million. As for her fleet, Venice disposed of more than three thousand ships of all types, manned by almost twenty thousand sailors. Doge Mocegino's statistics are certainly tinged with patriotic exaggeration – more recent and more realistic estimates of Venice's population put it at 110,000 at the beginning of the fourteenth century and 70,000 after the great plague. The population rose again later, but never beyond the earlier figure. Even so, making allowance for his natural tendency to amplification, Doge Mocenigo's account is striking: it represents a significant résumé of the progress of Venice during the preceding centuries.

Although the republic had been subjected to various hard tests, it had developed continuously during the fourteenth century. The increased tonnage of big cargo ships, whose average displacement was by now 700 tons; the forming of regular sea-communications with Flanders and England from the beginning of the century, after the spread of the Hundred Years War had made land-communications unsafe; above all, the increased demand for Eastern goods, all combined to strengthen Venice's position as a great international market – which she had been since the time of the Fourth Crusade. Venice sold the European merchants who waited on her quays not only spices and the traditional products of the East, but also slaves, for the households of the increasingly refined ruling class, copper for the new fire-arms, cotton, a more and more widely used material, sugar, which was beginning to emerge from the pharmacies into cooking, and the oil of southern Italy and Greece. Another product for which demand was soaring in the elegant high society of the fourteenth century was silk; Venice itself had begun to produce it, and the industry soon reached a respectable size. Commercial relations with the Germans were particularly active – for them Venice was the nearest and most natural point of contact with the East. There had been a German trade-centre in Venice since 1228, providing a warehouse for goods and a lodging-place for merchants, and during the fourteenth century the German community in Venice became considerable. In the early

fifteenth century the Emperor Sigismund and the Visconti tried vainly
to divert towards Milan and Genoa the trade-currents that flowed
down from Germany through the Brenner pass to Venice; until the
modern age and the growth of Trieste, Venice remained Germany's
port for the East. Not that German traders were by any means the only
ones to frequent Venice's quaysides and alleyways: no other city of
Christian Europe, perhaps of the entire world, was so markedly cosmopolitan. Venetian architecture and painting show this: they were as
receptive to the lessons of Continental and Northern Gothic as they had
been to Eastern styles. The Ca' d'Oro, the most famous example of the
Venetian Gothic style, was built between 1421 and 1440.

An important part of Venice's trade was, naturally, with the various
major Italian states. According to Doge Mocenigo, Venice annually
imported 48,000 rolls of woollen cloth and 40,000 of fustian from the
cities of Lombardy: 16,000 rolls of wool of various qualities from
Florence alone. In the opposite direction, salt and corn were important
Venetian exports inland. For a long time Venice had made sure of a
near-monopoly of salt, while she played a leading part in redistributing
the corn imported from Apulia and Sicily.

Even if it does not come up to Doge Mocenigo's enthusiastic description, Venetian prosperity seems fairly impressive. The more so
since during the second half of the fourteenth century Venice was almost
continually at war with her great rival, Genoa, and often suffered
military defeat. A first phase of the conflict, in which Venice was helped
by the Catalans, ended in 1353 with no real victory for either side, and
hostilities were resumed in 1378 after the Genoese managed to gain control of the key positions of Cyprus and Tenedos. The Genoese fleet
won a battle off Pola, and blockaded Venice; but in the hour of
danger Venice summoned all her energy and resisted desperately,
allowing the duel to end in a compromise peace, with certain concessions on the Venetians' part. This war, called the Chioggia War, of
1378 to 1381, had seemed to herald the beginning of the end for Venice,
but marks instead, as we shall see, the start of Genoa's decline: though
she won in military terms, Genoa was worn out by the struggle, and
more than ever rent internally by the traditional divisions within her
aristocracy. The burden of the war had been heavy for Venice too, and
she had had to fall back on types of forced loan – but the unity of her
ruling class helped her to overcome this hard test.

No sooner had the Genoese threat receded than that of Turkey became serious. But this time too Venice was up to the situation: by the
cunning use of diplomacy and arms she managed to assure herself the
control of the Dalmatian islands and coast (which she had temporarily
lost), to conquer new advance posts on the Greek mainland and in

Eubaea, and to smash the Turkish counter-offensive by defeating the fleet at Gallipoli in 1416. Five years later, Doge Mocenigo was able to pronounce his paean, full of facts and figures, to the glory of his city.

He was succeeded by Francesco Foscari, whose election to the office of Doge dragged through ten ballots and was perhaps the most competitive and dramatic of the city's entire history. There was a reason for this: now that Venice had survived the war with Genoa and resisted the first Turkish wave, she faced another difficult choice, heavy with consequences. On the death of Gian Galeazzo Visconti in 1402, many of the cities inland of Venice, which had been under his control, and had formerly been part of the Scaligeri domain – Verona, Vicenza, Padua – had with more or less good grace accepted protection from Venice. So Venice, which had had a foot on the mainland, around Treviso, since early in the fourteenth century, now unexpectedly found itself firmly established on land. A little later, a fortunate military campaign against the Emperor had given her control of part of Friuli also, and of the northern part of what is now the Veneto.

Should Venice – as Francesco Foscari argued – go further along this road of land-conquest, defying the violent reaction that was to be expected from the powerful nearby state of Milan, and letting herself get involved in the tangle of rivalries and wars that raged on the continent, or was it better to give up ? Since it decided this question, Foscari's election in 1423 marks a real turning-point in Venetian history: from that moment, although continuing to be a great sea-power, Venice also developed her new mainland rôle. In the first half of the fifteenth century Venice took part, with varying luck, in almost all the various wars of Italy, and in the long run made considerable territorial gains : Bergamo and Brescia in 1433, Ravenna in 1441, and in 1454 with the treaty of Lodi, the lands along the Adda, with the enclave of Crema.

There are good reasons for not considering this development of Venetian policy an about-turn from her previous course : gaining control of the land meant, among other things, putting an end once and for all to the disputes that had occurred with the inland communes about the regulation of the water flowing into the Adriatic ; so there was no more danger of the lagoon being silted up, or its natural conditions being disturbed in any way. Besides, the possession of the Alpine heights assured Venice a regular supply of the wood she needed to build her ships, and so allowed her to continue her sea-policy. In any case, in an age of famine, it was very much in Venice's interests to protect herself from the risk of importing almost all her food by sea. Yet the conquest of the land meant other things too: the Venetian aristocracy began to see the possibility of investment in land and property – an alternative to their old trading vocation. To Francesco Foscari the land had seemed the springboard Venice needed to carry on her great imperialist, maritime career ; but to his successors it became a shelter and refuge from storms. After the Turkish conquest of Constantinople, villas sprang up in the countryside around Venice. The most famous of them, a court frequented by noblemen and famous writers, was that built in the quiet hills of Asolo by Caterina Cornaro, in the second half of the fifteenth century. Before retiring there, she had been Queen of Cyprus.

GENOA, A CITY-FIRM

The Genoese empire in the Levant in the first half of the fourteenth century was certainly no smaller than that of Venice. Her victories over Venice in 1261 and 1298 had given Genoa a dominant position in the Bosphorus and the Black Sea. Genoa's colonies in the Black Sea – Caffa, won in 1266, and Tana – put her in control of the river-outlets by which the products of southern Russia were transported. Equally important to Genoa from the commercial point of view was the possession of the colony of Focea, with its alum-mines, which gave Genoa a near-monopoly in this indispensable colouring material. The Genoese also had their outposts in the Aegean: Chios and Lesbos. Lesbos was ruled by the Gattilusio family, who also controlled Lemnos and Thasos after 1247.

In the Western Mediterranean too, in spite of competition first from the Catalans and later from the Florentines, Genoa had firmly established bases. Although Venice had been the first to open up regular sea communications with Flanders and England, the Genoese dominated the Spanish market – at Seville they owned an entire quarter – and from Spain they set out for the towns and markets of North Africa. The first man to land on the archipelago of the Canaries was a Genoese, Lanzarotto Malocello. As for the North, though German trade flowed to Venice through the Brenner pass, Genoa also had an active share in it, through her neighbour Milan. Barcelona and Marseilles were not only rivals but also partners : Eastern goods unloaded at Genoa were able to go by way of Marseilles and continue along the Rhône to the interior of France, so avoiding the hazards of an Alpine crossing. On the return voyage from Marseilles or from Aigues-Mortes, Genoese ships carried Provençal corn or salt from Hyères, destined partly for Genoese consumption, partly for re-export.

So Genoa's trading-system had little cause to envy that of Venice ; and we have seen that her fleet proved militarily superior on several occasions.

Yet while Venice managed to survive the grave crisis of the fifteenth century relatively unscathed, the same cannot be said of Genoa. The reasons for this difference are to be found in the particular structure of Genoese society and communal life, which have already been mentioned. Throughout Genoa's history her ruling class kept unchanged the stamp of its feudal origins, and never formed a firmly unified corporate body like that which was sealed by the closing of the Great Council. It was never anything but an agglomeration of *alberghi* (*albergo* in this case being a sort of brotherhood of noble families, formed during the fourteenth century), of clans of families and their partisans, rivals one with another, each striving to secure itself the greatest possible influences on the town's political affairs. So in the eyes of the lower classes it lacked the prestige that a true political class must have, and encouraged in the people the hope of being able to make their rulers more malleable by force. Faced with the danger of the victory of a hostile faction, or that of popular subversion, the lords of the moment more than once placed the city under the protection of a powerful neighbour. So the history of Genoa in the fourteenth century is an incessant tale of revolts, struggles between groups, foreign interventions. When in 1339 the popular faction prevailed, and imposed the election of a doge, in the person of Simone Boccanegra, the oligarchic nobility immediately put the city under the wing of Archbishop Giovanni Visconti, lord of Milan. After his death Genoa suffered further violent internal struggles, and accepted French rule in 1396, until 1409. Then later, between 1421 and 1436, Genoa was once more under the Visconti, and under France again between 1459 and 1461. On the other hand, this political restlessness was no more than a screen to an underlying social immobility: in spite of attempts at change that came from below, Genoese political life continued to be the monopoly of a limited oligarchy of great families.

The same characteristics are to be seen in the economic sphere: private finances were in fact a good deal healthier than those of the republic, which, committed as it was to its large-scale maritime policy, and having used every kind of tax, duty, direct and indirect impost, to squeeze the last drop from the poorer classes, had to incur heavy debts and obligations, resorting to loans from private individuals, especially the wealthier citizens. The system was the same as that used in other Italian cities, particularly in Venice. It worked well so long as business profits and the city's good fortune in general allowed the Public Treasury to pay interest punctually to its own creditors. But when things began to get worse and there loomed the risk of losing not only interest but even part of the capital, citizens would only invest their money in state bonds and continue to trust the state if they had a great sense of devotion to the common weal. This existed at Venice but not at Genoa.

After the Chioggia War, which had swallowed up vast sums at Genoa as at Venice, public finances began to be threatened by disaster – by 1408 the state debt had reached the enormous figure of 2,938,000 Genoese lire – and creditors demanded maximum guarantees. They joined together in a syndicate, the Banco di S. Giorgio, in order that they could take over the administration of the public debt. But how could the new adminstrators guarantee a more regular payment of interest? The solution was to impose even harsher taxes and to entrust the Bank with the control of some of the state's tax-earnings. In this way, by making themselves administrators of their debtor's income and assuming the rôle of, so to speak, official liquidators, the creditors in partnership in the Bank assured themselves a solid guarantee. But when Genoese prestige and trade in the East began its downward curve, this guarantee was not enough. This happened during the first half of the fifteenth century: the fall of Constantinople in 1453 cut Genoa off from her flourishing Black Sea colonies, and was the final blow to an already gravely compromised political prestige.

In these conditions the Bank administrators demanded more : to be direct controllers of certain Genoese territories – colonies in the East, castles and land on the coast, Corsica – with freedom to exploit them at their own pleasure, and even to sell them. This was what happened to Leghorn, ceded to Florence in 1421, for cash. '(The Bank of) St George,' wrote Machiavelli, 'has placed most of the lands and towns of the Genoese empire under its control, governing and defending them and ... sending to them its governors, without the commune having to go to any trouble. And so it has come about that those citizens have lost their love for the commune ... and given it to St George.' It is hard to imagine a clearer example of what we mean when we talk about the consolidation of the corporative, privileged positions of the urban aristocracy: in Genoa we see a city, a 'republic', giving its finances and even its territorial sovereignty up to its richest citizens; we see a state transforming itself almost into a business, in which its great families are shareholders.

These great families were in fact the principal beneficiaries of the operation. Gradually, after the decline of Genoese trade in the East, economic difficulties grew, and small savers had to withdraw their money from the holdings of the Banco di S. Giorgio, leaving them concentrated in the hands of a small, powerful oligarchy of creditors, from which were to emerge the great dynasties of Genoese bankers who financed Charles v and Philip ii.

FLORENCE, FROM REPUBLIC TO PRINCIPALITY

In the early fourteenth century Florence's star was at its zenith. According to the description given us by Giovanni Villani, she was a city of 100,000 inhabitants, with a hundred and ten churches, thirty hospitals, and two hundred workshops, which every year produced from seventy to eighty thousand rolls of wool. Her forty banks handled huge sums and embraced the whole of Christendom and the Levant in their field of action. In the first decades of the century one of them alone, the powerful Bardi company, employed as many as three hundred and forty-six agents in twenty-five branches scattered here and there. Every year Florence consumed from fifty-five to sixty thousand flasks of wine, four thousand calves, thirty thousand pigs; in a world in which hunger was a permanent phenomenon she was, in short, a well-fed city. She was above all a well-taught city: Villani tells us that all the eight to ten thousand children of Florence could read and write, that between a thousand and fifteen hundred of them had learned 'algorism' and three hundred and fifty to six hundred attended the higher schools. The consequent basic level of literacy and culture was absolutely exceptional in the Christian West of the time. This must be remembered when one considers how fourteenth-century Florence could produce such a rich and genuine vernacular, 'bourgeois' literature. Among those boys who had learned grammar, rhetoric and algebra on the benches of Florentine schools were the historians Dino Compagni and Giovanni Villani, the story-teller Franco Sacchetti and the great Giovanni Boccaccio. This illegitimate son of a merchant and agent of the Bardi family in Paris was first sent to school at Florence and then to Naples to learn business. Would the famous realism of the *Decameron* have emerged without this apprenticeship and these years of travel ?

The internal organization of the republic was still regulated by the forms that the reform of 1282 and the '*ordinamenti di giustizia*' of 1293 had established; it was based on the principle of the participation of the greater and medium professional corporations in the management of public affairs, and on the swift and regular rotation of posts. But Florentine liberty and prosperity too had their Achilles heel, in the military weakness of a city whose inhabitants were too rich and too much concerned with the internal events of the commune and its parties to be good soldiers. The days of Montaperti and Campaldino, when the citizens of Florence had gone to battle personally, with their own cavalry bands, were past ; the trade of arms did not appeal to a people of craftsmen and merchants, and Florence was one of the first Italian cities to resort to the mercenary militias. Besides, the *contado* was too small to provide any great abundance of men at arms. The consequences of this military inferiority were seen in 1315, when the Pisan Uguccione della Faggiuola beat the Florentine troops at Montecatini, and in 1325 when Castruccio Castracani, a fourteenth-century self-made man who had become lord of Lucca, beat them again at Altopascio. On both occasions Florence had to call on the protection of her most powerful ally, the Angevin kingdom of Naples; and after the defeat of Altopascio, to entrust the city's seigniory to Charles of Calabria, son of King Robert. The danger later passed with the unexpected death of Castruccio in 1327, and Florence swiftly returned to her usual system of rule. Work on the construction of the Cathedral, which had been interrupted in 1323, was resumed, and in a few years Giotto's airy bell-tower rose up over the panorama of a city that was freer and more prosperous than ever.

But between 1340 and 1380 Florence's history was to be unpleasantly dramatic. There had been early warning-signs of the imminent crisis: in 1327 the Scali, a banking-house that, like many others, had committed itself to supporting the ambitious and capricious policies of the Angevins of Naples, had to declare itself bankrupt. But in the euphoria of that moment the Florentine bankers paid no attention and went on lending vast sums to both the King of Naples and the King of England. Then in 1339 the King of England decreed the suspension of payments, and the situation became catastrophic: one by one the great Florentine banking houses found themselves in desperate straits. The gravity of this financial and economic crisis and the fact that it coincided with a new reversal in foreign affairs – Lucca, which Florence had acquired in 1341 for 150,000 gold florins, now fell under Pisan rule – provoked a chain reaction among the citizens. For less than a year the seigniory was in the hands of an adventurer, Walter of Brienne, called the Duke of Athens. This experiment in seigniorial government collapsed amid general discontent, and the discords of class and party that had for a long time been fermenting within the city, made worse by the recent crisis, came out into the open. In 1343 the minor guilds, which had up to that time been excluded from the city's government, won the right to participate in public affairs alongside the greater and medium guilds. But in the following years their victory aroused a violent series of challenges and attempts at revenge on the part of the *popolo grasso* (the members of the greater guilds) and their political organization the Guelf party. The terrible plague of 1348, which drastically reduced the city's population, naturally aggravated existing social unease, and created new kinds. Now, following the craftsmen and small shopkeepers of the minor guilds, the disinherited masses entered the struggle. They consisted for the most part of immigrants from the *contado*, wool workers – the *'Ciompi'* – who made desultory attempts to organize themselves into a group. At the same time, war beat continually at the city's door, and several times in these years of crisis and social unrest Florence had to mobilize: the first time was in 1351, to repel the attack of the Milan Visconti, the second in 1362–4, against Pisa, and finally, between 1375 and 1378, against the Pope, on his way back to Rome, and anxious to extend his rule in central Italy as widely as possible. During this last war, called the War of the Eight Saints, which was, as we have seen, a severe blood-letting for the city's already disturbed finances, Florence was placed under an Interdict.

At this conjunction of profound social crisis, economic depression and psychological and religious agitation, the tensions that had been building up over three terrible decades burst out in one of the few episodes of Italian history that can be compared with the great city revolts of Flanders or England: the rising of the *Ciompi*. On the 19th July the *popolo minuto* or 'small people' surged into the streets, burned the houses of the chief citizens, hanged the police chief and forced the lords closeted inside the Palazzo Vecchio to come out; their places were taken by men of the minor guilds and the wool-proletariat. Their triumph was short: their chosen chief magistrate, the wool-carder Michele di Lando, himself became the accomplice of the counter-offensive of the *popolo grasso* although he immediately lost his position. But the new government, mainly composed of representatives of the minor guilds, had a brief existence. On the conservative wave that almost always follows revolutionary action, the Guelf party and the merchant oligarchy it represented managed to get back into power in 1382. So the long political and social crisis that had tormented the city for almost forty years, since the great bankruptcies, ended in the best way possible for the nobility and the privileged classes, and a new cycle of Florence's troubled history began: that of the consolidation of an oligarchic régime, and its development into a seigniory.

The families that counted at Florence were by now reduced to a handful: the Ricci, the Albizi, the Alberti, the Medici and a few others. They were divided by furious rivalries, and according to circumstances and luck, took turns in ruling the city. Even so, passing over the various political and family fluctuations and the changing fortunes of the contending clans, from 1382 Florence was ruled entirely by a small oligarchy of nobles and bankers. So after decades of unrest and upheaval Florence now had a relatively stable and socially homogeneous government; and stable governments, we know, are also the most efficient. So here were achievements, both domestically and in relations with other states. In the Italian wars between the end of the fourteenth century and the Peace of Lodi Florence was normally allied with Venice and against Milan; in spite of her chronic military weakness she manoeuvred ably and managed to make important territorial gains in the long run. The richest prize was Pisa, won in 1406, giving Florence her coveted access to the sea, and freeing her from her most persistent antagonist. Other conquests, or re-conquests, were those of Arezzo in 1384, Cortona in 1411, and Leghorn, ceded by the Genoese in 1421. Thus, what was to be the Grand Duchy of Tuscany took shape, though for the moment it was less like a state than a federation of towns under the tutelage of one dominant town. Within Florence, by far the most important exploit was the drawing up, between 1427 and 1429, of a land-register that provided the basis for a more equable and more productive distribution of taxation, and a restoration of the financial situation. Machiavelli wrote of this land-register that it was so made that 'the law, not men, bore the weight of it'. It reveals a detailed picture of the new Florentine prosperity, including the opulence of the oligarchy. The great families are inscribed in the register for sums that are far beyond the average. For example, in the quarter of San Giovanni there were only three families with a taxable capital of more than 50,000 florins : the Panciatichi, the Borromei, and, ahead of everyone, the Medici, with 79,472 florins.

So the scene was one of stability and efficiency. Florence entered a new period of prosperity and even opulence; and as in the past it was founded on the traditional mercantile and banking activities. Though the old banking houses of the Bardi and the Peruzzi had not survived the crisis of 1342, new ones had risen in their place, chief among them the enormously powerful house of the Medici, a model of business organization on an international scale. Though the old and glorious wool industry was in decline, and its early fourteenth-century annual production of ninety thousand rolls of wool now reduced to only thirty thousand, the new silk industry on the other hand was on the crest of the wave. Besides, the conquest of Pisa had opened Florence a way to the sea, and, at least in the first decades of the fifteenth century, she had considerable success in trying to make herself a sea power big enough to rival Genoa and Venice in the markets of the East. In this thriving time there was a return of the building fever that had characterized Florence in the early fourteenth century. In 1401 was held the contest for the doors of the Baptistry, won by Ghiberti; in 1421 Brunelleschi began work on building the Cathedral dome. The same artist and the same period produced the Pazzi chapel and the wonderful church of San Lorenzo. Private building went on together with public: the Palazzo Rucellai, the incomparable work of Leon Battista Alberti, was built between 1446 and 1451; the Medici villas of Careggi and Cafaggiolo were rebuilt by Michelozzo in 1434 and 1451. The list could easily be continued. The impressive presence of noble palaces in the city's streets and piazzas impressed on the minds and hearts of the citizens a respectful fear of the ruling oligarchy.

The rise of the Medici, who became de facto masters of the city in 1434, with Cosimo, did not so much open a new phase in Florentine history as consummate the forming and consolidation of an oligarchic régime, begun some decades before. From now on, certainly, Florentine chancellors and humanists could no longer, as they had in the days of the war against the 'tyrant' Gian Galeazzo Visconti, sing the praises of *florentina libertas*.

THE STATE OF MILAN FROM THE VISCONTI TO THE SFORZA

The long series of wars of the second half of the fourteenth century and first half of the fifteenth left Milan more enlarged and more strengthened than any other of the states of Italy. During the whole of the fourteenth century in fact, Milan's policy had been one of expansion towards every point of the compass: towards the North in the direction of the Swiss cantons, to ensure control of the Alpine passes, which were routes for trade with northern Europe; towards the South and the sea, with the aim of gaining possession of Genoa; to the East towards Piedmont and to the West towards Venice; finally, to the South-East towards Bologna, and beyond, towards central Italy. This expansionist policy was begun under Archbishop Giovanni Visconti (1339 – 54), whose achievements included the conquests of Bellinzona, the Angevin domains in Piedmont, Bologna, and for some years even Genoa. After his death, expansion was interrupted by the dynastic crisis that followed, during which many recent conquests were lost, but his grandson Gian Galeazzo took Milan further along the road of conquest. Between 1378 and his death in 1402, by means of wars and bold *coups de main* he managed to gain control not only of Lombardy and most of Emilia with the city of Bologna, but also won Verona and Vicenza from the Scaligeri, Novara and Vercelli from the house of Savoy, and Pisa, Siena and Perugia. The duchy of Milan – the ducal title was formally granted to Gian Galeazzo in 1395, by the Emperor Wenceslas – was the most powerful and formidable of the states of Italy, and the only one in a position to aspire to the rule of the whole peninsula. One may thus understand why the prime objective of the other Italian powers, and particularly Florence and Venice, was to reduce Milan's ambitions to a reasonable size. Gian Galeazzo's unexpected death and the new crisis that followed allowed them a chance they could not have hoped for: Venice, as we have seen, began her penetration inland, while Florence won Pisa. The Pope regained Bologna, and the other cities of central Italy that he had lost. Siena won back her liberty. In the wars of the first half of the fifteenth century Filippo Maria Visconti, who had prevailed over the other contenders to the duchy in 1412, was unable to win back much territory; in fact, as we have seen, he had to cede Bergamo and Brescia to Venice in 1433. Genoa offered the least resistance, and in 1421 once more fell under the protection of the Visconti. But once again it was a temporary occupation, lasting only until 1435.

So, after a century of wars, the state of Milan found itself restricted to the lands of Lombardy between the Adda and the Ticino, with the cities of Parma and Piacenza to the South and the Valtellina and the county of Bellinzona to the North, as an appendix. Within these more limited though still generous borders it remained one of the strongest and most solidly united Italian states. This became clear when Duke Filippo Maria died without leaving male heirs and the succession fell to his son-in-law, Francesco Sforza, a *condottiere* of proven skill and courage, but of obscure birth. At first it seemed that the prophecies of doom that had been made by many, including Filippo Maria himself, would be fulfilled: in the capital the citizen aristocracy took the opportunity of restoring the old liberties of the commune and proclaiming a republic, while the other cities of the state claimed their own rights. But after only two years this further and graver dynastic crisis was resolved, and in spite of resolute opposition from Venice Francesco Sforza managed to regain possession of all the lands of the state in their entirety. The hardness of this test had served to show how solid was the political organism created by the Visconti.

But what were the causes and factors of this success? Contemporaries, whether detractors or apologists of the Visconti, agreed in attributing their fortunes to the political structures of the state they had formed: to the fact that Milan was a 'seigniory' par excellence. To their enemies, the Visconti – above all Gian Galeazzo – were no more than bristling, warlike tyrants who reduced their subjects to the level of servants and whose only ambition was to violate Italian liberties. In consequence Milan was a sort of Sparta or Macedonia to Florence's Athens. Their apologists saw the state of Milan as the only part of Italy in which justice and 'peace' reigned, and where the old factions and local rivalries had been silenced by the energetic and enlightened action of their masters.

In fact, whatever their points of view, these judgements grasp an important aspect of the question. For there is no doubt that parallel with their policy of expansion, and as a result of it, the Visconti strove to create and consolidate efficient centralized administrative and fiscal institutions, and in this attempt they found it necessary to limit and crush the privileges and freedoms of the various communities, including those of the capital. Milan, as we have seen, tried to profit from the crisis following Filippo Maria's death by getting back her old prerogatives: but the brief and inglorious life of the 'Golden Ambrosian Republic', and its failure, showed how anachronistic this surge of citizen pride and local feeling was.

Even though it is right to emphasize the greater cohesion of the Visconti seigniory compared with the other Italian city-states, and the different relationship that existed between the capital and the other towns of the state, we should not forget that it never ceased to be fundamentally an inherited state, and as such, as is proved by the many dynastic crises that recurred regularly from the death of Archbishop Giovanni until the rise to power of Francesco Sforza, it was threatened as the other states were by local fragmentation and rivalries between men and between towns. There are other reasons for its power and solidity, and for the success of its seigniorial régime.

These reasons are to be found in the large resources of man-power and money that were available to the Dukes of Milan and allowed them to recruit the best mercenary leaders and the most experienced soldiers. Gian Galeazzo was able to embark on a colossal building programme like that of Milan's pretentious Cathedral, begun in 1389, or the Charterhouse of Pavia, begun in 1396, a Lombard Saint-Denis destined to house the tombs of the ducal family, without having to give up his ambitious and very expensive military schemes which he was pursuing at precisely the same time. The reasons for the Visconti's power are in the last analysis to be found in the healthy prosperity of the state and its economy.

As is the rule in Italian history, this wealth belonged largely to the towns. Milan of the fourteenth and fifteenth centuries was a city rich in resources and vitality. She was miraculously preserved from the great plague of 1348, and victoriously surmounted later epidemics, such as the terrible one of 1361. After the crisis that struck the fustian industry, her principal activity, apart from the traditional manufacture of arms, was the wool industry, the scale and organization of which had been modified on the model of Florence – it became more concentrated, and the work process was more closely adapted to the market. At Milan too there appeared the figure of the merchant-entrepreneur, *faciens laborare lanam*, and at Milan too banking and finance tended more and more to graft themselves on to manufacturing and trading. And it was these bankers who gave the Visconti the support they needed for their political ambitions. To procure this support for themselves they did not disdain to form bonds of kinship.

But the prosperity of Lombardy was not only that of Milan and the other main centres: it was also the fruit of the countryside and of the notable improvements and transformations that had taken place there during the fourteenth and fifteenth centuries; and in the context of a crisis as acute as that which afflicted Europe during this period, these developments are a splendid exception.

In fact, as has already been emphasized, the conditions for the drama of agrarian progress that was to unfold in the Lombard country-side almost without interruption until the nineteenth century had already been laid down in the period of the communes. The first great hydraulic and irrigation works – the Muzza canals and the *Naviglio Grande* – belong to the twelfth century, and the first mention of the *marcite*, those artificial meadows that characterize lower Lombardy, occurs in 1138. So already at that time the agriculture of Lombardy's most fertile areas distinguished itself from that of other regions of Italy by its higher technical level, and by being more of a corporate enterprise. But it was only from the mid-fourteenth century, spurred on by the crisis and the altered economic and food situation, that there began in the Lombard countryside a process of regulariz-ation and adaptation more complete and more successful than anything that took place in the rest of Italy. In other parts of Italy this return to the land had the air of a withdrawal, but in Lombardy it was a positive economic enterprise and an investment that paid off.

In the fourteenth and fifteenth centuries the cultivation of rice was introduced in wide areas of Lombardy, and that of woad spread around Voghera, the seeds being used in dyeing. During the same period mulberry-trees were introduced to the hill areas. In the mean time, supported by the seigniory's planning activity, the work of irrigation and canal-building went on and was intensified: in 1365 the canal from Milan to Pavia was opened; under Filippo Maria the Bereguardo canal was opened, and under Francesco Sforza the canals of Binasco and the Martesana were opened and work was begun on the Sforzesco Canal. Later, Leonardo da Vinci worked on projects for new hydraulic works. So lower Lombardy gradually took on the appearance we know: it became a land of dykes, canals and irrigated fields. This was the appearance it presented to Commines, late in the fifteenth century – a landscape *tout fossoié comme est Flandre*. The progress thus made in irrigation and the spread of artificial meadows allowed Lombard and Po valley farmers to develop the breeding and stabling of cattle far beyond the levels possible in the rest of Italy, in a subsistence agriculture that considered cattle primarily as instruments of labour. And they gathered the fruits of this progress: already in the fifteenth century the parmesan cheese produced in the countryside of Parma, Reggio and Lodi was one of the most prized Italian cheeses, and the butter of the Lombard plain was exported as far as Rome.

Those instrumental in this process of agricultural conversion and transformation were for the most part *homines novi* who had emerged from the ranks of the urban middle class or who came from the countryside itself. So it is easy to see how the control and distribution of property were also profoundly modified, in that there were an ever-diminishing number of feudal and seigniorial holdings. By means of lease-contracts that obliged the owner to refund to the leaseholder the expenses he incurred in making improvements, much property that had belonged to big landowners eventually changed hands. Lands belonging to the Church and to religious orders were particularly affected: in 1434 Enea Silvio Piccolomini, the future Pius II, lamented their relinquishment and financial disorder.

So, with its reclaimed fields, its stables, and its enterprising tenants, Lombardy and the neighbouring parts of the Po plain were already, in the mid-fifteenth century, the most progressive agricultural area of Italy. We shall see how much this contributed to its later prosperity and leading economic rôle.

THE KINGDOM OF NAPLES AND SICILY

After the peace of Caltabellotta (1302) the Kingdom of Sicily was no longer politically unified as it had been in the days of the Normans and the Hohenstaufen: for while the Angevins still reigned at Naples and on the southern mainland, Sicily was ruled by the Aragonese, who in 1323 became masters also of Sardinia. But if southern Italy and the islands were no longer a politically united whole, they were still, particularly in comparison with the rest of Italy, fairly homogeneous from the economic and social point of view.

This unity was primarily based on economic factors. As has already been stressed, agriculture was the fundamental and far the most important resource of the southern economy. A large proportion of the corn consumed in the populous, hungry cities of northern and central

Italy came from Apulia and from Sicily, which was long to remain one of Italy's granaries, and an even larger proportion of the wine drunk in Italy was 'Greek wine' or 'Latin wine', in other words from Campania or the neighbouring regions. Sicily also exported a considerable amount of cotton and sugar; the flocks of the Abruzzi produced wool and cheese; Aquila produced saffron.

The region was also united by its social and political institutions: in a largely agricultural economy feudal institutions and relationships had preserved themselves more or less intact, and with them, the political organization of a feudal type of monarchy. Above all, the South stood out from the general pattern of Italy – this too has already been emphasized – by the fact that it was less densely populated, and its inhabitants were less concentrated into towns. Although Palermo retained considerable importance as a centre of Eastern trade, it was no longer the triumphant metropolis of Arab and Norman days. As for Naples, it may have been the capital of a famous region and the seat of a lavish court, but it had only thirty thousand inhabitants, far fewer than the major cities of northern and central Italy, and its divisions into quarters, each one belonging to a different 'nation', made it more like an oriental than an Italian city. The Kingdom's trade and exports were mainly in the hands of foreigners: Jews, Catalans, Genoese, Florentines, and even Germans, who practically monopolized the Aquila saffron market. The same applied to finance, which was dominated by the great Florentine banking houses. It must be remembered that since the time of Charles d'Anjou's invasion these bankers had won favour in the eyes of the Angevin kings, and had secured the privilege of farming the bulk of the taxes and had even acquired considerable power in managing the Kingdom's political affairs. Niccolò Acciaiuoli, who up to his death in 1365 was the most influential person at court and the Kingdom's real political master after the death of King Robert, belonged to a family of Florentine bankers.

A society of this kind, anchored to its agricultural basis and lacking any alternative or compensating resources, was bound to suffer deeply from the effects of the general crisis of the century. In no other part of Italy were such vast areas now deserted that had formerly been cultivated: it is estimated that a third of the villages in the Kingdom of Naples were abandoned. In Calabria the level of population in the later sixteenth century was still far below what it had been in the fourteenth. In Sardinia the proportion of villages abandoned was even higher: about half, it seems; though there are no precise figures for Sicily, the situation there cannot have been very different. This widespread depopulation and the consequent decline of agriculture was not only due to plague and to famine, but also to the fall in prices of farm-produce that followed the plague and continued for many decades. A further factor was the increasing competition that many southern products, such as Sicily's sugar or the saffron of the Abruzzi, now had to face in the national market. This also explains the thoroughness with which certain areas where cereals had been grown were entirely converted to pasture-land. The most noticeable example of this process was the 'chessboard' of Apulia, a piece of Spanish '*meseta*' transported to Italy.

The crisis that began in the fourteenth century also had a profoundly disturbing effect on the social life of the South: this may be deduced from the fact that it had repercussions even on the level of political history. However much its prestige had been hurt by the humiliation it had suffered in the War of the Vespers, the Kingdom of Naples continued to play a main part in Italian politics up to the death of Robert d'Anjou in 1343. King Robert lost no opportunity of reasserting his position as a champion of Guelfism: he confronted every Imperial invasion of Italy from that of Henry vii to that of Ludwig of Bavaria; he put a stop to every Ghibelline pronouncement. It will be remembered that Florence herself, confronted by the menace of Castruccio, called on his protection. The Angevin monarchy's continued prestige may be measured by the brilliance of its court and its capital. Naples of the early fourteenth century, where the young Boccaccio lived, is vividly described in his story *Andreuccio da Perugia*; it may indeed have been unlike other Italian capitals, but it was no less splendid and illustrious. The contacts that the Angevin court kept up with Florence, through the bankers, and the presence at Naples of a wealthy Florentine community had attracted many Tuscan artists. These included Giotto himself, who in about 1330 painted a cycle of pictures, subsequently lost, in the Castel dell'Uovo; and Tino da Camaino, who executed the funeral monument to Charles of Calabria in the thirteenth-century church of Santa Chiara.

After Robert's death the scene changed radically: for the rest of the century the history of the Kingdom of Naples is a succession of struggles without quarter, of violent clashes between the various branches of the Angevin dynasty: that of Hungary, that of Durazzo and that of Taranto. During her forty years' reign the depraved Queen Giovanna managed to bury three husbands who had died in tragic or mysterious circumstances, before she herself met a violent end. But this in itself does not explain the radical change in the situation: dynastic conflicts were in the end no more than a reflection of the divisions and disunity of the baronial class, and these in turn the consequence of the current social and economic crisis. When their incomes dwindled, Neapolitan

feudal lords transformed themselves into 'adventurers' or actual
bandits, sought in war and plunder the profits they had lost, and forgot
their obligations of fealty to the King, while demanding ever-greater
concessions from him. The military exploits of King Ladislas (1400–14)
and the successes he obtained (for ten years he held the seigniory of
Rome, which had been abandoned by the Pope) succeeded for a time
in directing the barons' appetites outwards and in controlling their
aggressions. But after he died, in the reign of Giovanna II (1414–35)
the Kingdom fell back once more into feudal anarchy. The picture
of Aragonese Sicily at the same period is no different: after the death
of Frederick III in 1377 Sicily's story too is one of endless struggles
and dissensions between the nobles who belonged to the Aragonese
and Angevin factions.

The Angevins fought the Durazzo party; the Aragonese fought the
'Sicilians': thrones were struggled over by conflicting pretenders.
It is the same picture as that of the great feudal monarchies of Continental Europe: France at the time of Charles VI and the struggle
between Armagnacs and Burgundians: England in the Wars of the
Roses – a picture of disunity, blood and barbarism. With the difference
that at the end of these bloody vicissitudes there was no Charles VII or
Henry VII. Alfonso of Aragon, the prince who emerged victorious at
the end of the exhausting struggle, and in whose person the crowns of
Naples and Sicily were re-united, has come down to history as 'Alfonso
the Magnanimous'. In fact, under him and his successor Ferrante
the Kingdom of Sicily was once more an honourable member of the
community of Italian states, and his court became, as we shall see later,
one of the centres of Italian humanism, associated with the famous
names of Pontano and Sannazzaro. Naples was enriched with new
monuments, beginning with the triumphal arch of Castelnuovo, which
Luciano Laurana, the architect of the ducal palace at Urbino, built
between 1452 and 1460, in honour of the new dynasty. Later, in 1485,
Giuliano da Maiano built the noble Capuan gateway. But Alfonso's
generosity was shown above all towards the barons, with whom he
signed an agreement at the beginning of his reign, amounting to a
sweeping indemnity for all the usurpations and deeds of violence
perpetrated during a hundred years of feudal anarchy. At that date, of
the 1550 'universities' or local communities in the kingdom, only
102 belonged to the Treasury and the Crown: all the rest had fallen
under baronial jurisdiction, and were 'feudal' lands.

To make up for the shrinking of income that followed this massive
loss of Crown rights and jurisdiction – among other things Alfonso had
given up the *adoa*, a personal tax paid in lieu of military service – the
Aragonese monarchy had to increase the burden of taxes and tributes

borne by the peasantry. The peasants reacted, and between 1469 and 1475 the countryside of Calabria was the scene of peasant revolts more widespread and more determined than most uprisings in Italian history. They were of course crushed by fire and the sword. So, after a century of inner struggles and disorder, the Kingdom finally achieved peace within its own frontiers. But as we shall see, this peace was soon to be disturbed: not from below but from above, this time, in the form of sedition, not rebellion – the so-called barons' conspiracy of 1484. This too was soon defeated and repressed, but the barons' power, their alliance in a common cause, and their rebelliousness, were from this time on to constitute a permanent threat to the stability and even the unity of the kingdom.

THE BIRTH OF THE PAPAL STATE

What a strange city mediaeval Rome was! A loose agglomeration, half town, half country, much smaller and less densely populated than the large towns of northern and central Italy, not to mention the ancient Imperial metropolis that Rome had been, as the ruins scattered about her modest landscape bore witness. Rome had its own self-governing administrative and legal bodies, adorned with illustrious names, but effective power in Rome was held by the powerful feudal houses and factions, first among whom were the Colonna and the Orsini, who strutted about the streets with their gangs, and more than once forced the Pope out of the city. And yet this was the city from which ex-communications were issued, and the city before which emperors bowed low in the hope of a crown. There were days when the citizens of Rome could feel that their city was once again the real centre of the world: at the Jubilee of 1300, convoked by Boniface vIII, thousands upon thousands of pilgrims poured into Rome, jamming the streets so densely that a bridge collapsed under their weight. Then there had been the arrival of the Bavarian, with his picturesque train, and the unusual ceremony on the Campidoglio. One may almost say that mediaeval Rome led a double life: the humble plebeian life of every day, and that of great and solemn occasions.

One son of this Rome, who shared its double nature, was Cola di Rienzo, one of the most unusual figures of Italian history. The son of an innkeeper and a washerwoman, brought up among the peasants of the Ciociaria, he was a man of plebeian, instinctive tastes, and remained so even at the peak of his extraordinary career. When his good luck ran out and his body was hung up by the feet, all were amazed at his

incredible fatness. 'He looked like a huge buffalo or cow at the slaugh-
terer's' wrote an anonymous Roman chronicler. Power was for him
partly a means to heal the sore of his base origin: 'He gained colour and
blood,' says the same anonymous Roman, 'and he ate better and slept
better.' Yet this man had a deep love for his city, and was genuinely
and passionately convinced of his mission to restore it to the dignity it
had lost. From his earliest youth he had fed his mind with classical
writings, and had wandered restlessly among the remains of Roman
monuments, invoking the shades of great men of his past. 'Where are
these good Romans? Where is their perfect justice? . . . If only I could
have lived in their day.'

This strange mixture of extroversion and delusion, this learned
ignorance that so delighted the intellectuals, this combination of
naïveté and megalomania, together with the hold on men's minds that
the myth of Rome continued to exert, explain his extraordinary,
ephemeral success. In 1343 he went to Avignon as a legate of the people;
he returned with the title of Apostolic Legate to the Roman municipality, and the promise that a new Jubilee would be held in 1350.
This notably increased his popularity, giving him the ambition of
becoming ruler of the city. He did so in May 1347, when, after a
general tumult he himself had organized and instigated, the title of
Tribune of the Roman Republic was conferred on him. In this new
position Cola was not satisfied with putting the city in order and
ending the quarrels and factions of the barons. In his eyes Rome was
the capital of the world, and he, the '*liberator urbis*', could not neglect his
universal mission. So he sent messages to all the Italian princes and
towns, and announced for the Whitsun of 1348 a solemn meeting at
which the representatives of the cities and states of Italy were to nomin-
ate the new Emperor. For it was time to take the right of election away
from the German barbarians – time for Italy to be once more the
garden of the Empire. These were ideas that still struck a deep echo,
and not only in the minds of intellectuals like Petrarch.

But the solemn assembly of August 1348 was not held: Cola was
hated by the nobles, and lacked the support of the Pope, who regarded
his ambitions with trepidation, and in October 1347 he had to leave
Rome. So for the moment his career was over, but not without leaving
its traces – and the first to realize this was the Pope.

In his 'captivity' at Avignon the Pope had been chiefly concerned
with putting in order the administrative and financial machinery of the
Curia. Now he was faced with the problem of harnessing it to a state.
There had been one, in theory, since the time when Pepin had pre-
sented to the Pope the Byzantine territories won by the Lombards.
It was true that the territorial limits of the papal estates had for a long

time been vague, and it was only comparatively recently, in time of Innocent III, that they had become identified with the central part of the peninsula. In the mid-fourteenth century those territories were a no-man's or every-man's land, a mosaic of city-states and seigniories, communities of mountain-people or of monks. One of these, the republic of San Marino, survives to this day. But if this patchwork of jurisdictions and states in miniature could be given a powerful capital, then there might be a chance to make it into something more unified. And why could that capital not be Rome, to whose call, put out by an obscure, plebeian megalomaniac, so many lords had responded, and whose myth, as Cola had shown, was still so potent? And would that call not draw much more attention when it came from a pope, returning to Italy, as so many people had begged him to, establishing his home for ever in the capital of the Roman and Christian world and raising it to its former level? These were the plans that were being hatched at the Avignon Curia when, after previous attempts had failed, the sturdy Spanish Cardinal Gil d'Albornoz was sent to Italy, with the aim of restoring the Pope's temporal authority. At his side was Cola, who had survived a stay in Prague, at the court of Charles IV, and had been sent by the Emperor to Avignon. He now bore the title of Senator of Rome. But this time his triumph was even briefer: he entered Rome on 1 August 1354, and on 8 October he was stabbed to death during a riot. But Albornoz's mission was more successful: by ably exploiting the discord that divided the seigniories and cities of central Italy, and using as a lever the people's weariness, brought on by the recent plague and the continual wars, he managed to create the framework of a centralized state. The so-called Egidian Constitutions, which he proclaimed to a Parliament held at Fano in 1357, proclaimed the division of the state into seven provinces, each ruled by its own governor. So the Papal State took on the forms it was to retain for centuries, and the towns of central Italy – Narni and Spoleto for instance – were soon dominated by the massive forms of the fortresses Albornoz made them build, to prevent possible attempts at rebellion. The warlike Papal Legate died in 1367; ten years afterwards Pope Gregory XI was able to return to Rome and take possession of a state that embraced the whole of central Italy, apart from the territories of Florence and Siena and a few enclaves.

But the unexpected sequel of the Great Schism and the complications it provoked in the relations between the Italian states prevented Gregory XI and his successors from enjoying their increased estate. For several decades the Papal State, attacked at times by the Visconti from the North, at times by the Angevins of Naples from the South, once more fell prey to the anarchy that had reigned there before the arrival of Albornoz, and became the favourite hunting-ground of the mercenary leaders. Many of them in any case came from these regions: Braccio da Montone and Nicola Piccinino were from Perugia, Gattamelata from Narni, Sforza and Alberico da Barbiano from the Romagna. So it is not surprising that they should have seen these lands as the ones where they could most legitimately exercise their right of conquest, or that some of them actually succeeded in realizing these aspirations for a time. Braccio da Montone, for instance, held the seigniories of Perugia, Assisi and Jesi from 1410 to 1424.

It was only from early in the fifteenth century, with the death of Braccio da Montone and the reconquest of Bologna, and above all with the healing of the Great Schism, that the Papal State gradually began to find its unity and internal peace again, and the administrative and fiscal machinery set up by Albornoz could begin to work regularly. Its mechanism was extremely simple: it amounted to guaranteeing the landowners and nobility of the various towns and provinces the peaceful enjoyment of their incomes and privileges, while draining towards the Roman Curia the maximum possible amount of tax. So an ever more voracious capital was gradually imposed on an ever-drowsier province, as the artistic patronage of the Renaissance popes strove to revive the glories of the Roman republic, which had haunted Cola di Rienzo's hallucinations, Thus, while Rome prepared to embark on an era of rich and splendid monuments, the towns of the Papal State – Perugia, Assisi, Todi, Ascoli Piceno, Spoleto – were becoming dead cities or, if one prefers, cities of art, to conserve, as if in a glass case, the evidence of their vitality in the commune-era, and their present stagnation.

INTELLECTUALS AND THE CRISIS: PETRARCH AND BOCCACCIO

The general picture of the life and events of the Italian states between the early years of the fourteenth century and the mid-fifteenth century seems to conform to the definition of that period as an age of crisis. We have seen how the energy and good luck that had over the preceding centuries made the Italian states into the most prosperous and highly developed area of all Western Christendom now began to slow down and to meet obstacles. This state of affairs meant that within individual states the elements of lasting vitality were interwoven, more closely in some places than in others, with a tendency towards stagnation and withdrawal.

This double nature and instability of the fourteenth and early fifteenth centuries were noticed by the generations that lived through it, especially those that witnessed and were stricken by the Black Death. For reasons already made clear, the intellectuals were the only social class with antennae long and sensitive enough to respond to the confused ferment of politics and society; they sensed the change of climate more keenly than anyone else did, and found various ways to express the universal unease.

At this point the name of Petrarch naturally comes to mind. Francesco Petrarca was born at Arezzo in 1304 and died at Arquà in 1374: he was a passionately involved eyewitness of the Bavarian invasion, of the remarkable career of Cola di Rienzo – whom he sincerely admired, and corresponded with – of the terrible plague of 1348 and of innumerable wars. He was a restless traveller, and an administrator of unequalled fame among his contemporaries. He stayed in turn at the more important Italian and European courts, from the Pope's courts at Avignon to King Robert's at Naples (King Robert presented him with the poet's laurel wreath), Archbishop Giovanni's at Milan, and the court of the Republic of Venice. He was a lover of climbing expeditions and of wild landscapes, but also of the refinements and feather-bed luxury of seigniorial estates and country villas. This life of ambitions and disappointments, of travel from one temporary resting-place to another, of uncertainty and meditation, seems more than anyone's, and certainly more brilliantly than anyone's, the personification of the sickness of his century. His *Canzoniere*, the work which perhaps did more than any other to form the taste of generations of educated Italians up to the Renaissance and beyond, is the faithful diary of this long and varied life, with its bold but unhappy love affairs, its sensuality and its religious crises, its whole course wormed by doubt.

The united, well-organized universe of Dante's certainties was no more than a memory to Petrarch and the encyclopaedic and Aristotelian scholastic philosophy which had provided the foundation for the *Divine Comedy* also seemed old and worn-out. Petrarch preferred Plato, the philosopher of ideas and myths, to Aristotle, the philosopher of logic and physical science; he preferred St Augustine's *Confessions* to St Thomas Aquinas's *Summa*. Augustine was his chosen interlocutor in the *Secretum*, another of his works that is intensely introspective and autobiographical. Unlike Dante, the poet of the *Canzoniere* realized, however confusedly, that the sickness of his age did not represent a deviation and degeneration from the values and 'guides' that should have shown the way: it arose from the inadequacy, the withering of those values and guides. But what certainties and ideas could be put in the place of those whose day was over? Petrarch did not know, and knew he did not know. His natural tendency was not to escape this issue, but to find shelter and comfort within himself, in study and poetry, in the desire for glory and for death.

> 'What grace, what love, what destiny
> Will give me feathers like a dove
> That I may rest and rise up from the earth?'

The other great Italian of the fourteenth century was of course Giovanni Boccaccio, Petrarch's contemporary and admirer, who tried to have Petrarch appointed teacher of Greek at the university of Florence. But apart from these coincidences, the two great Italians of their day seem to have had no other characteristics in common. Boccaccio has for a long time been traditionally seen as the portrayer of the new urban middle class and its lack of prejudice, pushed as far as unbelief, its sense of fun, its vitality. He was indeed a member of that class: he was a bourgeois and a layman, who saw through every disguise or masking of reality, and considered and analysed things as they really were. Through the ten days of the *Decameron* a richly mixed crowd of people passes before us: pathetic blasé noblemen like Federico degli Alberighi; crafty, swindling merchants like Ser Ciappelletto, and merchants doomed to be cheated like Andreuccio da Perugia; clever men of the people like Masetto di Lamporecchio, and foolish ones like Calandrino; people who laugh and those they laugh at; opportunists and victims of 'Fortune'. The author almost always manages to stay detached from this 'theatre of the world', as both spectator and participant, and to impose on his story the pace and breadth of a secular, bourgeois age, emphasized by his elaborate Ciceronian style. He is able to do so because he has no illusions about any person's hopes of being the maker of his own life and destiny. These are subject to the whims and accidents of chance, that new and disturbing divinity of a disenchanted world, and the mistress of a century of plagues and wars. There are times when the intelligence or virtue of the individual prevails, and then Boccaccio records the victory with satisfaction; but at other times the individual is overwhelmed, and then, behind the narrator's impassivity, we feel a sense of dismay at this world, left the orphan and widower of Providence. He put himself in the position of a calmly objective recorder of life's dramas and chances; it was a difficult and exhausting mental standpoint, and a new one, demanding nervous energy and courage. Is it any wonder that Boccaccio too, in his premature old age, should have sought comfort and refuge in study and in piety?

But Petrarch and Boccaccio lived through the darkest and most dramatic years of this historical period. At the time of the Black Death they were respectively forty-four and thirty-five; one would never afterwards be able to forget the loss of the woman he loved, the other the heaps of dead bodies in the streets of Florence during those terrible days. The theme of death, one of the dominant motifs of the painting and iconography of the century (the frescoes at the Pisa Camposanto are a good example) was always to remain with them, together with that of the mutability and vanity of human things. But once past the troubled decades that followed the plague, and over the hurdle of 1378, year of the Ciompi uprising and of the war of all against all, a new and very active phase in the history of Italian intellectuals and culture began: the great age of Humanism.

4

___

1450–1550: Greatness and decadence

HUMANISM

The position that the intellectuals and the learned occupied as a social class in Italy during the late fourteenth century and the first half of the fifteenth, was even more prominent than that which they had held in the age of the communes and in Dante's time. The formation of much larger territorial units, provided with a complex administrative apparatus, the need for numerous diplomats and representatives to handle a state's complicated relations with others, and the growth of courts around the various lords – conceived as instruments of prestige and centres of political propaganda – were all factors that increased the demand for qualified intellectual personnel, and raised the already high value placed on their services.

The universities could hardly keep up with the increased demand: not so much because there were too few of them – for new ones were founded during this period, at Ferrara, Florence and elsewhere – but chiefly because they could provide nothing but the material and method of the scholastic, Aristotelian, encyclopaedic school, which had dominated them ever since their foundation. So they were no longer really capable of providing a modern type of training, adapted to the new requirements of the times. New schools of a private nature were therefore founded, at the courts, or in the homes of scholars: academies where, on the Socratic model, there was very direct communication between master and student, and where entirely new material was taught. The most famous of these schools was the Casa Gioiosa of Mantua, directed on new pedagogic principles by the Humanist Vittorino da Feltre, who taught a whole generation of students and future teachers.

The more famous and proven of the new intellectuals and Humanists were courted by the various city-states and their lords, and their careers took the form of a continual wandering among the main towns of Italy. This had also been Petrarch's experience: he may in many ways be considered the father of the humanities. Lorenzo Valla, for example, in his quite short life of fifty-two years, found the time to stay at almost all the most important cities and courts of Italy. He was born in Rome, moved to Florence when still young, and completed his studies there; then he left for Pavia, to teach at the university. He had to leave Pavia after incurring the enmity of his colleagues in the law faculty, and took refuge in Milan, with the Visconti; then he went to Naples in the service of Alfonso of Aragon, and ended his days back in his native Rome. Leon Battista Alberti, perhaps the most accomplished of Italian Humanists, also had a restless career. He belonged to a family that the Medici had banished from Florence, gained his doctorate at Bologna, and was able to go back to his home town in 1429. But he did not stay settled there for long: between 1431 and 1441 he followed the papal Curia in its peregrination from one to another of the cities where the difficult Council was held which opened at Basle and proceeded to Rome, then to Bologna, to Florence and, to Ferrara, where Alberti struck up a friendship with Duke Leonello d'Este. The fame he had won as an architect took him on other journeys and visits, until the end of his busy life in 1472. Among his major works are the Palazzo Rucellai in Florence, the Malatesta temple at Rimini, the church of S. Andrea at Mantua. It would take too long to describe the adventurous, unconfined lives of Francesco Filelfo and Antonio Beccadelli, called the Panormita, the two Italian Humanists most adapted to court life and expensive living.

These journeys and varied experiences, and the friendships and intellectual exchanges they gave rise to, strengthened the sense of fellowship that already existed among the Italian intelligentsia. Scholars were drawn closer together, until this solidarity became a full awareness of their particular function in the general pattern of Italian culture. This awareness was the starting-point of the great intellectual adventure of Humanism. Not until the Enlightenment was there to be another period of such energy and general enthusiasm, such a rich unison of ideas, such an atmosphere of dedicated search for truth.

Generally – this at least is the more accepted, conventional view – the Humanists are thought of as an army of scholars, untiring researchers, collectors of texts, whose historic merit consists essentially in having enriched and restored our knowledge of the Classical cultural heritage. If that had been all (and it was not) modern civilization's debt to the Humanists would still be inestimable. Without their discoveries, and their recovery of the past, their work of restoration, the later developments of European culture would be unimaginable. It is enough to think how much the Humanists' introduction of the study of Greek philosophy has meant to modern culture: by way of the Greek scholars who were asked to come and teach in the Italian schools and academies from the time of the fall of Constantinople at the end of the fifteenth century, the whole great heritage of Byzantine learning and philosophy, from Psellus onwards, became a part of Western European culture. We must realize how much it meant to be able to read the Greek classics in the original and in reliable editions, and how important was the rediscovery of Plato in his entirety, perhaps the greatest cultural event of the Humanist age, or that of Lucretius's *De rerum naturae*, found together with other important classical manuscripts in the cellar of a Swiss monastery, by Poggio Bracciolini.

Each text that was found and restored was diligently copied, and those copies became the centre of a whole trade: not the least important of the cultural workers of the age of Humanism was the seller of texts. One of them, the Florentine Vespasiano da Bisticci, shows in his *Vite* how much he respected and admired his learned clients, and how responsibly he plied his trade. In this way the first libraries were formed: that of the Convent of S. Marco in Florence owed its founding to the humanist Niccolò Niccoli; it included Boccaccio's personal collection of books; the Marciana library in Venice originated in a legacy from Cardinal Bessarione, one of the greatest Humanists of the age, and contained the books that Petrarch left to the Republic; the Vatican library in Rome was founded during the pontificate of Nicholas v (1447–55). But not even these developments in the production and distribution of books were enough to satisfy the hunger of a growing public: the invention of printing, if it was an invention, came at the right moment.

If Humanism had been no more than this enormous work of recovering the Classical heritage, its contribution to modern culture and civilization would still have been considerable. But it was more than this.

Through the work of restoration, textual editing and commentary, the most important and long-lasting acquisitions of Humanism took shape: some of the criteria still apply today in scientific research. Most important of all of these was the idea of the objective nature of research itself: no political, religious or emotional idol, no external consideration, should guide the scholar in his work. Woe to the scholar who mutilated or falsified a text! Philology became the basis and key of all knowledge, the critical edition a pre-condition for the reading of any text. The classic instance of the Humanists' new method and style of work was without doubt Lorenzo Valla's demonstration of the falsity of the celebrated donation of Constantine, the mediaeval document invoked by the Church to justify its temporal aspirations. This demonstration was founded entirely on textual and philological evidence. Knowing how to read a text now also meant being able to put it in the context of its period and give it a clearly defined place in the body of literature of which it was a part. So the philological dimension led to the historical. It was not a question of putting Plato and Aristotle against each other, but of understanding both of them, the one with the other. Aletheia, Truth, is the daughter of Chronos, Time, declares Leon Battista Alberti in his *Philodoxeos*; he was echoed by his compatriot, Matteo Palmieri, who wrote, *'veritatis profecto cognitionem dant tempora'* ('Time, surely, gives knowledge of truth'). This conjunction of philological method with the historical sense produced mental habits of wisdom and tolerance, which were later personified and exalted in the person of Erasmus of Rotterdam, the master of philology and of tolerance, and a product of Humanism.

The Humanists were fully aware of the newness and the importance of their discovery. They realized that their historic merit did not consist merely in having rediscovered and restored the texts of ancient authors, but in having recovered their method of working, their lack of idols and prejudices, their free and serene spirit. Sustained by this awareness, they looked back pityingly at the *media aetas* – the term was coined by the Humanists themselves – whose prejudices had prevented it from verifying philologically or reasoning historically. At the same time they exalted their own times and the intellectual revolution of which they happened to be protagonists. So a passion for the ancients generated a pride in being modern. Imitating the ancients did not mean repeating what they had said, but placing oneself before one's own world and one's own time with the same curiosity, passion and lucidity of judgement with which the men of classical times had faced their world. It meant researching, discovering new truths and building new roads. So pure science generated applied science.

In his *Trattato della Pittura* Leon Battista Alberti wrote that until his return to Florence from exile he had been convinced that 'weary' human nature would never again be able to recapture the productiveness and creative power of 'those prodigious men of antiquity'. But when he had returned to his own town and admired the works of Brunelleschi (*'Pipo architecto'*), Donatello, Masaccio, and the other great Florentine artists of the age, he realized that the moderns had surpassed antiquity, 'if we, without teachers, or any example, can discover arts and sciences that were never heard of or seen before'. One could not wish for a more eloquent testimony of the intellectual journey of Humanism.

'Arts and sciences that were never heard of or seen before' – the architects and engineers of the fifteenth century drew from the study of

Vitruvius the models for a new, highly original civil and military architecture; then they moved from the planning of a single building to that
of a whole city, rationally disposed and organized. Geographers and
cartographers, the greatest of whom was Paolo Del Pozzo Toscanelli,
a friend of Brunelleschi's, drew new representations of the world, which
were used by the navigators and explorers of the new world. Leonardo
da Vinci (1452–1519) translated into applied science his intuitions in
optics, mechanics and physical science in general. Yet we shall fall
into a grave error of historical perspective if we try to discover in
Humanism the origins of modern scientific thought. This was formed
later, by other and more complex means; and what is perhaps most
remarkable about the personality of Leonardo, the designer of futur-
istic machines and painter of disconcerting faces, is that he was so
exceptional, if not isolated. After him, Renaissance Italy was not to
produce any very significant discoveries in the field of science and
scientific thought. However, the great discovery made by Humanism,
that of the objective and pure nature of research, applies to every form
of human knowledge.

THE HUMANISTS IN ITALIAN SOCIETY

The preceding section has emphasized the importance of the influence
of Humanist culture on modern thought and civilization. Now we
must consider a more limited, historically circumscribed question,
but one that is no less important in a work concerned with Italian
history: that of the Humanists' relationship with Italian society and
the social climate of the Italian states, whose sons they were and in
which they worked. To put it in simple terms: what were their political
ideas, and how did they behave as members of society? This is not
an abstract question, but one that the Humanists put themselves and
tried to resolve. From Coluccio Salutati onwards the debate on whether
the active or the contemplative life was better was one of the main
threads running through Humanist literature. Most of those who took
part in this debate, particularly the Florentine Humanists, held that
the active life was superior: that the scholar should not shut himself up
in the isolation of his own study, but should care for his family, his
friends, his town; in other words, he should live the life of a citizen,
in the midst of his fellows. A famous work by the Florentine Humanist
Matteo Palmieri was called *Della vita civile*. Besides, for men who were
engaged in political life and held public offices, as many Humanists
did, the question did not even arise. Coluccio Salutati, besides making

efforts to get the leading Byzantine Greek teachers to come to Florence, was also Chancellor of the Republic, and employed all his talent and literary ability in exalting its freedom, and defending it against the arguments of the Humanists in the service of the Visconti. His successor was Leonardo Bruni, another leading figure, whose *Storie Fiorentine* and *Laudatio florentinae urbis* show how deeply he loved his city. Other Humanists took their involvement in 'civil' affairs as far as conspiracy. In 1453 Stefano Porcari died on the scaffold for having taken part in a conspiracy against Pope Nicholas v, who was himself a lover and patron of the *studia humanitatis*. The Milanese Cola Montano, leading spirit of the conspiracy to which Duke Galeazzo Maria Sforza fell a victim in 1476, also paid for his enthusiasm with his life. Pomponio Leto, most representative figure of the Humanist circle that constituted the Roman academy, and Bartolomeo Platina, who was later made prefect of the Vatican library by Sixtus iv, were also justly suspected of having conspired against the Pope. Naturally, not all the Humanists shared the Florentine Chancellors' republican conviction, or the various conspirators' ardent wish to kill tyrants. Some, like Antonio Lusco of Vicenza, were in the service of lords, and defended the idea of princedom against the propagandists of Florentine liberty. But almost all of them lived embroiled in the struggles and arguments of their day, accumulated experience of public life, and were led to reflect on the events of the time.

So it is legitimate to wonder whether the public activity of individual Humanists fused together and developed into the kind of collective, reformist political action, however complex and tangled, that existed during the Enlightenment. To find an answer to this question we must first ask ourselves if and how political or reformist activity was possible for intellectuals in the society of the fourteenth and fifteenth centuries. History provides the answer: Wyclif and Huss, the two great reformers of the age of the Church Councils and the struggle for Church reform, were both intellectuals, university professors; but that did not prevent them or their followers from becoming political agitators and arousing mass movements. Armed with a profound, consistent religious faith, they were firmly convinced that if it was true that society should be run according to God's laws, it first had to be cleansed of all abuses, the arrogance of the mighty, the corruption of bishops and prelates, the sufferings of the humble. Strong in this belief, they unhesitatingly drew the conclusion that they had to struggle for the reforms they wanted, calling all the faithful to the good fight; for this was God's commandment. We know that in a world where religion was considered the basis and the very essence of social life, and where the mental patterns of the masses were generally religious patterns, this was the only way anyone could really hope to alter the institutions and customs of a society. Social reform was only conceivable as reform of religion and the Church, and the raising of the humble as a revival and revolution of belief. This was the road trodden by Luther and, well into the seventeenth century, by the English Puritan revolutionaries.

But it would have been difficult for the Humanists to act in this way. Not only because Italian society was different, and differently organized, from Bohemian or English society, but also because their very position in society was profoundly different from that of Wyclif or Huss. As we have seen, they had elaborated an extremely modern form of culture, free from prejudices and idols; theirs was a very rich and refined intellectual experience. This intellectual superiority itself, and the full awareness of it that had ripened, conditioned them, and led them to see politics as a monopoly of educated and learned men, and the relationship between government and governed as a pedagogic, master-pupil relationship. Their ideal state was close to Plato's Republic: the state whose prince and magistrates were philosophers, or took the advice of philosophers. There was, certainly, the possibility of a bad prince, and then Brutus had the right to kill him; but only Brutus, or someone with his nobility of spirit and aristocratic Roman upbringing.

Nothing was more foreign to them than an idea of the world inspired by religious dogmatism: their disgust at the superstition of bigots and the corruption of the Church was equalled by what they felt for the intemperance and fanaticism of heretics. Poggio Bracciolini, who saw Jerome of Prague tortured at Constance, expressed deep admiration for this 'second Cato' and implicitly condemned his tormentors, but for Enea Piccolomini the behaviour of Huss and his followers was 'madness'. This attitude foreshadows the reaction of some Humanists to Savonarola and his attempt to reform Florence's religious and social life, and Erasmus's reaction to the Lutheran movement. Correspondingly, the Humanists were far from the idea that an improvement and 'reform' of society should be achieved by means of a complete upheaval, involving all social levels from the highest to the lowest, and all men, learned and unlearned alike. The people, in whom religious reformers saw the mouthpiece of God's will (and the *Ciompi* too had called themselves 'God's people'), were in their eyes the vulgar, enmeshed in their prejudices and enslaved by their passions, just as they had been in the eyes of classical writers. This was certainly not a point of view that favoured the rise of a corporate, harmonious 'reform' movement. For the Humanists, involvement in public affairs remained a matter of a noble, private decision; and so they did not assume their natural position as the leaders of the Italian people. All great revolutions, including intellectual ones, have their price.

ITALY IN THE LATER FIFTEENTH CENTURY

In the very brief space of time between 1449 and 1453 Western Christendom witnessed three great events : the final healing of the Great Schism, which had tormented the Catholic Church for almost a century; the end of the exhausting Hundred Years War; and the fall of the Eastern Empire, with the Turkish conquest of Constantinople. These events are so close together, almost contemporary with one another, that they seem designed to give us the impression of an achieved fulness of time : the conclusion of one historic cycle and the start of a new one. And in fact the Europe that began to emerge in the mid-fifteenth century, after the long labours that had begun with the four-teenth-century depression, was to a large extent a new Europe, in which an outdated reverence for the universal institution of the Papacy was becoming less and less important – the events of the Schism and the Council disputes had diminished its authority – and in which the massive reality of new national states like Henry vii's England and Louis xi's France, which emerged regenerated from the long test of the Hundred Years War, was becoming more important. It was a Europe whose eastern flank was exposed to the Turkish threat, and which was already gravitating towards the Atlantic : Lisbon, Antwerp, London and Seville were almost ready to take over from Venice, Genoa and the other Italian ports. In other words, it was a Europe that had all the time less room or justification for the privileged place Italy had so far held on the economic level and in the sphere of international relations, the place on which Italy had founded her fortunes.

But faced with this tendency, we must be careful not to anticipate history. The new European and Mediterranean pattern that took shape around the middle of the fifteenth century may have been heavy with unknown quantities and dangers for the future of Italian society; but it was no less rich in immediate opportunities. The threat of Turkey was not to be underestimated; and the shock provoked by the fall of Constantinople grew stronger as the years passed and the power-lessness of Christian Europe to react, in spite of the Pope's impassioned exhortations and repeated appeals for a renewal of the spirit of the Crusades, because more apparent. But on the immediate level of political and commercial relations, the consequences of the rise of Ottoman power in the Mediterranean were not so sudden or dramatic as one has been led to believe. Or not for all, at least. It is true that Genoa, suddenly cut off from her flourishing Black Sea colonies, suffered a grave blow that led her to hasten the process of converting her economy from a mercantile to a financial one – a process already begun with the founding of the Bank of St George. But Venice managed to find a *modus vivendi* with the new masters of the Levant. The loss of Negroponte and other advance posts in the Aegean and on the Balkan peninsula were compensated in part by the conquest of Cyprus, achieved at the expense of the Catalans and the Genoese, and even more valuable were the substantial exemptions and privileges obtained for Venetian merchants operating in Constantinople. After these agreements had been reached in 1479–80, hostilities between Venice and Turkey ceased for the time being, so that even the Venetian fleet observed perfect neutrality, and looked on impassively as the Turks tried to land at Otranto in 1480.

If nothing irreparable had yet happened in the East, however, in the West the international pattern of alliances after the end of the Hundred Years War and the healing of the Schism offered many opportunities and stimuli. The elimination of the main antagonisms that had characterized and complicated the European political scene for over a century had meant above all a relaxation of international tension, which was reflected within the pattern of Italian states. The forty years from the peace of Lodi in 1454 to Charles VIII's invasion of Italy in 1494 were a period of peace and stability for the Italian states, and the few wars that occurred were of a local character: for instance, that from 1482 to 1484 between Venice and the Duke of Ferrara, which ended in Venice's conquest of Rovigo and the salt-deposits of the Polesine. In these conditions, the generating mechanism of Italian wealth once again worked efficiently, and the mercantile and financial oligarchies of the cities took advantage of an international situation that was less oppressive and less loaded with unforeseen contingencies, in a Europe in process of reconstruction and economic development.

Germany, of course, went through a phase of general expansion during the late fifteenth century, and was, more than ever, a market that offered Milanese and Venetian businessmen considerable profits; when the German staple in Venice was destroyed by a fire in 1508, it was swiftly rebuilt, more spacious and efficient than before. As for France, the Lyons fair offered a wide field of action for merchants and financiers from Florence and other cities, in spite of the restrictions imposed by Louis XI and his desire to prevent the outflow of capital; and French documents of the period, beginning with the records of the States General of Tours in 1484, are full of lamentations at the '*sortie de l'argent hors du royaume*' in the direction of Italy. Among the main elements in the foreign trade of Italian cities in the fifteenth century were silk, in the production of which Lucca held an important place, and alum, which, after the loss of Genoa's mines at Focea, was provided by the deposits recently discovered at Tolfa, near Civitavecchia. These were mainly under the control of the powerful Medici banking house and of Genoese bankers. These two, in spite of competition from their Northern colleagues, the Fuggers of Austria and the Artaveldes of Antwerp, were still the major financial forces of Europe, in whose eyes they seemed the very personification of Italian wealth and industriousness.

So, though her wealth was now to a large extent the reflection of a new stage of economic development involving all the major European states, Italy was still a rich, highly-developed country at the end of the fifteenth century. 'Who does not know what Italy is ?' wrote Francesco Guiccardini in his *Storia d'Italia*, evoking the happy years of peace and stability – 'A province who is the queen of all others, because of her fortunate position, the temperateness of her air, the great number and skill of men ready for all honourable enterprises, the abundance of all things useful to mankind, the greatness and beauty of so many noble cities, the seat of religion and the ancient glory of Empire, and for an infinity of other reasons.' Italy was, in short, the richest, most cultured, most densely populated and most illustrious land of Western Christendom.

Italy possessed, besides, a wealth and culture one could see and touch. Like preceding waves of economic euphoria and dynamism, that of the later fifteenth century had its barometer in the enthusiastic urge to erect great public and private buildings; and this was encouraged by the patronage of courts and of city oligarchies. Without transforming this book into a history of art it is impossible to enumerate the buildings and works that enriched Italy's already considerable artistic heritage during the later fifteenth century. Filarete's Ospedale Maggiore in Milan, the Palazzo dei Diamanti at Ferrara, the completion of the Doge's palace at Venice, and Mantegna's decoration of the bridal room of the Palazzo Gonzaga at Mantua, to cite only a few familiar examples, all belong to these decades. In Florence alone, more than thirty *palazzi* and villas were built between 1450 and 1478; and in 1489 the imposing bulk of the Palazzo Strozzi was begun. Rome's building-boom was even more impressive – under the impulse of the Renaissance popes the city finally ceased to be that jumble of august ruins and hovels that it had been throughout the Middle Ages, and began to take shape as the unique city we know today, which developed under the wing of enlightened patronage and planning. When work was begun on the Palazzo Venezia in 1455, it was still a suburban site; but the great work of town-planning and pruning begun by Sixtus IV and continued by Julius II, with the cutting of the great arteries of the Corso and Via Giulia, made it one of the city's monumental centres. Near the Palazzo Venezia, on the Campidoglio, Michelangelo was soon to design one of the most decorative piazzas in Italy. Before him, other Florentine artists had already come to Rome to learn the lessons of antiquity, and leave examples of their modern work. Among others were Bernardo Rossellino, the architect of the Palazzo Venezia, Donatello, Antonio Pollaiolo, who made the tomb of Sixtus IV, and Fra Angelico and Sandro Botticelli, who both worked in the Vatican.

But more than Florence, and perhaps more than Rome even, it is the evidence of the small towns and minor courts that best helps us to realize how much conspicuous investment still represented the badge and emblem of power, social rank and wealth in the late fifteenth century. The small Montefeltro duchy of Urbino had a great palace, in whose courtyard worked artists like Piero della Francesca and the Flemish Juste de Gand; the small village of Corsignano near Siena was transformed into a city by Pius II, who was born there. Of this ambitious project remain a piazza and a name – Pienza – that are alone enough to evoke an image of the magnificence of Renaissance patronage.

So the process that formed and accumulated wealth in Italy was working once again. In terms of social history this meant, as we know, a further consolidation of those oligarchies of power and money that had been emerging during the past centuries, and which were the beneficiaries and the preservers of Italian wealth. In fact the history of the Italian states – of Genoa and its Bank, Rome and its Curia – is the history of the strength and the reinforcement of the existing internal orders and of the dominant oligarchies. In Florence too the history of the second half of the fifteenth century, from the Parliament of 1458 to the founding of the Council of Seventy in 1481, was a rapid series of turns of the screw designed to consolidate once and for all the victory of Medici rule and the power of the small oligarchy led by the Medici. The peaceful policy of equilibrium that Italy followed from the treaty of Lodi through the following decades encouraged this tendency and helped to make attempts at internal revolution more arduous, though these did exist: the 1453 Porcari conspiracy against Pope Nicholas V has already been mentioned, and so has that of Cola Montano in Milan in 1476. In Naples in 1484 there was an uprising of the barons against the Aragonese dynasty. But the most important and spectacular of these fifteenth-century conspiracies was that hatched by the Florentine Pazzi family in 1478, with the connivance and help of Pope Sixtus IV, against the city's rulers, the Medici. The blow was struck in the Church of Santa Maria del Fiore in Florence; Lorenzo, the lord of the city, managed to escape the assassins' daggers, but his brother Giuliano did not. But whether these fifteenth-century conspiracies succeeded in killing the tyrant who was their object, as Montano did at Milan, or failed, as the Florentine and Roman conspiracies did, none of them had any political result; nor for that matter did they set themselves any political aim. After they had succeeded or had been crushed, the city's political institutions remained unchanged, and the prestige of the lord, whether he fell victim to the attack or survived it, was heightened. In Florence the people raged against the conspirators of 1478, and one of them, the Archbishop of Pisa, was hanged on the wall of his church.

As Machiavelli was later to demonstrate clearly, there are men whose individualism and sectarian spirit make conspiracy a form of political struggle that leads nowhere and has no attraction for broader social groups. In the eyes of the mass of people, the fact that certain privileged citizens, for the most part members of great families, their minds dominated by humanistic or republican rancour and prejudice, should have decided to kill a lord, could only mean that they intended to take his place; so conspiracy amounted to no more than a proof that the oligarchic régime was unchangeable. If this was how things stood, it was better not to allow the benefits of peace that the domestic status quo had so far guaranteed to be exposed to pointless danger from a few ambitious and hot-headed men. Besides, every domestic upheaval jeopardized the delicate interrelationship of the Italian states, and the stability, peace and 'liberty' of Italy, compared with other countries. These were things it was in everyone's interests to preserve.

FLORENCE, CAPITAL OF RENAISSANCE STABILITY

The previous chapter has described a set of solidly established states, who tried, by means of a system of reciprocal guarantees and concessions, to conserve their respective spheres of influence and their respective interests, and a set of established men, oligarchies satisfied with their own opulence, and anxious to maintain the status quo. At this point we must consider to what extent such a situation helped to modify the social position of the intellectuals, those constant protagonists of Italian history. Did it accentuate that element of aristocratic aloofness and 'disengagement' that can be traced in Humanist culture? For an answer to this question we must concentrate our attention on Florence, capital both of Italian stability and of the Italian Renaissance.

All Italian school histories declare that the Florence of Lorenzo the

Magnificent (1469–92) was the index of the balance that existed between the Italian states, and the preserver of peace and 'liberty'. Lorenzo several times acted as a mediator, to dispel clouds that had gathered on the horizon, and to avert the return of a general Italian war on the model of those that had followed one another during the first half of the century. He intervened in 1478, when the failure of the Pazzi conspiracy looked as if it might be followed by a conflict between Florence and the Pope, helped by the Aragonese of Naples; and in 1482, at the time of the war between Venice and Ferrara.

But Florence's political hegemony was partly a result of her corresponding intellectual leadership – though this must not be understood as an absolute supremacy or monopoly, for the artistic and intellectual scene in Italy in the later fifteenth century was as lively and varied as it had been in the past. The Paduan Mantegna, who worked mainly at Mantua, is certainly a more interesting painter than Benozzo Gozzoli, the fantastical illustrator of the Palazzo Medici chapel ; and if such comparisons are meaningful, perhaps also more interesting than the famous Botticelli, with his slightly over-refined prettiness. Matteo Maria Boiardo, a nobleman who came down from his castle in the Appenines of Emilia to the Este court at Ferrara, which he entertained with the somewhat old-fashioned stories of his *Orlando innamorato*, was a rather provincial poet, who certainly lacked the compression and lofty expression of Poliziano, the leading poet and literary ornament of the Medici court. But on the other hand Boiardo's work is more genuine and nearer true poetry than are the rustic poems that Lorenzo the Magnificent wrote, with the affectation typical of a scholar and aristocrat approaching the common world. Finally, in the field of philosophical studies, the Aristotelian and Averroist school of Padua, which deeply influenced Pico della Mirandola, and which was to produce the passionate speculation of Pomponazzi at the end of the century, was certainly just as firmly founded and just as rich in its developments as Florentine Neoplatonism.

Talented artists, expert minds, famous universities and academies were to be found in all the Italian courts and cities: in the Milan of the Sforza, where Leonardo stayed and worked; in the Ferrara of the Este, in the Urbino of the Montefeltro, in Aragonese Naples. But nowhere except Florence was artistic and intellectual life so rich and so collectively intense that it became aware and proud of itself, of its own continuity, originality and power of attraction. 'What city', demands Salutati's invective against Loschi, 'not merely in Italy but in the whole world, is stronger within the circle of its walls, prouder in palaces, richer in temples, more lovely in buildings . . . Where is trade richer in its variety, abler in subtle understandings? Where are there more famous men ... where is Dante, Petrarch, Boccaccio?' In these lines the love of letters becomes an integral part of patriotic feeling and pride in being Florentine; and it is this awareness, which bursts from the pages of Bruni's *Laudatio florentinae urbis*, that gave Florentine culture an imperialist dimension, and increased its capacity of expansion and attraction. During the fifteenth century there existed a diaspora of Florentine artists throughout the towns and courts of Italy. We have already seen that the masters who began to paint the Sistine Chapel were Florentines. As for architecture, the mathematician Luca Pacioli, writing towards the end of the century, affirmed that anyone who wished to build had to turn to Florence; from Florence came Rossellino, architect of the Palazzo Venezia and of Pienza, Giuliano da Maiano, who designed the Capuan gateway in Naples, and worked at the Loreto Sanctuary, and Filarete, architect of the impressive Ospedale Maggiore in Milan.

But even more than her art and artists, the most effective instrument of Florentine cultural leadership was perhaps her language and literature. The habit of Italian Humanists – Leon Battista Alberti especially – of using both Latin and the vernacular in their works had certainly helped to make the Florentine vernacular more easily understood, more coherent and controlled than any other Italian vernacular: it was a highly literary language, and the language of intellectual Italy. Victory for the Florentine language was to be firmly sanctioned by linguistic theorists early in the sixteenth century, but it became clear during the fifteenth. Filelfo, who was born in the Marche, already affirmed that '*ex universa Italia etrusca lingua maxime laudatur*' ('In all Italy, the Tuscan language is most highly praised'), and when Bernardino da Feltre came to preach in Florence, he felt he had to apologize to his audience for his inability to express himself '*secondo l'arte del dir che sta a Fiorenza*' ('according to the art of speaking that exists in Florence'), but only '*secundum Evangelium*' ('according to the Gospel'). If non-Florentines expressed themselves in those terms, it is small wonder that Lorenzo the Magnificent should have exalted his 'mother tongue' as the 'idiom common to all Italy', and that Poliziano should have sung the praises of the 'abundant and refined' Tuscan language. In any case, it had been the language of Dante, Petrarch and Boccaccio: for the Humanists and scholars of the age, who considered language as a primarily literary matter, as an instrument of communication between scholars, this was a decisive argument, and the linguistic primacy of Florentine seemed the natural consequence of its literary primacy. It is no coincidence that among the first printed works produced in Italy, between 1470 and 1472, many were editions of the three great classics of Italian literature. Gutenberg's revolutionary invention thus also played its part in confirming Florence's cultural leadership.

Together with Florence's language and literature, the ideas of Florentine Humanism also spread. These were no longer the ideas of the days of Coluccio Salutati and Leonardo Bruni, the ideas of 'civil' Florentine Humanism. Since then, something had changed in the Florentine cultural situation, as it had on the political level.

The most interesting personality of later fifteenth-century Florentine culture is without doubt Giovanni Pico della Mirandola. He was a man of both boundless erudition and a rich, complex intellectual development – his youthful experience of Paduan Aristotelianism and Averroism was mingled with Florentine Platonism. His was a troubled, restless nature; and this was reflected in his life and in his works. In 1486 he wrote the *Oratio de hominis dignitate*, one passage of which is among the classic examples of Humanist prose and thought; 'I have made you neither celestial nor earthly, neither mortal nor immortal, because, free and sovereign artificer of yourself, you must shape and sculpt yourself, in the form you have chosen.' He ended his days as a follower of Savonarola. A more linear figure, less rich and complex than Pico, but even more representative of a certain cultural ethos, was Marsilio Ficino, formative spirit of the Florentine academy. He was in fact one of the major authors of the day, in contact with the greatest scholars of Europe, and his writings were eagerly awaited by a very wide public. He was a translator and a devoted student of Plato – a Plato filtered through Plotinus – and evolved a philosophical system that merged Platonism and Christianity, together with hermetic and magical elements, in the conciliatory ideal of a *pia philosophia*, a *Theologia Platonica*, as the title of one of his most important philosophical works puts it, according to which the scholar became reconciled with the Christian, and vice versa. Only one who knows can be in communion with God, who is infinite knowledge, and knowledge is an initiation reserved for a few. So the ideal of an aristocratic culture and a habit of intellectual detachment, tending towards contemplation, were gradually formed. The superiority of the active life, vigorously maintained by the first Florentine Humanists, was set in doubt and at times decisively opposed by Ficino and his school. Freed from his 'civil' bonds and obligations, the intellectual gave more emphasis to his own distance from the 'vulgar', and began to see his own social position not as a responsibility but as a priesthood, and his own activity not as work but as 'idleness' in the classical sense of the word: *otium*. The most eloquent example of this kind of disengagement is given by the life and career of Ficino himself: he was on good terms with the Medici and with their opponents; he supported Savonarola at the peak of his fortunes and was an ungenerous detractor in the hour of his disgrace. He always managed to appear imperturbable, and his basic attitude to public affairs was one of indifference or possibly opportunism.

So the long-term tendency of Florentine Neoplatonism was away from a public commitment; those aristocratic elements already present in Humanist culture were accentuated – Florence was the guardian of Italy's political establishment and also, to some extent, of her intellectual establishment. For the influence and reputation of Neoplatonism were widespread, and not confined to the specific field of philosophical studies and thought. Without it, a considerable part of the literature, taste and fashion of fifteenth-century Italy and even Europe, would be hard to understand. Neoplatonism is an important key to the origins of such literary phenomena as the popularity of Petrarchan poetry, or success of a book like Baldassarre Castiglione's *The Courtier*, which contains, together with other themes, a restatement of those disquisitions on the nature of love that had been dear to the Florentine Neoplatonists. More generally, it can be stated that Neoplatonism was the first real manifestation of an academic, worldly sort of culture, and as such marks an important stage in the history of the crisis of Italian Humanism; that is to say, it marks the beginning of the Humanists' renunciation of a 'civil', reformist commitment. Once again though, we must guard against anticipating history, particularly when it is a history as complex and contradictory as that of the Italian intellectuals, their relations with society and with the century. We have now to consider fifteenth-century Florence and Italy from another angle: as a society still rich in resources and vitality, and a culture engaged in backing up reformist activity. Florence was the capital also of this Italy.

SAVONAROLA AND CHARLES VIII

Mediaeval people were always very conscious of a century's approaching end – one thinks of the thirteenth-century prophecies of the Angelic Pope, and of the story of Celestine v. The millenarian idea that a new century should bring with it a new order and a regeneration of the whole human condition had long been current: it is expressed by Campanella, among others. The people of that time could only conceive of such a rebirth in religious terms; that is, as a 'reform' of the Church itself, the teachings of which constituted the very essence of the social bond.

The identification of thought with faith was so deeply rooted in the mass of the faithful that to their ears only the call of a believer and a man apparently inspired by God could seem really urgent and complete. This is why the idea of what we today call a 'revolution' or reform of society was to them closely associated with the idea of a restoration of the eternal religious values, and that is why revolutionaries of the Middle Ages and the first centuries of the modern era may so easily be mistaken for prophets, and at the same time for lovers of the good old days.

Not even the refined Italian fifteenth century made an exception to this end-of-century pattern. It must not be forgotten that during the first half of the century the urgent need for a reform of the Church had seemed evident to those generations who witnessed the Councils of Constance and Basle. Now, in the expectant atmosphere of the closing years of the century, the idea warmed into new life, and occupied men's minds and spirits.

During the last years of the fifteenth century, displays of a type of religious feeling full of anxiety and fear took place all over Italy, around the many impassioned preachers who travelled from town to town. But Florence, the most learned and cultured of Italian cities, was to be the scene of the most spectacular and turbulent religious revival. This may seem surprising until we remember that Florence was not only the capital of balance and Humanism – since the time of the Ciompi religious passions and popular resentments had smouldered in the town, and had at times burst into violent life; most notably, in the revival provoked by Bishop Antonino's preaching and charitable activity in the years 1445 to 1459, which deeply influenced the painting of Angelico. But no movement was as intense or had such results as that inspired by Gerolamo Savonarola, at the end of the fifteenth century.

Savonarola was born at Ferrara in 1452, and belonged, like Antonino, to the Dominican order. He settled in Florence during the last years of Lorenzo's reign and began his career as a preacher, with rapidly growing success. His preaching was exceptional in its animation, in the violence of its images and language, and in the boldness of its affirmations. At Advent in 1493, for example, he preached that the world was corrupt, and the Church was corrupt: its priests preferred the Classics to the Gospel, and had ears only for 'poetry and oratoric art', and 'where in the primitive Church there were wooden chalices and golden priests, the Church now has golden chalices and wooden priests.' The princes were corrupt, for their palaces and courts had become the refuge of rascals and wretches who thought only 'of new taxes, to suck the blood of the people.' The learned were corrupt, 'who, with many fables and lies, trace the genealogies of these wicked princes back to the gods'. The laws and the manners of the time were corrupt. What remedy should be invoked against the spread of so much villainy ? On this point too Savonarola spoke extremely clearly:

Oh Lord God, thou hast acted like an angry father. Thou hast driven us away from thee. Hasten the punishment and the scourge, so that we may soon be able to return to thee. Pour down thy great wrath. Do not be shocked by these words, brethren, but when you see that good men wish for the scourge, know that it is because they desire evil to be driven out, and the kingdom of Jesus Christ the Blessed to prosper on earth. To us today there is nothing left but to hope that the sword of the Lord will soon approach the earth.

It would be hard to find a clearer expression of the idea of the regenerating apocalypse and purging of the world, which at the end of that century stirred the minds and sensibilities of so many men.

And the 'sword of Christ' invoked by Savonarola, the 'flood' he threatened, the 'new Cyrus', avenging and mending, came. In September 1494, a little more than a year after the fiery Advent sermon, the armies of Charles VIII, with their Swiss troops and for-midable artillery, burst into Italy, meeting with hardly any resistance. In a few months it became clear that Italy had lost the 'peace' she had enjoyed for forty years, and with it the stability and 'freedom' that had been its sweetest fruits. The return of the 'barbarians' to Italian soil set loose all latent rancours and vendettas in a general upheaval: the Neapolitan barons, who had been quelled in 1484, raised their heads again: the Venetians were quick to lay their hands on the ports of Apulia; Lodovico il Moro, Duke of Milan, got rid of his nephew Gian Galeazzo, a rival to the dukedom. Pisa escaped from Florentine rule, and in Florence itself the Medici were expelled and a Republic proclaimed.

Who should have been its legislator if not Savonarola, who had foreseen the catastrophe and preached the need for reform and expi-ation? And he did not need much persuasion, but set out, in his *Trattato Circa il Reggimento e Governo della Città di Firenze*, a project for a constitution, partly modelled on the old institutions of the Florence commune, partly on those of Venice, and thus inclining more towards a wider or 'universal' government, as Savonarola put it, than to an oligarchic one. Savonarola's intervention in public affairs, and the political supervision he went on to exercise during the first years of the Florentine Republic, must not surprise us: what was the point of declaring Christ the city's lord, if His law was not to affect all aspects of communal life and be made concrete in public institutions and in modes of conduct? The laws of God did not admit exceptions and compromises, and a religious reformer could not exempt himself from being also a legislator. 'And if you have heard it said that states are not run with paternosters', Savonarola objected to his opponents, 'remember that that means the rule of tyrants ... the rule that does not relieve and free the city, but oppresses it. If you want a good government, you must submit it to God. Certainly I would not want to encumber myself with the state if it were not so.'

But God's commandment, which required governments to be pious and just and merciful, was not only imperative but universal. The 'complete' reform that had been begun in Florence had therefore to be spread to all Italy.

And you, people of Florence, will in this way begin the reform of all Italy; you will spread your wings in the world, to take to it the reform of all peoples. Remember that the Lord has given clear signs that He wishes to renew every thing, and that you are the people chosen to begin this great task, on condition that you follow the commandments of Him who calls you.

So for almost four years – from September 1494 to May 1498, in an atmosphere of general fanaticism, Savonarola's Florence experienced a violent, 'complete' and totally experienced reform, which involved everyone. It was something new and strange in the history of Italy. This must be realized if we are to appreciate the impact Savonarola's personality and actions made on his contemporaries in and outside Florence, and to understand that not only the humble but also the learned and the great felt attracted, to the point of wanting to partici-pate. Among them were Giovanni Pico della Mirandola, and also his nephew Gian Francesco, Savonarola's disciple and biographer; the famous doctor Antonio Benivieni and his brothers Domenico and Girolamo, the first a theologian and the second a writer of Platonic verses; the artists Giovanni della Robbia, Fra' Bartolomeo and Botticelli. It also seems certain that Luca Signorelli's great cycle of frescoes in the Cathedral of Orvieto was inspired by the events of Savonarola's career.

What attracted and inspired men of such high understanding was certainly not Savonarola's culture (when he tried to write of philo-sophy and doctrine he emerged as nothing more than a scholastic compiler), but his very extremism and warm-blooded immediacy, his 'learned ignorance', a quality to which intellectuals more than anyone are sensitive. Through his words and actions they began to realize their own isolation and the powerlessness of an aristocratic culture to satisfy the needs of a society in crisis. Later, when the brief episodes of Savonarola had already become no more than a past memory, this was even more evident, and it is certainly no coincidence that the two men of the following generation who had perhaps the most vivid sense of Italy's decadence – Michelangelo and Machiavelli – should also have preserved a keen interest in Savonarola. The first was a devoted reader of his works, and the second, although he had been one of the most detached and critical of Savonarola's hearers in his youth, found in him the stuff of the new prince, the 'legislator', the man who, if he had not been 'disarmed', would have succeeded in introducing to Florence a 'new order'.

Savonarola's reformist, republican experiment ended in failure. In July 1495 the French armies abandoned Italy, thus depriving the Florentine Republic of its most powerful ally and protector, and exposing it to its many enemies. There were enemies within, chief among whom were partisans of the Medici, who several times conspired to win back power, and enemies outside, the most implacable being Alexander VI, one of the popes who has gone down to history with the least odour of sanctity. He did not forgive Florence's loyalty to France or the reformist intemperance of Savonarola, whom he excommunicated in May 1497. Even so, Savonarola managed to keep the city's moral and political temperature high for almost two years more, and stayed in power. Instead of the traditional carnival festivities in 1497, an unusual ceremony took place at Florence: a burning of vanities; clothes, books and pictures ended up in the purifying flames.

But too many factors were eroding Savonarola's popularity: the slowness and indecisiveness of the war to win back Pisa (which did not surrender until 1509), the worries of the Florentine bankers, who were bound to the Roman Curia, the fact that those extraordinary events he untiringly foretold failed to materialize. He tried in vain to win back popularity with a last-ditch gesture: he declared himself ready to accept the challenge of his Franciscan enemies, who invited him to undergo ordeal by fire. On 7 April 1498, in the civilized, secular Piazza della Signoria, everything was prepared for the strange spectacle, but Savonarola put forward a number of pretexts and finally refused to undergo the ordeal. It was the end; and like all idols when they fall, he fell headlong. The next day he was arrested, and on 22 May hanged and burned at the stake.

After his tragic end the Republic survived another fourteen years, but its life was scarcely less inglorious than its collapse. Its foreign policy was irresolute, it was divided within by struggles between the various factions, and it put up hardly any resistance when in 1512 the troops of the Grand Captain Consalvo approached the city and brought back to it the rule of the Medici.

LOUIS XII's INVASION; VENICE AND AGNADELLO

We have seen that Charles VIII's Italian venture was a brief one. The chivalrous French King went the length of the country without meeting any resistance, but then found himself the prisoner of Italian diplomatic intrigue, and was faced with the danger of being cut off by the armies of the leagued Italian princes; he had to use force to open up his way back. His successor Louis XII thought it wiser to make diplomatic preparations before a fresh attempt on Italy: he allied himself with Venice and Switzerland against the duchy of Milan, to which, as an heir of Valentina Visconti, he was a pretender; and he made another agreement with Ferdinand of Spain, against the Aragonese of Naples, and allowing Cesare Borgia, son of Alexander VI, a free hand in the central Italian territories. Then he invaded Italy; but his military victories and territorial conquests did not prevent him too from falling into the toils of Italian diplomacy. He was driven out of Naples by the Spanish, who in this way moved permanently into southern Italy, and then incautiously – Machiavelli was to blame him for it – joined the League of Cambrai, formed by Pope Julius II against Venice (1509). In the end he found himself faced by a league of all the states of Italy and the Kings of Spain and England. This was the so-called Holy League, also promoted by Julius II. Its battle-cry, 'out with the barbarians', struck a general chord in a generation that had had a Humanist education. So Louis too had to cut his way out of the Italian trap (the battle of Ravenna, 1512) and get back to France, where he soon afterwards died.

Unlike Charles VIII's ephemeral invasion, the ten-year battle kept up by the French under Louis XII to get a firm foothold in Italy, and the failure of the attempt, imposed deep changes on Italy's political order. In 1512, on the eve of Louis's departure from Italy, the situation was very unlike what it had been ten years before. Southern Italy and the islands had by this time fallen irretrievably within Spain's sphere of influence and sovereignty; in central Italy the Florentine Republic had been beaten and, as we have seen, Spain had helped the Medici to come back and rule the city again. The Papal State on the other hand had grown bigger and stronger. In northern Italy the state of Milan no longer really existed as an independent political organism: after being subject to France for ten years it was now in the power of the Swiss; before long it would once more be occupied by the French, and eventually fall under Spain. Only Venice, who had held out single-handed against a league of all the Italian princes and the leading kings of Europe, had any claim left to consider itself a champion and representative of Italy's 'liberty', or what was left of it.

To contemporaries, this pride seemed fully justified: Venice had suffered military defeat at Agnadello on 14 May 1509, but had not only succeeded in avoiding the catastrophe that many observers considered inevitable: by able diplomatic manoeuvring she had managed to detach first the Pope and then Spain from the League, and so preserve her land-possessions, with the exception of recent conquests in Apulia and the Romagna and of the city of Cremona. And what is more, during the hostilities the peasants of Venice's inland territories and the people of the larger towns had never ceased to proclaim themselves '*marcheschi*' – this is confirmed by every source, including Machiavelli – and such towns as Friuli used what rustic weapons they had to resist the enemy and contribute to the restoration of Venetian control. Such an attachment of subjects and peasants to their master was so unusual that contemporary observers inevitably saw in it a deeper confirmation of Venice's internal unity and vitality: Venice's already flourishing myth gained new lustre.

This was what contemporaries, and sixteenth-century historians, thought. What should our opinion be? In a nutshell, that Agnadello and the war of the League of Cambrai were a great opportunity for Venice, which she missed. This is a question that must be investigated in depth – it is one of the crucial points of the history of Italy in the sixteenth century.

Immediately after Venice's defeat at Agnadello, the nobles and leading men of her various inland territories lost no time in shaking off the Venetian yoke and restoring the old town-freedoms, to their own advantage. They were particularly attracted to the Emperor Maximilian, and Germany's free, independent cities. Why could not Padua, Verona, Brescia and Udine be free cities, each ruling its *contado* once again, as Nuremberg, Augusta and Ratisbon still did? But the lower orders of townsmen and countrymen reacted against these rather anachronistic ambitions of restoring town-governments. They realized instinctively but clearly that this kind of restoration would strengthen the power of the nobility, and the town's rule over the *contado*; with innate common sense they saw that if there was a choice between a nearby ruler and a distant one, between a personal, direct rule and one that was more impersonal and indirect, the second was always to be preferred. So their loyalty to Venice and their stubbornness in declaring themselves '*marcheschi*' were above all a reaction against the oppressors nearest home, and their guerrilla resistance was a genuine peasant revolt. Among the proofs of this is the fact that when the peasants of Friuli rebelled they attacked not only the castles of the imperialist nobles but also some that belonged to nobles still faithful to Venice. The chronicler Priuli, though he is one of the main sources and props of the Agnadello myth, explicitly admits as much when he writes: 'Yet truly this was the cause of the rustic rising on behalf of Venice, that the citizens of all the towns of the inland territories were against the name of Venice, and were its enemies; and since the citizens and the countrymen were always against each other, the countrymen were for this reason favourable to the name of Venice.'

The peasants' spirits were further exasperated, and they were pushed closer to Venice's side, by the bitter experience of war and foreign occupation, with its trail of plunder, harsh rulers, cruelty. The hostility between the 'rustic', who lived from peace, and the soldier, who lived from war, was one of the basic themes of the rustic comedies written at this time, in the Paduan dialect, by Angelo Beolco, called *Il Ruzante*. This hostility too worked in Venice's favour. In the eyes of the peasants who had been cut to ribbons by German and French soldiery, Venice eventually came to represent the return to normality and peace.

So the psychological motives that led the peasants of Friuli and the rest of the inland territory to remain true to Venice and take arms against the supporters of the Empire were quite straightforward. It was not patriotism – what could that have been founded on, in any case? – it was love for their place of birth; it was not an acknowledgement of Venice, but fear of the feudal lord, hatred for the most immediate and tangible exploiter. Even so, however lacking in the conscious elements that biased historians have attributed to it, the peasant movement of 1509 and the years immediately following did constitute an appeal, and a drive towards the liquidation of the many remnants of town and family local rule that permeated the organization and structure of Venice's land-possessions. It was an invitation to Venice, and a chance for her to go further in transforming her dominions from a vague group of variously-ruled territories to a modern type of unified state.

But the chance was not taken: so in spite of the determined resistance and brilliant recovery, Agnadello marks the beginning of Venice's long decline. For, once she had regained possession of the inland towns and territories, Venice merely meted out severe punishments to those individuals and families that had most deeply committed themselves to supporting the Empire; but she deliberately renounced any attempt at reforming the pre-existing social arrangements and hierarchies. On the contrary, the local rulers and aristocracies were strengthened, with Venice's consent and support. A typical case is that of Udine, capital of Friuli, the region where the clash between the Austriaemulating nobility and the *marcheschi* peasants had been most bitter during the years of Agnadello; in 1513 there was a 'closing' (*serrata*) of the commune-council, which made the running of the town even more the monopoly of those noble families and powerful men who had been the first to turn against Venice in the hour of crisis and rank themselves with the enemy. With local variations, Padua, Verona and most of the mainland towns followed the same pattern. Once the crisis was over, the Venetian state went back to what it had previously been: a sort of federation of different cities and local powers, united only by a common subjection to Venice and to their own local aristocracy: a joint-ownership of Venetian and mainland aristocracies, in which the first were firmly pre-eminent in political matters, but the second kept many of its privileges, and both were careful to arm themselves against the possibility of unrest below, and disturbance of the existing balance and immobility. Gradually, following a tendency that can already be traced in the fifteenth century, the Venetian nobility converted into land more of the wealth it had won by trade, and Venice's whole economy increasingly withdrew from sea to land. As this happened, the conservative nature of the solution adopted after Agnadello, and its paralysing results, became more and more obvious. The much-praised 'balance' of the Venetian constitution, an integral and vital part of Venice's myth, was to be no more than a noble façade to this stagnation and decadence.

THE AGE OF LEO x

But though the Agnadello crisis had left Venice worn out, and though Savonarola's attempt at city reform had failed in Florence, there was one Italian state that was on the crest of the wave during this period: the Papal State.

Julius II, the successor of Alexander VI, may not be an outstanding figure in the history of the Church as a universal body, but he is important in the history of the Church state. For it was he who completed and regulated the work of extending and consolidating the central Italian territories under papal rule, a task that had been begun by Albornoz and carried on, through various difficulties, pauses and failures, through the fifteenth century. The way had been prepared for Julius by Valentino, Alexander VI's son, who had unified the Romagna and central Italy with French help, and made it into a solid domain. On his death, Julius II, a sworn enemy of the Borgia family, took over his inheritance and his ambitions. He conquered Perugia after a hard struggle, and reduced Bologna to subjection. Then, as we have seen, he promoted the leagues against Venice and against the French, both of which swelled his prestige.

Concurrently with these military enterprises and this work of extending the state's borders, Julius II also followed his detested predecessor in reinforcing the administrative and financial structures of the Papal State. The Curia's taxes were constantly increasing – in 1525 they were double what they had been in 1492 – and this made it possible to continue the policy of artistic patronage and great public works begun by the later fifteenth-century popes. No other period in the history of Rome, except the reign of the Emperor Augustus, has left such a deep mark on the city as Julius II's ten-year pontificate. In 1506, following Bramante's plan, and under his direction, work was begun on the new St Peter's, and was to go on for more than a century. In 1508 Raphael began painting the Vatican *Stanze*, and Michelangelo started work on the Sistine Chapel frescoes in 1512. While these masterpieces of Renaissance Rome were being created, ancient masterpieces were being brought up from under the ground. The discovery of the Laocoön group in 1506 is a famous example: one of the great events of the archaeological exploration that has gone on from the Renaissance up to the present.

Julius II's fortunate foreign policy, the Papal State's growing stature, and the splendour of its capital – Rome's population was by now up to one hundred thousand – were all reasons for the Roman Curia to become the main centre of attraction for Italian political and cultural life. This was Rome's position during the pontificate of Julius II's successor, Leo x.

Leo entirely lacked Julius's warlike and impulsive temperament, and when François I invaded Italy again he quickly reached an agreement with him, returning the recent conquests of Parma and Piacenza, and negotiating with him a concordat that gave the French Church a large measure of independence. But far from counting against him, this docility actually contributed to Leo's prestige in the eyes of a generation that had had too much war. Besides, he was a Medici: he belonged to the richest and most cultivated family in Italy, the family of Lorenzo the Magnificent, which had made Florence the unchallenged capital of Humanism and of Renaissance stability. After the troubled Republican interlude the Medici had just returned to Florence: so contemporaries saw Leo's election as sealing a happy marriage between Florence and Rome, between letters and Christianity, Humanism and piety; as such, it was bound to seem a happy event to those whom the Humanists had educated in the cult of Christ and Plato. In fact, under Leo x, the Roman court and Curia became a meeting-place and point of reference for most Italian scholars – it set the tone for the intellectual life of all Italy. From 1512 to 1520 the Pope's secretary was the Venetian Pietro Bembo, one of the greatest intellectual authorities of the time; among his works are the *Prose della volgar lingua*, which may be considered the first grammar of the Italian language. The College of Cardinals included men like Bernado Dovizi, another distinguished man of letters, and author of one of the most licentious plays of the age. Baldassare Castiglione, author of *The Courtier*, perhaps the sixteenth century's greatest literary success, stayed in Rome for a long time as Ambassador of the duchy of Urbino. Ludovico Ariosto also hurried to Rome as soon as he heard the news of the election of the Medici Pope. It was the time when he was bringing his *Orlando Furioso* to completion; but he was one of the few who left Rome disappointed. There were practically no important intellectuals of that generation whose lives were not in some way linked with Leo x's triumphant Rome, and who were not drawn there. And it is impossible to list all the painters who worked there: Rome was at this time far the most active artistic laboratory and workshop in Italy.

In the age of Leo x, or the century of Leo x, as Voltaire called it, Italian intellectual and artistic life reached such a level of shared intensity and homogeneity as never before. Few poets have been so generally and immediately understood and loved by their own contemporaries as Ariosto (the first edition of *Orlando Furioso* was published in 1516), and few painters as much as Raphael (who painted his *School of Athens* in 1510). This is of course a sign of their excellence and genius, but also of the very high degree of cohesive unity in the culture and taste of a generation, and its deep responsiveness to the artistic ideals of the age. For us, Raphael's Vatican *Stanze* are merely a masterpiece, but for a contemporary, who could easily see the many references they contain to the culture and situation of the time, they were also a compendium of his own world and aspirations. There are analogous reasons for the exceptional success of Baldassarre Castiglione's *The Courtier*, written in 1508–16. Its ideal of courtly completeness and its rarefied Platonism was recognized by the cultured public of the sixteenth century as a common ideal and model: the ideal of culture translated into a style of composure and intellectual self-control.

But a common ideal and taste presuppose a common language. The publication of the text of Dante's *De vulgari eloquentia* by Gian Giorgio Trissino, a scholar from Vicenza, was an event that gave new life to the idea of a court language. Two contrasting positions emerged from the discussions among the learned on the so-called language question: there were those like Bembo, who upheld the supremacy of Florentine and the language of Petrarch; and those like

Castiglione who defended a more composite language, a balance of regional usages. But underlying the debate and the different positions taken by its many participants was the conviction that a solution to the problem of the Italian literary language was now ready and possible, and the sense of the degree of fusion and unity the Italian intellectual community had reached, after centuries of refinement.

At this point it is well to remember the place the Humanist intellectuals had occupied in society, and the social function they had performed, or neglected to perform. What was true of the Humanists was even truer of the intellectuals of the age of Leo x. Nothing was more foreign to the learned men of that time than the idea of a common mission and responsibility towards the society they lived in. Even the demands of individual commitment, felt so strongly by the first Humanists, had become slight. The Italian language was conceived and desired solely as a means of communication among the learned, and the prevailing poetry was an eminently literary reflection of Petrarch.

The great test for this generation of intellectuals came with the Lateran Council of 1513–17, convoked by Leo x, and portrayed by Raphael in allegorical form in the paintings of the 'Incendio' *stanza*. It was Leo's intention, and the hope of many who followed the Council, that it would extirpate the abuses and superstitions that cankered the Church, and effect its 'reform', which had been spoken of since the Councils of a century before. The moment seemed ripe: the yearning for more modest and charitable forms of piety that had found expression in the religious ferment of the end of the fifteenth century, was still felt. In this period began some of the charitable enterprises that are usually seen as the first signs of Catholic reform. The best-known is the *Compagnia del Divino Amore*, which was formed at Genoa in 1497 and later operated in Rome and other cities.

But these hopes were disappointed. The Council not only failed to introduce substantial reforms but, in some respects, showed itself more responsive to the need for conservation than that for renewal. Among its more important decisions were the condemnation of Pomponazzi's theories on the doctrine of the soul, and its warning against the disturbing consequences that could be provoked by penitential preaching, which it restricted. The Medici Pope and his chosen colleagues still trembled at the recent memory of Savonarola.

It was thus proved that reform of the Church could not come from above, through Councils and under the guidance of learned men, and without the emotive, turbulent participation of the mass of believers. In the same year that the Council put an end to its labours, Luther nailed his ninety-five theses to the door of Wittenberg Cathedral.

NICCOLÒ MACHIAVELLI

The name of Niccolò Machiavelli has come up several times in the preceding pages. As secretary, or as we would say now, roving ambassador, of the Florentine Republic, the future author of *The Prince* was an interested witness of some of the most important events of his age. As a young man – he was born in 1469 – he listened sceptically to Savonarola's preaching; he was at Rome in 1503 when Alexander VI died, and a disputatious conclave elected his successor, the warlike Julius II. In 1509 Machiavelli was a witness of the war in the Veneto and the crisis of the Venetian state. But the experience which did most to form him was that of his repeated journeys and embassies to France. He was unlike many of his contemporaries and compatriots, who could not lose their engrained sense of the superiority of refined Italian civilization to French roughness, and attributed the victories of the armies of Charles VIII and Louis XII only to the power of their artillery and the 'fury' of a nobility and people imprisoned by outdated myths of chivalry. But Machiavelli immediately realized the political and social superiority of the unified and efficient absolute monarchy of France over the composite, heterogeneous organisms of the Italian states. He lucidly expounded this brilliant insight in his *Ritratto delle cose di Francia*. When Medici rule was restored in Florence, Machiavelli, who had been one of the secretaries of the recently-defeated Republic, and had been actively concerned in the organization of its forces and its administration, was naturally put out of office, and even imprisoned and tortured, since he was suspected of complicity in an anti-Medici conspiracy. He was freed after Leo X's election, but found himself excluded from public life; he retreated to his country home of San Casciano. His forced, painful idleness was only broken by journeys to Florence to take part in the learned conversations that took place in the gardens of the Rucellai family; but during this period he produced *The Prince* and the *Discourses*, two works without which the history of modern political thought would be inconceivable.

The material of study and meditation was provided, to use Machiavelli's pregnant phrase from the introduction to the *Discourses*, by the lesson of ancient things and the experience of modern ones. It was a question of extracting from that vast array of facts – the whole of history from antiquity to the present – certain laws or 'general maxims' which rarely fail, and permit a reasoned and organic view of the events of states and human societies. The method was that of the natural sciences, which had been Leonardo's and was to be Bacon's, applied to the human sciences and to politics. Political science ceased to be a contemplation of the perfect state and the good prince, becoming instead the experimental study of the social organism in its healthy and its corrupt forms, just as medicine is the physiology and pathology of the human body. This empirical and naturalistic approach alone makes Machiavelli a seminal figure in the history of modern political theory, and explains how, in spite of the anathema of superficial readers, his deep, subterranean influence worked on thinkers like Jean Bodin, Bacon, James Harrington and Jean-Jacques Rousseau himself, who described *The Prince* as the book 'of republicans'.

But the quality of a method is measured by its results, and the certainties that it reaches or approaches; and also in these terms Machiavelli's contribution was a major and revolutionary one. Synthesizing his various and complex arguments to the maximum possible degree, as we must here, we can say that Machiavelli considers two attributes necessary to a state if it is really to be a state. On the one hand, force: the capacity to defend itself against possible aggressors, and where necessary to 'enlarge' its own borders; on the other hand, internal cohesion: the correspondence between 'orders' and 'customs', between the force of consent from below and that of compulsion from above. History shows political organisms that only possessed the first of these conditions: the ancient Asiatic Empires for example, and the Turkish Empire of Machiavelli's own time. But their lack of internal cohesion and their despotic character made them giants with feet of clay. On the other hand, the free Greek city-states had had great internal solidity, and so in modern times had the Swiss mountain communities, the German cities, and Venice. But the sympathy that Machiavelli, as secretary of a Republic, naturally felt for those states did not blind him to the fact that their troubled borders were continually exposed to the risk of being overrun by their more powerful neighbours; the alternative was survival at the price of a jealous provincial isolation. Even Venice had risked losing the conquests of centuries in one day – Machiavelli himself had been a witness – and had eventually been forced to wrap herself in splendid isolation.

Neither had Florence fulfilled Machiavelli's conditions: during all her history she had been internally torn by factions, and had presented to the outer world a pitiful spectacle of military and political foolishness. So of all the states that follow one another through the course of history the only one that had combined military strength with internal cohesion, the exercise of arms with that of civil liberties, remained the great Roman Republic, before the rise of Caesar and the imperial decadence. But however much he was a son of Humanism and an admirer of Republican classical times, Machiavelli knew too well that even Republican Rome, like all political bodies, was conditioned by its time and circumstances; he knew that the inflexible law of historic cycles did not spare even the most august of states. So his task was not to linger in admiring description of classical civilization, but rather to look ahead and try to trace the features of a modern state, a 'new principate', which would not be a city-state, nor an empire of the Turkish or Oriental type. It was a difficult quest, particularly for an Italian of the early sixteenth century. The example of the great French monarchy, which Machiavelli contrasted with that of Turkey, already provided a hint, a possible term of reference, but it was not enough to solve the problem. Only history could do this: and Machiavelli could not foresee its course. For his greatness is not the often dubious and false greatness of the prophet and precursor, but the much more genuine greatness of the researcher and scientist.

But though it was a difficult search, he never for a moment ceased to feel committed to it, and *The Prince* and *Discourses* bear witness to the intensity and complexity of his commitment. Some years later, from 1519 to 1521, he tried to deepen his analysis by examining, in his *Arte della guerra*, the specific problem of military administration (he himself had been the organizer of Florence's citizen militia in 1506), and reached the conclusion that any state that wishes to command respect must dispose of its own arms, must be able to recruit reliable soldiers from among its own natives, without resorting to treacherous mercenaries. But if, as the example of Republican Rome indicates, the only good soldiers are those who fight for hearth and home, for whom their land is really a mother, what innovations and institutions have to be introduced in civil and social relations to transform the 'subjects' of great states into 'citizens', who would fight with the same passionate devotion as the ancient Spartans and the mountain Swiss? Once again the military question came back to the political one, and that in turn to the social one. Inevitably, the question of the character of the modern state remained an open one. Only one point was clear, which is in itself a true political discovery; that in those places where the process of political fragmentation and corruption had reached their limit, as in Italy, the 'new principate' was inconceivable without a total regeneration and an atmosphere of revolutionary tension. In a word, it was necessary to break every link with the past and set up a completely new order, to act with determination and, where necessary with the cruelty of a surgeon and a revolutionary. 'That a new prince must make everything new in a town or province he has taken' is the title of one of the chapters of the *Discourses*. In the last chapter of *The Prince*, perhaps Machiavelli's most famous passage, this revolutionary tension reaches its highest pitch. The call for the liberation of Italy from the 'barbarians' combines with that for a radical regeneration of political life and of the 'order' and *mores* of Italian life. This is the breaking-point of the Italian intellectual's traditional attitude: the self-satisfaction of the learned and civilized man is here transformed into an anguished sense of his own limitations, and detachment into militant commitment. Niccolò Machiavelli does not belong to the century of Leo x.

But the Medici, to whom *The Prince* was dedicated, were neither interested nor able to comprehend its spirit, let alone to put its suggestions into effect. For some years they left Machiavelli idle, entrusting him only with secondary and sometimes humiliating missions. Eventually, in 1521, he was commissioned to write the history of Florence. He brought his account up to 1492, and filled it with the bitterness of a man recalling a great past, with the certainty that this past cannot give birth to any future. He died on 21 June 1527.

ITALY IN CHARLES v's EMPIRE; THE SACK OF ROME

In 1519, after a spectacular and competitive electoral campaign, Charles of Habsburg was elected Emperor of the Holy Roman Empire. From his father he inherited Habsburg possessions in Austria and Flanders, and from his mother the crown of Spain; he was supported by the financial power of the Fuggers and the military power of the undefeated Spanish infantry; the new Emperor was a taciturn, reserved man, with a strong sense of the mission that destiny seemed to have entrusted to him; it is partly due to his strong personality, composed of energy and self-control, of Burgundian passion and Spanish sense of regality, of Flemish seriousness and German laconicism, that a restoration of the Empire seemed possible in a Europe by this stage divided by conflicts and by the interests of different states.

But an Empire like Charles v's, an accumulation of various peoples and disconnected provinces, could only exist if the universal character of its mission were constantly stressed. This universality – the mediaeval idea of a *respublica christiana* still struck some echo in the minds of sixteenth-century men – could only come from Rome; and the keys to mastery of Europe were to be found in Italy. So a truly Imperial policy had to be based on domination of Italy and on harmony between the Empire and the Church, led after Leo x's death by Adrian vi, formerly Bishop of Utrecht, and Charles v's own teacher. Charles's advisers, including his faithful counsellor the Piedmontese Mercurino da Gattinara, urged him to obtain these twin objectives. In any case the duchy of Milan, with its natural appendage of Genoa, was essential to the Emperor, so that he could set up quicker and safer communications between the Spanish and the German parts of his Empire. But Milan had once more fallen into French hands, in 1515, when François I invaded Italy in the wake of his predecessors and routed the Swiss at Melegnano. So mastery of Lombardy was the initial motive of the conflict between Charles v and François I for the mastery of Europe, a struggle that went on for almost thirty years, and took place mainly in Italy.

The first stages were disastrous for the French: on 24 February 1525 the French army was defeated at Pavia, and the King himself taken prisoner. It seemed as if Spanish rule over Italy had been established once and for all, at one stroke. At this prospect the Italian states, as at the time of the invasions of Charles viii and Louis xii, joined together in a league, which included not only François I, back from prison in Madrid, but also the new Pope, Clement vii, another Medici. The new phase of the war that followed was as rich in sudden reversals and surprises as any part of the troubled history of the sixteenth century. The Imperial troops who invaded Italy to oppose the league lost two commanders: first Frundsberg, a Tyrolean nobleman who died of apoplexy; then the Constable of Bourbon, a deserter from François I who was killed when the Imperial army had easily overcome the disunited leaders of the league, and were drawing close to Rome. Left leaderless (and without money), Charles v's army became a formless mob of soldiery that entered Rome without any order from the Emperor and, to the terrified amazement of Christendom, sacked the eternal city. Clement vii, shut up in the Castel Sant'Angelo, was virtually a prisoner.

The sack of Rome, which we can now see as the result of a series of unpredictable mischances, was however seen by many contemporaries as a fatal, omened event, a judgement from God and a manifestation of Divine wrath against the corruption and degeneration of His Church. The fact that one thousand years after the Visigoths it should have been Frundsberg's Lutheran *landsknechts* who had repeated the sack of Rome was also bound to seem a symbol of the division of Christendom, and a warning to put an end to it. Even before the Imperial troops entered Rome, members of Charles's entourage had mooted the idea of putting military pressure on the Pope to force him to call a Council. This had remained no more than a hypothesis, and something to be hoped for; but we shall see that from now on many men's minds were dominated by the idea of a Council that would put an end to the Protestant schism, by accepting its most justified demands for reform.

In this new climate the glories of the age of Leo x suddenly seemed faded and distant.

It was at Florence, land of Savonarola, Leo x, and the reigning Pope, that the psychological shock provoked by the memorable events of 1527 had the sharpest and most spectacular political repercussions. At the news of the sack of Rome the Medici were thrown out, the Republic was once again declared, and the city once more dominated by the atmosphere of religious and republican revival of the years of Savonarola. Christ was proclaimed lord of the city, the citizen militia was reconstituted, and in the atmosphere of general excitement and enthusiasm the popular and extreme parties, who were hostile to the oligarchy of great families, soon gained the upper hand. But the career of the last Florentine Republic too was to be a short one. A French expedition led by Lautrec met with failure beneath the walls of Naples, and the Genoese Republic, under Andrea Doria, moved over with its fleet and its money from the league to the Imperial side. These events decisively shifted the balance of power in Charles's favour, and cancelled out the psychological advantage that François i had gained by ably exploiting the propaganda-theme of Rome having been sacked and the Papacy outraged.

In 1529 peace was concluded anew between the King of France and the Emperor, who hurried to Italy to impose his rule personally. At a solemn congress held at Bologna, to which all the Italian states save Florence sent representatives, Italy's new pattern was laid down: Milan was assigned to Francesco ii Sforza, on condition that when he died the duchy should come under Imperial sovereignty once more; Genoa kept an independence more nominal than real, under the rule of Andrea Doria, and the other Italian states were drawn within the orbit of Spain. The Bologna congress was sealed by Charles v's receiving the Imperial crown from the hands of Clement vii, after he for his part had promised to restore Florence to the Medici. Now that the general situation had rapidly been stabilized, Florence was the only storm-centre, and suddenly found herself isolated and besieged. The fortifications that Michelangelo had helped to prepare were not enough to save the city from falling into Imperial hands. With the fall of the Florentine Republic and the return of the Medici, all Italy was securely under the Emperor's control, and a dramatic period in Italian history came to an end. It had begun with Charles viii's invasion and had seen the collapse of many hopes and many bold plans: Savonarola's project for a revival of the commune and of religion; the hopes that flourished at Leo x's court, of an alliance between literature and piety and a return to the happy stable time of Humanism; Machiavelli's vision of a total regeneration of Italian life on the model of the great foreign monarchies.

The history of these forty years was written by Francesco Guicciardini, a Florentine who had taken an active part in the events of the age and had fought on the side of those who had tried to dam the Imperial advance. His *Storia d'Italia* begins in 1492 and ends, significantly, with the death of Clement VII in 1533. It has the nobility and sadness of a classic epitaph, and every page is redolent with its author's melancholy awareness of writing a chapter that is already irrevocably over. Guicciardini was fourteen years younger than Machiavelli, whose friend and correspondent he had been; he had lived long enough to see the sack of Rome and the events of the terrible year 1527, the congress of Bologna and the end of the second Florentine Republic, and long enough to draw from these events the bitter, final lesson of knowing himself to be a lonely survivor. The *Ricordi politici e civili*, which he devoted himself to after his retirement from politics, and which, like his other works, he did not bother to publish, are an account of this state of mind, and of the nobility and lucidity with which a great son of the intellectual tradition of Florentine Humanism was able to face changed fortune. There are pages of this work that have led some to see Guicciardini as a detached and even cynical figure. But surely such affirmations as: 'Pray God that you may find yourself where victory is', so open, and in the last analysis so naïve, may only be made by one who has lived intensely, and shared the convictions and aspirations of his age.

THE INTELLECTUALS AND THE COUNCIL

For more than twenty years after 1530 the general European scene was dominated by the Franco-Imperial conflict. The peace agreed between Charles V and François I in 1529 was soon broken (1535), restored (1538) and broken once more in 1542. Again, hostilities were concentrated in Italy. But they produced no significant modification of the pattern introduced at Bologna. And even though the Franco-Habsburg conflict was still the *leitmotiv* of European politics, it no longer entirely dominated the scene as it had in the previous decade. For other problems now complicated European politics and made the diplomatic game and the relations of the great powers more complex.

In the East the Turkey of Suleiman the Magnificent was on the offensive: the Turks occupied Rhodes in 1522, and by winning a battle at Mohacs in 1526 became a threat to Vienna. With the help of Berber corsairs from North Africa, Turkey evidently hoped for naval supremacy in the Mediterranean. In Germany the Lutheran schism had by now become a great movement that struggled for the autonomy and freedom of the German nation; and the Protestant princes who consti-tuted the Smalkaldic League (1531) were a political force whose existence Charles could no longer ignore.

In this complex and contradictory political context the idea of what we might call a great Imperial and ecumenical revival made headway at Charles's court. The Turkish threat revived the ancient but never wholly-forgotten myth of the Crusade: Charles conquered Tunis in 1535, and made a very unsuccessful attempt on Algiers in 1542. At the same time the Protestant secession brought back into circulation the idea of a Council, but one that, unlike the Lateran Council called by Leo x, would be no mere reassertion of prestige, but a serious, commit-ted attempt to restore the unity of the Church and the peace of Christ-endom, on the basis of internal reform, and with the collaboration of all interested parties. Pressure had to be brought to bear both on the Papacy and on the Smalkaldic League; and this was the direction in which Charles's policies worked in the decade 1530–40, using as levers the more moderate Catholic and Protestant elements.

In all Europe, but perhaps more in Italy than elsewhere, this prospect of a return of the Empire and of the ecumenical spirit excited hopes and expectations. Everything contributed to make it an inspiring and a credible prospect. A reformed and reconciled Christendom, ready to take up the banner of the Crusade, would have been able to give back Italy her place as the centre of Europe, to give back the Church and clergy their authority and piety, and the Humanist intelligentsia its cosmopolitan position and authority. At our distance of centuries these hopes seem illusions: the Mediterranean was ceasing to be what it had been for hundreds of years, and the unity of the Church had by that stage little chance of surviving in a Europe composed of nation-states. But that was not how people of the time saw the situ-ation: not all Italian intellectuals were as clear-sighted as Machiavelli or Guicciardini; and many of them used all their energy, piety and intelligence in the effort to bring about a reform and reconciliation of the Church.

'Italian evangelism' is the blanket term that usually covers the various currents and groups that worked towards Church-reform and a reconciliation with Protestantism. It had various centres and various tendencies. At Naples a circle formed around the Spanish scholar Juan de Valdès, who in 1540 published his *Alfabeto cristiano*, a short work preaching indifference to all dogmatic formulations and all the outer manifestations of religion. Enthusiastic members of this group were the Apostolic protonotary Piero Carnesecchi; the Humanists Marc'Antonio Flaminio and Aonio Paleario; Caterina Cybo, Duchess of Camerino; the Marchese Gian Galeazzo Caracciolo; the Bishop of Salerno, Seripando; and Bernardino Ochino, one of the most famous preachers of the age and general of the Capucins, a new order stemming from the Franciscans. Other important centres of Italian 'evangelism' and conciliation were the Republic of Lucca, where the theologian Pier Martire Vermigli worked; Ferarra, with the Duchess Renata of France, a daughter of Louis XII and of Anne of Brittany, who had married Ercole d'Este, at whose court Rabelais and Calvin were welcomed, and where there was a lively circle of sympathizers with Church reform; Verona, with its Bishop Giberti; Modena, with the Humanists Molza and Castelvetro, two authoritative intellectual figures of the day. But the most important breeding-ground of new ideas and new religious tendencies was probably Venice; there, the presence of a flourishing German colony, and the Republic's tolerance, made it easier for northern European ideas and books to circulate. Venice gave Italian 'evangelism' one of its most eminent figures in the nobleman Gaspare Contarini, and was for a long time the home of the Englishman Reginald Pole, who was universally considered a sincere and convinced partisan of religious conciliation, until he compromised with the persecutions of Mary Tudor. An important figure inland in the Veneto was the Bishop of Capodistria, Pier Paolo Vergerio, former German nuncio, who devoted himself to organizing Lutheran churches on a firm basis. Finally, it is impossible to overlook the name of Vittoria Colonna, widow of the Marchese of Pescara, the victor of Pavia; she was a sensitive and searching poetess, the friend and confidante of some of the leading Italian Protestants. These are only a few of the names in which Italian 'evangelism' and Protestantism were rich. Bishops and pastors of the faithful, scholars who had reflected on the great lessons of Erasmus, famous preachers, courtiers, aristocrats: there was no sector of the Italian intellectual or ruling class to which hopes for reform and for religious peace had not penetrated. But it was an élite, out of touch with the radical religious and popular discontent that existed in many parts of Italy. This élite had inherited from the previous generations of Italian intellectuals a deeply-rooted aversion to outward ritual display, and to the zeal and intolerance of the new reformers and the fanaticism of the crowds that followed them. With few exceptions, their ideal could only be one of a reform introduced from above, and an ideal aristocratic piety.

Yet when Cardinal Alessandro Farnese was elected Pope in 1534 with the name of Paul III it seemed that the moment of Italian 'evangelism' had arrived. The first nominations he made to the College of Cardinals, such men as Contarini, Sadoleto, Pole, the Neapolitan Carafa, and the Frenchman Du Bellay seemed a clear indication of his reforming spirit; and even more encouraging was the decision to form a commission, in which the newly nominated Cardinals were widely represented, charged with studying a plan of possible Church reform. This commission performed its task: in 1537 it produced the *Consilium de emendanda Ecclesia*, which may be considered the charter of Italian Church reform, both for its proposals to extirpate abuses, and also for its limitations and timidity – among other things it proposed a censorship of books, and the banning from schools of Erasmus's *Colloquia*. In the same year Paul III, welcoming Charles v's invitations and yielding to his pressure, decided to convoke a Council. But five years passed before the relevant Bull emerged, for disagreements had arisen over the city to be chosen. In the end the choice was Trent, a Catholic city, but within the territory of the Empire, and close to the borders of Protestant Europe. But in the mean time many things had changed.

In 1536 François I had resumed hostilities in Italy, and for some years the situation had once more been uncertain. In the Mediterranean the Turkish fleet had defeated the Venetian fleet off Prèveza, in 1538. In Germany the Smalkaldic League gave no sign of disarming, and it was now clear that Charles v, engaged on three fronts, had to readjust his ambitious Imperial policy. But the event that did more than any other to modify the situation and introduce a radical note was the success of Calvin's preaching at Geneva and beyond. Faced with this wave of radical reformism the Papacy's line became more rigid; and the Empire was soon placed in the position of having to support this new policy. So, many of the conciliatory hopes of the previous years were destined to vanish before long, and many of the illusions retained by intellectuals to collapse.

Breaking-point was reached in the years 1541–2. The Regensburg conference between Catholic and Protestant delegates, at which Contarini and Pole participated on one side, Melanchthon on the other, failed ; this was followed by the Pope's founding of the Holy Office. So the Council approached under gloomy auspices: even before its opening session the witch-hunt of counter-reform had begun, and many men found their consciences at the crossroads between return to orthodoxy and a final farewell to it. Some ardently took the second course, among them Pier Martire Vermigli, Bernardino Ochino and the Humanist Celio Curione, who were among the first to take flight from Italy.   Many were to follow them in the coming years. But there were also recantations, and silent but painful bendings of conscience. For both the heretics and fugitives, and for those who returned to the orthodox fold, or at least made a show of doing so, the crisis of 1541–2 represented the end of many generous and noble illusions.

One of those who had had many contacts with Italian 'evangelist' circles had been Michelangelo; the artist returned to Rome a survivor of the exciting but bitter adventure of the siege of Florence. Discussions of his supposed secret Protestantism have had their day; yet it is hard to escape the sense that the theme of that strange master-piece, the *Last Judgement*, painted between 1536 and 1541, is the same as that which inspired the anguished meditation of Luther and Calvin: the theme of God the Judge, with His hand raised above a mass of naked human flesh, marking the unalterable line that divides the lost from the saved. This fresco bears the marks of its years: the years of Michelangelo's hard, agonized old age, and of the last great exploit of the Italian Renaissance, its last lost battle. That group of men who, from 1530 to 1540, had tried to translate into reality the teaching and message of Erasmus of Rotterdam broke up and scattered: the event marks the true end of the Renaissance in Italy. With this failure, the intellectuals as a group and an élite cease to perform the tasks of binding together and of setting an example, which had been theirs since the beginning of the commune period.

THE CONSOLIDATION OF SPANISH RULE AND THE ADVENT OF THE COUNTER-REFORMATION

In the decade 1530–40, in spite of the continual wars, there were no substantial changes in the territorial and political pattern of Italy that had been laid down at Bologna, unless one counts the formal and entirely predictable absorption of the duchy of Milan into Charles v's Empire. But there were changes from 1544 to 1559, the fifteen-year period between the peace of Crépy and that of Cateau-Cambrésis, which put a final end to the Italian wars and the Franco-Habsburg duel for European supremacy. These changes amounted to the birth of one new state, the duchy of Parma and Piacenza, and the disappearance of an old one, the republic of Siena.

We have already seen how that corridor of land made by the territories of Parma and Piacenza, on the border between Emilia and Lombardy, had on several occasions from the time of the Visconti to that of Julius II passed from the hands of the state of Milan to those of the Church state. The question was resolved once and for all in 1545, when Pope Paul III managed to persuade Charles v to make the two cities into an independent duchy for his son, Pier Luigi Farnese, and so to enrich the map of Italy with one more little state. As for Siena,

during the last phase of the Franco-Spanish war she had openly
declared her support for France, and had let the Florentine republicans
use Sienese territory as a springboard for an attempt to win back
Florence from the Medici. Siena was defeated by the combined action
of Florence and Spain, and from 1555 was no longer a free republic
but an integral part of Florence's domain, save for the coastal strip of
the so-called garrison-state, which was assigned to Spain. This was
decided with the treaty of Cateau-Cambrésis, the final confirmation
of Spanish rule over Italy. When Charles v abdicated and his Empire
was divided, the Italian possessions were assigned to Philip ii, who
instituted a Council of Italy in 1563, to superintend and co-ordinate
the actions of the various viceroys and governors installed at Palermo,
Naples and Milan.

Besides the Siena war, there were other cases of resistance to the
gradual Spanish takeover: but they were fairly local, and often took,
besides, an equivocal form. In this respect the most troubled years
were 1546–7, when there were uprisings at Naples against the proposed
introduction of the Spanish Inquisition, which we shall look at later.
There were also three conspiracies in those years: at Genoa, where
the Fieschi family, supported by France, tried to shake off the rule of
the Dorias; at Lucca, and at Parma. At Lucca the gonfalonier Francesco Burlamacchi tried to draw his city and other Tuscan cities into
an attempt to overthrow Medici rule; its clearly republican character
and the atmosphere that generated it make it the most interesting and
significant of these conspiracies. For we must remember that Lucca
had been one of the capitals of Italian 'evangelism', and one of the
towns whose heretical agitations were most anxiously watched by the
guardians of orthodoxy. At Parma on the other hand the conspiracy
that led to the killing of the Duke, Pier Luigi Farnese, was fomented
by the Spanish, alarmed by his ambiguity and his aspirations to
independence: which goes to show that conspiracy was a political
weapon that could cut both ways.

So one by one the last strongholds of the 'liberty' of the Italian
states fell. Spain ruled at Palermo, Naples and Milan, and was in
close alliance with the Papacy, which in turn dominated a considerable
part of the peninsula. In practice, Spain exercised a kind of protection
and control over almost all other Italian governments, particularly
those of Genoa and Florence: in short, she was in political control of
Italy.

At the same time as the consolidation of Spanish rule, the work of
religious restoration went on. From the opening debates of the Council
that began its work at Trent in 1545 it was clear that the group who
attended in the hope that it might represent one more chance for a

reconciliation with the Reformation would easily be defeated by the firmly ranked, orthodox, zealously anti-heretical Italian and Spanish bishops. Pope Paul III was quick to grasp the first opportunity – a plague that broke out in Trent in 1547 – of moving the Council to more trusted and closer Bologna, a city of the Church. This decision deeply irritated Charles V, caused new tension between Church and Empire, and paralysed the work of the Council, which, after a brief session from September 1551 to April 1552, was not resumed until 1562. But there was no pause in the repression of heresy: under Julius III (1550–5) and even more under Paul IV, the Neapolitan Cardinal Giampiero Carafa, it was increasingly harsh. At the same time, the powers of the Holy Office and the field of action of the new and extremely powerful Company of Jesus were every day extended. The point was reached when even those members of the Holy College known for their temperate and conciliatory opinions were subjected to the Inquisition of the Holy Office : Cardinal Morone and Cardinal Reginald Pole, for instance. Even though Pole had made up for his Erasmian and 'evangelist' past by his co-operation with Mary Tudor's persecutions, he was deprived of the post of papal delegate to the Council in 1557. The following year saw the publication of the *Index of Prohibited Books*; how stunned the survivors of the age of Leo X must have been to learn that among the works a good Catholic was forbidden to read were not merely those of the notorious Machiavelli, but the *Decameron*, and *De monarchia*, by Dante, father of Italy !

Pius IV (1559–65) was a moderate, at least in comparison with his zealous predecessor, Paul IV. But by this stage the work of repression and intimidation had gone far enough for him to be able to reopen the Council, and to close it in December 1563 with the solemn acceptance of the *Professio fidei tridentinae*, which officially announced the Counter-Reformation.

Italian 'evangelism', already weak and sorely tried, could not stand up against the tempest that raged against it: there was soon a split between those who chose a complete break with the Church and those who submitted, out of fear or by way of subtle intellectual manoeuvres, to Tridentine orthodoxy. Flights from Italy followed at the same rate as recantations.

It is impossible to give the complete list of those who fled from Italy in those years: among them were Bishop Pier Paolo Vergerio, who crossed the border in 1549; the Neapolitan Marchese Galeazzo Caracciolo, two years later; Castelvetro; the noble lady Olimpia Morata; Diodati of Lucca, a famous translator of the Bible; Lelio Sozzini of Siena, with his nephew Fausto; Biandrata, the Saluzzese doctor, and many others. Some of these émigrés, like Caracciolo, became prominent and respected members of the churches of Geneva and Zurich; but others, probably the majority, journeyed on to more distant places and more radical ideas. A determining factor in this was Calvin's doctrinal intransigence, and the incident of Serveto's martyrdom. One of the Italian exiles, Castellione, argued in his *De haereticis an sint persequendi*, written on the occasion of Serveto's martyrdom, that one could not deplore the papists if one followed their very methods. So many of the Italian heretics left Geneva and sought refuge in England, Poland and Transylvania, where some of them played a leading part in the religious events of the later sixteenth century. But their break-away from Geneva and Calvinism was above all a question of ideals; many shared Serveto's rejection of the Trinity, others, like Fausto Sozzini (Socinus) went even further, to preach the need for a religion free of any dogmatic constriction, free of rules: a wholly inward faith. In some ways, this was the idea of religion that had been advanced since the first years of the century by Juan de Valdès and his circle. But the new, changed circumstances in which it was now proposed made it also an invitation to tolerance. As such, Socinianism has traditionally been recognized as an influential element in the origins of modern liberalism.

But if religious practices and outer manifestations were matters of indifference, why not accept them and submit to them, while taking care, before the tribunal of one's own conscience, to practise a true private religion, stripped of tinsel ? This in fact was the solution found by many who had not felt strong enough to leave their own land and the things they loved, even though they were deeply reluctant to accept the new forms of Tridentine Catholicism. Before he eventually chose exile, Fausto Sozzini himself had lived for many years in Italy, hiding his own beliefs under a mask of formal obeisance to current usages and rites. Calvin was certainly not able to share this attitude; and it was he who coined for it the name 'Nicodemianism', after the man 'who went to Jesus by night'. His apostle's intransigence and his jurist's habit of mind could not follow all those meanders and mental shifts that were open to intellectuals with a highly complex history and a tradition of extreme mental refinement behind them. But if he had lived a few years longer he would have seen that the last sons of Renaissance civilization were capable not only of compromises with others and with themselves, but also of intellectual consistency, taken to its ultimate conclusion. In 1567 the apostolic protonotary, Piero Carnesecchi, ascended the scaffold – and others were to follow him. Carnesecchi went to his execution wearing an immaculate shirt and a new pair of gloves; in his hand he held a white handkerchief.

5

1550–1600: Decadence and greatness

THE ST MARTIN'S SUMMER
OF THE ITALIAN ECONOMY

During the sixteenth century Europe began its march towards the position of world supremacy in technological, intellectual and political matters that it was to pride itself on, and to use during the following centuries. The first and most striking aspect of this leap ahead was of course the impulse given to European navigation and commerce by the great voyages of discovery, and by the opening up of regular trade-routes between Europe and what were to become, or had already become, European colonies. For a long time historians have handed down the traditional idea that this development of Atlantic and colonial trade drastically altered the rôle of mediators between East and West that the Mediterranean sailors had held for centuries, and so hastened the decline of the Italian ports' trading activities, which were already sorely tried by the naval supremacy acquired in the first half of the century by the Turks and Berbers. Recently, however, this traditional view has been modified; historians are now more cautious in speaking of a decline in Mediterranean trade during the sixteenth century.

It has for example been discovered that the ancient spice-route via the Red Sea and the Mediterranean, which had been almost entirely disused since the Portuguese navigators had discovered a way to reach the East Indies directly, by sailing around Africa, returned to regular use from 1550 to 1570, which allowed Venice to compete with Lisbon once again in providing Europe's markets with this essential and very expensive product. It has also been established that from about 1587 – a time when France was in the grip of religious wars, and the struggle between Spain and the Dutch rebels at its height – Genoa became the port of disembarkation and sorting-centre for the galleons, loaded with precious metals, which the Spanish monarchy sent from Barcelona to provision its wars and finance its ambitious foreign policy.

In the last quarter of the century English and Dutch ships made their appearance in the Mediterranean, and the systematic freebooting they engaged in was no less of a danger and inconvenience to the Italian ports than the competition they brought. Even so, this new period in the history of the Mediterranean did not represent a clear loss for Italian trade and prosperity: the Tuscan port of Leghorn was able to profit considerably from English and Dutch commercial activity in the Mediterranean.

In the general picture of sea-trade in the sixteenth century the rôle and place of the Mediterranean was certainly not what it had once been: but the diminution was relative, not absolute. The truth is that the increase in the total volume of goods and commercial opportunities during the century was reflected in the Mediterranean, though to a lesser extent than elsewhere, and contributed to a liveliness that had no cause to envy past centuries. So in spite of all the handicaps and difficulties of the moment, Italy and her ports also benefited from the new circumstances, and shared in the wealth of the new Atlantic Europe.

But the development of trade and navigation is only one aspect of Europe's leap ahead in the sixteenth century. Another, equally heavy in its consequences, was the so-called 'price revolution', which originated in the ever-vaster amount of American silver imported. It worked as a stimulus for European commercial enterprises, and contributed to the general process of expansion. Italy too was affected by the price revolution, from about the 1570's, and by the climate of euphoria. Economically, the last decades of the sixteenth century and the first of the seventeenth were an active period for the Italian states: their St Martin's Summer (Cipolla's term). During these years the Genoese bankers reached the summit of their financial power; the silk industry, and others specializing in the production of luxury goods, worked at a steady pace; speculation became frenetic, to the point of becoming betting, pure and simple; and a new, spectacular building boom took place in Italy's towns. Innumerable churches, town houses and country villas appeared: as always, speculation and investment in new property went hand in hand. The general animation of the time is also reflected in the population curve, which, in spite of the plagues that struck this or that region or city, showed a distinct rise. This was partly because the later sixteenth century was a time of peace and natural recovery after many years of wars and upheavals.

But since the price revolution stimulated new economic activity in the countries of western Europe, it also acted as a solvent of existing social relations, and, gradually, as the midwife of new social groups and classes. This was a long and difficult process, but many developments would probably have been impossible but for the price revolution and its major contribution to the rise of new groups and men, and to the corresponding decline in the power of the old privileged classes. The price revolution was a key factor in Holland's rapid emergence, in the English revolution, and in the hovering of the French bourgeoisie between integration within the *ancien régime* and revolution. In Italy the price-revolution was a less general solvent; such fluidity as there was affected only the lower strata of society – mass-vagabondage and banditry, typical marks of the disturbed and fermenting sixteenth century, were very characteristic of Italy too. But as far as the traditional terms and fundamental traits of Italy's social structure were concerned – the relationships between town and country and between privileged and subordinate groups, the strength of local patriotism – there were hardly any modifications. It is true that the Italian economic St Martin's Summer produced its parvenus and *nouveaux riches*, but their integration into the ranks of the establishment was relatively swift and complete. Italian society kept the unity (and the elasticity) it derived from its origins and development. Italy – at least that part which had been the scene of commune civilization – had never had a real feudal system, nor a third estate, but a single, united establishment of privileged persons, of *signori*, as they were and still are called by the humble and by peasants, who apply the term indifferently to those who have power and those who have money. The price-revolution did nothing to split this solid bloc of interests and social groups that had survived for centuries. On the contrary, the position of the established order had for some time tended to grow stronger, and during the sixteenth century this tendency was reinforced, and became more evident, both on the level of political institutions and on that of social life. Social gaps became deeper, social relations were crystallized in the forms of etiquette, public offices and power became increasingly the monopoly of a limited aristocracy.

But these considerations may seem abstract and unfounded unless we reinforce them by a precise examination of particular local situations, while keeping in mind as a convenient framework the general lines of development that have been traced.

THE SPANISH TERRITORIES

The Neapolitan barons who had rebelled against King Ferrante in 1484 had supported the French during the Italian wars of the early sixteenth century. And the French, for their part, had done all they could to encourage the barons' traditional intolerance of the central power. Consequently the Spanish victory and the absorption of Naples into the territories of the Spanish crown had also been a victory for absolutism against the tendency of a feudal order to split and fragment power. Don Pedro of Toledo, who was sent from Madrid to Naples a few years after Lautrec's expedition of 1529, held the title of viceroy, but in fact there was concentrated in his hands a degree of power such as none of his crowned predecessors in Naples had commanded. And he exercised this power. Those barons who had helped Lautrec's expedition were inflexibly punished with death or exile, and their goods confiscated and redistributed among followers of the Aragonese.

If it had shown itself unbending against offenders, the Spanish monarchy and its viceroy knew also how to reward those who had stayed faithful to it; Spanish absolutism was far from contemptuous or punitive in its treatment of the privileges and rights of the Neapolitan baronage. Twice, in 1510 and in 1547, the violent reaction of Naples, instigated and sustained by the barons, prevented the Spanish from introducing the Inquisition to the province. In other words, they resigned themselves to doing without an instrument of control and government whose effectiveness had been abundantly proved in its mother country. At the same time the existing representative bodies of the kingdom, Parliament and the elected assembly of Naples, were composed almost entirely of nobles, and kept all their prerogatives, including the right of consultation whenever new taxes were introduced. The main offices of the province, the Council of State, the collateral Council, the Regia Camera Sommaria, were also, according to a law of 1550, composed mainly of natives of the region, and were also to a large extent the perquisite of the nobility. The nobles had the opportunity of following a military career and serving the King, and many of them did so, especially from the end of the sixteenth century, distinguishing themselves on the battlefields of Flanders and of the Thirty Years War. In this way the Spanish monarchy acquired not only valiant fighting-men, but also a safety-valve that let off the Neapolitan barons' remaining aggressions.

So the assertion of the viceroy's powers had not brought any *qualitative* change in the kingdom's traditional political structure. This continued to be basically a diarchy of baronage and crown, or, rather, an absolute monarchy tempered by baronial elements. Besides, the same principle reigned at Madrid; it was not surprising that the province should be governed on the same principles as the mother country. But when had such a political structure been capable of containing the development and fermentation of new forces and new social relationships?

After the terrible blood-letting of the fourteenth and fifteenth century crisis, the fabric of southern society was healing, and the general tone of social and economic life regaining strength. From about 1530, the time when the territory ceased to be the scene of clashes between the French and the Spanish, Naples too had its St Martin's Summer. There is no better evidence of this than the population-curve; from 1532 to 1599 the number of 'heads' liable to taxation rose from 315,000 to 540,000, excluding the city of Naples, which began to acquire the status of a great metropolis in these years. At the end of the century the population of Naples had reached two hundred thousand: it was the liveliest and most populous city of Europe. Its appearance underwent profound changes: until a short while ago the city's main street still bore the name of Pedro of Toledo, the Spanish viceroy who built it.

The sixteenth-century colony of Naples is no exception to the rule whereby an impetuous rise in population and accelerated urban development coincide with favourable economic circumstances and vigorous production. The part we know best, thanks to very recent studies, is Calabria; and the data provided all agree in indicating that population increase and economic expansion went together. In fact the doubling of the number of households between the account of 1505 and that of 1561 (from 50,669 to 105,493) is paralleled by the figures relating to the production of silk, the region's principal resource, which also doubled. There were substantial increases also in the cultivation of cereals and olives, and in livestock. If, as appears most likely, these figures represent a general tendency of the southern economy, it is not hard to understand how the region was able to maintain and even increase its traditional exports of farm produce to the markets of northern Italy. Even though assessments vary, the available figures and accounts combine to give the picture of a widely active foreign trade. And it must be remembered that this was a time when prices were rising to a revolutionary extent.

In this situation, and in a society at least provisionally freed from the nightmare of need and feudal anarchy in which it had lived so long, greater possibilities of development and social advancement were open to the intermediate social groups engaged in trade, finance and the professions. It is true that the sectors of the community concerned with trade and credit were still dominated by foreigners to the region, as they had been since the days of the first Angevins; the only difference being that the Jews had been expelled by Pedro of Toledo – in this as in other things a faithful executant of his Catholic King's orders – and had been replaced by Genoese. These, in payment for the support Andrea Doria had given Spain at the critical moment of Lautrec's expedition, had greatly benefited from the distribution of land and favours following the reprisals against the pro-French barons. But even so, in spite of the privileged position of the Genoese, there would have remained wide margins of development for the Neapolitan trading and professional middle class, especially in the capital, if only it had not found itself up against the obstacle of the existing political structures. In the elected council of the people of Naples, for example, there was only one people's representative for every five representatives of the nobility; and Ferdinand the Catholic, like all his successors, rigidly refused to allow the vote of the people's representative to equal the five votes of the nobility.

In May 1585, when the impression made by the revolt in the Low Countries was most vivid, and there were ripples of unrest in all the Spanish possessions, some sectors of the Neapolitan middle class put themselves at the head of a general insurrectional movement that burst out in the city, following a rise in the price of bread. They proposed that the representatives of the people should be given an equal voice with the barons. But without success: the revolt was systematically crushed, and as many as twelve thousand citizens – an indication of its breadth – forced to leave the city. There was no chance of another such attempt.

By now the times were changing again, and the short St Martin's Summer drawing to its end. Towards the end of the sixteenth century there were signs that the economic situation was getting duller and deteriorating. After the plague made a dramatic reappearance with the great epidemic of 1576, the years of famine followed with increasing regularity, the birthrate dropped, and the mood of economic euphoria, which the price-revolution had encouraged, faded. In these new circumstances the privileged sections of the community were naturally led to consolidate their own positions as landowners, and we find that the barons made more frequent attacks on the prerogatives of the community, while the Church – the new activist Church of the Counter-Reformation – systematically rebuilt and reorganized its own territorial possessions. At the same time the state increased the already heavy burden of taxation.

The combined force of these various pressures was in the end bound to arouse a general sense of unrest and dissatisfaction at the lowest social level. So at the end of the century there were uprisings and revolts in Naples. The most famous is that inspired and led by Tommaso Campanella, who in 1599, in his native Calabria, put himself at the head of a heterogeneous mass of social and political forces, held together by his millenarian announcement that the 'new century' was to bring a new 'change of state'. The attempt was routed, and Campanella began his long years of imprisonment.

But the clearest sign of discontent among the peasants was banditry. This was, indeed, an endemic phenomenon: in the attempt to get rid of it the viceroy Pedro of Toledo had already had to condemn eighteen thousand people to death, though on his own admission he had failed to bring the whole kingdom back to order and tranquillity. But the extent of banditry, and the forms it assumed in the last two decades of the sixteenth century were something that had not been known before. As in the neighbouring Papal State, Neapolitan banditry in the years 1585–92 and 1596–1600 was a truly mass phenomenon, involving broad strata of the rural population, not only the more desperate, uprooted people, but also better-off farmers and many of the minor clergy. Operations against the main bandit leaders like Marco Sciarra who was active in the Abruzzi soon took on the air of full-scale wars, with towns taken first by one side then by the other, battles and sieges; the bandit movement was only defeated when the viceroy of Naples and the papal government joined forces.

In a social context characterized by the beginnings of economic depression and by a tension that pushed political attitudes and sympathies to the two extremes of conservatism and subversion, the margin of action of intermediate forces grew narrower all the time, and their demands for 'reform' had less and less chance of gaining acceptance. Antonio Serra, a Calabrese, spent much of his life in prison, where he wrote a treatise on economics, pinpointing the province's difficulties in the shakiness of its native merchant and manufacturing class, and the corresponding backwardness of its political institutions. But in the conditions of the time his voice inevitably remained unheard. Certain bourgeois circles of Naples, whose most authoritative representative was the jurist Giulio Genoino, tried to involve the viceroy, the Duke of Ossuna, in a policy of reform; but the attempt never had much chance of success. The Duke of Ossuna was accused of treason by the barons at the court of Madrid, and was recalled in 1618. From then on, as we shall see, the southern social crisis mounted steadily towards the great crisis of 1647.

In its broad outlines the history of the province of Sicily during the sixteenth century is not very different from that of Naples. In Sicily

too the constitution was a diarchy, a partitioning of viceregal and
baronial spheres of influence. The barons, who were in almost entire
command of the island's Parliament, rebelled twice in two years,
1516 and 1517, against the first viceroy sent by Ferdinand, Moncada,
and made it clear from the outset that they would not tolerate intru-
sions in the field of what they considered their rights and prerogatives.
Moncada's successors took careful note of this, and the Duke of
Olivares himself is said to have reminded them that 'in Sicily, with the
barons you are everything; without them, nothing'. There in the
southernmost region of Italy, where Charles v's Imperial absolutism
had been brought to a halt, Philip II's bureaucratic absolution also
had to stop.

Yet even Sicily had its short St Martin's Summer; from 1501 to
1583 the population of the island, excluding Palermo and Messina,
rose from 502,761 to 801,401, and the exports and prices of corn, the
island's main resource, kept at a steady level. But in Sicily too the
favourable conditions lasted too short a time to make any breach in
the pattern of social relationships and the existing political structure.
Sicily suffered three years of famine from 1575 to 1577; a period of
hard times and economic decline set in. At the end of the century
Sicily had more or less ceased to be a big cereal exporter: this was
partly because of the population increase, and because of competition
from corn produced in northern Italy, and corn imported from the
East; but another factor was probably the impoverishment of the
soil. It had been exhausted by agricultural methods that, because of
the social structure of the countryside, had remained backward.

Among Spain's possessions in Italy, Lombardy, as we have already
seen, was particularly important because of its geographical position.
Control of Lombardy provided rapid communications between the
Mediterranean and Germany, and thus constituted an essential link
in the Habsburg system. For this reason, it was without doubt the
Italian province that had suffered most from the wars of the early
sixteenth century: Marignano and Pavia were two of the famous battles
fought in Lombardy. The same situation was later repeated in the
early seventeenth century, when the hostilities of the Thirty Years War
broke out, and the Valtellina and Monferrato became key positions,
bitterly contested by the two antagonists. But in the long intervening
period, on the other hand, the years of 'Spanish dominance', Lombardy
gained many advantages from its position. The nearness of Genoa, and
the position of primary importance that the Genoese banking oligarchy
had acquired in Charles v's Empire, helped to make Lombardy one
of Europe's economic nerve-centres. So in the later sixteenth century
Milan became one of the favourite markets of the great Genoese

bankers, some of whom made their own homes there, and built sumptuous palaces. The most famous of these is the Palazzo Marino of 1558. Milan's population grew from eighty thousand in 1542 to a hundred and twelve thousand in 1592, and the city witnessed a lively outburst of building activity. And unlike the rise in population in Naples, that in Milan was founded on a solid basis of flourishing crafts. The traditional Milanese industries – wool, silk, small-scale metal work, luxury cloths – were all intensely active. So was the more recent and promising printing industry.

But as we know, the main and most reliable resource of Lombard economy was provided by the agriculture of the fertile Po plains. For them too the second half of the sixteenth century was a happy period, in the course of which the wounds of war healed and the career of progress begun in the time of the communes was resumed at a quicker pace. It is no coincidence that the two great agricultural experts of the age, Agostino Gallo and Camillo Tarello, were both from Brescia, a province bordering on the state of Milan, and typical of the Po region, nor was it a coincidence that their works make frequent reference to the highly developed farming systems of lower Lombardy.

In a society whose wealth was mostly in the form of land, property, whether acquired recently or long before, was bound to be the criterion of respectability and political prestige. The Lombard nobility, who were assured an adequate share in main government posts and administration by Charles v's 1541 Constitutions, and who had their stronghold in the Senate that had been set up on the model of the French parliaments of Louis xii, were above all a group of landowners, and considered themselves as such. This is proved by the fact that in 1593 the College of Jurists, the training-ground of civil servants, excluded men engaged in trade. But the Lombard nobility was a social and political class that was very unlike the Neapolitan or Sicilian baronage; not only in the substantial size of many of its estates, but also in the way it saw and used its position as a privileged, ruling class.

Cardinal Carlo Borromeo, Archbishop of Milan from 1565 to 1584, and one of the major personalities of Italian religious history, was instrumental in forming this attitude and making the Lombard nobility aware of it. Borromeo was the nephew of Pope Pius iv, another Milanese, and when Pius died he left Rome and the Curia for Milan, determined to make his city a capital of the Counter-Reformation. He arrived in time to consecrate the new cathedral, which had been begun almost two centuries before, and had just been completed. With his mixture of intransigence and activism, energy and piety, he was an obvious personification of post-Tridentine Catholicism; no-one could have approached his task with a better chance of success. And his rule of the Milanese Church left a deep mark on the intellectual and religious life of the city and the state. The first thing he wanted was a clergy in his own image: zealous, industrious, austere and dynamic; to this end he embarked on a root-and-branch reform of his diocese, allowing no established position to stand in his way, and tolerating no resistance, though this brought him into conflict with the Spanish government. Even the old order of the Umiliati, which had been so closely linked with the beginnings of the Lombard wool-industry, was dissolved. Its place was taken by the new, powerful Jesuit order, later installed in the Palazzo di Brera, who were given important responsibilities in the field of teaching. The struggle against heresy was also, of course, pursued to the bitter end, with no blow spared.

But the work of Carlo Borromeo and of his nephew Federico, who succeeded him as ruler of the diocese in 1595, was not confined to the internal reorganization of the Church and the restoration of orthodoxy: they bravely and energetically grappled with every aspect of public and community life, from the field of culture (the Biblioteca Ambrosiana, one of Milan's great cultural institutions, was founded by Federico) to that of charitable work and welfare, vitally important in an age of widespread begging. The Borromeos also restored the considerable lands and properties of the Milanese Church.

This multifarious and energetic activity left a long-lasting mark on the religious and social life of Lombardy: the Borromeos are the ultimate source of that breed of industrious Catholicism, which may have been paternalistic, but was also compounded of social responsibility, that for a long time characterized the Milanese and Lombard ruling class. We may define it as a sense of the rich man's mission. Activism and paternalism for a long time remained, and still do remain, characteristic traits of the Milanese spirit and way of doing things. They originate in Carlo Borromeo who, by restoring the cult of St Ambrose, was the first to infuse his fellow-citizens and flock with the awareness and pride of being Lombards, and at the same time assiduous workers in the Lord's vineyard.

THE GRAND DUCHY OF TUSCANY

During the wars of 1537-59, Cosimo dei Medici, as we have seen, was able to extend the bounds of his state to the point where they almost reached those of present-day Tuscany. Of the towns and territories that now comprise Tuscany, only the Republic of Lucca, the Duchy of Massa Carrara, which was under the Cybo family, and the coastal towns of the garrison-state remained outside Medici rule. The most important acquisition had been that of Siena and her lands.

Such a territorial expansion demanded a transformation of the structure and very character of the Medici seigniory. A new balance had to be found. In particular, it was necessary to break with Florence's traditional policy of considering subject territories and towns as appendices of the capital, as its hinterland: a better-balanced and more homogeneous territorial and political organism had to be brought to life. This had been the road Lorenzo the Magnificent had begun to move along, and where he was followed by Alessandro dei Medici (1530–7), Cosimo (1537–74) and Ferdinando (1587–1609).

The old city magistracies and professional corporations continued to exist in theory, but were deprived of practical authority. Effective power passed into the hands of the so-called *pratica segreta*, a small team of civil servants who worked under the constant control of the city's lord. They led a bureaucracy in which provincials gradually came to outnumber Florentines. The size of this bureaucracy, and its political importance, constantly increased, so that a building became necessary to house its central offices: between 1560 and 1580 the architect Giorgio Vasari superintended the building of the Uffizi, a few yards away from the Palazzo Vecchio. The contrast between the character of these two buildings, the practical sobriety of the earlier one, the swaggering exuberance of the later, is the most effective illustration of the whole parabola of Florence's history, from its mercantile commune origins to its Grand-Ducal finale. The Palazzo Vecchio itself was not what it had once been, the home and symbol of Florentine liberty: inside it, the ducal apartments had been rearranged by Vasari, the Principality's official architect, and the building's severe façade contrasted with the preciosity and sophistication of its interiors.

So, under the unifying and levelling impulse of the Medici and their bureaucracy, the state of Florence was transformed into a duchy, or rather, into the Grand Duchy of Tuscany, from 1569, when Cosimo managed to acquire the title from the Pope and have it confirmed by the Emperor. During the transformation, Florence lost not only the limitations but also the resources she had derived from her city-state character; at the same time, she failed to acquire the characteristics of a modern absolute state. One should look less at the bureaucratic administrative structures and institutions and more at the social classes and forces behind them, which conditioned the way they worked. From this point of view Florence and Tuscany at the end of the sixteenth and beginning of the seventeenth century show a marked tendency to withdrawal and economic stagnation.

To summarize the process, one can say that it was precisely at the end of the sixteenth century that Florence ceased to be a great financial and productive centre, as it had still been early in the century, and became a residential city of *rentiers* and civil servants, as it still is today. This radical metamorphosis is reflected in the crisis and the weariness of the merchant-aristocracy, who had been the creators of Florence's opulence and greatness.

This decline is another process that one must guard against seeing as more dramatic and sudden than it was. It took a long time: up to the early years of the seventeenth century Florence's silk exports remained steady, and Florentine bankers were still important figures at Lyons. During the wars of religion many of them moved to Paris, and the links they formed with the court of Catherine dei Medici persuaded many of them to turn themselves from independent financial operators into tax-lessees and agents in the service of the French Crown, or even to become courtiers; many of them ended by seeking naturalization. The marriage of Maria dei Medici, daughter of the Grand Duke Ferdinand, to Henri IV, accentuated this tendency; and so a new wave of Florentine immigrants settled in France, after the wave of republicans who had taken refuge there in the first half of the century. There is no room here to go into the effect this influx of highly qualified intellectuals had on French political history: Cardinal de Retz was a member of the Gondi family.

At the same time as many Florentine merchants and financiers were becoming French citizens, others, on the other hand, like the Corsini of London and the Gerini and Torrigiani of Nuremberg, at last returned home. But both the first and the second were contrasting manifestations of a single process: the conversion of the Florentine merchant and banking aristocracy into a group of *rentiers* and landed proprietors at home and abroad. In Tuscany at the end of the sixteenth century land was the most eagerly sought form of investment. So large estates were formed, by private individuals who bought land with the capital earned from trade; by churches and ecclesiastical bodies, which the active administrators of the Counter-Reformation period were constantly expanding, with the accommodating support of the authorities; by chivalrous and military orders such as the Knights of S. Stefano, founded in 1561 by Cosimo, as a force to fight the Berbers; and, finally, considerable estates were formed by the Grand-Ducal family. Together with this concentration of property into large estates, inheritances by elder sons and ecclesiastical mortmain tied up increasingly wider areas of land; at the same time there was a race for noble titles and privileges. Unlike what happened in other Italian states such as Lombardy or the Veneto, this rush for land was not accompanied by any attempt to improve agriculture. There has been no deep research into the subject, but it does not seem that Tuscan agriculture of the later sixteenth century can be described as anything but static. In their new rôle of landed proprietors, the Florentine and Tuscan ruling class turned out to be as poor in initiative and imagination as they had been enterprising and resourceful in banking and trade. Their administration was, on the whole, orderly and diligent, but niggardly. Where their ancestors had shown a taste for and a pride in opulence, they had a taste for parsimony. There is probably no other Italian city that built less than Florence in the sixteenth century. Florence's baroque buildings can be counted on the fingers of one hand.

The single exception to this general withdrawal was the remarkable prosperity of the city and port of Leghorn, from the last twenty years of the sixteenth century and throughout the seventeenth. In 1577 Ferdinand proclaimed Leghorn a city, and provided it with valuable port machinery; it soon attracted a cosmopolitan, industrious population of Jews, Byzantines and Englishmen. The tolerance and even favour shown by the Grand Dukes to these immigrants, and the later founding of a free port, certainly helped to make Leghorn one of the most active ports of the Mediterranean, used particularly by the English and the Dutch. Both Genoa and Marseilles felt the effect of its competition. Leghorn was also one of the main centres of freebooting, a further factor in its activity and prosperity.

But Leghorn was an exception: being a trading and transit port, it had few economic links with the Tuscan hinterland; Leghorn's relation to the inland region has justly been compared with the present relation of Singapore to Malaysia or that of Hong Kong to China. In general, the late-sixteenth century Grand Duchy of Tuscany was a state that lived from rents, and administered, with a certain degree of prudence and good sense, the wealth it had built up over the centuries – both its material and its spiritual, cultural wealth.

Florentine intellectual life of the second half of the sixteenth century still demands respect and admiration. One of the great figures of the period is Galileo Galilei, whose father, Vincenzo, was a distinguished musician and musical scholar and one of the founders of the Florentine *Camerata*, which is traditionally credited with reviving Italian musical life and with originating the Opera. Perhaps Galileo's mathematical genius owed something to his father's musical talent: the love of order, measure, proportion and harmony.

Even so, if one considers late sixteenth-century Florentine intellectual life as a whole, paying more attention to the norm than to the exceptional summits, it is bound to seem less energetic than it had been; it shows a marked tendency to withdraw into contemplation of its own past. Encouraged by the Grand Duchy's paternalistic patronage, academies were founded in this period – the Florentine Academy under Cosimo, and the Crusca Academy under Ferdinand – and they were the scene, and the means, of this retreat. From the start, their principal mission was the valuation, or over-valuation, of the city's cultural heritage, its literature, authors and language. Carlo Lenzoni wrote a defence of the Florentine language, later imitated by Salviati in his *Orazione in lode della fiorentina lingua*; Vicenzo Borghini was a keen student of Florentine literature, and probably the first Dante-specialist in the history of Italian scholarship. In 1612 the members of the Crusca Academy published the first edition of their *Dizionario*, in the effort to crown the supremacy of the Florentine tongue, and put an end to the language problem, which had been debated throughout the sixteenth century. Another leading figure was Giorgio Vasari, a native of Arezzo. He was not only the official architect of the Grand Duchy, but the author of the *Lives of the most excellent Italian architects, painters and sculptors*, which was both the first attempt at an organic history of Italian art from Cimabue to the sixteenth century, and, particularly in its first edition of 1550, a fairly explicit defence of the supremacy of Florentine art.

In this satisfied contemplation of their own past, the Florentines certainly displayed a pride in being the heirs and continuers of that past; but even stronger perhaps was the feeling that the great period of Florentine civilization was ending – a sense of nostalgia and help-lessness. There was also a certain provincialism, a tendency to close in on themselves with a self-sufficiency and aloofness that was the exact contrary of the mental openness of the great Florentine artists and intellectuals of the past. So 'Florentinism' was born at the time when Florence was already ceasing to be one of the great intellectual capitals of Europe, and becoming an Italian province.

PIEDMONT AND THE HOUSE OF SAVOY

It may seem surprising that this history has so far contained no more than occasional and fugitive references to Piedmont and its lords of the house of Savoy, who were one day to be the Kings of Italy. But this omission has been deliberate, and the reasons for it will soon become clear.

The term 'Piedmont' dates from the twelfth century, and originally referred to the confined area between the curve of the Alps and the upper course of the Po; only later was it extended to all the foothills of the Italian side of the Alps, from Aosta to Nice, excluding only Saluzzo and its territory, an independent marquisate later annexed to the French Dauphinate. It is difficult to argue that the history of this extreme fringe of the peninsula should be considered part of the history of Italy before the sixteenth century. Piedmont was in fact part of a territorial organism which had its capital at Chambéry, and was ruled by a family of distant Burgundian origin. Its borders extended as far as the Rhône and the shores of Lake Geneva. Even Geneva was part of the territories of the dukes of Savoy up to the first decades of the six-teenth century and the eve of the Calvinist revolution. On the other hand, their domain did not include some territories that we are now used to considering not merely as obviously Italian, but even as Piedmontese – such as the fertile plains to the east of the Sesia, with the cities of Novara and Vercelli, and the hilly district of Monferrato, which had for hundreds of years been an independent duchy, and in 1536 was assigned by Charles v to the Gonzagas of Mantua. On that occasion the house of Savoy gained only the city of Asti, once a flourishing commune and a city of enterprising businessmen.

Since it commanded the eastern chain of the Alps the Duchy of Savoy was for hundreds of years one of those buffer states, or marches, of which there were so many on the political map of mediaeval Europe. (Navarre and Lorraine were others.) It was, in the language of the age, 'the gate of Italy', but not yet a part of Italy. The Italian language alternated with French, from place to place and valley to valley. When Emanuele Filiberto, inspired by the decree of Villiers Cotterets under François i, decided to make the use of the vernacular obligatory in legal documents, he was careful to specify that this applied to both the languages in current use, Italian and French. Here may be found the origins of the bilingual habit, and clear bias towards French, that characterized the rulers of Savoy up to the time of Cavour and Vittorio Emanuele ii.

Not only geographical and linguistic reasons put Piedmont on the fringe of Italy: Italy, particularly the northern and central parts, was the most densely urbanized geographical area of all Europe. This could certainly not be said of Piedmont, even if the Piedmontese Jesuit Botero proudly declared that his country was one great city 'three hundred miles around' – an elegant way of recognizing, as he in fact did, that it had no 'cities of extraordinary size'. At the beginning of the sixteenth century Turin was little more than a fortified hamlet, and even at the end of the century, when Emanuele Filiberto had made it the capital of the Italian part of his possessions, the population of Turin was only forty thousand, far smaller than that of any of the other major Italian centres. But though it had few towns, Piedmont was rich in small communities and castles. 'There is no part of Italy where the estates and castles are more numerous or bigger,' wrote Botero. There were free mountain communities and great and small feudal estates that kept strong powers of jurisdiction and constriction over their 'men'. Emanuele Filiberto tried in vain to abolish the many survivals of serfdom in his states: the peasants were either unable, or in many cases did not bother, to pay the price demanded of them for their liberty, and serfdom was not finally abolished in Piedmont until the eve of the 1789 revolution. At this point a comparison is inevitable with the Bolognese *liber paradisus* and the other collective liberations that had taken place in the communes of Italy since the thirteenth century. This is a reference that enables us, however approximately, to measure in chronological terms the social gap that separated Piedmont from the most precocious and advanced parts of Italy.

But time was narrowing this gap. While, as we have begun to see, the arrival of Spanish rule began a stage of stagnation and enfeeblement for the Italian states, backward, under-developed Piedmont still had, precisely because it was backward and under-developed, a wide margin of development and much latent energy. The signs of this were soon evident. In the second half of the sixteenth century the Duchy of Savoy certainly preserved a greater degree of independence and political initiative than most of the other states of Italy. Duke Emanuele Filiberto manoeuvred skilfully between Spain, which was involved in the effort to reconquer the Low Countries, and France, which was internally torn by the wars of religion. He profited from their mutual desire, after the settling of accounts at Cateau-Cambrésis, to avoid yet another reopening of hostilities in Italy. By these means Emanuele Filiberto, the victor of Saint-Quentin, won back his Italian states in 1559, after twenty years of French occupation; he managed to consolidate his position quickly, and even to get French garrisons to withdraw from some of the Duchy's strongholds, such as Turin itself. His successor, Carlo Emanuele I, went further in the same direction, and in 1588, when the wars of religion were at their height, won the marquisate of Saluzzo and held it against the French counter-offensive; he reached an agreement with Henri IV, ceding to France the alpine valleys of Bugey, Gex and Bresse in exchange for Saluzzo. On the other hand, the attempt to win back Geneva with a surprise attack in 1602 was unsuccessful, and even more so the later attempt to win Monferrato, against the will of the Spanish. But we can look at these events in their place. For the moment it is enough to observe that in the later sixteenth and early seventeenth centuries the Duchy of Savoy seemed to many observers to be the only Italian state that had kept its own independence intact from the omnipresent Spaniards. One of these observers was the poet Alessandro Tassoni, who in 1614 dedicated his *Filippiche contro gli Spagnoli* to Carlo Emanuele I.

The facts show that there were many exaggerations and illusions in these panegyrics, which were in any case largely occasioned by circumstances. But, setting aside the hypothetical possibility, not considered seriously even by its rulers, that the Duchy of Savoy could occupy a leading position in Spanish Italy, there remained the fact that a new and relatively efficient territorial and political entity had asserted and consolidated itself in a corner of Italy that had all through the first half of the century been a battlefield for foreign armies and as such had seemed destined to remain what it had been for centuries, a land of local loyalties and feudal fragmentation.

From this point of view of internal policy and the strengthening of constitutional bodies, the work of Emanuele Filiberto had really left a lasting mark. It is true that progress had also been made under the French occupation, with the creation of two parliaments, at Chambéry and Turin, and with a noticeable advance in unifying the laws of Piedmont. It must not be forgotten that the French rulers of Turin had included a man as enlightened and modern as Guillaume Du Bellay. But though Emanuele Filiberto had spent his youth fighting the French, once he had regained possession of his states he was intelligent enough to continue the work of his ex-enemies, reinforcing ducal power in relation to feudal and local rule. It had after all been a Savoyard, Claude de Seyssel, for some time Archbishop of Turin, who had at the beginning of the sixteenth century sung the praises of the *grande monarchie de France*.

It is hard to see Emanuele Filiberto's internal policy as anything but a systematic effort to introduce and strengthen in his states the principle of the subordination of individual interests and privileges to the central power; the policy that had indeed made France a great monarchy. The sight of the disruption and confusion into which political and religious strife had thrown his great neighbour in the wars of religion strengthened him in this principle, and led him to give his absolutist leanings the colours of Tridentine orthodoxy. The parliaments instituted by the French were preserved (only their name was changed to Senate) and the Duke used them as an effective instrument to bring about the gradual triumph of common law and royal justice over the various local usages. Certain of these local laws still allowed for cases of murder to be settled by a cash payment on the part of the murderer, a system that amounted to an encouragement and guarantee of impunity to powerful men who wished to administer their own justice, as they commonly did. While authority was given to the new parliaments on the French model, the old feudal representative bodies, based on the French States General and provincial parliaments, were deprived of power. The foundations of a more systematic and modern administrative structure were laid, by means of the creation of provinces and prefectures and of the council of state. Together with legal and administrative reforms, monetary and financial ones progressed: a new, single royal coin was minted, and the Exchequer was reorganized, being split into two parallel bodies, at Turin and Chambéry, in 1577.

But the most important of the reforms promoted by Emanuele Filiberto was the military reform that brought about the formation of a militia of twenty thousand infantrymen, recruited on a system of territorial conscription, and stationed in local bases. This had considerable political importance: it was a new blow struck at the privileges of the noble and feudal class, whom the Duke now no longer had to rely on to provide men in case of war.

Finally, the new absolute monarchy of Savoy did not neglect economic matters: provisions in this sphere included the attempt to abolish serfdom, the founding of a bank, directed by Genoese financiers, to control financial affairs, encouragement given to the trading concerns of Nice, and to the silk, printing and glass industries. Although Emanuele Filiberto had persecuted the Waldensian minority of the Alpine valleys of the Pellice and the Chisone, he encouraged Jewish merchants and bankers to settle in his state, to help its economy, which displeased the Roman Church.

So the two aspects of the French type of absolute monarchy, its repressive, severe watchfulness on the one hand, its innovatory dynamism on the other, were reproduced by the Savoy monarchy. But for the moment, under Emanuele Filiberto, the second was more in evidence than the first.

VENICE AFTER AGNADELLO

The history of Venice after Agnadello is, in spite of everything, one of decline. 'In spite of everything', because the most recent tendency among historians has been to react against the catastrophic picture given by eighteenth-and nineteenth-century historians, and to emphasize those elements of vitality and resilience that the political and economic organization of the Republic did certainly give signs of during the sixteenth century. This latest historical interpretation contains a corrective element that we must accept, but not to the point of reversing the earlier judgement. From a long-term point of view the history of the Venetian Republic in the sixteenth century describes a descending curve, which is especially clear to anyone who looks at it retrospectively, from the viewpoint of the end of the century.

To begin with a general statement: at the beginning of the seventeenth century Venice was no longer a great Mediterranean power. Not only was her position in the Mediterranean drastically reduced and weakened by the new, vigorous competition of the French and the Dutch, but even in the Adriatic, which the Republic proudly considered its 'gulf', Venetian freedom of movement was seriously restricted. Lodged in the islands of the Dalmatian archipelago, encouraged and protected by the Austrian Habsburgs, the Slavonic pirates were able to disrupt Venetian trade gravely; and Venice's inability to put an end to their raids provoked complaints from Turkey, and the not unjustified claim that Turkey itself should take over the task of policing the sea, since Venice seemed incapable of doing so. So, caught between the Turkish anvil and the Habsburg hammer, Venice was in a very delicate situation, which threatened to destroy her position as a major sea-power. Added to this was the threatening presence of the Spanish, rulers of Milan and dominant over all Italy, on Venice's eastern frontier.

This situation did not of course arise overnight, but by stages, through a dramatic process that had its moments of glory for Venice. In the war of 1538–40 Venice was defeated by the Turks, and lost Nauplia, and Monemvasia and other Aegean islands; for thirty years afterwards she thought it best to follow a reserved, isolationist policy. Then in 1571 the fleet of the Holy League inflicted a crushing defeat on the Turks at Lepanto, a victory to which the Venetian fleet made a decisive contribution; it seemed as though Venice was abundantly revenged. However, for Venice at any rate, Lepanto was a victory that led nowhere. In the end, Spain's uncertainty and hesitation in pursuing the Eastern Mediterranean struggle led the prudent Venetian diplomats to make peace with the Turks once more, in 1573. It was a compromise peace: Cyprus, which the Turks had occupied after a bloody struggle, was finally lost, together with other lesser possessions in Albania and Epirus, and Venice had to pay a considerable indemnity.

Apart from the heavy financial burden of war, Venice's main motive in seeking an agreement which her allies saw as a betrayal was her anxiety to retain those commercial outposts in the Mediterranean on which Venetian prosperity had been founded. Not only tradition and habit but also realistic commercial considerations led Venice to take this decision. It is not in fact true, as has long been said and believed, that the great geographical discoveries and the consequent opening of new sea-routes had brought about the collapse of Venice's lucrative eastern trade, particularly in spices. It should be said, rather, that this trade had its ups and downs during the century, according to changing economic and political circumstances. Although in 1504 the Venetian galleys returned without spices from Alexandria and Beirut, and although Venice had to buy her own pepper from Lisbon in 1515, the traditional spice routes via the Mediterranean and the Red Sea came back into favour from 1550 to 1570, and Venice took advantage of this. Later, when Spain had conquered Portugal, Philip II offered Venice the monopoly of the trade in the spices that arrived at Lisbon; but this time too the consideration of their prevalently eastern interests persuaded the Venetians to refuse. Not until the early years of the seventeenth century were spices classified as goods from the West rather than from the East.

Understandably, the Venetian aristocracy was strongly attached to its own traditional eastern trading activities; but we must not suppose it wasted time and energy in regretting the glorious days of the Fourth Crusade. Its shrewder and more alert members, at any rate, realized that such regrets were vain, and that new methods and new attitudes were needed to face the present and its agonizing questions. Proof of this is given by the variety of economic projects that took shape in Venice in the sixteenth century: for although they were varied they had the common aim of transforming Venice from the market-city it had been to a centre of production, on the model of other Italian cities. The most important of these new Venetian enterprises was undoubtedly the wool industry, which soon became considerable, and a challenge to inland wool-centres: in 1602 production reached 28,729 rolls of cloth. More typically Venetian products were the glass of Murano, and other luxury products, for which the refined upper classes of Europe were to rely on Venice for a long time. And finally, of course, there was the great development of Venetian typography in the sixteenth century. At its peak, 113 firms were active, large and small, some of which, from Manuzio to Giolito, occupy an important place, not merely in the history of printing but in that of sixteenth century culture.

All these great economic enterprises helped Venice to remain a great metropolis, and even to become more of one. In 1565 the population reached the remarkable figure of 175,000, and even after the terrible plague of 1576–7 it remained around 140,000. As the population rose, the number of Venice's buildings increased. Many of the famous Venetian palaces, such as that of the Corner family, belong to the sixteenth century, and so does the arrangement of St Mark's

Square in its present form. Sansovino's Loggetta of 1537–40 was followed by the same architect's Library (1536–54) and Mint (1537–45), and the architecture of the square was completed with Scamozzi's new Procurator's palace of 1586. One could almost say that on the eve of its decline Venice was anxious to hand down to posterity the image of itself in its extreme splendour.

But Venice's industrial boom and the animation it brought to the city's economic life was not so much the beginning of an effective process of conversion, but more the effect of favourable circumstances, of that brief euphoric period that was, as we have seen, a St Martin's Summer for the Italian towns. As such, it lasted for a relatively short time; by about 1570 the wool industry already showed signs of flagging, and the private shipbuilders and fitters, who were geared to producing outdated types of ships, also began to decline. In these conditions the soundest and in some senses the most profitable investment was still property, especially in the form of estates on the mainland.

The continued rise of population in the town and on the mainland made the problem of providing food increasingly acute. Proof of this is the fact that from mid-century maize was grown in the Veneto (maize yields more than corn, and is cheaper), and major schemes of land-improvement were put through. A probably over-optimistic estimate speaks of half a million fields around Treviso, formerly uncultivated, now reclaimed. In any case, whatever the scale of the process, there can be no doubt that the tendency of the Venetian aristocracy to acquire estates on the mainland, already in evidence in the late fifteenth century, was accentuated, and became a headlong rush for land. During the sixteenth century 257 villas – four times as many as in the fifteenth century – were built in the countryside around Venice, and most of them belonged to Venetian aristocrats. They included masterpieces of Palladian Neoclassicism, such as the Villa Malcontenta at Mira (1560), the Rotonda at Vicenza, the Villa Badoer at Rovigo, and the splendid Villa Barbaro di Maser, with frescoes by Veronese. In 1588, according to an estimate by the Venetian patrician Piero Badoer, half of the land around Padua, 18 per cent of that around Treviso, and three per cent around more distant Verona, were owned by citizens of Venice. In the mean time the income earned by the *decima*, a land-tax imposed equally on lay and ecclesiastical property, rose from 33,000 ducats in 1510 to 134,000 in 1582: a notable increase, even taking into account the inflation produced by the price-revolution.

In the present state of our knowledge, it is difficult to establish with any accuracy who took part in and benefited from this rush for property on the mainland. The most plausible hypothesis that can be extracted from the data available is that land-investment was confined to a fairly narrow circle of great families, and that in consequence the transformation of Venice's aristocracy into a landowning class was accompanied by a reduction in its numbers: it became an increasingly exclusive élite of privileged persons. Telling signs of this tendency had appeared on the political level ever since 1538–40, the time of the Turkish war, when young men of the leading families were admitted to the *Maggior Consiglio*, even though they were under the prescribed age of twenty-five, as long as they were able to pay a price of twenty thousand ducats. The Council of Ten, assisted by a small group of representatives of the leading families, called the *zonta*, had become increasingly the ruler of the city's public life, and even of its foreign policy. There had been some reactions on the part of those sectors of the nobility who thus found themselves restricted to the fringes of power: in 1582 the party that called itself the *giovani* managed to obtain the suppression of the *zonta*, and a reduction in the powers of the Council of Ten. But this was not and could not be anything more than a temporary victory, a momentary check to an irresistible process: economic decline is rarely dissociated from political hardening of the arteries.

So the sixteenth century was a period of decline for Venice. But it was also a period of greatness: greatness in the economic sphere, for as we have seen, Venice's economy was adaptable and had considerable powers of recovery; greatness of the Venetian ruling class, who were to give further proof of vitality and courage in the days of the Interdict; the greatness of the victorious Venetian fleet at Lepanto; but above all, it was a time of cultural and artistic greatness. Not only was mid-sixteenth-century Venice the chosen city of Palladio and Veronese, those two supreme masters of a decadent age, but it also conserved a wider margin of intellectual freedom than any other Italian city in the Counter-Reformation period. It was no coincidence that the Venetian aristocracy produced Cardinal Giuseppe Contarini, the compiler of the *Consilium de emendanda Ecclesia* in 1537, and one of the most prominent Catholic reformists; and no coincidence that Venetian printers produced the first Italian translation of the Bible in 1532. Her close commercial ties and many human contacts with Germany meant that Venice was more exposed than any other Italian city to new ideas and the new reformed faith. At the same time her substantial, lively printing trade and book trade, and the nearness of the famous University of Padua, made Venice a natural reference point and centre for new currents of thought.

Among the artists and *literati* of sixteenth-century Venice stands out the disconcerting figure of Pietro Aretino, who spent the last thirty years of his life there (1527–56), and bestowed on the city the title of 'Lady Pope of Italian cities'. But his superabundant personality must not allow us to forget the crowd of lesser figures, exiles, drifters, victims of persecution, who took refuge in Venice and helped to give its intellectual life a cosmopolitan liveliness. The printers who worked in Venice in the sixteenth century included men from every part of Italy, from Florence, Naples, Siena, Bergamo, and even from France; and each of them had his own network of colleagues and associates. Neither did Venice adopt an exclusive attitude towards artists: Jacopo Sansovino, who may be considered the creator of St Mark's Square, was a Florentine.

The liveliness and receptiveness of Venice's intellectual life, which the city managed to preserve in part even after the closing of the Council of Trent, successfully resisting the introduction of the Index for a long time, helped to nourish and revive the myth of Venice, which was already deep-rooted in Italian public opinion of the time. At the end of the sixteenth century it was more than ever alive and flourishing, and was strengthened not only by Venetians like the historian Paolo Paruta, but also by foreigners who had become naturalized Venetians, such as Jacopo Sansovino's son Francesco, who in 1581 wrote a treatise on *Venezia città nobilissima*, which achieved wide circulation. Thanks to these writings, and many others deriving from and inspired by them, whole generations were to see Venice as the last refuge of the 'liberal' government and freedom that other Italian cities had either never known or had lost. This dreamy myth contained a touch of nostalgic and commemorative patriotism; it was, among other things, a new display of the provincialism that characterized the cultural ethos of all Italian states – Florence, Naples and Milan as well as Venice – at the end of the sixteenth-century. But it also contained the perception and awareness of a continuing tradition, a style and a dignity that were not lacking. The days of the Interdict, and Paolo Sarpi's political and intellectual battle against Rome and the Counter-Reformation, were not far ahead.

GENOA AND ITS BANKERS

When faced with the alternatives that the Franco-Habsburg struggle, which lasted until Cateau-Cambrésis, put before the states of Italy, Genoa was the first and readiest of sixteenth-century states to make its own choices. In 1528, just after the sack of Rome, when Charles v's armies were fighting those of François I on Italian soil, Andrea Doria took power, broke the traditional links of alliance that had in the past bound Genoa to France, and went over to the Empire and Spain. It was a final decision: unlike Venice, which was to follow a prudent policy of isolationism in the effort to preserve such freedom and independence as was compatible with her growing weakness, Genoa was from now on to accept the fact that she was unconditionally a part of first the Imperial, later the Spanish sphere of influence. And since she was the first to make this dramatic choice, she was able to draw the maximum possible advantage and profit from it, speculating on her geographical position, which she made a natural meeting-point between the Empire's Mediterranean and Continental territories. For Charles v and Philip ii, possession of Genoa meant the possibility of swift communications between Barcelona and Milan, and between the Mediterranean and central Europe. The Genoese were well aware of this, and made a lucrative business out of their loyalty to the Habsburgs.

Genoese businessmen had already frequented Spanish ports and trade-routes regularly in the preceding centuries. Now, however, their penetration was more thorough and on a larger scale. They rented out ships to Charles v, made sure of the monopoly in imported Spanish wool, and in the manufacture and distribution of soap ; above all, they advanced capital to the Spanish Crown, and gained in return tax-leases, seigniories and estates in Spain and Naples, honorary posts and positions of high responsibility. Andrea Doria himself, for example, became Prince of Melfi, and Ambrogio Spinola was given the title of *generalissimo* of the Spanish army, which he led to victory against the great Maurice of Orange, in the Low Countries.

But it was in the second half of the century that Genoa's political and economic association with Spain began to bear most fruit. The Genoese bankers survived the first of the Spanish Crown's series of bankruptcies in 1557, if not unscathed, at least less harmed than their great competitiors, particularly the Fuggers. Their position on the international money market was thus strengthened. Another fortunate coincidence for them was the outbreak of the insurrection in the Low Countries, and the consequent decline of Antwerp. This in fact led to a readjustment of Mediterranean routes: from the 1570's Genoa became the centre for the receiving and sorting of American silver, which left Seville and Barcelona for central and northern Europe. So by way of Genoa and Genoese bankers passed the vast quantities of cash needed to maintain the armies fighting in Flanders, and to finance the Habsburg *Weltpolitik*. This offered them new and un-dreamed of possibilities of speculation and profit; in the expectation of cargoes of American silver from Seville the Genoese bankers were ready to advance vast sums, sure of being repaid with due interest, when the silver arrived. So Genoa took over the place of Lyons and Antwerp as the greatest western financial centre, and controller of the international exchange market, which had until recently had its centre and clearing-house at Besançon, in Franche Comté. From 1579, the Besançon fairs were moved to Piacenza, a city relatively close to Genoa, and continued to operate there for the rest of the century and longer, under Genoese control. There, huge sums were dealt in: according to some, necessarily approximate, estimates, thirty-seven million *scudi* in 1580, and forty-eight million a few years later. There was, it is true, the risk of insolvency on the part of the Spanish Crown, which was deeply in debt; and other bankruptcies did in fact follow the spectacular one of 1557, with alarming regularity. But the Genoese bankers, as we have seen, knew how to protect themselves against such risks, and what they lost as speculators they won back, at least in part, by making sure of new taxes or land-concessions.

So no city profited more than Genoa from the wave of activity that the sharp stimulus of the price-revolution provoked in the European economy. Other crafts and small manufacturing activities – such as those of coral, silk and paper – followed in the wake of the bank, developed, and reached a high level of prosperity.

But no other city of Italy shows more clearly how this sudden upsurge of energy and activity failed to undermine already existing relationships, but rather helped them to solidify and crystallize, a process that had been going on for a long time. The prosperity of Genoa in the second half of the sixteenth century was in fact above all that of the Genoese financial oligarchy, ranked firmly around the Bank of St George; and as the city prospered so the aristocratic nature of the social and political organization of the city and the régime was accentuated and became more obvious. Andrea Doria's *coup d'état* of 1528 was in some respects itself a further reinforcement of the oligarchy. Behind the screen of an elaborate constitutional reform, by which the system of election was combined with that of choice by lot, Doria himself was given the rôle of ruler and mediator, and the 'old nobility' to which he of course belonged, and which included the great families and dynasties of bankers connected with the Bank of St George, was given a clearly defined seniority over the 'new nobility', which consisted mainly of men in trade and industry. The 'new nobility' reacted against this treatment, and the way was prepared for the conspiracy planned by the Fieschi family in 1547 and the agitation it provoked among the people. But this second coup failed, and gave the implacable and irreplaceable Andrea Doria the pretext for a new turn of the screw in the direction of oligarchy. For it was decided that a quarter of the members of the *Consiglio Maggiore* should no longer be chosen by lot, but by the governors of the Bank of St George, and that the smaller *Consiglio Minore* should also cease to be chosen by lot from among the city's patricians, but should be elected by the reformed *Consiglio Maggiore*. Only in 1576 did the 'new nobility' win a partial victory in the form of a revision of the Genoese constitution in their favour, and a reduction of the tax-load that had been placed on them. But although this last adjustment of the constitution made some difference, Genoa's political life was by this stage too deeply conditioned by established interests, and by the economic rule of the financial oligarchy controlling the Bank of St George. From 1576 until the end of the Republic, the Genoese constitution underwent no further substantial changes, and internal political struggles gradually ceased, which was less an indication of equilibrium than the end of a process of crystallization that had been going on for centuries.

Genoa at the end of the sixteenth century presents more than ever the unusual spectacle of a city ruled more by the criteria of a business than by those of a state. What was most striking was the disproportionate contrast between the European prestige of Genoese financiers, and the feebleness of Genoa as a political body. The same city whose leaders lent vast sums to the King of Spain could hardly suppress the rebellion of the Corsican mountain people, and would have found it very difficult to do so without the help of the Spanish. This, the most municipally conscious of Italian cities, and the most impervious to outside influences, was the same city that first sent its navigators to sail all the routes of the world and then became the home of one of the first international money-markets in modern history. Is it going too far to see in this development the symbol of all Italy's history in the later sixteenth century ?

ROME AND THE CHURCH STATE

Rome was the centre of the revived, ambitious and active Catholicism of the Counter-Reformation, and the capital of an extensive state, which, with the acquisition of Ferrara in 1598, reached as far north as the course of the Po. Under the popes of the second half of the sixteenth century Rome continued on its brisk progress towards becoming a metropolis, begun in the pontificates of Julius II and Leo X. No other Italian or European city, not Venice, Paris or London, underwent such a radical process of expansion and re-planning during the sixteenth century. Fifty-four churches were built or rebuilt, sixty new noble palaces, twenty villas, houses for fifty to seventy thousand people, and two entire quarters were built, thirty new roads were opened, and three aqueducts restored, so that, through the thirty-five public fountains, the whole city, even at its highest points, was ensured a regular water-supply. These are the bare figures of Rome's building-boom. When one adds that these developments included the cupola of St Peter's – the last stone of which was placed in position on Christmas Day 1589, to the salute of cannon from the Castel Sant'Angelo – the Vatican palaces, the Lateran, Montecavallo (now the Quirinale) and the Collegio Romano, no-one at all familiar with the buildings of present-day Rome will hesitate to accept the sincerity of those sixteenth-century travellers who, when they returned to Rome after a long absence, swore that they no longer recognized the city. Not only were they deeply impressed by the new buildings, the straight streets radiating from the great squares; they also felt lost and sometimes sad at the disappearance of a familiar street, corner or urban landscape dear to them. For, as always, the urge to build was accompanied by the urge to demolish. In order that the Jesuits' Collegio Romano could be built, a whole quarter was razed to the ground in 1581–2. Nor did the demolition gangs stop at fairly recent buildings: the ruins of ancient and mediaeval Rome were not safe either. The stones of Ponte Sixto came from the Colosseum, and some of the marble of the Vatican from the church of Sant'Adriano, which in its turn had been a mediaeval re-working of the old Curia Romana, the august seat of the Senate. So we can understand Raphael's protests at the indiscriminate demolitions for which Bramante, the *maestro ruinante* was responsible, and the bitterness of Rabelais when in 1536 he witnessed the major works of destruction and rebuilding that took place on the occasion of Charles v's glorious entry into Rome. In the sixteenth century too it was true that '*la forme d'une ville change hélas plus vite que le coeur des mortels*'.

This exceptional city had an exceptional population. Not so much in terms of numbers – though only Naples and Venice exceeded Rome's population of 115,000 – as in its mixed composition. The Eternal City, with its priests, pilgrims and unmarried men, was the only city of Italy in which the men greatly outnumbered the women, which helps to explain the massive development of prostitution and the fame of Roman courtesans, second only to those of Venice. Rome was also unique in that its temporary population of tourists, pilgrims, adventurers, outnumbered the permanent population, especially on Jubilee occasions; and immigrants of more or less recent date outnumbered the natives of Rome and Lazio. A description of 1576 takes a cross-section of 3,495 inhabitants of Rome and records their places of origin: 2,922 were foreigners who had recently come into Rome from every part of Italy and from abroad – they were Spaniards, Frenchmen, Poles, Turks and so on. This census did not include the Jews, who had been relegated to the ghetto by Paul IV, and were counted separately. They were a numerous colony: 1,750 persons; and they increased in the second half of the century, to about 3,500. It is true that Jews were forbidden to live in any other city of the Papal State save Ancona. But, quite apart from considerations of their economic utility, the presence of Jews in Rome could be allowed, for among that cosmopolitan population it caused no scandal.

With its Curia, its Cardinals, its innumerable inns, its courtiers, the crowd of petitioners around each of the various courts, Rome certainly produced less and consumed more than any other Italian city. It was more a question of waste than of consumption: Rome's wealth was poured into churches and palaces, and flung away on the holidays and ostentatious luxury of an almost entirely parasitic economy that lived off its own fat. A large part of the money spent at Rome, and that provided for the ambitious international policies of the popes, their artistic patronage and expensive schemes for the city's development (the building of St Peter's alone cost one and a half million silver *scudi*, a sum equal to the state's income for a year) came from outside. The tributes and collections made in every part of Catholic Christendom may no longer have assured the income they had once provided, but the popes could always resort to bankers, first those of Florence and later those of Genoa, and they could above all rely increasingly on the tax-earnings of the state. All through the century the earnings of the *Camera Apostolica* showed a constant rise; from 1526 to 1600 the total tax-yield for the whole Papal State more than doubled, taking into account the devaluation of money. The work of absolutist centralization achieved by the Counter-Reformation popes, by Sixtus V in particular, has often been described and praised; the *Congregazioni* were formed, and central and peripheral administration was generally reorganized. But the most important aspect of this centralizing activity, and the one that gave most tangible results, was taxation. In any case, one can hardly talk of 'absolutism' if this term is applied, as it often is, to a governmental programme designed not only to bring about a higher degree of centralization, but also to favour the social promotion of the bourgeois and lower classes and their activity. There was in fact scarcely any trace of this in the church state of the later sixteenth century.

It is true that some of the oldest and most unruly of the great noble houses were forced to renounce many of the privileges and prerogatives that made them independent potentates, and their rents, caught between the fork of the price-revolution and the new papal tax policy, were drastically cut down, sometimes to the point of ruin. But the new-rich and the new nobles who took their place, and the 'country merchants' to whom they let their estates, were no slower than they had been in trying to unload their economic difficulties on to their 'men' and their peasants. So in the Papal State, in the second half of the sixteenth century, there were many displays of 'baronial reaction', of a systematic attack on the surviving liberties of country-folk, the collective systems of villages and of the communities in forests and pasture-land, the traditional forms of patronage and representation. This attack often went with a growing tendency to replace firmly-settled farmers with casual labour of a seasonal nature, provided by migrants from the depressed mountain areas.

The ever-increasing pressure that the consumer-city and the machinery of the state placed on the countryside was in the long run bound to provoke discontent and acute tension. The desperate protest of the people, augmented by the effects of terrible, recurrent famines, flowed together with the resentment of nobles reluctant to accept papal absolutism and taxation, to produce one of the most formidable outbursts of banditry in Italian history. Alfonso Piccolomini on the one hand, Duke of Montemarciano near Ancona, and connected to the great Orsini family, and Marco Sciarra on the other, a man of low birth who called himself *'flagellum dei missus a deo contra usurarios et detinentes pecunias otiosas'*, and was said to rob the rich to give to the poor, represent the two spirits of the wave of criminal anarchy that swept over the whole Papal State from 1577 to 1595, and even threatened the capital itself more than once. The tomb of Cecilia Metella, at the city gates, was a bandit hideout for a long time. Nothing had any effect on the many thousands of men who had taken this desperate course; not mass-executions – five thousand men were executed from 1590 to 1595 alone – not Sixtus v's iron-handed policy, nor his attempt at a concerted action in co-operation with neighbouring powers. When he died in 1590 brigandage subsided for a time and then returned worse than before. Only in 1595, when the famines had become less acute, did it begin to decrease, though never to the point of disappearing entirely: the fire went on smouldering beneath the ashes.

The vicious circle of taxation, baronial reaction, famine and banditry, in which the society of the church state was caught up during the last decades of the sixteenth century, made a deep mark on its economic institutions and even on its productive capacity. At the end of the century some parts of the state had begun to go downhill, and their decline became more marked during the next century. The cultivated land around Rome was the first to decline: in the nineteenth century travellers saw almost deserted stretches of land, devastated by malaria, where in the sixteenth century there had been relatively well-populated farmland, which helped to provide the capital with food. The same applies to the Maremma around Tarquinia, which had been considered one of the state's main sources of corn. But from the beginning of the sixteenth century the process of decay and depopulation, which had already begun in the late Middle Ages, accelerated into a sudden collapse. Besides the general causes that have been hinted at, there were more particular local circumstances that helped to speed the process: in particular, the increasing tendency of the big landowners of the Roman countryside to turn arable land over to pasturage. Already in the sixteenth century the Romans devoured a great deal of lamb and sheep-cheese, and it was more profitable to provide them with those things than to sell cheaper bread to the people. So in the countryside around Rome, as in England at the time of Thomas More, sheep drove men from the land. But where men and cultivation and woods receded, malaria advanced. The papal government tried to deal with this situation by taking measures to encourage the cultivation of cereals, and by starting to drain the Pontine marshes, under Sixtus v. But in the long run these attempts were not enough: the fate of the Roman Campagna was by now sealed.

The picture of decay presented by the agriculture around Rome and in the Maremma of Lazio is of course a particular case: there were areas of agrarian progress in the sixteenth-century Papal State, especially in the northern provinces, whose economy gravitated towards the Po. In the country around Bologna, for example, hemp was widely grown, with notably advanced techniques. But in general the picture is one of stagnation, on the brink of decline: heavy taxation, baronial reaction, banditry and famine were followed sooner or later by penury and distress. And if the first were removed or reduced, the second remained. It is significant that the Papal State, which still exported corn in about 1570, had to import corn from other regions and even from abroad, with increasing frequency, during the following decades. In about 1590–4, a time of grave famine, corn from the Nordic countries began arriving for the first time at Civitavecchia.

'The prince not only lays his hand on the people and draws blood from them . . . having drawn their blood with taxes, he destroys their spirit by taking from them every chance of profit, which might enable them to pay their taxes.' The work from which this quotation is taken concludes with the well-known words of Pliny : '*Latifundia Italiam perdidere.*' The writer cannot be suspected of prejudice: he is the Jesuit Giovanni Botero.

THE INTELLECTUALS IN THE AGE
OF THE COUNTER-REFORMATION

The experience of those intellectuals who had lived and worked in the years from the pontificate of Leo x to that of Paul iv had been a dramatic one. The election of a pope from Italy's most cultured city and from a family of artistic patrons had aroused hopes which had been confirmed by the first years and actions of Paul iii's pontificate, but had suddenly collapsed before the reality of the Church's division and the resurgence of intolerance on both sides. In the climate of the Counter-Reformation and post-Tridentine Catholicism it became clearer every day that any conciliatory suggestion or any nostalgia for Erasmianism were anachronistic. The choice now was between an open break with orthodoxy or full submission, for whatever motives and with whatever outward mask; it was difficult to emigrate, and equally difficult to stay.

But what happened was not merely the drama of one generation, that of Contarini and Pole and of Michelangelo, the generation who had continued to place their hopes in the Council up to the last minute. What took place was the failure of the intellectuals as a class; they now ceased to be a unifying force and example for the disunited people of Italy. The learned lost their prestige and their rôle. During the sixteenth century the intelligentsia and culture of Italy went through the deepest crisis they had known up to that time.

It would of course be naïve and simplistic to suppose that this crisis was immediately translated into a lowering of the level of Italian intellectual and artistic life. The heritage of the Renaissance was too abundant and too recent for it not to go on exerting a strong attraction and influence. Yet the crisis did exist, even if it was shown by the dissipation and frittering away of a creative vein rather than its exhaustion, and took the form of restlessness, not that of paralysis, which would have been impossible. So the unity, fusion and harmoniousness of Renaissance culture were shattered.

The first loss of unity was geographical: the 'Florentinism' of the *accademici della Crusca*, the revival of the Ambrosian spirit at Milan under the Borromeo family, the Venetian patriotism of Paruta and Sansovino have already been mentioned. Naples moved in a similar direction: there, the historian Di Costanzo was concerned with defining and celebrating a tradition of local glory. All these are instances of withdrawal into provincialism and dialect, which would be accentuated in the next century. The masks representing various cities, which appeared on the stage of the *Commedia dell' Arte*, were an extreme manifestation of this spirit. Such city-patriotism, born within the walls of academies, protected and encouraged by the patronage of princes, was bound to lack the vigour and authenticity of Italian town traditions. Nothing is further from the real spirit of Florence than the Florentinism of late sixteenth-century *litterati*.

This development of separate local cultures is only one symptom of the general fragmentation of Italian intellectual life; the process is most evident in the figurative arts, which were so open to experimentation and so deeply stamped by the various regional traditions. However broad and comprehensive the term 'mannerism', which usually covers the artistic tendencies and styles of the period, it cannot be applied to every product of an extremely varied and restless artistic activity. The art of the later sixteenth century ranges from religious paintings to the first still-lifes, from the great pictorial cycles illustrating the glories of this or that princely house to miniature portraits, from the stone colossi of Ammanati and Bandinelli to the elegant statuettes of Cellini and Giambologna, from the sullen style of Vignola's Church of the Gesù to the grace of Palladian villas, from Tintoretto's *luminismo* to the rather glossy finish of Veronese's paintings. The prevailing mood was one of experimentation, in which the search often became an end in itself, producing a multicoloured series of possible solutions. Typical of this experimentalism was a fastidious concern for detail and for the particular, and the consequent tendency of the major arts to borrow the techniques and modes of the minor ones: painting often became decoration – as in Giulio Romano's *trompe l'oeil* works at the Palazzo del Tè of Mantua, the temple of Italian Mannerism – sculpture became jewellery, and architecture became garden-design and the art of directing parties, splendid entrances and funeral ceremonies. The Baroque had almost arrived: the enormously prolific Bernini produced his first work in 1625.

Literature too was dominated by variety of expression and affected experimentation. All literary genres were cultivated, some pushed to the limits of their expressive capacity, and all treated with the extremist taste typical of experimentalism, which in itself foreshadows the Baroque. With the Neapolitan Giambattista Della Porta, comedy became as grotesque as was possible, and already tended towards the modes and forms of the *Commedia dell' Arte*; the tragedies of Giambattista Girardi Cinzio, an author Shakespeare was to draw on considerably, inclined towards bombastic bluster; the *novelle* of the time were romantic and exotic. Even autobiography became adventure fiction, with Cellini's famous *Life*. Poetry allied itself with music, and opera was born. The first was *Dafne*, performed at Florence in 1595.

So the panorama was varied and luxuriant; but it lacked the fixed points and the outstanding exploits of the age of Leo x. The only literary work of the later sixteenth century to have resisted the assaults and erosions of time is Torquato Tasso's *Gerusalemme Liberata*. But it cost Tasso immense effort and anguish to master and impose unity and discipline on the restless world of his emotions and tastes: his piety and sensuality, his Counter-Reformation scruples and his natural extroversion. The difficulty of Tasso's poetic task and of his restless life are a confirmation of the intellectual extravagance and wastefulness of the age he lived in.

Having briefly surveyed the intellectual state of Italy in the age of the Counter-Reformation, we must now see what the immediate and long-term results of that movement were. It is traditional to lay most emphasis on the reaction against Renaissance rationalism and immanentism: the Inquisition censored Paolo Veronese's festive version of the Last Supper, the Jesuits conducted a relentless campaign against the execrated memory of Machiavelli, Giordano Bruno died at the stake and Campanella was imprisoned. These events are almost too well-known. It is therefore worth emphasizing that its repressive police action was not the only side of Counter-Reformation cultural policy; for the Counter-Reformation Church was concerned not merely with triumphing over a defeated enemy but also with recovering its heritage and so reconstituting, to its own benefit and under its own control, a new intellectual community. The influence of the Society of Jesus exemplifies this ambition: the Jesuits were designed to be a new, unified body of intellectuals who had absorbed the lesson and the techniques of Humanist pedagogy and philology and would thus be capable of taking the place of the Humanists in courts and schools, and of exerting in society as a whole the same dominant influence. Even the execrated Machiavellian view of politics could be taken over, once it had been reduced to a mere technique of power: Botero and other Jesuit theorists embarked on the difficult task of working out a political theory that would advance Christian principles.

This effort made by the Counter-Reformation Church to restore the cultural heritage of Humanism to its own advantage, and to invest its own intellectuals with the prestige and the rôle of earlier Humanist and lay thinkers, was a vast undertaking that extended to all disciplines and all provinces of knowledge. In the philological field, for instance, this period saw the Sistine edition of the Vulgate; in art the development of sacred archaeology, following the discovery of the Roman catacombs; in history the publication of Baronio's *Annales ecclesiastici* from 1588 to 1607; and in science the reform of the Julian calendar under Gregory XIII. This last achievement was a complex and laborious scientific operation that involved a committee of experts, and was made possible by wide consultation with universities and international scientific circles; it was defended against its critics by Tycho Brahe and Kepler. Finally, particular emphasis should be given to the reform of polyphonic music, which is connected with the name and work of Pier Luigi di Palestrina, the man who was able to give a voice to the truest and most reticent kind of religious feeling experienced by the leading personalities of the Counter-Reformation.

These varied enterprises make an impressive picture. However, the Church's impartiality was too transparently an instrument, its cultural autonomy too limited, its ambitions too fanciful and its dynamism too often mere activism for any real hope of success in its ambitious project. Nor were the most highly reputed representatives of Counter-Reformation culture – Sirleto, Baronio, Possevino, Botero – outstanding enough to exert a strong power of attraction. They were scrupulous scholars or able polemicists, but remained in the end men of the Church and its party.

In these circumstances, the ambition of gathering varied, scattered intellectual tendencies around the Church and around revived post-Tridentine Catholicism, to resolve and reconcile in orthodoxy the contradictions of a feverish era, were without much chance of success. In fact, not only did the Church in general fail to reach its objectives, but its failure only increased the age's lack of direction or unity, the sense of unease and the readiness to embark on new ventures and experiments. The Italian intellectual community was more fragmented and dispersed than ever; in the last years of the sixteenth century and the first of the seventeenth, strange personalities and lives abounded: libertines, intellectual adventurers, travellers, utopians. To this category belongs Giulio Cesare Vanini, who died at the stake at Toulouse in 1619, after a life of travel, apostasy and intellectual intrepidity; or the Florentine Francesco Pucci, who, after travelling from the Low Countries to Transylvania, died on the way to Rome, where he had intended to submit to the Pope a project of his for reconciliation between the churches; or Marc'Antonio De Dominis, publisher of Sarpi's *Storia*, an apostate bishop who died in the bosom of the Church but was condemned to the stake posthumously. And one cannot overlook the roving, adventurous life of the greatest painter of the age, Caravaggio.

In an age that was both disoriented and conformist, both provincial and cosmopolitan, the price of intellectual individualism was often extravagance or eccentricity. But we must be careful not to confuse the few true heroes of this difficult age with the many eccentrics. Caravaggio was not the only one of these heroes.

GIORDANO BRUNO AND TOMMASO CAMPANELLA

Giordano Bruno was born at Nola in 1548 and joined the Dominican order at Naples at the age of eighteen. But the cloister was ill-suited to his ardent spirit and mind, inclined to question the most sacrosanct truths of faith. He soon aroused the suspicions of the Inquisition, which led to his flight from Rome and the start of the long pilgrimage that was to be the rest of his life, first across Italy from Rome to Nola, Savona, and Venice, then across Europe, from Geneva to Toulouse, Paris, Oxford, Wittenberg, Prague, Helmstadt and Frankfurt. It was not until 1591 that he crossed the Alps back into Italy: he was summoned by the Venetian patrician Giovanni Mocenigo, and came to stay in Venice. But it was the least fortunate of his many sojourns: he was denounced to the Inquisition by Mocenigo himself, arrested and taken to Rome, where, after a long and dramatic trial, he was condemned to the stake. He was executed in the Piazza del Campo dei Fiori, on 17 February 1600.

Thus outlined, Bruno's life may seem like that of many other adventurers and bold spirits of that turbulent age; and so it was, in a sense. He was a Calvinist at Geneva, a Lutheran at Wittenberg, and wished to become reconciled with the Catholic Church when he returned to his homeland. Throughout these changes he remained all the time what he himself called 'an academician without an academy', whose temperament was rebellious and unpredictable. But if we look deeper and examine not merely his adventurous life but the tormented course of his thought, we find that what appears in others as eccentricity is in him true intellectual heroism, drawn from the firmness of his convictions, and his own respect for them.

For, amid the many layers and deposits of thought with which Bruno's restless mind occupied itself, there was one fixed point: his rejection of the Aristotelian and Ptolomaic concept of the universe, his acceptance of Copernican theories, and his extension of those ideas on the philosophical level. In an infinite universe populated by an infinity of worlds, there are no concentric heavens or spheres, and any point may be the centre of the universe. And since our world is not the hub of the universe, man dissolves into the eternal process of nature, where every birth is a death and every past is present. Bruno's dictum is well known:

> *Quid est quod est? Ipsum quod fuit*
> *Quid est quod fuit? Ipsum quod est*
> *Nihil sub sole novi.*

In this cosmic and tragic view of reality, which many have seen as a foreshadowing of Spinoza, the old God is no longer the creator or unmoving mover of things, but the spirit of the universe, poured and diffused into all things: God becomes Nature. In this framework, what importance could the hair-splitting of differing sects and creeds have? From the contemplation of the infinite unity of the universe the philosopher drew a sense of the transcience of things and human opinions, and at the same time a sense almost of dizziness, in which there was some dismay but also enthusiasm, a 'heroic exaltation' close to the feeling of one who discovers and explores new, unknown lands. 'Time takes away everything and brings everything,' wrote Giordano Bruno. 'Every thing changes. Nothing is destroyed: there is only one (being) that cannot change, and is eternal, and may eternally endure. With this philosophy my soul becomes greater and my intellect is magnified.'

Such a vision of the universe contained the roots both of scepticism and of the historical method: it could lead to opportunism or to heroism. But in Giordano Bruno the second prevailed. When taken before his judges he at first retracted the supposed errors he was accused of, but then once more protested his innocence and his right to freedom of thought. He replied to his death-sentence with words that recall those of Socrates: 'You probably feel more fear in pronouncing judgement on me than I do in hearing it.'

Similar in many ways to Giordano Bruno's life was that of his contemporary and compatriot Tommaso Campanella. Born at Stilo in Calabria in 1568, Campanella also joined the Dominican order, and soon left the cloister for a life of wandering. He was tried a first time by the Holy Office and sent back to his native Calabria. As the year 1599 approached, the idea that the conjunction of the stars and the advent of the new century would prepare the world for a total regeneration led Campanella, as we have seen, to arouse and lead an uprising, which was of course crushed. He was arrested again, and escaped death by feigning madness. But he was not able to escape imprisonment, which lasted for twenty-seven years, until it was commuted into a closely-guarded sort of liberty. He was drawn into new schemes and conspiracies, and in 1634 emigrated to France, where he died in 1639. During his last years, this man who had formerly hoped for the triumph of the Spanish monarchy dedicated one of his works to Richelieu and wrote in celebration of the birth of the future Sun King.

Campanella's life too was eccentric and strange; his strangeness seems at times to border on lunacy. He declared that his forehead was, like that of Moses, adorned with seven protuberances or mountains, and he changed his own prosaic name into the finer-sounding 'Squilla'.

From his own studies and astrological beliefs he drew the firm conviction that he was a prophet of a new age, and the chosen instrument of a general purification and universal reform. Strong in this certainty he offered his services as magician and messiah to the King of Spain, the Pope and the King of France, at various times, when he was not determined that he himself, leading the rebellious Calabrians, would achieve the splendid utopia of the City of the Sun. But we should recognize the method in his madness, and remember what Campanella himself said: 'The world went mad through sin, and wise men, thinking to cure it, were forced to speak, act and live like madmen, even if they thought differently in their own privacy.'

In fact Campanella's astrology was also an attempt to bring religious phenomena into the framework of merely natural events: it foreshadowed the modern scientific view of the universe as a chain of laws. And his prophesying represented an awareness of the modernity of his own time and its 'pregnancy' with new developments. 'These new appearances of ancient truths, new worlds, new systems, new nations, are the principle of the new age.' These remnants and resurgences of mediaeval learning and a mediaeval attitude are in Campanella's thought combined with an extremely modern and scientific attitude towards reality. He had learned from his master Bernardino Telesio that reality was nature, and that only the senses and experience could open the doors of its mysteries. His irritations with those who continually invoked the 'authority' of the Classics, and Aristotle in particular, was equalled by his certainty that one could only approach truth by reading the great book of Nature with one's own eyes. 'I learn more from the anatomy of an ant or a piece of grass,' he declared, '. . . than from all the books that have been written since the beginning of time'. It is not hard to see why a man who expressed himself in these terms should, in 1616, when he was still in prison, have come to the defence of Galileo who had been asked by the Holy Office to give up his defence of Copernican theories.

6

A century of stagnation

ITALY ON THE FRINGE OF EUROPE

With its gold and its infantry, with the prestige of a great international power, and with its Catholic orthodoxy, the Spain of Philip II not only commanded the respect of the Italian princes and states, but seemed to many of them, after so many decades of wars and upheavals, the only guarantee of stability and calm in Italy. Under the wing of Spain the Genoese bankers had traded and prospered, the Papacy had achieved the victory of Lepanto and the Medici had finally established their rule over Florence and Tuscany; the whole peninsula had enjoyed several decades of peace. 'Italy,' wrote the Florentine historian Scipione Ammirato, 'has not felt that oppression she feared, but has for many years enjoyed the greatest happiness that has ever been.' And he was not alone in thinking so.

Towards the end of the sixteenth century, however, the international situation had changed, and there were signs that Spain's prestige had begun to decline. The rebellion of the Dutch provinces was followed by the resounding defeat of the Invincible Armada, and this by the accession of Henri IV, and France's dramatic return to its position as antagonist of the Habsburgs of Madrid and Vienna. Some Italian princes took advantage of the new situation by trying to loosen the bonds of subjection and protectorate that bound them to Spain, and to win back a wider margin of autonomy and political initiative. When Ferdinando de'Medici negotiated the marriage of his daughter Maria with Henri IV, and sought to persuade Clement VIII to recognize the new King of France, he showed clearly that, as far as the circumstances and the Spanish domination of Italy allowed him, he was keen to resume the traditional line of friendship with France that the Florentine Republic had followed. Carlo Emanuele I of Savoy went further, and in 1610 formed a league with Henri IV, committing himself to a joint attack on Lombardy; but this plan was frustrated by the French

King's unexpected death. Meanwhile, writers and propagandists stoked the flames of anti-Spanish feeling among the educated class. In 1614, in his *Filippiche contro gli Spagnoli*, Alessandro Tassoni wrote: 'The monarchy of Spain is a sleeping ogre, a vast, flabby, vulnerable bulk, a colossus of straw', and Philip's formidable officers nothing more than 'knights errant, used to feeding on coarse bread, onions and roots, and to sleeping peacefully in their rope-shoes and shepherd's cloak'. We find a similar tone in the writings of Trajano Boccalini, the most brilliant 'journalist' of the age.

These anti-Spanish arguments and hopes found their widest echo and audience in Venice – where Boccalini had in fact taken refuge. 'Venice's' sea was infested by Slavonic pirates who operated under Habsburg protection; she was troubled by competition from the Adriatic cities of the Papal State, and hemmed in on the landward side by the pincer-shaped territories of Habsburg Austria and Spanish Lombardy. Venice had always suffered more than accepted Spanish rule over Italy, and if in the past her attitude had been prudent and even passive, she now understood that further concessions were impossible. So when in 1605 the new Pope, Paul v, encouraged by Spain and using the arrest of two ecclesiastics as a pretext, placed Venice under an Interdict, and the Governor of Milan mobilized troops on the frontiers, Venice replied by expelling the Jesuits and firmly reasserting her own sovereignty in ecclesiastical matters. In the struggle that followed, Venice was able to stand firm until French mediation – hoped-for and accepted, but not solicited – brought the dispute to a conclusion that satisfied Venice's claims. A leading spirit of Venice's resistance was Doge Leonardo Donàa, formerly Ambassador Extraordinary to Rome, and an eminent representative of that party of 'young men' who had for some time been critical of the fence-sitting of Venice's foreign policy. Another was the Servite friar Paolo Sarpi, who, as theologian of the Republic, countered the virulent propaganda campaign unleashed against Venice by Rome and Spain (to which Campanella himself contributed, with his *Antiveneti*). Sarpi was able to make use of a wide range of contacts throughout intellectual Europe, including Gallican and Protestant circles. His great erudition and open-mindedness had procured him the friendship of men of letters and statesmen: of the English Ambassador to Venice, Sir Henry Watton, a devout disciple of the Reformation, of the French historian Jacques de Thou, and of Galileo himself. But he was aided above all by his aversion to the Catholicism of the Counter-Reformation, and by his sympathy for the demands for moral reform and reconciliation that came from the Protestant countries. Both these feelings are strongly present in Sarpi's greatest work, the *Istoria del Concilio tridentino*, published in

London in 1619. In this work, as in all his others, he showed that he was still a worthy and faithful son of his city, the most tolerant of the Italian cities of the sixteenth century, and the most hospitable to men and ideas.

The *succès d'estime* Venice won during the Interdict dispute had its sequel. In the difficult situation that followed the assassination of Henri IV, she used boldness and cunning to score another round against the Habsburgs, obliging them to withdraw their protection from the Slavonic pirates, who thus ceased to threaten Venetian sea-routes. During the same years, Spain was forced to renounce any prospect of revenge on Carlo Emanuele I of Savoy, who, with as much rashness as good luck, had taken arms against the Governor of Milan, to assert his own right to the Monferrato lands, which formed an esssential part of the territories of the Gonzagas of Mantua.

But these successes won by Venice and by Carlo Emanuele I were the last true demonstrations of independent initiative that the Italian states showed Spain. By this stage the international picture had again altered: Henri IV's death had meant a shrinking of France's counter-balancing presence, and now the accession of Ferdinand II, a pupil of the Jesuits, to the Viennese throne marked the resurgence of the militant Counter-Reformation, and the start of the Thirty Years War.

The first stage of this conflict was favourable to the Habsburgs, in Italy as elsewhere. Spain's domination of the key position of the Valtellina both assured the connection of Lombardy with the Habsburg territories of Austria, and completed Venice's geographic isolation. Her resistance, helped once again by Carlo Emanuele I and by France, could not alter the situation; also in vain were Savoy's attempts, encouraged by conspiracies within the city, to gain control of Genoa, most pro-Spanish of Italian cities.

Even the vicissitudes of the Thirty Years War – the general pattern being one of French counter-offensive until the victorious peace of Westphalia – brought about no significant changes in the political and territorial arrangement of the peninsula, except in Savoyard Piedmont, which had joined the Habsburg camp, and found itself in consequence invaded by the armies of Richelieu and for many years reduced practically to the status of a French protectorate. The anti-Spanish revolts of Sicily and Naples were, as we shall see, repressed; and at the date of the treaty of Westphalia Italy still lay mainly within the orbit of Spain's influence. But by that time Spain was no longer a great power, and so, as far as the Italian states were concerned, the disadvantages of political dependence or semi-dependence were not even| balanced by the advantages of an effective protectorate. Little by little, during the second half of the century, the decline of the Spanish Empire became more and more evident, and Italy came to the notice of the new rising political star of Europe, the France of Louis xiv, as one of its most vulnerable points, and one of the areas most suited to displays of force or less demanding military exercises. An instance of the second category is the French expedition of 1674 to the aid of Messina, which was in revolt; the French abandoned the city to harsh Spanish reprisals as soon as they met English opposition. The bombardment of Genoa in 1684 by a French naval squadron was, on the other hand, a display of force.

As for Venice, the glorious days of the Interdict had long since passed. Turkey returned to the offensive with an exhausting war of more than twenty years' duration that ended in the conquest of the Isle of Candia in 1669. The Venetian patricians, after long hesitation, decided to make an alliance with Vienna, in the hope of a doubtful revenge. So in the wake of the resounding victory of Sobieski under the walls of the Austrian capital, Venice joined the Holy League, and thus aligned herself with the new Habsburg policy of movement towards the East. The territorial advantages obtained by this alliance were ephemeral. (Venice managed to recover possession of the Morea from 1699 to 1718.) A permanent legacy from this date on, however, was the growing pressure of Vienna on the Balkan peninsula and the Adriatic, and the ever-stronger competition Venetian trade had to face from Trieste. Campoformio and the end of the Republic were not far off.

To complete our survey of Italy's place in the seventeenth-century European scene, we must take a brief look at the Papacy. Its loss of authority as an international arbitrator, and the eclipse of its prestige serve better than anything to symbolize and summarize the marginal rôle Italy was reduced to in the new Europe of the nation-states. None of the protests raised by Pope Innocent x against the religious clauses of the Treaty of Westphalia was taken into consideration by the European powers, while in the second half of the century no one was very surprised to see Louis xiv laying down the law to the conclaves. In his *Siècle de Louis XIV* Voltaire wrote: 'Certain rights, many claims, a political tradition, a little patience: that is all that today remains to Rome of ancient power, who six centuries ago wished to subjugate the Empire and Europe to the tiara.'

THE ECONOMIC CRISIS OF THE SEVENTEENTH CENTURY

From the first decades of the seventeenth century the characteristic rhythm of Italian economic enterprises is a sharp fall followed by a stagnation that goes on for the rest of the century. This may safely be stated: it is confirmed by all the data we have.

Venice, which in 1602 still produced twenty-nine thousand rolls of woollen cloth per annum, was producing two thousand by the end of the century; Milan had between sixty and seventy concerns active in the wool trade at the beginning of the century, and five in 1682; in the same period Genoa saw the business of her port reduced from nine to three million tons, and the number of looms employed by the silk industry from eighteen thousand to two thousand five hundred; Florence produced twenty thousand rolls of woollen cloth per annum from 1560 to 1580, and by the mid-seventeenth century was producing only five thousand. The same story is true of Cremona fustian, Calabrian silk, and the alum of Tolfa, which from 1620 onwards found practically no sale in the markets of Europe. One could go on with further examples.

The stagnation of production and export was naturally accompanied by that of trade. The diminution and final extinction of the spice trade, which the Venetians had managed to defend against the Portuguese and Spanish, but not against the Dutch, with their bases in the East Indies, is only the most obvious and classic example. In fact, the sea-traffic of all the Italian cities, with the exception of Leghorn, felt the repercussions of the crisis. At the end of the seventeenth century the fleets of the various Italian cities amounted to only 7 or 8 per cent of European shipping, against the 26 per cent of England and the 17 per cent of Holland: the days of Italian primacy at sea were really gone for ever. Another indication of Italian economic stagnation in the seventeenth century which it is hard to question is that provided by the price-curve: there are not many full accounts that are worthy of consideration, but they are so consistent that they are enough to show a clear downward trend. This is more pronounced in the sector of manufactured goods than in agricultural products or in raw materials.

Finally, to recapitulate and summarize the situation, we have the demographic statistics of the century. On the whole, between the last decades of the sixteenth century and the first of the eighteenth, it seems that the population of Italy remained stationary, or increased to a hardly relevant extent. In Sicily, for example, the 1,070,000 inhabitants of 1570 became 1,123,000 by 1714. Elsewhere, with the exception of Piedmont, which experienced, as far as we can judge, a rather more lively population increase, Italy more or less followed this pattern. As an explanation of this relative stagnation one must take into account the plague that, in successive waves and in different areas, afflicted the peninsula. That of 1630–1, which Manzoni vividly evokes in *I Promessi Sposi*, terrorized not only Lombardy but also Piedmont, the Veneto, Emilia and Tuscany; that of 1656–7, on the other hand, struck the southern regions, and Sardinia and Liguria. The only region of Italy to escape relatively unscathed from this awesome series of scourges was Sicily; but Sicily, most particularly the eastern part, was rent apart by the terrible earthquake of 1693, to the devastations of which the numerous buildings reconstructed in the late Baroque style in Catania, Syracuse and Noto, still bear witness. But epidemics, natural catastrophes, famines (that of 1680 in Sardinia reduced the island's population by a quarter, according to the census figures), occurred also in the sixteenth century, without profound lasting effect on the tendency towards population-increase. The fact that these compensatory reactions are not found in the seventeenth century leads one to suspect that the deepest roots of population stagnation should be sought in the general conditions of economic life and in the seriousness of its depression. In this connection one should look for an exact date for the beginning of such stagnation; if, as certain incomplete figures indicate, it was already under way before the 1630 epidemic, the hypothesis is confirmed, and the theorizing along Malthusian lines that may be found in late sixteenth-century writers such as Serra and Botero takes on greater meaning and relevance.

The sharp collapse of manufacturing activity; the shrinking of trade; deflation and a static population; the spread of begging and pauperism: the economic picture of seventeenth-century Italy is solidly of a piece – it must leave any observer with the impression that the crisis it illustrates and proclaims is something noteworthy and decisive, which may be singled out as one of the key-points of Italian history. So in fact it is. We must therefore try, in so far as it is possible in an experimental discipline such as history, to define the crisis.

We must first of all realize that in the century of the Thirty Years War the whole of Europe, in varying measure, suffered from economic recession and social instability. So the Italian crisis was a part of the more general European crisis; but it was made more acute by the fact that, as we have seen, the peninsula occupied a marginal position in the Europe of the time, not only politically but also economically. That large part of Italy that was subject to Spain was burdened with a tax-load that reached and often exceeded the limit of contributive capacity. Naples and Milan were asked to contribute exorbitantly to the political ambition of the Duke of Olivares and to the chronic bankruptcy of the finances of the Spanish Crown that resulted from it. Besides, the fact that Italy was within the Spanish area of influence certainly helped to cut her off from the main currents of Atlantic and colonial trade. There remained the Mediterranean, it is true; but in this sea too, English, French and above all Dutch ships were the only ones able to face the risk of privateer-warfare, and to challenge Turkish power successfully. So they gradually took the place of the fleets of the Italian cities in the traditional activity of commercial exchange between Europe and the East. The point was reached where many Venetian merchants preferred hiring ships flying the English flag to fitting out their own. The only Italian sea-town to profit from the new situation was the port of Leghorn, whose good fortune culminated in its transformation into a free port in 1675.

Yet references to the economic and political state of Europe are not enough to explain the economic crisis of Italian society. Besides reflecting external and general factors, this also had internal reasons: the inability of Italian economic activity to adapt itself to the new international context – its slow reactions.

At the risk of over-simplification, the argument may be summed up in a formula. It can be said that in the seventeenth century that mechanism of Italian prosperity and opulence, whose characteristics have been remarked on several times in the preceding pages, jammed and ceased to work. In an age when the markets were invaded by colonial products and by English woollen cloth, and commerce was on an increasingly larger scale, it was no longer possible for Italian merchants and manufacturers to make high profits by exploiting the rarity of their goods, even if they had a monopoly. Impossible also was a type of manufacturing activity encapsulated within the narrow limits of a guild, and almost entirely based on the search for quality and the demands of a relatively small clientele. Dazzling cloths imported from abroad cost a good deal less that the prized Venetian and Florentine cloths, with their out-of-date sobriety. Even on the level of the trade in high-quality and luxury goods, the royal factories of Colbert's France became feared competitors in the second half of the century, thanks also to the experience brought them by the emigration of Italian workers and technicians. These men were indeed much sought-after, and as Braudel has shown, the story of the attempts made to attract the glass-workers of Murano to France has the flavour of a detective story.

In these circumstances, those who owned the available residues of capital were more than ever encouraged to take the

traditional way of tying it up in land and in conspicuous investment.*
It is perhaps no coincidence that the most parasitic and rent-rich
city of Italy – Rome – should also have been the city where the great
Baroque architecture of Bernini and Borromini gained its finest
artistic victories. Rome was not alone however, and with the exceptions
of Florence and Venice – haughty cities jealous of their own architectural traditions – the Baroque, most expensive of all the architectural
styles that have succeeded one another in the history of Italian art,
triumphed everywhere. It appeared at Naples, at Turin, at Genoa,
in the earthquake-devastated part of Sicily, and in the villas outside
towns and in the country. The number of these villas increased steadily
throughout the seventeenth century: in the Veneto alone we can count
332. Certain of them – the extreme example is the villa of the Palagonia
family at Bagheria near Palermo, whose 'lunatic asylum' display
aroused the Olympian Goethe's indignation – demonstrate how their
builders' and owners' taste for waste could sometimes become obsession
and megalomania.

Naturally, it was more difficult for the wealth of the nobility and the
privileged classes to generate more capital when it was tucked safely
away in luxury goods or converted into buildings, and the parasitism
and polarity already very characteristic of Italian society, especially in
the towns, were accentuated. Pauperism, vagabondage and prostitution
were widespread in seventeenth-century Italy. The only way for many
to escape degradation was to find some pretext to enter the narrow
circle of a court, a guild, a great household, as a 'client'. The *Commedia dell'Arte* figure of the opportunist servant, perennially famished,
or that of the priest of plebeian or peasant origin who, like Manzoni's
Don Abbondio, embraces an ecclesiastical career more from a vocation
for easy living than out of human charity, are typical of the real Italy
of the period. So are the *'bravi'*, who were indistinguishable from
bandits, save in having the protection of powerful men.

The seventeenth-century Italian economic scene is thus generally
dark, but there are some glimmers of light. It is not always quite true
that tying up capital in land was in every case a kind of non-investment,
compared with the more dynamic and profitable activities such as
commerce and manufacturing. This is for example not the case of
those farmers of the Lombard plain who during this century applied
themselves to making better use of their land, increasing the acreage
cultivated for fodder. (Nor was this a passing phase: by the early
eighteenth century this acreage had increased by 200 per cent since the
mid-sixteenth century.) There were other islands of progress: the

* Conspicuous investment refers to investments one can see, 'show-off' projects:
palaces, galleries, gardens, etc.

farmers of Emilia who, according to a Bolognese agronomist in 1644, had succeeded in bringing the growing of hemp 'to an exact and singular perfection', and introduced important modifications of agricultural technique and machinery; there were also the proprietors of land around Venice, who transformed their villas from holiday-places into centres of efficient farming. By so doing they helped to break with a tradition by which farming had been considered exclusively from the point of view of provisioning, or else as speculation – they gave life to a more long-term kind of investment with wider-spread profits: a healthier, more modern type of economic enterprise.

Certainly, these examples are too scanty, and too little known, to justify over-general or hasty conclusions. Yet they seem enough to allow one to say that already in the seventeenth century a process of transformation and renewal had begun to take shape; in the next century it spread through the whole Italian countryside, constituting a genuine reversal of tendency in the history of a country in so many ways dominated by the presence of its towns. It is also true that the areas of agricultural progress, where they can be picked out with any certainty, remained limited to northern Italy and the Po region. But this is only a foreshadowing of the way in which, as we shall often notice later, modern Italy was born and developed: by way of an increasingly accentuated subordination of the more backward regions to the more advanced, of the South to the North. The disparity between the two halves of the country was, as we know well, an inheritance of past centuries; but during the seventeenth century the scissors are opened even wider. The developments and events with which the next section is concerned may explain the phenomenon.

ANTI-SPANISH REVOLTS IN SOUTHERN ITALY

Of all the Spanish dominions in Italy, the South was the one that had to contribute most massively to the Spanish monarchy's financial effort during the exhausting Thirty Years War. If Milan was the kingdom's rampart and as such felt the consequences of war directly, on her own soil, Naples had to pay for the privilege of having the war far from her own frontiers, by providing as many soldiers and as much money as she could. This was a constant rule of Spanish policy and of its great strategist of the moment, the Duke of Olivares. It was applied thoroughly. Raids were organized in the southern countryside, to procure the troops needed by the Habsburg armies. The men collected in this way were taken often in chains, to the ports of embarkation and to the fronts of Germany, the Valtellina, Flanders. But even more than men, the Spanish monarchy needed cash – enormous amounts of cash. This also it succeeded in procuring. According to the reliable accounts of a banker of Genoese descent, Cornelio Spinola, war contributions absorbed every year the enormous sum of three and a half million ducats; in only the first year and a half of his viceroyalty, the Duke of Medina managed to put together seven million ducats. Of these *'asistencias'* a considerable part was taken north to Milan, and thus constituted a clear loss for the southern economy.

To obtain the sums it needed, the central power naturally turned to the weapon of taxation, and wielded it vigorously. Between 1636 and 1644, ten new indirect taxes were imposed, and many extraordinary contributions were demanded. But little by little, as the number of heavy taxes grew, the amount collected by each one diminished. In an economic situation characterized, as we have seen, by a lasting stagnation of productive activity, there was in fact a limit to the contributive capacity of the kingdom, beyond which it was not possible to go. In these conditions the viceroy had no other way but to find private bankers ready for a financial operation with great risks attached to it, but with the incentive of possible profits of a highly speculative nature. One such was Bartolomeo D'Aquino, a former merchant who was, according to a contemporary, 'a man caring little for God and Saints'. The central power would be indebted to him and the other financiers associated with him when the money it needed had been raised.

This was the way this speculation worked: in exchange for sums they advanced, D'Aquino and his partners received many shares in excise duties and state dues. Because of the progressive diminishing of revenues obtained by taxation, these had depreciated, and most of their holders were unable to realize more than a sometimes derisory part of their face value – when they were not actually compelled to get rid of them. But, thanks to their connections and prestige, D'Aquino and his colleagues were able to get them discounted at their face value. This, as may easily be understood, opened the way to enormous profits and possibilities of speculation. The ruin of many thousands of small savers and investors was transformed into the wealth of a narrow circle of speculators and privileged persons, and an immense operation of plunder and transference of wealth could thus be taken to its limit.

But that was not all. A part of the profits realized by D'Aquino and his privileged clientele was invested in buying the right to farm or even in actually purchasing those same duties and excises on consumption and trade from whose revenue they had made such profits. This naturally offered them new possibilities for speculation: and as tax-exactors they showed themselves as severe as they had been casual in handling public money. Another destination for the profits of this financial operation was, naturally, investment in land, and the purchase of titles and rights of feudal jurisdiction. As far as the latter were concerned, things were once again made easier by the financial difficulties of the central power, which, notwithstanding opposition from the 'universities', did not hesitate to allow many state lands to become feudal, and thus be placed under private jurisdiction. So a new, more numerous and more rapacious titled nobility was formed, and titles of nobility proliferated. It was the job of genealogists – another typical profession of the Italian seventeenth century – to compose illustrious family trees for these parvenus. For D'Aquino they did not hesitate to make use of St Thomas Aquinas.

To summarize what has so far been described, we may say that, so long as they were able to face Madrid's financial demands, the Spanish viceroys who succeeded one another between 1620 and 1648 were willing to dispose of that part of sovereignty that was within their competence, and to put up for auction, to the profit of a privileged few, the state machine itself. So when taxation was at its highest, central organization was at its lowest: the severest oppression coincided with the greatest disorder. A further worsening of the situation, and disorganization and disorder would have become anarchy.

There had been previous warning signs of this tendency. In certain of the more turbulent and quarrelsome sectors of the nobility there flourished again the traditional spirit of dissidence, which had emerged in the familiar forms of aristocratic conspiracy (the Pignatelli conspiracy, 1634) and of political flirtations with France, sworn enemy of Spain and the Habsburgs and protectress for many years of the southern baronial opposition. But these attempts were fairly easily repressed or absorbed: however bitterly some of the nobility might resent the current promotion of parvenus, the baronage in general had profited widely from the circumstances and speculations of the moment, and had indeed won large prizes in the lottery of rights, favours and concessions to which the state had been forced.

But from 1646 on, events moved faster, and control of the situation increasingly escaped the Spanish government. The viceroy, on the verge of bankruptcy, was compelled to arrest D'Aquino, attempting to make him a scapegoat to general indignation. The manoeuvre only partially succeeded, and a little later the same viceroy, realizing the extreme precariousness of the situation, submitted his resignation. His successor found himself facing a situation that was by now explosive. On 17 July 1647, following the imposition of a new tax on fruit, the people of Naples came out into the streets. From the capital the insurrection spread into the provinces; and so began what may be considered the most notable of the few revolutionary episodes of Italian history.

As always happens in upheavals of any magnitude, the forces and interests set in motion were various, and their aims did not always coincide. First were the common people of the capital, with their improvised captains and tribunes, their desperate but inconclusive radicalism, their anger and confusion. Then there were the middle-class citizenry, with their more considered political aims and direction. To begin with, under the influence of the aged Giulio Genoino, in his day counsellor of the Duke of Ossuna, this class aimed at a 'reform of the kingdom' in a popular, anti-baronial sense; on this basis they were prepared to reach a compromise with Spain. But Madrid's intransigence and the consequent aggravation of the situation persuaded them, under the leadership of the armourer Gennaro Annese, to take up progressively more extreme positions, culminating in the proclamation of a Republic in October. Another element was the diplomatic involvement of Mazarin's France, for whom the rebellion was no more than one incident and front in the far wider anti-Spanish struggle. Finally, linked with French policy, were the ill-judged efforts of Duke Henry of Guise. After the proclamation of the Republic, he arrived at Naples, and managed to get himself recognized as 'Duke' of the Republic itself. But his unexpected overtures to the baronage and his amateurism soon lessened his ephemeral popularity, and contributed to the loss of direction and final defeat of the revolutionary camp. In August 1648 the Spanish, under the command of John of Austria, managed to regain control of Naples and snuff out the rebellion.

There was, as one can see, an extremely complex interweaving and interaction of forces. But it becomes simpler when one looks at the two extremes of the forces and social classes involved in the struggle: on the one hand the baronage, which had abandoned every whim of opposition and ranked itself solidly in defence of the king and its own privileges, and on the other, the antifeudal peasant movement in the provinces. These – barons and peasants – were the motive 'wings' of the opposed ranks of conservatism and revolt, and it was their frontal conflict that in the last analysis largely determined the outcome of the struggle.

This was most bitter. The peasants, drawn up and led by survivors of the battlefields of the Thirty Years War, gave proof both of their desperation and of their determination to fight and win. It was not merely a *jacquerie*, but also a peasant war. Country and town were conquered, entire provinces put under peasant control, and the baronial military contingents defeated in many battles and skirmishes. The dismay that these successes aroused among the barons appears clearly in the words of the most powerful and terrible of them, the Count of Conversano. '*Yo estoy desperado,*' he wrote in January 1648, '*estamos perdidos.*' But in the end, after the defeat of the revolt in Naples, even the peasant guerrillas had to submit, and the machine of feudal repression was able to move into action. The revenge was frightful and pitiless. Intended as a deterrent, it was determined to demonstrate that nothing had changed and nothing could change. And in fact that is how it was to be: for a long time yet the southern countryside was to remain, between the two poles of baronial arrogance and peasant indifference, chained to a destiny of immobility; the society founded on this immobility was to find itself cheated of any possibility of progress or modernization. The defeat of the revolutionary movements of 1647–8 marks an important date in the prehistory of the southern problem.

The history of the viceroyalty of Sicily in the first half of the seventeenth century is, like that of Naples, a story above all of heavy duties, special contributions, *arrendamenti*; in one word, of taxation. And it is consequently also a history of revolts. But these, unlike those that had taken place on 'the continent', remained for the most part confined to the towns, and were thus exclusively the business of the lower and middle classes who lived in them. The first was that of Palermo of August 1647: a typical famine-revolt, which was crushed within one month by the combined action of the baronage and the viceroy. The second, that of Messina of 1674, had its roots in the traditional resentment of this city towards Palermo, and also in the rivalry that divided the leaders and most prominent families of the town. This revolt, as has been mentioned, furnished the pretext for a new French intervention, which, by the way in which it was made, and even more by the way it was abandoned, helped to make the city's surrender and return to Spanish rule inevitable.

FROM GALILEO TO VICO: THE TWO CULTURES OF SEVENTEENTH CENTURY ITALY

In this chapter it seems unnecessary to state who Galileo Galilei was, or to go over the events of his life, from his teaching at the universities of Pisa and Padua, to his trial and condemnation of 1633, and then to the solitude of his last years and death, in 1642. It seems superfluous also to remark on the place occupied by his personality and his discoveries in the modern scientific revolution and the movement, to use Alexandre Koyré's happy phrase, 'from the world of almost to the universe of precision'. Brought up on Neoplatonic and Pythagorean ideas, his starting point, which was also that of Bruno and Campanella, was the acceptance of the Copernican hypothesis and the rejection of Aristotelian physics and cosmology. But at the point where Bruno stood still in amazed contemplation of the infinity of the universe, he penetrated within it, to organize and measure it; and at the point where Campanella had recourse to astrology and the game of the conjunction of the stars to explain the rules underlying the concatenation of phenomena, he sought them in mathematics. He considered that the only possible knowledge of reality was that offered by the exact and natural sciences, and that the philosopher could only be a scientist and mathematician.

'Philosophy,' he wrote, 'is written in this great book that lies continually open before our eyes (I mean the universe), but which cannot be understood if one does not first learn to understand the language and the characters in which it is written. It is written in the language of mathematics, and the characters are triangles, circles and other geometrical figures, without which it is humanly impossible to understand a word of it; without these it is a futile journey through a dark labyrinth.'

But the mathematician and scientist in their turn, insofar as they were aware of the theoretical importance of their discoveries, were bound to be philosophers; and in fact, when the Grand Duke of Tuscany asked Galileo to return from Padua to Pisa, Galileo claimed from him not only the title of mathematician but also that of philosopher, 'professing that he had spent more years studying philosophy than months in pure mathematics'. He did not do so out of pique or out of misplaced ambition, but because he did not conceive of mathematics as the integration of an already existing body of knowledge but as the foundation of a new knowledge. By the same token, the Aristotelianism he fought against was not only a scientific hypothesis of the structure of the universe that had been superseded and belied by observation, but also, in those who remained obstinately faithful to it, a manifestation of mental laziness and obscurantism. The struggle for a new science was thus inevitably joined to that more general struggle for a renewal of culture and thought. In other words, one could not be 'modern' in the study and practice of the exact and natural sciences, and reactionary in other fields of thought. Modern culture, founded on the new 'sciences' of Nature, had to have the coherence and unity of the great Classical and Humanist cultures that Galileo had abundantly absorbed.

This call for unity of knowledge was to be richer in its consequences than any other argument or stand of his thought and his own difficult life. It was for this that the greatest of his contemporaries, from Bruno to Sarpi, saluted him as a pioneer and a new Columbus (a common paragon in the pamphlets of the age), and it was for this that the Church condemned him.

In spite of the admonition he received in 1616, in 1632 he published his *Dialogo dei massimi sistemi*, the true manifesto of modern scientific thought, written in the same limpid, triumphant language as Descartes' *Discours de la méthode* four years later. If human knowledge is infinitely inferior to that of God as far as *extent* is concerned – goes one of his most famous and most quoted assertions –

'in *intensive* understanding . . . that is, understanding perfectly, I say that the human intellect understands some (propositions) as perfectly, and has of them a certainty as absolute as Nature herself can have; and such are the pure mathematical sciences . . . of which the divine intellect knows infinitely more propositions, since it knows them all, but I believe that human knowledge of those few propositions it understands equals the divine in objective certainty, since it succeeds in comprehending necessity, beyond which it does not seem that there can be greater certainty.'

Meanwhile Galilean teaching had begun to bear its first positive fruit. The work of Federico Cesi, a student and patron of science, peculiarly gifted as a cultural organizer, produced the *Accademia dei Lincei* at Rome, which Galileo himself joined in 1613; its programme consisted essentially in the consolidation and planned continuance of Galileo's scientific programme, and of his anti-Aristotelianism. Cesi's efforts were certainly not in vain: around the *Accademia dei Lincei*, or at least in connection with it, a truly remarkable group of intellects gradually collected. Among these were the Milanese mathematician Bonaventura Cavalieri, the physicist Evangelista Torricelli of Faenza, the mathematician Benedetto Castelli of Brescia, all names well-known to students of the history of science. Galileo's trial and the ending of the Academy's activities after Cesi's death in 1630 were setbacks, but the Galilean and Lincean tradition was later resumed and developed by the Florentine *Accademia del Cimento* (founded in 1657) and the Neapolitan *Accademia degli Investiganti* (founded in 1663). A generation of great mathematicians was followed by one of great doctors, including such illustrious names as the Florentines Viviani and Redi and the Bolognesi Bellini and Malpighi – the important contribution made by the latter to the sciences of biology and embryology is well known.

In the field of scientific study and experiment, then, the lesson of Galileo has been understood and put into practice. As we have seen, however, the exact and natural sciences were not a specialization for Galileo, but the foundation of a 'philosophy' and of a whole new culture

As such, their progress was for a long time conditioned by the extent to which they were able to effect a profound renewal of the whole Italian intellectual atmosphere. But the obstacles along this road were many and solid. The pressures and the vigilance exercised by the spirit and the authority of the Counter-Reformation were too strong, the isolation and provincial fragmentation of Italian culture too pronounced, and its rhetorical habits and old idols too firmly installed.

This was of course particularly true of the humanities, but these, in many men's eyes, were still what was really meant by culture. Political science, for example, continued to be studied in a Counter-Reformation, Aristotelian spirit, as an abstract and scholastic accumulation of precepts of the correct art of government, for the use of princes. The various seventeenth-century writers of treatises on the *ragion di stato* supposed that they were circulating, through the filter and disguise of Tacitus, the unprejudiced counsels of Machiavelli. In fact their arid casuistry could not be further from the political realism and naturalism of the Florentine secretary, and his attempt to confer on politics the dignity and sureness of an experimental science. In the same way, literary theorists and critics continued to think in terms of 'kinds', and to cultivate an essentially rhetorical, aristocratic idea of literature. This largely corresponded to the prevalent taste and practice: much Italian prose and poetry of the seventeenth century is in fact essentially a rhetorical and oratoric exercise, even if it is an oratory which often maintains a high level of experimentation and refinement. Marino's *Adone* (1623), a masterpiece of refined *preziosismo*, had a wide influence, and the lesson of simplicity and modernity conveyed by Galileo's prose was understood by few who were not writers and expounders of scientific matters.

So between scientific culture and traditional humanistic culture was fixed a chasm, which eventually resolved itself into the relative isolation of the first, and into the weakening of its power to break down and renew. As we shall see, it was only during the eighteenth century, and with the bursting into Italy of the Enlightenment, that this gap was to be partly filled in. Influences towards cultural renewal and reunification were already filtering through from beyond the frontiers; but their advance also was slow, and hindered by many obstacles.

The most powerful of these influences was certainly that of the new Cartesian philosophy. Most important, it was this that allowed the philosophical implications and the message contained in Galilean teaching to become explicit, 'clear and distinct', and their reviving power to be set free. So it is natural that the first Cartesians or, as they were called, *'renatisti'* of Italy should have been men of science, more or less directly linked to the Galilean school. Tommaso Cornelio of Cosenza was a teacher of mathematics and member of the Neapolitan *Accademia degli Investiganti*, as was Giovanni Alfonso Borelli, author of a *De motu animalium* in which he took up the well-known mechanistic theses of Descartes. Leonardo da Capua on the other hand was a doctor, and also a member of the *Investiganti*. He was not only the member of his profession to be attracted by the new Cartesian philosophy: according to the account of Ludovico Antonio Muratori, so was the great Malpighi. But alongside the mathematicians and doctors there also appear intellectuals of Humanist extraction among the Italian Cartesians: the Neapolitan lawyer Franceso d'Andrea, the Sardinian poet Carlo Buragna, the Calabrese philosopher Gregorio Caloprese, teacher of the greatest Italian poet and 'Arcadian' of the early seventeenth century, Pietro Metastasio. A Sicilian nobleman, Tommaso Campailla, even had the idea of writing a philosophical poem to illustrate the new 'renatist' philosophy.

The Italian Cartesian school was increasing in extent: but this did not necessarily mean a corresponding increase of intensity and profundity in its original activity – that of an avant-garde and destroyer of the theories it opposed. Far from it: as often happens in such cases, the development was in the opposite direction. Increasingly evident among the Italian Cartesians was the tendency to lay greater emphasis on the more traditional, more easily absorbed ideas of their master, rather than the more original and radical ones. To many of them, Descartes now appeared more as the theorist of the *res cogitans* than that of the *res extensa*, as an assertor more of innate ideas than of clear and distinct ones: more a metaphysician than a physicist. In this way, by being brought closer to Plato and the metaphysics of innateness, Descartes was to some extent absorbed into tradition, and the mainstream of Classical and Renaissance thought; he was made more assimilable but also more inoffensive. What was obscured or even altogether lost was the most revolutionary aspect of his thought: his faith, that is, in the sciences and in reason as keys to a complete understanding of human reality. Once again the old Humanist culture showed itself most unwilling to be dethroned by the 'new sciences'. Besides, if one wanted to be an out-and-out Cartesian one risked waking one day to find oneself in the embrace of 'the impious and rash Spinoza'.

From Descartes to Plato, then, was the return journey made by such men as the Neapolitan philosopher Paolo Matteo Doria; in his youth he studied physics and mathematics and fell very much under the influence of Descartes; then as he grew older he turned to social and more strictly philosophic studies and to the recantation of his 'juvenile' Cartesianism. His is the characterization of Spinoza quoted

above. But this intellectual journey was above all made by Giovambattista Vico, one of the most robust and scintillating minds in the
history of Italian philosophical culture.

A contemporary and friend of Doria's, Vico also came close to
Descartes in his youth, to move gradually away later. In one of his
first works, the *De antiquissima italorum sapientia* of 1710, he emphasized
that the mathematical sciences, being entirely a product of the human
mind, had indeed the virtue of exactness – but he did so mainly in
order to underline their arbitrary and conventional character, their
abstraction. From this position it was a short step to overturning the
order of priority in which Descartes had put the sciences, and to
affirm the superiority of the solid humanities – history, poetry, oratory
– to the mathematical abstractions of the new sciences. Vico himself
had already partly taken this step when in his university oration *De
nostri temporis studiorum ratione* (1708) he had affirmed that 'the most
serious harm done by our type of study is that, all intent on studying
the natural sciences, we give little weight to moral science, above all
to that part of it which deals with human intelligence and its passions,
as far as it is concerned with civil life and eloquence', and that 'among
us the admirable and excellent study of political matters is almost
entirely neglected'. Besides, were not laws, customs, the myths and
fables of poets (that is, the concrete expression of the political, moral
and imaginative sphere) themselves products of the human spirit, and
did not the principle of the conversion of truth apply also to them,
since, as we have seen, it had been applied to mathematics? Furthermore, surely the only world man could attempt to reach full knowledge
of was that which he had himself constructed: the world of history.
As for the natural world, it could be known only to God, its Creator;
man had to be content with that approximate and conventional
knowledge of it that the exact sciences provided him with.

Morals, politics, eloquence – the humane sciences – became more
and more Vico's prevailing if not exclusive objects of interest. In the
Scienza Nuova, his major work, written in one sustained burst in 1729–
30, and subsequently several times reworked, he traced a great and
fascinating panorama of man's historic development through the
various 'ages', from the primitive barbarism of the 'monsters' to the
'heroic' age of warriors and poets, and that of philosophers. But not
even the world of history and men was self-sufficient: it could not be
exhaustively known from within. Like the world of nature, it too had
phases of 'flux' and 'reflux', and ultimately Vico's historicism falls
within the same limits he had placed around the innovating boldness
of the natural sciences.

Vico was discovered, as is well known, in the Romantic era, thanks largely to Michelet. The brilliance of the *Scienza Nuova* and its affirmations about the historical origin of language and of poetry and the historical, communal meaning of the great epic poems – Vico was among other things one of the first to put Homer in historically correct terms – and the general historical basis of his thought were by that time able to find a sympathetic public, ready to receive and appreciate them. So it was said that Vico had not been understood by his time, but had been vindicated by posterity.

But perhaps in the enthusiasm of this discovery other and possibly more real and organic aspects of the Neapolitan philosopher's work may have been overlooked: the anti-Cartesianism that is its starting-point, and the reaffirmation of transcendence that is, in the end, what it arrives at. In the preceding pages it has often been emphasized how, in a world that still had no idea of progress, the figure of the revolutionary may sometimes be confused with that of the traditionalist. But in the first decades of the eighteenth century, when Vico was working on his *Scienza Nuova,* the Enlightenment faith in progress was already beginning to spread through Europe.

7

Italy and the Enlightenment

ITALY AND EUROPE

From the time of the treaty of Cateau-Cambrésis until the early
eighteenth century, the political map of Italy underwent no significant
changes. In northern Italy the duchy of Savoy had succeeded in
annexing some marginal parts of Monferrato, and in central Italy the
Papal State had acquired Ferrara in 1598 and absorbed the surviving
independent principalities of Urbino in the Marche, in 1631, and of
Castro in upper Lazio, in 1649. This was all, or almost all. On the
whole the political arrangement and internal frontiers of Italy had
remained unchanged for almost a hundred and fifty years, and the
irksome guardianship of Spain had kept the ambitions and initiative
of particular states on a close rein. The French domination of Europe
in the later seventeenth century had the same effect. It must not be
forgotten that after the treaty of Cherasco in 1631, Piedmont, the most
dynamic and warlike of Italian states, had been reduced to little more
than a French protectorate.

This situation changed radically in the early years of the eighteenth
century. The War of the Spanish Succession of 1700–13 reduced Spain to
the rank of a secondary power, and put a constraint on the ambitions of France under Louis XIV: the doors of Italy were once again open
to the play of widely-varied forces. In the framework of the policy of
European 'balance' ushered in by the treaties of Utrecht and Rastadt,
Italy's mosaic of little states and faded dynasties deprived of power
made it a favourite field of action for the diplomacy of the great powers
in their incessant work of adjusting and balancing the interests of
various states. If any power had to make concessions, or if its candidate
for this or that European throne was defeated by the candidate of some
other power, there was always an Italian duchy or state in which the
defeated candidate could be lodged. So there was hardly any international conflict, from the War of the Spanish Succession to those for

the Polish and Austrian successions, which did not bring about some change in the political arrangement of Italy. Within a few decades, some Italian states passed several times from one master to another. Sicily, for example, passed from the house of Savoy to Austria, and then to the Bourbons of Naples, all between 1714 and 1734, while the duchy of Parma, where the Farnese dynasty expired in 1731, was held by the Bourbons, then by Austria and then by the Bourbons again, between 1734 and 1748. It would take too long to reconstruct these changes in all their detail and chronological succession: we shall return to them later, with the histories of the particular Italian states during the century. For the moment it is enough to say that at the date of the treaty of Aquisgrana (1748), which concluded the War of the Austrian Succession, most of the Italian states were ruled by a different nation or dynasty from that which had ruled them at the beginning of the century. The state of Milan had passed from Spanish to Austrian rule; Mantua had lost its independence and had also been absorbed into Austrian Lombardy; Parma, formerly ruled by the Farnese family, was under the Bourbons; at Florence the Medici dynasty had expired in 1737, and the city was a Lorraine seigniory; Sicily and the Kingdom of Naples, after two hundred years of Spanish rule, had won back independence, under the Bourbons; and Sardinia no longer belonged to Spain, but to the house of Savoy. The only states that were still under the same rulers as before were the Este duchy of Modena, the Republics of Venice, Genoa and Lucca, Savoyard Piedmont, and of course the Papal State. From this general rearrangement in the second half of the eighteenth century until Napoleon Bonaparte's invasion Italy enjoyed a long period of peace, and there was no change in the political arrangements made at Aquisgrana.

But the new dynasties and boundaries, and the changes these brought about in the power-relation of various states, were not the most important result of the upheavals Italy was subjected to in the first half of the eighteenth century, nor was even the shrinking of the area under foreign rule, now reduced to Lombardy. What mattered most was that the isolation and provincialism in which Spanish rule had kept Italy for two hundred years was now at an end. The new rulers of Florence, Naples and Parma may have been foreigners to the lands they had been assigned, but for this very reason they were a good deal more European and less provincial than the old ruling houses. As for the Austrian administrators of Lombardy, they were, as we shall see, infinitely abler and more modern in outlook than the previous Spanish rulers and viceroys. It is no accident that the Italian states that display the most vitality in this period are Austrian Lombardy and the other states ruled by new foreign dynasties. The others, such as Venice,

Genoa, Piedmont and the Papal State, which kept their old rulers and systems, continued, to a greater or lesser extent, to decline, in provincial isolation.

But during the eighteenth century Italy was not merely brought politically further into the Europe of the age of balance and of family pacts; it was also economically integrated into a market at the centre of all the main trade-currents of the time.

The sea was the most important vehicle of trade. We have seen that Italy's first free port had been the very active Leghorn. Venice had followed the same course in 1661, but the timidity and reservations with which the decision was taken greatly reduced its effects and results. During the eighteenth century however the idea of the free port spread widely. The example was given by Trieste in 1717; then the free port of Ancona was founded in 1732, and as in the cases of Leghorn and Trieste, results soon followed: while, on an average, fifty-seven ships a year came into port in the five-year period 1727–31, in 1732–6 the average was a hundred and eight, and, although the statistics show oscillations, the number of ships continued to rise during the rest of the century, reaching an average in 1792–6 of a hundred and sixty-nine. Other free ports instituted during the century were those of Civitavecchia in 1748 and Messina, to which Charles of Bourbon gave back the privileges it had lost after the revolt of 1674.

As well as the development of the ports and of sea-communications, corresponding progress was made in roads and land-communications. During the eighteenth century the most important event in the eventful history of Italian roads was probably the building of the first coach-route across the Alps, completed in 1771 by Maria Theresa's government. This road came through the Brenner pass to the Po plain and then went by way of Modena and the Appenine pass of the Abetone, as far as Florence. This new artery passed through almost all the territories of the house of Austria or of princes of the same family (the house of Lorraine in Tuscany) or allied to it (the Este of Modena), and it inevitably exerted a strong power of attraction. There were many attempts and projects designed to link other centres and ports with this route. Francesco III D'Este had a coach-route built from Massa to Modena, and Leghorn and Pistoia were joined by a navigable canal. On the other hand, the project of connecting Milan with the new road by the waterways of the Po, put forward by the Milanese mathematician and man of letters Paolo Frisi, came to nothing.

In this way Italy strengthened her economic bonds with Europe: her ports and Alpine coach-routes brought her firmly within the European circuit. But what must be particularly emphasized is that Italy became reintegrated within the European economy at a time when that economy was going through one of its most exuberant phases of expansion. The eighteenth century was of course the time of the 'agrarian revolution', which transformed wide areas of the European countryside, and it was also the eve of the great English industrial revolution. It was the century of Physiocracy and Adam Smith, and the age when the pure science of Galileo and Newton was transformed into the applied science of Watt and Arkwright. It was the age of enlightenment; after the long, tormented crisis of the seventeenth century, modern bourgeois Europe had set out to dominate and conquer the world.

This was the Europe of which Italy was every day a more essential part, and this the prosperity she benefited from. But we must see to what extent internal impulses and developments responded to stimuli and demands from outside.

AGRICULTURE AND REFORM

Agriculture was the sector of the Italian economy and Italian society that most directly benefited from Italy's involvement in the European market. It could not have been otherwise: the days when Italy supplied Europe with luxury and oriental goods were, as we have seen, gone for ever. Eighteenth-century Europe demanded from Italy the agricultural products required to feed its ever-growing population, and raw materials for its factories.

Italy provided both. Above all, raw silk; a good part of the raw material used by the prospering textile factories of Lyons came from Piedmont and Lombardy. The South too was a major silk-exporter, especially Calabria, even though this trade seems, from the scanty data available, to have undergone a drastic reduction. On the other hand, southern Italy's export-trade in oil increased dramatically. Oil was not only a foodstuff, but was also used increasingly by the Marseilles soap-factories. An average of 51,974 '*salme*' was exported annually from 1760 to 1764, and an average of 95,648 in 1790–4. Besides silk from Piedmont and Lombardy and oil from the South, Italy exported corn and wine, in years when there was a good harvest. The European popularity of certain characteristic Italian wines dates from the eighteenth century; Sicilian Marsala, for instance, which was launched on the European market thanks largely to the initiative of an Englishman, John Woodhouse.

The growing European demand for agricultural produce and raw materials, combined with the demands of a domestic market that was also expanding, naturally provided a powerful stimulus for Italian agriculture. All available data, the prices of produce, land-values, rents, indicate that agriculture was reanimated, and became better organized commercially. In the Mantua region the prices of corn, maize, hay, rice and wine all show, to a varying extent, and with the irregularity typical of farm-produce, a distinct rise. The same pattern emerges from an analysis of prices in the Vercelli region. Here, in the major rice-producing area of Italy, the price of land tripled from 1761 to 1790, a clear sign that farming was all the time becoming more of a business. The agreement of all available data make it unnecessary to give further examples. It is on the other hand worth noticing that the movement of Italian prices corresponded with that of European prices in general, a further sign that Italy's economy had become integrated, once and for all, into that of Europe.

Gradually, a massive drift to the land took place; it is best illustrated by Italy's population-figures for the century. Again as in the rest of Europe, the population of Italy rose – from 13–14 million to 18 million, it has been estimated. What should particularly be noticed is that on the whole this increase affected the countryside more than the towns, and that this represents a symptomatic reversal of the usual tendency.

It is true that the population of some Italian cities increased during the century: Naples, for instance, the most highly-populated European metropolis of the age, had 400,000 inhabitants by the end of the century; Palermo rose to 140,000; Rome had 162,000 in 1740. The development of Turin was exceptional: the city had been made the capital of a warlike kingdom with a strongly centralized administration, and between 1702 and 1761 its population rose from 43,000 to 92,000. Catania, another of the Italian ports to take advantage of the favourable economic circumstances, almost trebled its population, which increased from 16,000 to 45,000, between 1713 and 1798. But in some other cities the population remained stationary, or even fell: in the first category must be included even hard-working Milan (114,000 in 1714 and 131,000 in 1796), in the second, Venice (from 138,000 in 1702 to 137,000 in 1797), Florence and Genoa. To give a general picture, around the year 1770 there were twenty-six centres with a population greater than 20,000, of which five had more than 100,000, a situation that had not substantially changed since the sixteenth century.

The countryside presents a very different picture. In Piedmont, the density of population rose from 44·18 per sq. km. to 56·40, in the brief period 1700–34. On the Venetian mainland the density per sq. km. rose from 68·7 to 73·5 between 1776 and 1790, while in Lombardy there was an absolute population increase of 25 per cent, from 900,000 to 1,112,000, between 1746 and 1766. The population increase in the Kingdom of Naples, and in the other regions of Italy, was also considerable.

This return to the land was such a profound and general phenomenon that people soon became aware of it. Agriculture was fashionable in eighteenth-century Italy. The poets set their fables in Arcadia, and poems were even written on the cultivation of rice and hemp. Agricultural academies and societies multiplied; the best known was the Florentine *Accademia dei Georgofili*, founded in 1753, the 'supreme council' of Tuscan landowners. Innumerable works were written on agriculture, and many of the leading figures of eighteenth-century culture concerned themselves with its revival. These included the great Genovesi, whose preface to the treatise *L'agricoltore sperimentato*, by the Tuscan Cosimo Trinci, includes this eulogy of farming, which is by itself enough to give a vivid picture of the enthusiasms of the century.

This art alone exercises the body, revives its strength, allows it to breathe a more buoyant air, prolongs its life . . . it nourishes sweet hopes, simple and honest affections, generates the humanity and sweetness of a life that is companionable, but without masks. It is the enemy of cunning, of arrogance, of wars. If God Himself made it the task of unfallen man, why should we suppose that it may not be the amiable occupation of the fallen? I am tempted to believe that our very detachment from it and our devotion to empty ponderings may be one of the punishments to which our foolishness is on this earth condemned.

To speak of a return to the land is not to exhaust the subject, however. What type of return was this, and what forms did it assume? Were they those of a traditional, non-intensive farming, intent on grasping from the land – from as much land as possible – the maximum produce, and from those who worked on the land the maximum labour, with the minimum expense and payment? Or those of an intensive, rational agriculture, founded on an economic calculation of investment and earnings, a more modern, bourgeois agriculture? In fact, both tendencies were at work, and were often interwoven, even within a single state. The agrarian history of eighteenth-century Italy is one of land-reclaiming and hydraulic projects, but also of indiscriminate deforestation and equally indiscriminate attacks on common land and pasturage. It is a history that embraces both the enlightened projects of the Lombard landlords and the seigniorial reaction and rapacity of the southern ones, both the introduction of new crops, and the unthinking spread of cereal-growing to poor, marginal areas. It includes both the birth of capitalistic agricultural concerns and the survival of the old absentee estates. These contradictions and contrasts must be borne in mind if one is to understand the evolution of eighteenth-century agriculture; and not only that, but other developments too.

The men and the social forces that played a part in agrarian progress, and worked towards the development of a capitalist system in Italy, soon realized that it was not enough to promote land-improvement schemes, to introduce new crops and better techniques, nor even to free the corn-trade from restrictions. The fundamental question was to strike at the root of the whole system of an economic *ancien régime*, and so to free more dynamic and modern forces. It was a question of cutting down and restricting the rents received by parasitic absentee landlords, aristocrats or churchmen; a question of ending the anachronistic institutions of fidei-commissum and mortmain, which kept vast areas of land in an absurd state of inalienability. But those who wished to achieve such goals had to be prepared to face and fight the all too predictable reactions of the privileged, to be ready to strip them of their positions of power within the state, to cut down their prestige and authority. It was necessary to deprive the nobility of their remaining powers of jurisdiction, to reduce the Church's influence in state affairs and in forming public opinion, and to suppress town-guilds. In one word, 'reform' was needed.

So the question of the land came back to that of the state: if it was to be victorious, or even no more than effective, the struggle against the *ancien régime* had to be transferred to the economic and political level, and there had to be a general mobilization of enlightened public opinion in the battle for reforms. But in the century of the Enlightenment the natural leaders of public opinion were the 'philosophers', the intellectuals. We must concern ourselves, yet again, with the eternal question of the intellectuals' rôle in Italian history.

ITALIAN INTELLECTUALS
DURING THE AGE OF ENLIGHTENMENT

As well as being politically and economically integrated within Europe, Italy shared in the 'cultural revolution' of the century. The term may seem hardly pertinent, and even impertinent, and so it is, to some extent. Yet we must remember that the history of eighteenth-century culture does not consist merely of a list of its intellectual leaders and the summits reached by them; it is also a history of the first promotion of culture on a mass scale in modern Europe. This is what men of the age meant when they spoke of 'enlightening' philosophers and their victorious, irresistible progress.

Italy was no exception, and also had to face the demands of a rapidly expanding cultural market. To realize this, one has only to look at what happened in the book trade, which went through a boom. Publishers and printers multiplied, and their catalogues grew fuller; books were printed in considerably larger impressions; periodic publications became more numerous all the time, and more specialized: there were literary reviews, reviews of 'agriculture, art and commerce' and of medicine, ladies' magazines, story-magazines, memoirs, gazettes, encyclopaedic publications and so on. Foreign works were translated copiously and swiftly. Italian printers were not daunted by the enormous bulk of Diderot and D'Alembert's *Encyclopédie*: two editions soon came out, the first at Leghorn and the second at Lucca. Voltaire's *Histoire de Charles XII* was translated in 1734, only three years after its publication in France, and Rousseau's *Nouvelle Héloise* in 1764, two years after the first edition at Geneva. Many of these translations came out in pirated editions that declared fictitious or imaginary places of publication (Philadelphia, Amsterdam, Cosmopolis) to escape the censor's vigilance. Where not even this ruse was possible, people could always buy the work in the original; for by the eighteenth century many educated Italians could speak and even write French. The memoirs of Goldoni and Casanova, Galiani's writings on economics and Baretti's literary criticism, were all in French. This wide knowledge of French, and to a lesser extent of English also, naturally encouraged the circulation of foreign books in Italy, and gave more work to the censor. Between 1758 and 1794, Venetian frontier officials stopped twelve consignments of Rousseau's works and nine of the works of Helvétius. But their labours were not very effective.

This boom in books was accompanied by one in the theatre. Most of the great theatres of Italy date from the eighteenth century. La Scala in Milan was inaugurated in 1778 and the Fenice in Venice in 1790. With these famous names go a host of lesser ones, several dozen in Venice alone. Playwrights were fully employed, and it is possible to understand how one particularly successful writer, Carlo Goldoni, took on and performed the task of providing his public with sixteen new plays in a single season.

The formation and growth of a new public forced the producers of culture, the intellectuals, to emerge from their isolation, and faced them with new problems and responsibilities. How could they communicate with this new public? Above all, in what language? As in all periods of intense general activity for Italian culture and the Italian intelligentsia, the old problem of the language arose again. All save a few diehards were agreed on the need to purify the language of seventeenth-century bombast and long-windedness, and to break with the affected academic tradition of a narrowly conservative purism and Florentinism. Some, such as Pietro Verri and Cesare Beccaria and the contributors to the Milanese review *Il Caffè* went further, to declare that the Italian language would derive considerable advantage from a judicious adaptation to the vocabulary and syntax of the triumphant French language.

Because if we could express our ideas better by italianizing French, German, English, Turkish, Greek, Arabic or Slavonic words, we should not refrain from doing so out of fear of Casa or Crescimbeni or Villani, or of many others, who have never thought of setting themselves up as tyrants of the minds of the eighteenth century. . . . We protest that we shall use in our pages the language understood by cultivated men from Reggio Calabria to the Alps.

In short, a modern Italian, even though gallicized, would be a more functional, more fruitful and in the end more national instrument of communication than a slavish literary language. It was, perhaps, an extremist position, but precisely because of this, it has the merit of making clear the fundamental terms of the problem, that is, the necessity of bridging the gap between the language of the clerks and that of simple men, between literary and spoken Italian.

This enterprise could only be brought to a conclusion by a long process of practice and gradual refinement, and the century had passed before the results had reached final maturity. In the mean time, even writers who were clearly aware of their responsibility towards their public continued to avail themselves of makeshifts. Goldoni, for example, often had recourse in his plays to a 'polite', refined form of Venetian dialect, as a more satisfying and richly communicative solution than a stereotyped literary Italian.

But if the problem of *how* to speak and communicate with readers and audiences could not be resolved, or only with doubtful provisional solutions, the question of *what* to say left little space for doubt. What the new public of the age of reason demanded from their men of letters, their booksellers and the compilers of their periodicals was to be educated and kept informed of the advances achieved by the new enlightenment in every field of knowledge. This public demanded a modern, up-to-date and versatile culture, and a healing of the traditional gap between humanistic and scientific studies. Italian thinkers and writers strove to answer these needs; and a brief survey of their subjects and titles will give some idea of the breadth and seriousness of their attempt.

In the first place we find a considerable number of works devoted to what was the 'new science' par excellence of the Enlightenment: economics. Cesare Beccaria wrote on the *Elementi di economia politica*, and his friend Pietro Verri produced *Meditazioni sull'economia politica*. The strange, talented Venetian monk Gian Maria Ortes wrote *Dell' economia nazionale*, and the Neapolitan Genovesi *Lezioni di commercio e di economia civile*. But economics, however new, was a vast subject: hence the publication of works designed to illustrate particular aspects and problems, from money-systems and their 'disorder' (Verri, Beccaria, Galiani) to the corn-trade (Bandini and Galiani) or fishing (Pagano), not to mention the series of writings on agriculture that have already been referred to. Closely related to economics was geography; there was a copious literature of travels and descriptions of places: travels in Russia (Algarotti), to Constantinople (Casti), in the distant and free Americas (Mazzei). There were descriptions of exotic, distant lands, but also of places which were near but no less unknown, such as those accounts of the southern regions of Italy by Giuseppe Maria Galanti, Francesco Longano and other Neapolitan writers, who were the first to cast some light on that world of poverty and backwardness. Then there were works of science, such as those of the physician Lazzaro Spellanzani, or popularizations such as Algarotti's celebrated *Newtonianesimo per le dame*, works of statistics, technology, the applied arts; in short, every kind of writing designed to contribute to the *pubblica felicità*. This is probably the expression that recurs most frequently in the titles of eighteenth-century works: there is *Della pubblica felicità* by Ludovico Antonio Muratori, *Riflessioni sulla pubblica felicità relativamente al regno di Napoli* by Giuseppe Palmieri, *Della felicità pubblica considerata nei coltivatori di terre proprie* by the Piedmontese Giambattista Vasco. The list could be made much longer.

We have been able to give no more than a brief summary of eighteenth-century literature, with no attempt at considering the value of the questions it discusses, or the various positions that emerged from the debate; the amount, and the utilitarian, mundane nature of this literature must not lead us to suppose that it was a second-rate, repetitive output, destined for mass consumption. Some of the works that have been mentioned, such as the economic writings of Galiani and Ortes, earn an important place in the literature of the Enlightenment by their originality and vigour of thought. Cesare Beccaria's *Dei delitti e delle pene* was another important work, whose lucidly classical title announces the precision with which it is thought out and written. This peroration in favour of the abolition of the death-penalty was one of the great literary successes of the age: it was translated into several languages, aroused lively discussion, and even earned its author the offer of a post from Catherine of Russia.

Nor should we think that the passion for the 'new sciences' that pervades Italian culture of the Enlightenment brought about a paralysis or abandonment of traditional humanistic disciplines; how could this have happened in an age when almost all writers were accustomed to dealing with a variety of subjects? Even setting aside this consideration, it is undeniable that the work done in the traditional disciplines and in scholarship in eighteenth-century Italy is impressive.

Let us consider history, for example. It is no exaggeration to say that the work of the great eighteenth-century scholars, above all of Ludovico Antonio Muratori, to whom we owe the compilation of the *Rerum Italicarum Scriptores*, still the main implement for students of the Middle Ages, marked a decisive stage in the development of Italian historical studies. But the work of historians was not confined to erudition and the collection of source material: works such as Giannone's *Storia civile del Regno di Napoli*, Pietro Verri's *Storia di Milano* and Muratori's *Antiquitatis italicae mediae aevis* are excellent. The Jesuit Tiraboschi produced the first organic history of Italian literature, and Lanzi the first history of Italian art since Vasari's. The compilation of these works was made possible by a gigantic labour of learning and research, which, among other things, re-discovered authors and texts that earlier scholars had ignored or condemned. The outstanding example is the proscribed and execrated Machiavelli, whose works were published in an almost complete edition for the first time in Florence in the 1780's.

So the work of historical research continued with undiminishing vigour. What did however change profoundly was the spirit in which it was conceived and undertaken. Muratori, to take the greatest and most representative example of the century's academic achievement, was not, as historians often are, nostalgic for the Good Old Days; instead, he took every opportunity of proclaiming his pride in being a son of the cultured and enlightened eighteenth century. For this reason he did not seek in the past the consolation of lost glories and greatness, but the roots of the evils and abuses that he fought against: the temporal appetites of the Church and the superstition of the masses, the privileges of the few and the sufferings of the many. What interested him, therefore, was not Roman history, with its wars and literary pomp, but the obscure, arduous history of the Middle Ages, with its Guelf and Ghibelline factions, the local patriotism of towns and municipalities, the struggles between magnates and the people. Here was the source of what was good and what was bad in the Italian community and Italian civilization, for which there was no point in constructing a more illustrious ancestry. The historical study of Muratori, as of Verri and Giannone, is thus a civil history, which renews the great tradition of Machiavelli and Guicciardini.

Finally we must mention eighteenth-century literature. Not merely to complete the picture, but also because it was an essentially social literature: one that was profoundly and severely aware of its own responsibility in forming the education and taste of a public of new, enthusiastic readers. It is no accident that two of the 'fathers' of eighteenth-century writing, Alfieri and Goldoni, were principally dramatists: writers who chose an eminently public literary form. Alfieri practised his art more violently, in a more dogmatic spirit. He was an aristocrat, a traveller, an impenitent lover and an undisciplined reader, but gifted with a passionate capacity for identifying himself with what he read in Plutarch or Machiavelli. He populated his tragedies with characters made in his own image: his tyrants and his tyrannicides are united by a common restless energy. By writing about supermen and rebels he created an anti-conformist drama that denies every idea of the theatre as entertainment.

Carlo Goldoni's plays, on the other hand, remain highly entertaining, but their social function is, though less overt, no less effective. It has been noted that Goldoni's heroes (if the term can be applied to his anti-heroic characters) are for the most part Venetian merchants and bourgeois, concerned with exercising their professions with the same affectionate wisdom as they run their own families, while his nobles, with their vacuous haughtiness, are always presented as the representatives of a world and system of outdated values, in a state of decomposition. But this is not all: what is more important is that Goldoni saw himself as a writer of plays for an 'Italian' public, to which Venetians and non-Venetians, the bourgeois and the common people, the learned and the less learned all belonged. It was this that gave such newness and originality to his theatrical innovations, by which he set out to graft on to the old instinctive, popular *Commedia dell'Arte* the discipline of the theatre as a cultured, literary phenomenon, with the aim of forming and educating a new theatrical taste for the majority. Goldoni's success in this attempt has lasted until the present day, and should perhaps be considered one of the finest victories of the Italian Enlightenment.

The third great literary figure of eighteenth-century Italy is the Abbot Giuseppe Parini, whose fame is linked above all to a verse-satire called *Il Giorno*, in which he describes the futile day of a young nobleman of Lombardy. Parini is a writer with a solid background of Classical culture, extremely sensitive to problems of form and of the language proper to literature. He was intolerant of any experimentation, and the severe literary discipline he imposed on himself naturally made his work measured and self-controlled. This very reticence makes his satire of the nobility persuasive and highly effective as social comment.

This necessarily brief and summary survey of eighteenth-century culture brings us back to the starting-point: to the question whether or not the intellectuals of the eighteenth century played any part in forming and developing an enlightened public opinion, and assisting the battle for reforms. What has been said so far indicates that the answer must be affirmative. Italian intellectuals were united by the Enlightenment; once more, as in the past, they formed a spiritual community. Together with this unity, they rediscovered their social rôle and sense of collective responsibility for society, which had largely been lost. Insofar as they succeeded in being Europeans, they remembered that they were also Italians, at a time when that meant, above all, becoming aware of the backwardness of Italy, and the urgent need to make up lost ground.

8

The age of reform

HABSBURG REFORM: LOMBARDY

We have already seen that Lombardy, particularly its lower, irrigated part, was one of the regions of Italy whose agriculture was most highly developed and modern. We know too that this had been the result of a long process of agrarian improvement that had begun in the age of the communes and continued almost uninterruptedly up to the threshold of the eighteenth century, surviving unharmed, or with slighter damage than elsewhere, the two great depressions of Italy's economic history, in the fourteenth and the seventeenth centuries. In the eighteenth century, particularly the second half, this progress was not only kept up, but entered its liveliest phase. It is no exaggeration to say that it was in the later eighteenth century that Lombardy emerged as the economic leader of Italy, which she remained throughout the nineteenth century, until our own day.

Once again, the part that profited most from this fresh wave of agrarian progress was the irrigated lower part, the country of rice, of 'marcite' or water-meadows and of large-scale stock-breeding. Here too the favourable economic situation and the rise of agricultural prices had a stimulating effect, and lower Lombardy's enterprising landowners and farmers were once again backed up by state initiative in building infrastructures. All this helped to make the lower Po valley a model of rational modern agriculture; the Englishman, Arthur Young, who travelled from Milan to Lodi at the end of the century, and was a good judge of such matters, was reminded of the most highly developed country areas of his own nation. In the part of the plain that was not irrigated, in the hilly areas, and in the part around Mantua, which had recently been incorporated into the state of Milan, the level of life and of agricultural productiveness was nearer the Italian average, and less well sustained. But one new element with a great future was the cultivation of mulberry trees, which spread increasingly, and was accompanied by the development of a domestic industry specializing in the first processes for the treatment of wild silk, which, as we have seen, was Lombardy's main export. So even the least advanced areas of Lombard agriculture were becoming part of a pattern of trade, and benefiting from the favourable economic situation.

This general development of production was not accompanied by any corresponding social advance; social relations and political institutional structures remained rigid. Most of the land belonged to great estates, which were the property of the nobility and of ecclesiastical orders. In fact, 75 per cent of the estates larger than forty hectares, and 100 per cent of those larger than a hundred hectares, belonged to the nobility or the clergy. In the Mantua area 50 per cent of cultivable land was divided among 437 big landowners and 543 religious institutions, while the rest was broken up among 24,000 small or medium-sized proprietors, mainly small ones. There was therefore only a very small bourgeois farming class, which was confined to the land-holders of lower Lombardy. But these men, though they were largely free to run their holdings as they wished, and had good opportunities of earning and accumulating wealth, still remained dependent on the landlord, and found themselves part of a system of social relations and attitudes that made their social promotion to the bourgeois level a difficult process. The bourgeois elements in the towns found themselves in a similar situation. The wealthiest among them, the 'farmers' of taxes, which they administered on behalf of the state, had made their fortunes by profiting from a system of taxation that claimed tribute from the humble, while touching the privileged lightly or letting them off altogether. These tax-exactors were thus typical representatives of a third estate, integrated within the system of the *ancien régime*. The problem that faced the Austrian administration under Maria Theresa and Joseph II, and with which it grappled, was to adapt the system of social relations to the level reached by forces of production.

It was an imposing task, which took fifty years and involved the co-operation of a team of extremely able people. These included the Tuscan Pompeo Neri, who was in charge of the land-register compiled under Maria Theresa, Gian Rinaldo Carli, an Istrian, who was chairman of the upper council for the economy, Pietro Verri and Cesare Beccaria, both Milanese, who performed various delicate tasks concerned with state administration. Parini too played a part: he was editor of the '*Gazzetta di Milano*' under Maria Theresa, and under Joseph II superintendent of the new public schools that had replaced those run by the Jesuits. So the best brains of Lombardy, and not only of Lombardy, were enlisted in the courageous innovatory effort of the enlightened Habsburg despotism.

The starting-point for all successive reforms was Maria Theresa's land-register, which had been begun in the reign of Charles VI and then allowed to lapse, owing to the resistance shown by the privileged sections of the community. It was completed by a specially formed commission, between 1748 and 1755, and finally put into effect in 1760. In spite of its limitations, and the exemptions that survived, this register provided the Habsburg government with a precise instrument for making a wholesale transfer of the tax-load on to land and property, and relieving the burden of personal taxes and taxes on trade. On the other hand, the valuation of land had been made once and for all, and landlords were thus safe from subsequent increases of the taxes levied on their property if they made improvements and increased their incomes. This meant that cultivation was extended to a great deal of previously neglected land: for once, the process of taxation was economically productive.

The reform programme had begun well, and continued from 1760 to 1790 at a brisk pace. Hardly any sector of public life or the structure of the state remained unaffected. First of all, local government was restructured, on the basis of an administrative division of the state into provinces and communes; this had the double aim of quelling the conflicts between town and country, by including both of them in a single territorial unit, and of handing over local administration to those landowners who, because of the new land-register, now made a sizable contribution to the state's income. It was in fact laid down that the 'deputies' of the various local councils were to be chosen exclusively from among those who paid the land-tax.

The reform movement worked inwards towards the centre, concentrating above all on financial administration, with the creation of a higher council for the economy in 1765, replaced in 1771 by a chamber of magistrates aided by a department of accounts. Also in the financial sector, the reform of direct taxes was followed by a reform of indirect taxes, and of the 'royalties' received by the tax 'farmers'. These men had protectors even in Vienna, and the struggle against them was a hard one, in which Pietro Verri played a leading part. In the end it was successful: in 1770 the 'farmers' ' lucrative activity was taken over by the Public Treasury. Up to this point reforms had been chiefly concerned with reorganizing taxation, and with the rearrangement of the administration, which was a necessary precondition of tax-reform. But from 1771 there was a fresh wave of reforms aimed at other sectors and levels of society and of the state. The first problem to be faced was that of relations between the state and the organization of the Church, and the related question of teaching and schools. Many monastic schools were closed down and their incomes taken over by the Treasury to be used for the reorganization of public schools. The Jesuit order was dissolved and its schools closed. In contrast, greater authority was given to the University of Pavia, one of the strongholds of Italian Jansenism, whose teachers included Alessandro Volta and Lazzaro Spallanzani. This was not all: a series of chain-measures abolished the guilds, restrictions were imposed on fidei commissum, the Inquisition tribunal was banned, and a monetary reform was undertaken. We must also remember the great progress made in road-building and communications: in 1776 Milan was linked with the Adda by the Paderno canal. To complete the picture of the last years of Maria Theresa's government, there was a harmonious relationship between the arts and public patronage; the neoclassical theatre of La Scala was opened in 1778, and the Cannobiana theatre a few years later. Under Maria Theresa the people of Milan were, wrote Pietro Verri, as happy 'as it is possible to be under absolute rule'.

But the period of enlightened despotism in Lombardy was not yet over: with the accession to the Viennese throne of the vigilant Joseph II (1780–90) it entered its most intense phase. In 1786 Milan was overwhelmed by a 'torrent of innovations', to quote the historian Custodi. New and severer jurisdictional measures were introduced, the territorial limits of the provinces were adjusted, customs duties reformed, and the free movement of goods within the state decreed; all the old established bodies within the state, including the venerable Senate, were abolished. All this took place as part of a meticulous process of bureaucratic centralization. As it approached the end of its course, Austria's enlightened despotism showed itself increasingly enlightened but also increasingly despotic. The people of Milan felt this, and Joseph II was not as popular with them as Maria Theresa had been, as Pietro Verri states in his work *Riflessioni sullo Stato di Milano nell'anno 1790*. Verri, one of the protagonists of the reform movement, seems now disheartened and worried.

This sense of unease can probably be explained by the fact that the administration, in spite of its impressive effort at reform, had not sufficiently encouraged the formation, within the society it had reformed, of social forces sufficiently powerful and self-aware to carry on the work of reform themselves. Perhaps in spite of their energy and thoroughness, those who put through the programme of reform were guilty of timidity, in restricting it largely to financial and administrative questions, and only rarely extending it to the economic sector. It is for example significant that the most incisive and 'bourgeois' reform, that concerning the free movement of goods within the state, was one of the last to be put into effect. But it must also be emphasized that success was hard to achieve, owing to the immaturity of a bourgeoisie that had for too long been used to forming a part of the system, and to the power of the aristocracy to resist – it was prepared to accept a rationalization of its supremacy, but not to give it up, entirely or in part. A revolution from above only has some chance of success when it can break through at a chosen moment, with the sustained help of independent action from below, and with the emergence of new social forces. In Lombardy in the eighteenth century a nearer approach to this break-through was made than in any other part of Italy. But it was not achieved; for that, other shocks and upheavals would be necessary.

HABSBURG REFORM: TUSCANY AND MODENA

After the Medici dynasty died out in 1737, Tuscany, as we have seen, was assigned to Francis II of Lorraine, Maria Theresa's husband. He did not move from Vienna, and the country was ruled by a council of regency until 1765. Even in this period the reformist tendency of the new dynasty became evident. In the economic field, the free exportation of corn from the Maremma was decreed in 1738; in administration, measures limiting fidei commissum and mortmain were introduced; in the field of Church-state relations, ecclesiastical censorship of books was abolished, and favours were conceded to the prosperous Jewish colony of Leghorn. But the true period of Lorraine reformism in Tuscany began with the accession of Peter Leopold, who, like his brother Joseph II, was steeped in Enlightenment culture and Jansenist ideas.

Peter Leopold's programme of reform also availed itself of the services of an array of able, trained specialists, outstanding among whom were Francesco Gianni, and Pompeo Neri, who had worked on Maria Theresa's land-register. The reform programme aimed above all at achieving a complete freeing of the market both of land and of produce. Between 1766 and 1773 a series of scaled measures made the internal and the export trade in corn completely free, abolishing the network of internal restrictions and tolls that had hindered it. At the same time another series of measures freed the land by dealing a mortal blow to the institutions of fidei commissum and mortmain. By these actions the Lorraine government not only advanced the good principles of triumphant physiocracy but also the interests of the landowners, who wanted to sell, to export, and to swell their possessions, to the cost of the religious and chivalrous orders. From that time on, free trade became one of the economic and political dogmas of the Tuscan landowners. Parallel with this work of economic liberalization, Peter

Leopold and his colleagues completely restructured the systems of administration and taxation. For the cutting of economic bonds and the end of the city's privileges in matters of food and provisions demanded that power be transferred and disseminated from the capital to the countryside. The magistracy of the *conservatori della giurisdizione del dominio fiorentino* (preservers of Florentine rule) which had up to that time presided over the affairs of the countryside, and the analogous institutions that existed in the other major cities of the state, were abolished. In their place, local administrations were set up in each community, having considerable autonomy, and being composed largely of local landowners and squires. The tax-structure also was simplified and decentralized, with the establishment of a single land-tax, and the abolition of still existing exemptions. The tax-load was thus more equably distributed. Budgets were made public.

In Tuscany too the greatest strides were made in the struggle against ecclesiastical privileges. On the model of what Joseph II was doing at Vienna, and with the help of the vigorous Jansenist element in the Tuscan episcopacy and clergy, Peter Leopold went so far as to propose a reform of the Church during the last years of his reign. But the innovations suggested by Scipione de'Ricci, Bishop of Prato and of Pistoia, and the ideas of clearly Jansenist inspiration that he put forward, met first the hostility of the mass of the rural population, who saw themselves cheated of the symbols and beliefs of their traditional faith, then that of the clergy, who met in council in Florence in 1787, and declared themselves against the continuation of the experiment. The Grand Duke had to give in with a good grace, and the Tuscan Jansenists had to choose between retracting their errors or persevering in them to the point of embracing, some years later, openly democratic and Jacobin ideas.

In spite of this failure, Tuscan reformism and enlightened absolutism had many positive achievements to its credit by the late 1780's. Besides the measures already mentioned, the government could boast of the abolition of city guilds, decreed in 1781, of works of land-reclamation in the Val di Chiana and elsewhere, a noteworthy series of public works and, last but not least, the abolition of the death penalty and of torture. The instruments of torture were publicly burned, and Tuscany could claim to be the first country of Europe to put Beccaria's ideas into effect.

But what has been said of Lombardy also applies to Tuscany. The agriculture of Tuscany was nothing like that of lower Lombardy, it is true, and since it was in a more backward state the breaking-point that has been spoken of could only be seen as a long-term objective. It was not merely a question of clearing the way for those forces whose weight naturally pushed in the direction of the renewal of traditional structures and the modernization of agriculture; first, those forces had to be created. However long this process would be, a necessary stage was the modification of traditional agricultural contracts and relationships, and in particular the system of *métayage*, which had dominated the Tuscan countryside for centuries.

Francesco Gianni showed himself aware of this when in 1769 he presented the Grand Duke with the 'instructions' in which he proposed that the lands of the Conservatorio di San Bonifacio, a great charitable institution, should be leased out in semi-perpetuity, in such a way that the leaseholder, for an initial sum and an annual rent paid to the Conservatorio, acquired all rights in the land. Gianni's openly declared aim was to put 'the land in the hands of those who work it, above all', and so to encourage the formation of a class of independent landowning farmers. The suggestion was made by the Grand Duke himself, as his own personal wish, but those who had put the idea forward and supported it soon had to recognize that the resistance along this road was not small or insignificant.

The squires and landowners, whose weight in the society of Tuscany had been considerably increased by the recent reforms of local administration, certainly wished for the large estates of lay and ecclesiastical charities to be brought onto the market, but wished to benefit from the operation themselves. The land in question, they argued, should not be let but sold, and the new proprietors should run it according to the traditional system of *métayage*. *Métayage* was, they said, the cornerstone of Tuscan society: woe to anyone who made any attempt on it. These interests found distinguished supporters in the Accademia dei Georgofili, the high council of Tuscan landowners. Here is how one of them, Ferdinando Paoletti, spoke out against the mooted possibility of public authority stepping in to adjust the relations between master and peasant:

The right of property cannot exist without liberty. . . . Whatever arrangement offends or alters this liberty also offends and alters property. . . . If the traditional terms of our contract are changed by positive laws, liberty and in consequence property will immediately be affected . . . social laws must tend only to safeguard the rights of property; the tutelary authority must be the protector, not the regulator of private interests. . . . In any public administration whatsoever, agriculture and all that relates to it must bear on its brow the sign '*noli me tangere*'.

Paoletti was not alone in upholding such views. Pompeo Neri himself did not think very differently, which explains his opposition to Gianni's plan.

This resistance did not prevent the experiment from running its course in the following years; land belonging to charities, to ecclesiastical orders, and finally, even land belonging to the ruling house, went the same way as the estates of the Conservatorio di San Bonifacio. But the opponents of the scheme managed to slow it down and partly to nullify its effects by managing things so that in more than one case land, instead of being leased to those who had worked on it with their own hands, was sold en bloc, which was of course to the advantage of those with more capital. If we add that many of the new leaseholders were later probably forced to give up the land assigned to them, it is easy to see why the operation launched by Gianni had, in the end, no significant results. On the land of the Conservatorio di San Bonifacio itself, in 1779 only 25 per cent of the rent came from leaseholders who had previously been *métayers*, while 62 per cent came from members of the nobility and bourgeoisie, and from country brokers and traders. Five years later, in 1784, the disproportion had increased to 19 per cent and 69 per cent.

The Tuscan landowners not only lacked capital, in many cases, but also the farsightedness and courage needed to undertake a large-scale work of agricultural reform. So in the end they chose the shorter way, and to the uncertain profits of a long-term investment preferred the safer, more familiar profits to be gained by putting harder pressure on their peasants. This is shown by the fact that the peasants remained heavily in debt to the landowners, and in some cases more than previously. The squires of Tuscany were ready to support the government's reforms so long as these coincided with their own interests, but came out in opposition as soon as reform threatened to graze that touchstone of Tuscan society, *métayage*. In the long run the effect of such reform as had been achieved was bound to diminish progressively.

During the last years of his reign, Peter Leopold hinted at the introduction of a constitution that would include an assembly charged with exercising its own control over the state's financial administration. But in a society where the quantitative increase of production had been contained within the framework of traditional, if not archaic, agricultural relations, it is unlikely that such a constitution would have been anything but a twin of the Accademia dei Georgofili, more a hindrance than a tool for the enlightened ruler.

Modena too belongs to the area of Austrian reform. For Duke Francesco III d'Este was bound by family and political ties to the Viennese court, and his main colleagues were trusted members of the Austrian government. Besides, his state was crossed by new roads: the Abetone and the road towards Massa, which made its position too important for Austria not to wish to control it. At Modena also, therefore, the reformist measures of Maria Theresa and Joseph II were applied.

Here too steps were taken against mortmain, monastic schools were suppressed, war was waged against the tax 'farmers' and, finally, a new land-register was completed in 1788, on the basis of which the whole tax-system was revised. But at Modena too there was one barrier that was not passed: the struggle against the 'farmers' achieved no more than the substitution of local ones for the Milanese. At Modena too, the blows struck against the property and privileges of the nobility were a good deal less severe than those against ecclesiastical property and privilege.

BOURBON REFORM: NAPLES, SICILY, PARMA

In the Kingdom of Naples too, agriculture profited from the century's favourable circumstances. The population increase (to nearly five million inhabitants by the end of the century), the consequent broadening of the market and the rise in prices were factors in the development of production in the southern countryside, as elsewhere. There is a regrettable lack of available data, and little research has been done in the field, but it is hard to imagine that the substantial increase in agricultural exports did not reflect a similar increase in production and a trend towards more profitable and more commercial types of cultivation such as oils and silks.

These different forms of progress undoubtedly acted as a stimulus towards a modernization and rationalization of the Kingdom's farming structures, and towards the removal of the heavy feudal encrustations that still weighed on landowning. Had these influences been helped by the co-operation of the social forces that were most concerned, towards a transformation of this kind, they might have cut deeply into the whole texture of southern life. But, as we shall see, such a cooperation existed only in a very small degree.

First of all, there was no hope that the baronial class would act so as to encourage this transformation. Unlike the Lombard landowners, and even the squires of Tuscany, the southern feudal lords, entirely lacking any tradition of business and trading, and long since used to living in the capital and at court, saw their rents only in terms of the prestige they brought and the extravagance they allowed. It is not surprising therefore that in the long run many of them found themselves in difficulties, and were compelled to sell part of their estates to parvenus of various origins, to peasants of substance, to businessmen and professional men. The documents of the period in fact show that these social groups continued to amass property throughout the century.

These new-rich were without doubt a more dynamic class, less paralyzed in their economic ventures by taboos and social fetishes. But the obstacles that were placed in the way of their rising further were such that their energies were often wasted and dissipated on the way. First of all we must remember that the landownership they had achieved was rarely free of feudal types of taxes and obligations; in consequence many of them found themselves engaged in a struggle on two fronts, against the claims of the local baron, who laid claim to pre-eminent rights over all the lands within his jurisdiction, and against the community of the local people and their organizations, who demanded the perpetuation of the communal grazing rights they had enjoyed since time immemorial. Even if the bourgeois landowner emerged victorious from this hard struggle and, as did happen in certain cases, managed to enforce his right to a full and free control over his own land, even to the point of enclosing it, his difficulties were not yet over.

Unlike nobles and ecclesiastics, bourgeois landowners were forced to pay taxes, and these were neither few nor light. The new Bourbon dynasty, with its regal ambitions and pompous monuments, was no less extravagant than the previous Spanish administration, and the tax system introduced by the Spanish had not been substantially modified.

The sector of economic life that bore the heaviest weight of taxation was certainly trade. The export duties on oil and silk, for example, were extremely high, not to mention the corn 'bills'. But in the last analysis these taxes too fell on agriculture: the merchants were forced to make up for the depredations made on their profits, to the cost of the producers of the goods they acquired. One of the merchants' most frequent methods was the 'verbal contract' by which the merchant made a cash advance to assure himself the right to buy at harvest-time, on the basis of the official price, which was fixed each season by the local authority, and was lower than the normal market-price.

Encumbered by the surrounding feudal institutions, weighed down by taxes and exposed to middlemen, the bourgeois landowners were hindered from developing their properties, and many of them found themselves reduced to the traditional method of exploiting peasant labour to the utmost. So instead of combating the baronage they ended by joining it, inheriting its attitude, and, in the long run, its absenteeism, So in the southern countryside that element of demarcation and conflict between the classes, which might have brought about a resolution of the crisis, was gradually worn away.

For in such a loosely united society, the relations between various social groups tended in any case to crumble into a cloud of local, personal disputes and litigations, an atmosphere in which a horde of lawyers, notaries and pettifoggers flourished. Like its immense, dolorous capital, whose streets bustled with the frenetic, inconclusive activity of a varied, disparate crowd of princes and *lazzaroni*, powerful men and social outcasts, southern society revolved about a vacuum. It was unable to produce from within itself the energies that could have revived it.

But that which could not emerge under its own power from within, could have been provoked from outside, if the government had been bold in its reforms and had acted incisively. But we shall see that this was not the case.

The new king, Don Carlos of Bourbon, who succeeded to the throne of Naples in 1734, had an exalted view of his own position as a monarch. In this he was a true Bourbon and descendant of Louis xiv, from whom he inherited a taste for building on a monumental scale. His was the driving spirit behind the palaces of Caserta – a true southern Versailles – and Capodimonte, and he encouraged the archaeological excavations of Pompeii, one of the great cultural events of the century. But Don Carlos had enough political sense to realize that in the enlightened eighteenth century the glory of a king was measured by the breadth and depth of his reforms. For this reason he surrounded himself with able, enlightened ministers, most notable of whom was the Tuscan Bernardo Tanucci, who, when the King had to give up the throne of Naples for that of Spain in 1759, became the leading member of the council of regency responsible for governing the Kingdom during the minority of the new King, Ferdinando iv.

The most effective reforms made by the Bourbon monarchy and by Tanucci were those in the field of state/Church relations. The immunity of ecclesiastical property from taxation was reduced, the Inquisition and the right of sanctuary were suppressed, the wealth of numerous monasteries was confiscated, mortmain was restricted, and a concordat was drawn up, which put the relations between the monarchy and Rome on a more equal footing. This reform policy, characterized by severe hostility to the papal Curia, was in entire harmony with the juridical training and lawyer-like outlook that prevailed among the Neapolitan intellectuals. They had been taught by Pietro Giannone, author of the *Storia civile del regno di Napoli*, whom the Church had persecuted and driven into exile and prison.

But in the Kingdom of Naples even more than elsewhere, the privileges of the clergy and the ecclesiastical orders, however enormous and encumbering (there were seventy-five thousand priests and monks in the Kingdom, and their rents came to between two and a half and six and a half million ducats), were only a part of the 'system'. Implacably pursuing them, almost exclusively, could and in fact did mean choosing the easiest and most exposed target, while the main citadels of the *ancien régime* remained unharmed and unattacked.

Very little was in fact done to dismantle the privileges and 'feudal abuses' of the baronage, to reform the fiscal and administrative apparatus, to attack the parasitism of the capital in relation to the provinces. The general land-register launched by Don Carlos of Bourbon in 1741 could have provided the foundation for this complex work of reform, but instead, because of the imprecise way in which it was drawn up, and even more because of the firm resistance it met in the capital and in the provinces from those whose privileges it threatened, it turned out to be a very imperfect instrument. Other isolated and disconnected measures produced only partial successes of little significance, and in the end the work of reform undertaken by Don Carlos and his team came to an end without having harmed the structures of the *ancien régime* or alleviated, let alone removed, its abuses.

We can see how intolerable and engrained those abuses were from the dreadful famine of 1764, when Naples drew crowds of starving people, the living evidence of the conditions in which the vast majority of the Kingdom's population were forced to live, conditions, Genovesi was to say, worthy of Hottentots, not of the inhabitants of highly-civilized Europe. This tragic spectacle was a traumatic experience for a generation of intellectuals that was perhaps the most brilliant in the long history of southern culture, the generation of Genovesi, Palmieri, Galanti, Filangieri and Pagano. Unlike the previous generation, who had grown up in the spirit of Giannone's anticurialism, and with a largely legal education, the Neapolitan intellectuals of the later eighteenth century had been brought up on the writings of the Enlightenment and on political and economic studies. Their master, Genovesi, held the first chair of political economy, or rather 'trade and mechanics', in Italy. Starting from these premises, they were quick to develop the conviction that the Kingdom's problems and crises could only be solved by means of a struggle without quarter against all feudal abuses, of the clergy, of the barons and of the capital, and by means of a regeneration of society from its basis, agriculture.

Their hour seemed to have arrived in the 1770's, when the court was dominated by the new queen, Maria Carolina, a dynamic daughter of Maria Theresa, who had joined a masonic lodge, and assumed the position of a protectress of new men and new ideas. Some of them were given public posts and consultant positions. Giuseppe Palmieri, for instance, was made director of the High Council of Finance. But they soon realized that the resistance of the powerful classes and the financial difficulties of the monarchy overshadowed all proposals or ambitions for reform. Palmieri was perhaps the most bitterly disillusioned of all: his project for the reform of export tariffs on oil and silk was discussed at length but never put into effect, and the law that he succeeded in bringing out in 1791, which was intended to tax feudal estates and give preference to the needier farmers, achieved nothing positive or practical either. In any case, apart from its meagre results, Neapolitan reform of the 1780's and 1790's was a late fruit: by this time many were beginning to look beyond the frontiers of the Kingdom and of Italy, to France and its revolution.

A special case is that of Sicily, which had a separate régime within the Kingdom, being ruled by a viceroy, and having kept its parliament. The barons, although many of them were forced to let their fiefs to parvenus of peasant extraction, the so-called *gabellotti*, were much more unified than those on the mainland, and were traditionally used to considering themselves as the island's only representatives, and their deeply-rooted privileges as subject to no outside power. The clash between the Sicilian barons and the monarchy's proposals of reform was therefore a frontal one. It reached its climax in the years 1781–6, when the Marchese Caracciolo was sent to the island as viceroy. He was a pupil of Genovesi's, who had frequented the salons of Paris and returned from them deeply imbued with the spirit of the Enlightenment. He managed to obtain some successes, particularly in the struggle against the privileges of the Church and the more patent abuses of the feudal system. Even so, he was in the end forced to give up the struggle without bringing to fruition a scheme for a land-register, which would have provided the basis for a true abolition of feudalism. His successor, the Prince of Caramanico, who stayed on the island until 1794, followed a more moderate line of action, with the result that in Sicily too the age of reform passed without producing notable results. The most important, perhaps, and the one that had the furthest-reaching consequences, was of a negative kind: the new impulse given to the traditional Sicilian spirit of independence. Once again the barons had a good hand – they were able to make their defence of their own interests seem like a fight to the end to save Sicily from foreign interference.

In 1748 the Duchy of Parma was also assigned to the Bourbons, in the person of Filippo, a son of Elisabetta Farnese, and son-in-law of Louis xv. He entrusted the education of his son to Condillac, and the affairs of the state to a Frenchman, du Tillot, who followed a policy of reform designed essentially to strike at the privileges of the clergy and to promote the establishment of manufacture. To this end he encouraged the immigration of foreign workers and technicians. But this aroused the resentment of many of the common people, who were incited by the nobility and by the court, which after the death of Filippo was dominated by the influence of the Duchess

Maria Amalia, a daughter of Maria Theresa, who was bitterly hostile to the French party. In 1771 popular discontent burst out in violent demonstrations, after which du Tillot was forced to resign. So at Parma too the experiment of reform ended prematurely, and largely failed.

THE STATES WITHOUT REFORM

So far we have looked at the states of Italy that were affected by the eighteenth-century wave of reformism. But there was another Italy that was either completely untouched, or else no more than slightly and superficially skimmed by this wave. And this was not some irrelevant little backwater, but a considerable part of the peninsula.

To this unreformed Italy belong, above all, those states that had largely preserved a traditional structure, characterized, as we know, by a clear division between the dominant city and its territory, and by the economic and administrative subordination of the latter to the former. With the exception of the minute Republic of Lucca with its 120,000 inhabitants, this was the case of the Genoese state. After trying in vain to get the better of the guerrilla uprising led by Pasquale Paoli in Corsica, Genoa had to cede the island to France in 1768, and was reduced, territorially as well as politically, to a city-state, retaining only its occasionally disputed control over the narrow coastal strip of the Riviera. But Genoa was most a city-state in its internal political institutions, which had changed little since the reform of 1576; the city was still under the absolute rule of the banking oligarchy ranked around the Bank of St George. The numbers of this oligarchy had shrunk, so that it had the character of a limited caste, but its enormous financial power allowed it to keep its control over the Republic, leaving to the impoverished nobility and the 'gentle' class the minor posts and tasks in the diplomacy, administration and army, so making use of them to restrain potential popular unrest.

At Venice too, by now reduced to a shadow of the mercantile power it had been, the crisis in the traditional political structures took the form of a narrowing and petrifying of the ruling oligarchy. By this time the families that practically monopolized the heights of power had dwindled to fifty or so, while the remnants of the nobility, the so-called *Barnabotti*, had been reduced to great distress, and had to be content with the meagre earnings of a small coastal trade or with the salaries of minor jobs on the mainland, perhaps swelled by more or less legal tips. The governing bodies, particularly the *Maggior Consiglio*, were at the same time gradually losing their authority, and attempts to restore some of their vitality, such as that made in 1761–2 by the nobleman Angelo Querini, with the support of the *Barnabotti*, were in vain. However, unlike Genoa, Venice had considerable, wide territories, and the way was open to her, at least in theory, towards an adjustment and re-balancing of the relations between capital and mainland. But the conditioning of the past was too strong, and the Venetian oligarchy continued to consider the mainland as an appendage of the city, and to subordinate all chances of development to the city's interests. Venice's territory was without roads, isolated from the outside, divided within into a series of circuits, which were closed by a customs system originally designed to ensure the provisioning of the capital and the sale of its imports; it did not even constitute a true territorial unity, but was a federation of towns, each of which played the lord over its surrounding countryside, and was in turn dominated by a narrow local oligarchy. They were united only by a common rancour towards the bureaucratic and inefficient absolutism to which they were subject. In an age when it was increasingly realized that a modern state could only exist on the basis of a rational and fair territorial administration, this kind of division into watertight compartments was very anachronistic, and it led to a general asphyxia of economic life. It is not surprising that in such a situation there should have been centrifugal tendencies: towards Lombardy in Brescia and Bergamo, towards Austria in Friuli.

These were the warning signs of a crisis that was not far off, as even the Venetian patricians seemed to realize; at least, they behaved as if they realized. Their foreign policy seemed to have no aim but to camouflage the existence of the Republic, and all their acts seemed dominated by that *terreur de l'avenir* which, according to a foreign observer, had gripped the city known throughout Europe for its hectic carnival and for its free behaviour.

This terror of the future did not cause Venetians to forget their attachment to their city. A deep love for Venice is evident in the paintings of Guardi, Canaletto, and the other painters of the city, in the music of Albinoni and of course in Goldoni's plays. The same sentiment is exemplified by the great walls put up by the Republic during its last years of life, to protect itself against the sea, from which it had drawn life, and from which it could now expect nothing but storms. These were the fortifications that protected Venice from the recent flood of November 1966.

The Papal State remains to be mentioned. In the eighteenth century the Papacy's international prestige touched its lowest point ever. Pius VII, whom Napoleon Bonaparte drove out of his state and forced into imprisonment and exile, was not the first pope of that period to suffer humiliation at the hands of those who were for the moment in power. Before him, Clement XVI had in 1773 been forced to dissolve the Society of Jesus, and Pius VI had made a pilgrimage to Vienna in 1782, in the completely hopeless attempt to dissuade Joseph II from his anti-Church policy. We must add the long series of measures limiting the prerogatives and privileges of the clergy, which the popes of the eighteenth century had to suffer from all or almost all the governments of Europe and Italy, and which, apart from everything else, played a considerable part in aggravating the Papal State's already chronic financial crisis. Deprived of what had remained of its international prestige, the Papal State was on practically the same footing as any other of Italy's states, and it was universally considered one of the most backward and badly governed of them.

The panorama it offered to the foreign visitor, beginning with the capital, seemed to embody the antithesis of all that a 'civilized' society should have been, in the eyes of enlightened eighteenth-century opinion. At Rome, Montesquieu said, '*tout le monde est à son aise, excepté ceux qui travaillent, excepté ceux qui ont de l'industrie, excepté ceux qui cultivent les arts, excepté ceux qui ont des terres, excepté ceux qui font du commerce*'.* This description may be highly coloured, but is not entirely unfitted to a city of 140,000 inhabitants who included thousands of beggars and thousands of priests. The rest of the state was for the most part the image of its capital. Going northwards from Rome, the eighteenth-century traveller first encountered the stretches of the Roman countryside and the Maremma of Lazio that had been left desolate and devastated by malaria, then advanced into Umbria and the Marche with their sleepy countryside and their cities and towns where time seemed to have stopped in the days of Albornoz. Only in Ancona, the state's most active port, was there any sign of improvement, which increased as the traveller made his way into the territory of the so-called 'legations'. The countryside here, with its tree-lined roads, its fields planted with hemp, and its irrigation, presented a very different picture from that around Rome, or in the other provinces of the state. At its centre was Bologna, a city of 70,000 people, which, besides having a famous university and a considerable manufacturing activity, was also considered the state's 'land port', sited as it was on or near the junction of important roads and rivers. But the relative prosperity of the northern province was almost entirely the reflection of the general prosperity of the Po area, and as such was a weak rather than strong point for the Papal State. As soon as the chance emerged, centrifugal tendencies were to be expected here too. By what may seem a paradox,

---

* 'everyone is at ease, except those who work, those who own businesses, those who cultivate the arts, those who own land, and those who trade'.

but was not, they began to appear at the very moment when the Papacy gave signs of wishing to embark on a policy of reform, under the pontificate of Pius VI (1775–98).

Pius VI was very unlike his predecessors, in energy and in temperament; he had something of the Renaissance popes' ambitions as a patron of the arts and builder of monuments. His pontificate produced, among other things, the Palazzo Braschi, the opening of the Pio Clementino Museum and the resumption of work on draining the Pontine marshes. But his ambitions of reform had less success. The reform of tributes, designed to simplify exaction and to restrict existing immunities, foundered before the considerable, predictable resistance that was shown it; and its organizer, Cardinal Ruffo, had to resign from the post of General Treasurer. As for the land-register undertaken in 1777, it contained within itself the seeds of its failure, being based on the landlord's own declarations of their property. Only in the legation of Bologna, under the energetic guidance of Cardinal Ignazio Boncompagni Ludovisi, was the land-register drawn up on the basis of an accurate, expert estimate, and it aroused municipal jealousy and anxiety among those who saw in the threat to their privileges an attempt on the city's prerogatives and freedom. It thus provided the first opportunity for the appearance of those centrifugal tendencies that have been mentioned.

It should not greatly surprise us that this took place under the banner of a narrow and cautious conservatism. That a government whose watchward had for centuries been *quieta non movere* should now undertake a policy of reform was bound to seem, to the owners of property, a betrayal. As for the others, who were not landlords, their mistrust of the government was too ancient and too deep to be modified by the unexpected spectacle of a pope with reformist ambitions.

A SPECIAL CASE: SAVOYARD PIEDMONT

Piedmont was the only one of the Italian states of the eighteenth century able to take an active and profitable part in the complicated diplomatic and political manoeuvres of the first part of the century. For the War of the Spanish Succession offered Duke Vittorio Amedeo II a long-awaited chance to break the vassalage to France to which his state had been condemned for decades. During the first stage of this war Piedmont was allied with France, but broke off the alliance in mid-conflict, in 1703, going over to the Austrian side, and so helping to increase Louis XIV's isolation. It was a good political choice: at the end of the war the treaties of Utrecht and Rastadt recognized the Duke's royal title, and assigned him Monferrato, Alessandria and Sicily. (Seven years later, however, this last conquest had to be exchanged for poorer and more backward Sardinia.) The successor of Vittorio Amedeo II, Carlo Emanuele III, carried on his unscrupulous and profitable policies. He allied Piedmont with France in the War of the Polish Succession, and with Austria in that of the Austrian Succession, choosing the winning side in both cases, with the result that in 1748 Piedmont had succeeded in incorporating a considerable part of the rich territories of neighbouring Lombardy, reaching as far as the Ticino. Piedmont's centre of gravity thus moved farther east, towards the Po plain, and towards Italy. But we should guard against seeing eighteenth-century Savoy expansionism as any kind of anticipation of the national policy of Cavour and Vittorio Emanuele II. The goals of Vittorio Amedeo II and Carlo Emanuele III were not national but territorial ones, and their conduct was dictated entirely by questions of opportunity. Proof of this is the fact that in the War of the Austrian Succession they chose the alliance with Maria Theresa and the limited territorial advantages this brought, rather than the French alliance and d'Argenson's plan, which, in a sense, anticipated the policies of Napoleon III in Italy, guaranteeing Lombardy within the framework of a general readjustment of Italy's balance.

Parallel with Piedmont's expansion and the strengthening of its military and diplomatic prestige, the modernization of the state's internal structures went ahead. Vittorio Amedeo II had been alternately the ally and the enemy of Louis XIV, but had always remained his admirer and emulator. In 1717, as soon as the royal crown was securely his, he issued a series of edicts to reform the whole state administration, modelling its structure on Colbert's French system. A Council of State ruled over the various departments, there was a General Council of Finance, and a network of superintendents spread about the various provinces, to ensure the central power's control over them. Made strong by these instruments of government, the King was able to give a free reign to his political actions, whose tendency was to affirm the monarchy's pre-eminence and its rôle of arbiter among the various 'orders' of the state. The clergy's large privileges and immunities were cut down, and their rôle in the traditional activities of public assistance and teaching was made more limited: alms-houses and hospitals run by the state gradually took the place of the clergy's scattered charitable institutions. At the same time the University of Turin was given greater authority, and its teaching body renewed, traditionalists being replaced by men steeped in Gallican and even Jansenist ideas. The nobility too saw their privileges considerably cut down and their lands, included in the land-register decreed by Vittorio Amedeo II, subjected to more regular and punctual taxation. This accelerated the transformation of the nobility from a class of squires and semi-independent feudal landlords into one of army officers, diplomats and government functionaries; although nobles were easily outnumbered by the bourgeois and parvenu element in the field of administration.

To complete the similarity with the France of Louis xiv and Colbert, there was an outstanding series of public works. New roads and canals were opened, and the port of Nice, which then constituted the kingdom's only access to the sea, was enlarged. The development of the state's capital was particularly intense, which accounts for the dramatic population-increase already mentioned. During the eighteenth century Turin acquired the symmetrical and regal character that still gives its historic centre a different appearance from that of any other Italian city. The greater part of the buildings erected in this period, the Superga basilica, built to celebrate the victory of 1706 over the French, the Palazzo Madama, and many others, were the work of a Sicilian architect, Filippo Juvara, whom Vittorio Amedeo brought to Turin, and who was something of an Italian Mansart.

The complex governmental activity of the new Savoy monarchy was most intense during the first thirty years of the century, and was thus earlier than that of the other reformist Italian rulers. When Vittorio Amedeo reformed the administration of his state, gave power to the University of Turin and struggled against the abuses of the clergy and the nobility, the Medici still ruled Florence, Naples had not yet been restored to independence, and the happy period of Maria Theresa's reforms had not yet begun in Lombardy.

However, the difference is not merely one of chronology but also, more important, one of kind. For the measures taken by the Savoy monarchy belong, as we have seen, within the pattern of a classic type of absolutism like Louis xiv's, rather than that of the enlightened despotism of eighteenth-century princes such as Joseph II. This is clear above all if one considers the sector of economic policy: Piedmont saw nothing like the liberalization of the market of land and produce that was in fact achieved in Lombardy and Tuscany, and Piedmont's economic life went on developing mainly within the limiting context of city mercantilism and restrictiveness. This certainly did not help bourgeois fortunes and enterprises, which were however substantial, especially in the provinces that had formerly belonged to Lombardy, where rice was grown widely, and a rent-system of a capitalist type generally practised. The export trade in raw silk, which was the major resource of the agriculture of much of Piedmont, was hindered by a government policy aimed at encouraging the development of Piedmontese silk-manufacture, and the small groups of people connected with it. The result was that the bourgeois classes were encouraged to 'integrate' into the system of absolute monarchy, by way of government offices and the acquisition of noble titles, and that the centralized, bureaucratic structure of the state gradually repressed the germs of reform that had been hatching in the very texture of society. In the long run, even the reformist energy of the monarchy was in turn checked, and in fact this regressive tendency already emerged during the last years of the reign of Vittorio Amedeo II. In 1727 a concordat was signed that meant the virtual renunciation of the anti-curialist policy previously followed; in 1736 the exile Pietro Giannone was arrested and imprisoned, and a number of the university teachers of most advanced views dismissed. In the following decades the reactionary tendency became more marked, reaching its extreme in the reign of Vittorio Amedeo III (1773–96). While in Milan, Florence and Naples the reform movement was at its height, in Piedmont every progressive proposal was dropped, and Turin became the greyest of Italian capitals, the one that was most effectively shielded from the light of progress by its barriers of censorship and conservatism, the stolid barracks of Enlightened Italy.

Savoy absolutism still retained some impetus only in its contact with the archaic social structure of Sardinia; but in this case too its actions were sporadic and disorganized, and succeeded more in provoking the resentment of the powerful classes whom reform had disturbed than in drawing the approval and support of other social classes.

It is not surprising that the more restless spirits sought to escape from the stifling atmosphere of Piedmont in the later eighteenth century. The first famous instance of the Piedmontese intellectual emigration was Alberto Radicati di Passerano, an aristocrat who, after a hectic and spendthrift youth (he was married at seventeen, a widower at nineteen and remarried at twenty-three) threw himself wholeheartedly into the service of Vittorio Amedeo II, believing that he was to participate in a great work of political and religious reform. But he was disillusioned by the concordat of 1727, and his protests and intemperance forced him to leave the state and become a traveller and adventurer, first in England and then in Holland, where he died in 1737, after having set down in his writings his dream of a religion restored to the purity of a natural deism and a society brought back to the state of nature. But the prince of Piedmontese rebels and *émigrés* was Count Vittorio Alfieri, even though his rebellion was confined within the limits of an individual act of anarchic protest. Peevish, as aristocratic writers are, Alfieri aimed his protest one moment against the conservatism of the Turin court, the next against the excesses of the Paris Revolution, at all times against the vulgarity of the 'plebeians' and of the 'sesquiplebeians', the term with which he stigmatized the bourgeois and parvenu classes. But it was not necessary to have the temperament of Alfieri or Radicati to find the atmosphere of Savoy and Piedmont unfavourable: men of less exceptional mettle and less brilliant intelligence were driven into exile, prison or silence. These included the astronomer Lagrange, who had been one of the founders of the Academy of Sciences, Francesco Dalmazzo Vasco, author of writings on economics and politics, and the Abbot Carlo Denina, a scholar of integrity.

In short, from the political and intellectual point of view, Piedmont was a depressed area of eighteenth-century Italy, a fact which it is difficult to reconcile with the rôle it was to play in Italian history during the next century. But in this connection it must not be forgotten that the Savoy kingdom was the most seasoned and tested of Italian states. The Piedmontese nobility, unlike that of other states, was not composed of aristocrats and bourgeois who had returned to the land during the centuries of stagnation and economic depression, but was an ancient nobility that drew from its chivalrous origins the habit of command and obedience. The King himself was the descendant of feudal lords who, like their compeers beyond the Alps, had worked for centuries to impose their authority as absolute sovereigns. Turin had never been a city on the Italian model, ruling over the surrounding countryside, but was an old fortified place that had relatively recently been transformed into a capital. In other words, Piedmont's historical development had to some extent been a repetition, on a smaller scale, of that of the great states north of the Alps: the transformation of a feudal monarchy into an absolute monarchy, effected by the continuity of institutions and customs. The history of the formation of the Savoy state had not shown either the early spring or the prolonged autumn that had characterized that of the cities and states of commune-Italy. Piedmont was the oldest and most seasoned of Italian states, but also in a sense the youngest and most flexible.

9

The French Revolution and Italy

JACOBIN ITALY

The analysis that has been made in the previous chapter of the Italian
states in the eighteenth century has shown clearly that the area of
enlightened reform was confined to certain of them: to Austrian
Lombardy, Lorrainese Tuscany and the Kingdom of Naples. Almost
all the rest of Italy was excluded. Furthermore, by the 1780's the reform
movement in Naples, Parma and even in Florence was on the wane
and showing signs of fatigue and reaction. Only in Lombardy, under
Joseph II's impulse, did it still retain any impetus.

So it is not true, as some nationalistic historians have maintained,
that the French Revolution of 1789 interrupted, with its 'excesses',
an ordered movement of progress, or that without this vast and influential event the goals of the social and political reform of Italy would
easily have been reached and passed. In 1789 the cycle of Enlightenment reform was more or less closed, and some of the men who had
supported it were moving towards more radical solutions: so they did
not hesitate to make the immortal principles of the Revolution their
own. This was the case of what we may call the 'left wing' of Neapolitan
reformers, and of most of the Jansenist clergy. Pietro Verri himself,
though far from having a revolutionary temperament, regretted that
the shining French example had met misunderstanding and even
hostility among his compatriots. He commented bitterly:

> French ideas serve as a model for other peoples. . . . What will happen to
> Italy? We are immature and not yet worthy to live under the reign of virtue.
> Because of our desire to be cunning we are, like the Greeks, the rejected
> people of Europe, after having been its masters.

But naturally, those who most rapidly and unconditionally espoused
the cause of the French revolutionaries were the younger generation.

They organized and took part in the enthusiastic, improvised revolutionary attempts and movements of 1794–5 in Piedmont, Bologna, Palermo and Sardinia. Luigi Zamboni, a law student who was one of the organizers of revolt in Bologna, was only twenty-three when he was executed in 1795, and Emanuele De Deo, hanged at Naples in 1794 for conspiracy, was twenty-two. The ideals of these young men may approximately be defined as 'Jacobin'. Rousseau was their favourite author, the Constitution of the year one their political model. The fact that in the France of the Directory the Jacobins were going through a difficult time did not stop them looking to the sister Latin country as the only possible liberator of Italy.

Besides, France already had a foothold in Italy. Corsica's struggle for liberty had been followed passionately by enlightened Italian opinion, and among the enlightened Pasquale Paoli had been one of the most popular men of the century. Now that Corsica, an Italian land by language and tradition, had become French, and France had become revolutionary, the idea of making the island a common feature of the French revolution that had taken place, and the Italian one to come, soon developed. In 1790 Filippo Buonarroti, a descendant of Michelangelo and a 'Jacobin' student at the University of Pisa, moved to Corsica and there started the publication of a periodical, the *Giornale patriottico di Corsica*, which may be considered the prototype of the press of the Italian *Risorgimento*. In 1794 France, which had been at war with Austria and Piedmont for two years, and had already annexed Nice and Savoy, occupied the Oneglia territory, and Buonarroti was appointed Commissaire. He took the chance to move his headquarters from the island to the mainland, and established closer contact with other representatives and centres of Italian patriotism. But his Jacobinism and Robespierrism earned him a recall to Paris and several months of arrest. When freed, he went on planning the Italian revolution, and tried, by his writings and conspiratorial action, to win to the cause the members of the Directory and the most prominent members of the Army of Italy, including its commander, another Corsican, Napoleon Bonaparte. In the mean time he played an active part in the *Babouviste* Conspiracy of the Equals: for him, the cause of the Italian revolution was one with that of French Jacobinism. But his attempts failed, both in France and in Italy: almost simultaneously the Conspiracy of the Equals was discovered and the armistice between France and the King of Sardinia was signed at Cherasco. Buonarroti was arrested, and his Italian friends who, following his instructions, had set up a revolutionary community in the Piedmontese town of Alba and sent out a call to Piedmontese and Lombard revolutionary forces, had to give up their plans. Alba itself, according to the terms of the armistice, was handed back to the King of Sardinia.

Buonarroti had been the first to try to reconcile the cause of Italian revolution and the interests of the new Thermidorian France; but it now seemed that no such partnership was possible, between the anxieties of a revolution that was not yet begun, and the concern for respectability and stability of one that was already accomplished. As far as Italy was concerned, the foreign policy of the new France seemed no different from that of the *ancien régime*: once the 'natural frontiers' had been reached, with the acquisition of Nice and Savoy sanctioned by the armistice of Cherasco, and when France was sure of its military control of Piedmont, the Directory seemed concerned with raising on the other fronts the military force necessary to bring Austria to the conference table. It was natural to suppose that this treaty would affect Italy only in so far as it would involve an adjustment of the balance between the two major continental powers.

But in periods of revolution and civil war the most logical predictions are often proved wrong, and the course of events takes unimagined directions, especially when such an exceptional personality as Napoleon Bonaparte is concerned. The new commander of the Army of Italy was certainly not the man to be satisfied with the secondary rôle assigned him by the Directory. Between May 1796 and April 1797, in less than a year, he achieved an unprecedented series of military victories, occupied the whole of northern Italy, pushed as far as the gates of Vienna and forced Austria into peace discussions at Leoben. Napoleon had won from the Directory a liberty of movement and initiative which he used to promote his own personal policy in Italy.

On the whole, this policy did not differ from that of the Directory, and it was always subordinated to France's national interests. But, unlike the Paris Directors, Napoleon realized that a steady French influence in Italy could only take root if the aspirations to reform and independence nourished by the Italians who had greeted his armies as liberators were satisfied. It seems to have been on his advice that in September 1796 the general administration of Lombardy, which he had set up in place of the previous régime of military occupation, held a competition for a dissertation on the theme 'Which of the free governments is best suited to the happiness of Italy?' The cream of the Italian intelligentsia took part, including Melchiorre Gioia of Piacenza (who was the winner), Ranza and Botta from Piedmont, the Venetian Fantuzzi, the Florentine Ristori, the Roman Lattanzi and the Neapolitan Galdi. Frenchmen too took part, including Rouher, and a titled poet, Giovanni Fantoni. The solutions proposed were very varied, between the poles of unitary republic, 'one and indivisible', on the French model, and federative republic. But all the dissertations had a common tone of faith and hope. It was however a big step from outlining plans of independence and unity to putting them into effect, and events were to show that Italy's confusion was far more complex than the Jacobins and patriots of 1796 thought.

THE 'SISTER REPUBLICS' AND THE REACTION OF 1799

To begin with, the hopes of those Italians who had saluted Napoleon as the liberator of northern Italy seemed to be at least partially justified by events. From October 1796 to March 1797 a series of congresses were held, at which the representatives of the duchies and legations Bonaparte had removed from papal sovereignty participated. The aim of these congresses was to define the constitution of a 'Cispadane (i.e., south of the Po) Republic', which took the tricolour as its flag. In June this new-born republic was merged into the larger political organism of the Cisalpine Republic, whose capital was Milan, and which also incorporated the Venetian territories of Brescia and Bergamo, the Valtellina, the duchy of Massa Carrara, and the Romagna. So for the first time since the days of Gian Galeazzo Visconti, a powerful state with a flag of its own and an army of its own (the so-called 'Italian legion') existed in northern and central Italy, and could reasonably hope to constitute a centre of attraction and agglomeration for the areas that would later be freed. But every hope of this kind was very soon disappointed. In June 1797 Genoa, which provided the Cisalpine Republic with its natural access to the sea, became a republic in its own right, the Ligurian Republic, and so tied itself down to its old particularism. Venice and the Venetian mainland east of the Adige were on the other hand assigned to Austria by the treaty of Campoformio in October 1797, in spite of the hopes and the protests of Venetian and Cisalpine patriots. Finally, early in 1799, Piedmont was annexed by France.

But even within its original confines, the Cisalpine Republic, with its three and a half million inhabitants, could have constituted a field of action broad enough for an experiment in civil and political reform of national relevance, if it had not been for the heavy French domination. Like the other sister republics, the Cisalpine, in spite of its nominal independence, never for a moment ceased to be subject to a military occupation, with all its consequences: constant requisitions, impositions of very high contributions, which eventually threw the finances of the young state into disorder, the plunder of works of art.

Its rulers, who had in any case been personally chosen by Napoleon, never had effective freedom of movement in relation to the envoys of the Directory, and those who tried to procure some, by refusing, for example, to ratify a treaty of alliance with France that included provision for a very high indemnity to be paid, were abruptly dismissed. This was not all: the Cisalpine constitution had been based on the French constitution of the year three, with its two-chamber system and its suffrage based on tax contributions. In a country whose third estate was not very substantial or aware of itself, and where no revolution had redistributed wealth, this meant handing over power to a limited social group, consisting mainly of noblemen and professional men: people for whom, barring a few exceptions, the fear of the new was in the end stronger than impatience with the old. This entirely suited the plans and desires of Napoleon and the rulers in Paris, who were hostile and mistrustful of the unitarism and extremism of Jacobins and *anarchistes*. But it was less in harmony with the deep, even if unconscious longings for reform that pervaded Italian society.

Yet even with these limits the Cisalpine Republic's two years of existence count for something in the history of modern Italy. For the first time the barrier of municipalism had been broken and Italians of various regions found themselves associated in the assemblies and bodies of a general government. For the first time an Italian city, Milan, of which Stendhal was fond of calling himself a citizen, had taken on the position of a true capital, with its journalism, its clubs, its intellectual life. It represented the gathering-point of the scattered Italian intelligentsia. This political and intellectual enthusiasm was, for the reasons already suggested, only partly translated into concrete governmental activity. Even so, there were some achievements, such as the final abolition of fidei commissum and mortmain, the institution of civil marriage, the delegation of registry tasks to local authorities, the secularization of numerous religious orders and societies. It was too much for an ordinary administration, and too little for a revolutionary government. For this reason the Cisalpine Republic did not succeed in putting down deep roots in Italy.

Similar comments may be made on the other two republics, the Roman and the Neapolitan, that were set up when Napoleon had already left Italy for Egypt, after reopening hostilities against the Pope and against the Bourbons of Naples. The Roman Republic began life in February 1798, and it too had a constitution modelled on that of the year three, and entirely dictated by a French commission. Up to the end it was essentially a protectorate, and its only important acts were the abolition of fidei commissum and the placing of the Jews on the same level as other citizens. The Neapolitan Republic had an even shorter life: it was proclaimed in January 1799, after Championnet's troops had defeated the Bourbon resistance, and only lasted five months. The most notable feature of its very short existence was, as we shall see, its glorious end.

After so many French victories the fate of the Italian countryside was in fact falling into other hands. In the spring of 1799 the Austro-Russian army, under the command of Suvorov, spread across the Po plain, while from Calabria Cardinal Ruffo was getting ready to lead his *sanfedista* bands to the reconquest of Naples. A few months later the French were driven out of Italy, keeping only the stronghold of Genoa. But the victory of the armies of the anti-French coalition would not have been so swift if it had not been aided from within. For during 1799 there developed a popular and peasant guerrilla resistance to France in most parts of the Italian countryside – in Piedmont, in central Italy, in the South. Strange men came to the fore in this cruel rustic war: bandits like the famous Fra Diavolo, who operated among the peasants, ex-officers and foreign agents such as, respectively, Lorenzo Mori and Waugham, who, together with their shared mistress, Alessandra, 'maid' of Valdarno, led the army of Arezzo that attacked the cities of Tuscany and Umbria to the cry of *'viva* Maria!', massacring Jacobins and Jews. And there were cardinals like Fabrizio Ruffo, who landed in Calabria with a handful of men, but reached Naples with an army of peasants and *'lazzaroni'*, the Army of the Holy Faith.

So Italy had its *Vendée* without having had a genuine revolution. But it was perhaps for this reason that the reaction of 1799 was so general and savage. The fanaticism of the peasant bands who raged against the French, the Jacobins and the Jews contained the desperation and rage of those who had once again been disappointed, of men who vented their anger as they could, against whomsoever they could. The princes had spoken of the 'public happiness' and the Jacobins had evoked agricultural law, but in the end the century of enlightenment and revolution had passed without anything in the conditions of their lives having really changed. They now celebrated the century's end in an atmosphere of pandemonium, and took an ephemeral revenge.

The city hit most furiously by the wave of reaction was Naples. Hemmed in by Cardinal Ruffo's forces by land and the English fleet under Nelson by sea, the Neapolitan patriots and republicans resisted valiantly for some days, barricaded in the city's forts, until they were offered an honourable capitulation. The terms of the agreement, which guaranteed their safety, were however rejected by Nelson; and a massacre took place. Some of the major figures of the culture and aristocracy of Naples fell victim to the reaction of 1799: Admiral

Francesco Caracciolo, the noblewoman Eleonora Fonseca de Pimentel, the scientist Domenico Cirillo, the jurist Francesco Conforti, the political writers Mario Pagano and Vincenzio Russo. The last named, a doctor, was the author of a collection of *Pensieri Politici*, in which, with a revolutionary's passion and lucidity, he had outlined a society founded on agriculture and on equality, and restored to virtue and democracy: the programme of a revolution that had not even been attempted.

NAPOLEONIC ITALY

In the spring of 1800, with the successful gamble of the battle of Marengo, Napoleon opened the way to the reconquest of Italy. He was now no longer a young and unknown general with a Jacobin past, but the most respected and most feared man in France, First Consul and, within a few years, Emperor. He no longer promised liberty, equality and revolution, but the stability and order of a modern, efficient administration. This was a prospect which, in Italy as in France, was bound to meet with the agreement and favour of a public opinion that had witnessed too many revolutions and *coups de scène*. Jacobin enthusiasms and hopes had been crushed in 1796–9, and as for reactionaries, and those nostalgic for their old rulers, a few months of Austro-Russian occupation, and the fanaticism of the Army of the Holy Faith had been enough to discredit them. The vast majority of Italians saw peace and stability as the first prerequisites of progress and reform, and for almost fifteen years Napoleon was able to provide them with these things and thus guarantee Italy the possibility of an ordered but intense development.

The most important of the Italian states during the Napoleonic period was without doubt the Italian Republic, which was solemnly proclaimed at Lyons in January 1802 by an assembly of Italian notabilities convened by Napoleon; after Napoleon assumed the title of Emperor it was transformed into a kingdom. At its foundation the Italian Kingdom comprised the territories of the old Cisalpine Republic, but later, following Napoleon's victorious military campaigns, it became a fairly impressive territorial unit, extending to the Veneto in 1806, the Marche in 1807 and the Trentino in 1809. Like the Cisalpine Republic it always remained essentially a satellite state. Napoleon, who had taken the title of President of the Republic at Lyons, was also the King, and the viceroy he had placed in Milan, his stepson Eugène Beauharnais, tried in vain to persuade Napoleon to concede him effective powers of decision. If Milan should catch fire, Napoleon wrote to him, you should await my orders and in the mean time let it burn. When in 1805 the Kingdom's legislative body was bold enough to ask for a reduction in the recently introduced registration tax, the omnipotent Emperor promptly dissolved it, and never summoned it again. The Kingdom's financial and fiscal policy in fact remained subordinate to French military needs: out of a budget of eighty-six million in 1802 forty-nine million went to war expenses and payments to France. Besides money, Napoleonic France demanded men, and resorted to compulsory conscription, an innovation that was certainly not popular in a land of few military traditions.

The territorial organization of the Italian Kingdom too was based on the centralized Napoleonic French system: the state was split up into departments, to each of which a prefect was sent. The legal codes, of course, were those of Napoleon. Transplanted to Italy, a country over which the revolutionary wave had passed without leaving deep marks, the institutions and laws of the Napoleonic establishment had, however, considerable power to break and to renew; and authoritarian centralization and levelling of administration did represent a step ahead from the previously existing fragmentation and the favouring of towns at the expense of the countryside. As for the Napoleonic civil code, it was far from representing, as it did in France, a conservative crystallization of already formed bourgeois relationships – it served instead as the midwife of these very relationships.

So from the point of view of economic development the life of the Italian Kingdom was active. The difficulties with which the expenses of war had burdened the Treasury had forced the government into the old revolutionary expedient of selling national property, on a vast scale. This property consisted for the most part of the estates of ecclesiastical bodies, which the state had taken over. In addition, the Napoleonic code had put a final stop to the laws of primogeniture and fidei commissum, which had unfrozen another considerable portion of the Kingdom's land, and helped to make the land-market yet more active. The chief beneficiaries of the resulting redistribution of property were the new men of the bourgeoisie. In the Bologna area, for example, the bourgeois landowners held 24 per cent of the cultivated land in 1789 and 40 per cent in 1804, while in the same period the nobility's percentage had fallen from seventy-three to fifty-eight. Some of the state's property was however bought by members of noble or famous families, including the Cavour family who, after the purchases made during the period of French occupation, took over the Lucedio lands and the famous Leri estate from the Borghese princes in 1822.

So everyone, bourgeois or noble, invested in land. Throughout the

Napoleonic period the prices of agricultural produce continued to rise, and to give considerable profits. But for anyone who wished to make a fortune and raise his social standing there existed other opportunities beside the acquisition of public property. Napoleon's armies needed to be clothed, shod, armed, and Napoleon's continental strategy demanded, in Italy as elsewhere, the execution of major public works, particularly roads. The most notable road built in this period, but not the only one, was the Simplon, which connected Milan with Switzerland. Public building and the provisioning of armies thus offered new fields of business and speculation for the new bourgeois Italian industrialists. The continental blockade against England, which Napoleon set up in 1806, certainly damaged certain sectors of production, particularly the export trade in raw silk, the decline of which was further hastened by competition from the factories of Lyons. But other sectors, such as the wool, leather, linen, mineral and arms industries, were less gravely affected by the blockade than is commonly supposed, and it is not impossible that in some cases the blockade may even have acted as a stimulus and as a protective barrier. It was probably in these years that the most advanced part of the Po area reached that 'point of break-through' previously mentioned: from that time on the bourgeois classes began to stand on their own feet.

The territories of northern and central Italy that did not belong to the Italian Kingdon – Piedmont, Liguria, the duchy of Parma, Tuscany, Umbria and Lazio – were annexed one after another, between 1800 and 1808, incorporated directly into France, and transformed into French departments. Like the Italian Kingdom they were subordinate to France (or rather, in this case, entirely dependent), and they too suffered from the continental blockade, which had hit Genoa and Leghorn particularly hard. But the painful consequences of the blockade were offset, in some cases more adequately than in others, by the modernity and energy of French administration and legislation, compared with the previous governments. For we must remember that with the exceptions of Tuscany and Parma, the territories annexed by France had barely been touched by eighteenth-century reformism. Here more than anywhere else, then, Napoleonic rule was bound to come as a violent but healthy shock-treatment.

The history of the Kingdom of Naples during the same period was more complex and richer in its motifs. The Bourbon dynasty, restored by the reaction of 1799, had done little to maintain the loyalty of those who had fought for it, or to win the sympathies of its opponents. It confined itself to a policy of simple administration. So when at the beginning of 1806 Napoleon, the victor of Austerlitz, declared the end of the Bourbon monarchy, no one came to its defence; and this time the entry of the French into Naples met far less opposition than in 1799. The conviction that the reforms that had been spoken of for decades could be delayed no longer, the awareness that the new Napoleonic régime hated disorder and Jacobin excess, nostalgia, among some, for the Republic of 1799, and among others the fear of its return, all combined to make the way smooth for the French, and to surround their return with many hopes.

These hopes were not, on the whole, disappointed; the decade of French rule, during which Joseph Bonaparte and Joachim Murat (from 1808) occupied the throne of Naples, has remained in Neapolitan memory and historic tradition as a happy time, almost tinted in the colours of myth, as an interlude of good government amid a century of bad rule. Unlike the 1799 republic, this régime was not felt to be foreign to the country. Murat in particular followed a consistent policy of employing local ability in administration, and limiting the interference of French functionaries.

Above all, the Napoleonic kings gave the Kingdom's men of property exactly what they asked and no more: a more efficient administration and apparatus of state, and reforms tailored to their interests. The charter of these reforms was the law of 2 August 1806, the 'abolition of feudalism', on the basis of which all powers of feudal jurisdiction still existing in the Kingdom were suppressed, and the state's sovereignty affirmed everywhere. But though this meant a revolution from the legal and administrative point of view, things did not greatly change in terms of social relations. The feudal lords may have ceased to be *signori*, but they had become owners of their land *pleno jure*, a new condition that in many cases allowed them more freedom of action than they had had before. They had also been indemnified for the loss of those feudal rights that had been taken away from them. So the abolition of feudalism did not make very important changes in the existing distribution of land, nor in fact had that been its aim. Neither did any great changes result from the sale of ecclesiastical lands, confiscated by the state in the Kingdom of Naples as elsewhere. Recent researches have shown that 65 per cent of the property sold fell into the hands of about two hundred and fifty buyers, almost all of them noblemen, high state officials, including many Frenchmen, and the rich bourgeois. Immediately after the abolition of feudalism came the law on commune demesnes, which declared, among other things, that part of these lands should be apportioned to the peasants; but this law, too, did little to change the situation in the countryside. It remained practically a dead letter. So the great estates of men of property and the tiny, subsistence holdings of the small landowners remained the two poles of a general backwardness, and there remained a social abyss between the privileged and the *cafoni*. In southern Italy the development of intermediate social strata, of an agricultural and town bourgeoisie, was in fact slower during this period than it was in other regions of Italy. There were few industrial or manufacturing concerns, and a high proportion of those that did exist were due to foreigners, especially Swiss. Furthermore, in a seafaring country the effects of the continental blockade were inevitably more sharply felt, and in fact did much to increase the already very high prestige of land investment. Even if feudalism had been removed, the ownership of land, of a great deal of land, constituted every parvenu's passport to respectability. So the French decade left Naples modernized in its governmental, administrative and fiscal institutions: but with its social structure essentially the same; and its backwardness was all the more evident if compared with the progress that had been achieved in the northern regions.

The only two regions of Italy that remained outside the area of French rule and influence were Sardinia and Sicily, where the Savoy family of Turin and the Bourbons of Naples respectively took refuge. The Bourbons however had to come to terms with the English military occupation, especially from 1811, when Lord Bentinck was sent to Palermo as minister plenipotentiary and military commander. Bentinck was a Whig, and firmly convinced that the struggle against Napoleon had to be conducted not merely on the military level but also on that of politics and propaganda. To this end, exploiting their traditional spirit of independence and their aversion for the Bourbons, he managed to persuade the Sicilian barons to accept a watered-down version of the Napoleonic abolition of feudalism, and a constitutional régime on the English model, with an upper and a lower house. This operation was a fairly intelligent way to convince the Italians that the fall of the Napoleonic usurpers would not necessarily mean a complete restoration of the Bourbon monarchy, and to set up the model of the English constitution and Parliament as an alternative to Napoleonic centralization and Caesarism. Bentinck's work, as we shall see, did much to ensure that the Italian Napoleonic régimes did not survive their founder's defeat.

THE END OF NAPOLEONIC RULE

Before the arrival of the French and the Napoleonic code it was difficult for any Italian who was neither noble nor fairly well-off to pursue an intellectual career. The easiest road, however paradoxical it may seem, was a career in the Church. This explains why eighteenth-century Italy, like France at the same time, was so rich in priests and abbots whose ideas were far from orthodox, and who distinguished themselves by the reformist ardour of their writings and their attitudes. Ludovico Antonio Muratori, whose historical works had taken up the Machiavellian view of the Papacy as an obstacle to Italy's progress, was an abbot. So was Parini, author of an ode which stigmatized as barbaric the practice of castrating the boy singers of the Sistine Chapel. So was Gian Battista Casti, adventurer and author of erotic verses. Then in the last years of the century there was a whole series of Jansenist and Jacobin bishops and priests; some of them, like the Bishops Serrao and Natale, and the priests Pacifico and Falconieri, fell victim to the reaction of 1779. Military and university careers were a good deal more closed than the Church. So for anyone not disposed to take orders there only remained the typically Italian, or rather southern Italian, career of the law.

After 1796 things changed radically. For the sons of the nobility and the bourgeoisie there now opened, above all, the glorious path of a military career in Napoleon's armies, together with the chance to acquire a more modern education in one of the many military academies Napoleon was founding in Italy. We shall see later that many of the patriots of the Risorgimento served their political and military apprenticeships in the ranks of Napoleon's armies. But other possibilities were also now open to the more gifted: the enlarged, more powerful universities, the academies of art, the conservatoires, the specialized schools, the *lycées* instituted on the French model, the administration, and, finally, journalism. Ugo Foscolo, certainly the most interesting and restless Italian intellectual of the time, followed all these careers: he was a soldier, a journalist, a university professor with no academic affectations; his life is almost a summary of the history of Italian intellectual activity during the Napoleonic era.

So, above and beyond the boundaries between states, a new, fresh body of intellectuals was taking shape, who took an active part in civic life, and who were instrumental in creating a national public opinion. Ugo Foscolo has already been mentioned: his epistolary novel *Jacopo Ortis* was one of the bedside books of the new generations between revolution and restoration. But more than of literature one thinks of the new, explosive phenomenon of journalism. One of the most authoritative newspapers of the Napoleonic period was called the *Giornale italiano*; it was edited by Vincenzo Cuoco, a Neapolitan and the author of an essay on the revolution of 1799, who later emigrated to Milan. The title of his paper was not a vain one, for whether it was dealing with politics, with literature, with economics or with educational problems, the *Giornale italiano* genuinely addressed itself to a national public opinion.

But a public opinion, besides expressing itself in literature and in cultural debate, tends naturally to give itself a political organization. In the general conditions of the age, and in Italy more than elsewhere, this could only take the age's typical forms, those of secret societies and sects. So in the North was formed the society of the Adelfia, whose followers included many army officers, and of which Filippo Buonarroti was a member. In the Kingdom of Naples the *Carboneria* group was active; it recruited its followers from the army, from the provincial bourgeoisie, from the clergy and in some cases from the common people. Another secret society was the Guelfia, which was spread throughout the Papal State and the Romagna. It is hard to say exactly what the political tendencies of these associations were: ex-Jacobins worked and conspired beside conservatives who were nostalgic for the *ancien régime*, supporters of Napoleon beside his opponents, French agents with English agents and Bourbon partisans from Sicily. The very structure of the societies, divided into separate cells which had no contact with one another, and organized according to a system of successive levels of initiation, made them open to the most varied infiltrations; and the aura of mystery that surrounded them made widely differing interpretations of them possible even for their own adherents of lower rank. This explains why a false Bull of Pius vii was believed, in which the Pope, who had been exiled and humiliated by the French, invited believers to join the *Carboneria* society. Broadly speaking, the secret societies and sects of the Napoleonic period were above all a channel into which urges towards independence and constitutional aspirations could flow. By means of these secret societies a confused and sometimes indiscriminate desire to participate in public and political life was displayed on the part of a recently-formed public opinion still undergoing its first experiences. Since this was their nature, the sects and secret societies only succeeded in influencing the course of events minimally when the Napoleonic régime in Italy fell.

When at the end of 1812 news reached Italy of the disastrous retreat from Russia and the grave losses suffered by the Italian troops who had joined in the campaign, it began to be clear to many people that Napoleon's days were by now numbered. The battle of Leipzig banished every doubt. From this moment on the exclusive political and diplomatic aim of the Napoleonic rulers in Italy, from Eugène Beauharnais in Milan to Joachim Murat in Naples, was to detach themselves from Napoleon, in the hope of assuring the survival of their crowns and kingdoms and to repeat in Italy the operation which allowed Bernadotte to keep the Swedish crown. On the other hand, the sense that Napoleon's days were numbered gave fresh impetus to the hopes for independence and constitutional rule that were current among the political groups and in Italian public opinion. There were two lines, that of the governments and that of Italian patriotism, which could have met and interwoven. But they did not, and the result of this missed meeting was the successful restoration of the old rulers.

In Milan the agitation aroused by the party of so-called pure Italians brought about the assassination of the Italian Kingdom's Finance Minister, Prina, on 20 April 1814, and fatally jeopardized the efforts of Eugène Beauharnais. He had broken away from Napoleon and signed an armistice, wishing to preserve the Kingdom and ensure its independence. The result of the assassination was not that which its contrivers had hoped for, but the pure and simple restoration of Austrian rule in Lombardy.

In Naples, on the other hand, it was Joachim Murat who, by rejecting the constitution which the *Carbonari* insisted on, and trusting exclusively to the arts of diplomacy, deprived himself of the most valuable trump card he might have held: the support and agreement of the Kingdom's public opinion. His impulsiveness was another factor in his downfall: during the Hundred Days he came back to the side of Napoleon, whom he had deserted at Leipzig. Gambling on an impossible recovery, he led an army into northern Italy, but was driven back by the Austrians. Only then, *in extremis*, did he agree to a constitution: but it was too late. Forced to leave the Kingdom, to which the Bourbons returned, he made a last desperate attempt, landing in Calabria in October 1815, with a small group of followers; he was captured and shot. His courageous death no doubt contributed to his posthumous popularity: a 'Muratist' current persisted in the Naples region up to the time of national unification and even beyond. It expressed an awareness of the reforms achieved in the Kingdom by the decade of French rule.

10

Restoration and Romanticism

THE RESTORATION AND THE MOVEMENTS OF 1820-1

The principle of legitimacy proclaimed by the Congress of Vienna was applied to Italy with zealous and bureaucratic punctiliousness. Save for a few not very important adjustments of frontiers, all the dethroned dynasties were restored to their territories: the house of Savoy in Piedmont and Sardinia, the Bourbons in Naples and the house of Lorraine in Tuscany. Exceptions were not made even for those states in miniature, the duchies of the Po valley: Francesco IV d'Este returned to Modena, and Maria Louisa, who was to be Napoleon's not inconsolable widow, to Parma, on the understanding that when she died the state would be restituted to the branch of the Bourbon house that had formerly ruled it. In the mean time they became sovereigns of the former republic of Lucca, which, when they returned to Parma, in 1847, was incorporated into the Grand Duchy of Tuscany. Together with Lucca, the other Italian states that suffered from the new organization of Italy were the two republics of Genoa and Venice. The fact that they had become republics some centuries before the French Revolution, and had therefore a better title to legitimacy than any of the Italian rulers except the Pope, could not save them from the fate to which their internal weakness had for a long time been leading them. Genoa became a part of Savoy and Piedmont, which thus achieved one of its main expansionist aims, and Venice was combined with Lombardy to form the Lombard-Venetian Kingdom, ruled by a viceroy appointed from Vienna, and entirely absorbed within the international conglomeration of the Habsburg Empire.

On the whole, though the new division of Italy was simpler than the situation that had existed before Bonaparte's first invasion, it was a conspicuous backward step from the situation of the Napoleonic period, especially as far as the lands of the Po plain, the most advanced part of the country, were concerned. For what had been the Italian Kingdom was once more split up into the Lombard-Venetian Kingdom, the two duchies of Modena and Parma and the Papal State. The consequences of this may easily be imagined.

As the old political frontiers were restored, so were customs barriers. The goods that came down the Po from Lombardy to the sea, or by the Brenner pass in the direction of Modena and Tuscany, were forced to pay as many import and export taxes as there were states which they had to cross. Except for Tuscany, which remained true to the free-trade principles of the days of the Grand Duke Leopold, all the other states, to a greater or less extent, practised restrictive policies in the interests of their capital and court and of the coalition of interests at their head. One of the consequences of this was that smuggling was rife on all the frontiers, and interwoven with the chronic banditry of some regions. The northern borders of the Papal State were particularly seriously affected. Economic frontiers not only existed between states but also within some of the larger ones: up to 1822 a customs barrier on the river Mincio divided Lombardy from Venice, and another was placed between the Empire's territories in Italy and those north of the Alps. The elimination of these barriers did not, however, free Venetian-Lombard trade from the handicaps it suffered, or from its subordination to Austrian and Bohemian competition; in fact, its difficulties were later aggravated by the forming of the *Zollverein*. A similar situation prevailed in the Savoy territories, where one customs barrier divided Piedmont, and another stood between Piedmont and the newly acquired Ligurian territories. The abolition of the Ligurian Republic in 1818 did little good to the trade of Genoa, which had emerged sorely tried from the continental blockade, and was subjected to keen competition from Trieste and from Leghorn. The Turin court continued to base its policy on rigidly restrictive and protectionist criteria. No wonder that in these conditions anti-Piedmontese feeling was strong in Genoa, or that Genoa, together with Leghorn, became a stronghold of republicanism during the Risorgimento. Genoa was of course the town of Giuseppe Mazzini.

The Restoration was not merely political, then, but also economic. Even so, there were limits to what could be restored. It may have been possible to replace dynasties on the thrones they had lost, and to reconstitute old frontiers, and it may have been possible to reopen the doors of schools and courts to the Company of Jesus (though some governments, such as the Grand Duchy of Florence, refused to do so); but it was practically impossible, or at least very difficult, to erase the deep changes that twenty years of French rule had made in the very texture of society, in the relations between men and between classes.

The only Italian government that repealed the Napoleonic codes in their entirety and revived the previous confused and backward legislation was the Turin government, which was also the first to recall the Jesuits, with all pomp, and to resume discrimination against the Jewish and Waldensian religious minorities. Elsewhere, greater caution was observed. Such men as Vittorio Fossombroni, who led the Tuscan government during the Restoration period, Luigi de'Medici, the main collaborator with the Bourbons of Naples, and even Cardinal Ettore Consalvi, Pius VII's Secretary of State, not to mention the Habsburg officials in the Lombard-Venetian Kingdom, who had learned in the school of Joseph II, realized that a total restoration of the old status quo was an impossible and dangerous task. In places where the Napoleonic codes were repealed, as in the Lombard-Venetian Kingdom and Tuscany, the rulers were careful to substitute new legal codes permeated with the eighteenth-century reformist tradition and with Napoleonic legislation itself. In Naples the repeal of the Napoleonic codes was even more nominal.

In the same way the question of the national property sold during the Napoleonic period was also treated cautiously. Only a small proportion could be restored to its old owners, generally religious communities and charities. Even in the Papal State these bodies had to be content in many cases with an indemnification, and so finally lost possession of their old estates to those whom they had considered usurpers. Things went the same way with the feudal privileges and rights that had been abolished. In this case too it was difficult to turn back and cancel what had been done. In particular, it would have been quite impossible to retie the innumerable intricate bonds that had been cut by the abolition of feudalism in the South; and in fact no one considered this course. On the contrary, the anti-feudal legislation of the Napoleonic régime was extended to Sicily, which thus experienced, well into the Restoration period, the delayed effects of the revolution and the French occupation.

The policies of the Restoration governments thus oscillated between the two extremes of a legitimist intransigence of principle and an accommodating flexibility of action, between the unrealistic attempt to govern *against* the new classes and social groups that had emerged from the crisis and collapse of the old order, and the equally unrealistic attempt to win their trust and support. In both cases, whether threatening or blandishing, they succeeded only in giving proof of their own weakness, and in encouraging the opposition that was hatching at the meetings of political societies. 'In the eyes of furious men', wrote Stendhal in his *Promenades*, 'concessions are nothing but a proof of the weakness of the government that makes them'.

In this connection the case of Naples is perhaps the most illuminating. The preservation of what we may call the bourgeois conquests of the French decade was counterbalanced: important concessions were made to the Church with the concordat of 1818, and others to the court and the financial circles connected with it in the business of taxation and customs. This contradictory and ambiguous line of government, combined with a pinched economic situation and difficulties in the market for farm produce, resulted in wide discontent. In March 1820 the news that the King of Spain had been forced to accept a constitution was enough to provide a gathering-point for powerful political and social forces.

With the complicity, or rather the help, of the army, which included many Muratist officers, the insurrection that began at Nola on the night of 1–2 July swiftly spread into the provinces, reached the capital, and within a few days forced King Ferdinand to accept and swear to the Spanish constitution. But the speed of this victory indicated the weakness of the forces of resistance rather than the unity and vigour of the forces of 'movement'. Divisions within the victorious revolutionary camp soon emerged, to hasten, or even determine, its defeat. There were political divisions between the officers who belonged to the *Carboneria*, and the Muratist old guard of those who had risen to positions of importance during the French decade; there were social divisions, of which political differences were mainly a reflection, between the agricultural bourgeoisie of the provinces and the professional and official bourgeoisie, and between the bourgeois class as a whole and the peasants. Finally, there was a territorial division between the mainland and Sicily. In Sicily the revolutionary movement had had from the beginning a separatist character, and on this ground it soon came into conflict with the new constitutional government. Mutual antagonism came to a head in October 1820 when the new Parliament, which had met in Naples, cancelled the agreement previously reached with the Sicilian Junta and sent General Pietro Colletta to the island, in an essentially repressive capacity.

These contradictions of course helped to undermine the strength of the revolutionary camp, and to paralyze its actions; they were the deepest reason for its failure. The King's duplicity was another factor: after accepting the constitution and acting ambiguously towards the new government, he was sent to Ljubljana to avert the threat of an Austrian intervention; instead, he requested it. But the Austrian expeditionary force only had to appear at the frontier in March 1821 for the constitutional army to scatter, and so leave the way wide open for the complete victory of the Restoration.

The Austrian intervention in the Kingdom of Naples persuaded the secret political organizations of Piedmont, who also had their main strength among army officers, to accelerate the revolutionary preparations that had been under way for some time. On 9 March the garrison of Alessandria, a stronghold of conspiracy, raised the tricolour above its own barracks; and the example was followed during the following days by other detachments, including that of the capital. The rebels' chief demand, or at least that made by the majority of them, and by the politically most aware, was, as in Naples, for the Spanish constitution. But they also put pressure on the monarchy to lead the way towards the reconstitution of a Kingdom of northern Italy, not shrinking from the prospect of fighting Austria. But though this was a more demanding and less locally-minded programme than that of the Neapolitan rebels, the range of forces set in movement was narrower, and the Piedmontese insurrection of 1821 remained more confined within the ambit of a military *pronunciamento* and secret conspiracy. Also, as in many conspiracies, there was an element of naïveté – before launching the insurrectional movement its promoters had had meetings and discussions with the heir to the throne, Prince Carlo Alberto, who they knew did not share the reactionary attitude of most of the court. But he had remained ambiguous and elusive before the uprising, and later disappointed all the patriots' expectations, when King Vittorio Emanuele I abdicated and he took on the duties of a Regent. He was sandwiched between pressure from the rebels, who made him swear to the Spanish constitution of 15 March, and from his uncle, Carlo Felice, a rigid upholder of legitimist principles: after many hesitations Carlo Alberto eventually yielded to his uncle's suggestions, and handed over power to him. With the help of Austria, Carlo Felice soon succeeded in getting the better of the constitutional army, and re-entered the capital in the fulness of power, as an absolute monarch.

The defeat was followed by reprisals; a series of trials took place in many Italian capitals. The trials in Milan of the members of the *Carboneria* and *Federati* groups, who had been in close contact with the Piedmontese rebels, were particularly spectacular for the number and quality of the accused. Among those condemned were Federico Confalonieri, a brilliant Milanese nobleman who had been prominent in the 'pure Italian' movement and was distinguished for his economic enterprises and for his patronage of the arts, Silvio Pellico and Pietro Borsieri, both contributors to the *Conciliatore*, Alessandro Filippo Andryane, emissary of the untiring Buonarroti, and Colonel Silvio Moretti, a vigorous Napoleonic officer. At the Naples trial too, many of those condemned were professional soldiers, thirty of whom received the death penalty.

But many succeeded in taking flight from trial, and went into exile. The first wave of Italian political emigration included the Lombard economist Giuseppe Pecchio, the Neapolitan general Guglielmo Pepe, who had taken part in the 1820 uprising, and the poet Giovanni Berchet. Most of them continued their activity abroad, in conspiracy, or by fighting on the battlefields of Spain and Greece, like the Piedmontese Count Annibale Santorre di Santarosa, one of the originators of the Piedmont *pronunciamento*, who died in Greece in 1825. Others, like Raffaele Rossetti, father of the Pre-Raphaelite poet, and Antonio Panizzi from Modena, future director of the British Museum, eventually became assimilated into their countries of immigration.

So the Restoration was triumphant, and within its context the forces of reaction gained the ascendancy. In Naples Medici had to resign, and was replaced by the Prince of Canosa, a champion of the most intransigent legitimism. In Rome, the victory of the 'zealot' cardinals in the conclave of 1823, which elected Leo xii, brought about the dismissal of Consalvi. This fury against the defeated, and this malicious thirst for revenge, was a further proof of the Restoration's weakness, short-sightedness and pettiness. But the ranks of its opponents, the political societies and the liberal movements, were also weak. Not only because the battle had left them prostrate and bereft of their best intellects, but also because, as the moment of battle had made clear, their ideas were inconsistent and contradictory, and because of their tendency to improvise and their lack of deep roots.

This double weakness was bound to produce stagnation, and Stendhal's *Promenades dans Rome*, among other works, presents a stagnant society of sceptical cardinals, generous but fatalistic working people, blasé police ministers and young liberals, who, after going to hear Giuditta Pasta at La Scala, meet in a café to talk 'about music, love and Paris'. While waiting for things to change one could take advantage of the *douceur de vivre* that the Restoration, like all old régimes, offered. But would they really change? Unlike his compatriot Lamartine, Stendhal knew the history, character and resources of the Italians too well to be in any doubt of this, or to suppose that they would submit to being, as his Roman barber said, 'ruled by priests' indefinitely. 'I do not believe that I am being utopian,' he wrote in the *Promenades*, 'if I say that revolution will break out in Italy in about 1840 or 45.'

CULTURE IN THE RESTORATION PERIOD; MANZONI AND LEOPARDI

One of the signs that the Restoration stagnation was not to last long was the fact that, as Stendhal and others observed, every person 'in the least cultured' was in opposition. Anyone who has read this far and knows what the position of the intelligentsia had been in Italian history will be able to realize how much this opposition meant. For there are in history permanent conditions that are hard to reverse and during the Risorgimento the rôle and place of the intellectuals in Italian society remained what it had always been. We may even go so far as to say that without the stimulus and the unifying power that they exerted it is doubtful whether a bourgeoisie as weak as that of Italy would have emerged victorious. For the Italian bourgeoisie had, traditionally, a narrow, corporative attitude and a lack of political consciousness. The rule that presided over the birth and development of the modern socialist movement also applied in this earlier period: the germination of a collective political awareness and demand for rights is not always spontaneous, but must often be produced or at least stimulated from outside. This is the point of view from which it is most convenient to approach the problems of Italy's cultural history in the period of the Risorgimento.

The new element in European culture of the first decades of the nineteenth century was, as everyone knows, Romanticism. In Italy it made its official appearance in 1816 with the publication of a letter from Madame de Staël, inviting Italian writers to become aware of the new literary currents north of the Alps, and to translate the works of the major authors of the day. The invitation was accepted, and in Italy too there appeared ballads and historical novels set in the Middle Ages, poetry was discussed as an expression of the spirit of the people, the claims of the imagination and of spontaneity were defended against those of the intellect and of literary discipline, and the claims of history and tradition against those of the arbitrary tyranny of conceptualization and reason. The contributors to the Milanese review *Il Conciliatore* proclaimed themselves 'Romantics'; many of them, after experiencing the rigours of Austrian censorship, learned also about the Imperial prisons, after the rebellion and trials of the year 1821. In fact the great majority of the Italian Romantics took part in the liberal and patriotic opposition to the restored régimes, and it is not hard to understand why they could not be sympathetic to those aspects of Romanticism whose tendency was to identify the Romantic movement with the ideology of the Restoration. With them the sense of history never or very rarely led them to oppose the past and the present, the *ancien régime* and revolution, the Middle Ages and the modern age, nor did it lead to a sentimental exaltation of the spontaneity and immediacy of simple people, an idolizing of ignorance and hence a justifying of paternalism. In other words there was no Friedrich Schegel and no Chateaubriand among the Italian Romantics. Since Italy was still dominated by the narrow bigotry of the Restoration, the ideas and demands of eighteenth-century rationalism and utilitarianism still had much of their original impact and persuasive force: the new Romantic school could not set itself in opposition to them, but could only stress the need for a corrective attitude and a deeper understanding. It was not enough to be against the old régime and on the side of progress; it was also necessary to single out the forces able to bring the new order to light, to define the obstacles in the way, and to work out a battle-plan adapted to the true possibilities of Italian society. This had been the lesson propounded by Vincenzo Cuoco in his book on the Neapolitan revolution of 1799, and it found an audience. The Romantic generation was one of political intellectuals, not only in that it provided many of those who took part in conspiracy and in the political movement of the Risorgimento, but also, above all, in that they were aware of the responsibilities and conditions that political action implied, and acted like politicians. To this however should be added that responsibility and moderation, to paraphrase a famous passage of Manzoni, cannot always be cleanly and perfectly separated. This applies both to the Italian middle class of the nineteenth century and to its intellectuals.

Manzoni's name does not arise by chance. Besides being the most famous of the Romantic generation, the author of *I Promessi Sposi* was also, even if he was not a declared partisan of the Romantic school, able to represent its evolution and its points of view more richly and with more awareness than anyone else. As a young man he was an anti-clerical disciple of the Enlightenment (he was a nephew of Cesare Beccaria), but under Fauriel's influence he gradually approached the new Romantic culture, and in 1810 declared himself a Catholic again. But his Catholicism was tinged with Jansenism, and was a faith felt and practised more as a moral system than as a cult.

In the same year he returned to Italy from his long stay in Paris, and in his native Milan he followed and encouraged, without directly participating in, the struggle of the Romantics and the *Conciliatore*. On the occasion of the Piedmontese uprisings of 1821 he wrote an ode hoping for their victory and the coming of an Italy 'united in arms, heart and altar'. Yet it was not by such displays of attitude in writing or action that Manzoni played such an important part in the forming of a national public opinion, but through his whole work as a writer, and above all as a novelist. The novel, as a new literary genre destined for a new, wider public, once more raised, for those able to grapple with it, the eternal question of the language, of the need to fill the gap between the literary and the spoken language and provide a language that would be, to use Manzoni's own words, 'a means for the communication of all sorts of ideas between all Italians'. This was no easy matter, if an old Jacobin patriot like Luigi Angeloni, having decided to write a work to incite the Italians to the revolutionary struggle for democracy could find no better way of writing it than in an affected, fourteenth-century, purist Italian, and if two such genuine poets as the Milanese Carlo Porta and the Roman Gioacchino Belli were forced to resort to their respective dialects to make poetically plausible the everyday world and common people they were drawn to.

Manzoni not only faced this problem but solved it. The language of *I Promessi Sposi*, which was one of the factors in the novel's enormous success, is precisely that Italian 'for everyone' that the author had sought and which he had succeeded in elaborating by a hard, prodigious labour of literary discipline and of winnowing and whittling away. He produced an Italian that was effective without being dialectal or provincial, communicative without being stereotyped, and made vigorous by everyday middle-class usage.

The content corresponded to the form: the story of *I Promessi Sposi* is the personal story of Renzo and Lucia, a betrothed couple whose marriage is hindered by a series of adverse circumstances until the very end, set against a great historical panorama of Spanish-ruled Lombardy in the seventeenth century, the age of the wars of the Valtellina and Monferrato, and of the great plague of Milan. More exactly, Manzoni's masterpiece is a historical novel in which history is turned around from its usual position and seen from the point of view of simple people, the victims of the ambition and oppression of the powerful, the intricacies of state matters, wars and famines. To all these scourges they oppose their immense human resources, their work, their courage, their mistrust in the justice of the powerful and their trust in that of God. In the pages of Manzoni we hear the true voice of the Italian people, as they have been shaped by the centuries, with their resignation but also their vitality. Critics of Manzoni have mentioned his 'paternalism', or rather his 'cult of the people'. They may be right, but it must be added that no-one before him had raised – let alone solved – the problem of 'the people' and of a popular literature. Few later writers, in changed circumstances, have raised the problem with so much understanding of it; and none has solved it at such a high and noble level of artistic expression.

The success of *I Promessi Sposi*, which still continues, was immediate and enormous. It provides permanent evidence of the power of the new Romantic culture to spread and to attract, and helps us to recognize its historical rôle and the part it played in forming a national public opinion. But of those who came under the influence of Romanticism, yet still disputed and discussed it, not all looked back to the past. There were also men of very clear and open minds and fairly advanced ideas, like Giacomo Leopardi, one of the greatest Italian poets of all time.

He was born in 1798 in a sleepy little town of the Papal State, of a noble and reactionary family (his father, Count Monaldo, was known as the writer of one of the most aggressively legitimist pamphlets). Handicapped by nature – he was a hunchback – he consumed his adolescence in a 'mad and desperate' study of the classics in his father's library. Together with the ancient authors, the works of enlightened and materialist French writers of the eighteenth century, Rousseau, Voltaire and Holbach, were the companions of his studious youth. In any case, the lesson of the first, as Leopardi understood it, was not much different from that of the second: they converged in the ideal of a magnanimous human race that was republican, free of superstition, close to the purity of its nature. These are the ideals, profoundly different from those of the Romantic school, which most frequently emerge from the poetry Leopardi wrote before 1819. From their height he contemplated and judged the world and its evil age. No-one felt as strongly as he did the tedium (*noia*) of living under the Restoration.

But it was possible to hope that the 'dead century' in which he was fated to live might shake off its torpor and 'rise' to 'famous deeds' as he hoped in the song '*Ad Angelo Mai*', or was its shame irredeemable? The defeat of the 1821 insurrections, the increasibly painful awareness of his own deformity, and his isolation all helped to incline Leopardi increasingly towards the rejection of every illusion and every consolation. Human unhappiness was not merely a feature of the nineteenth century but of every age and every human condition, and tedium the unwelcome, faithful companion of every living being, from the wandering shepherd in the loneliness of Asia to the highly-civilized Parisian. Only death could put an end to tedium, and it was only in death that man, persecuted by his blind, cruel step-mother, Nature, could hope to find peace.

Clearly, in a vision of the world so wholly materialistic and pessimistic, there was little enough room for interests of a political character. But after many years of political near-apathy Leopardi was roused by the coming of Liberal Catholicism on the Italian political scene.

The affirmation that the cause of human progress could not be separated from that of religion, as the 'new believers' claimed, was one that could only disgust Leopardi deeply. For him, it was not through the consolation of myths and superstitions but, on the contrary, through a manly and pitiless contemplation of their own unhappy state that men could attain the strength and solidarity they needed, to fight the one battle that he thought worth fighting: the common battle of the human race against the offences and burdens of nature. This is the message of *La Ginestra*:

> *Nobil natura è quella*
> *Ch'a sollevar s'ardisce*
> *Gli occhi mortali incontra*
> *Al comun fato, e con franca lingua,*
> *Nulla al ver detraendo,*
> *Confessa il mal che ci fu dato in sorte,*
> . . .
> *Tutti fra sé confederati estima*
> *Gli uomini; e tutti abbracci*
> *Con vero amor, porgendo*
> *Valida e pronta ed aspettando aita*
> *Negli alterni perigli e nelle angosce*
> *Della guerra comune.**

It is a high and lasting message which we, men of the atomic age, can understand, and which deeply perturbs us. But contemporaries, involved as they were in the long and urgent tasks that their age imposed on them, could hardly understand or reflect on it. It is to them and to their laborious advances that we must now turn back our attention.

ITALY AND THE JULY REVOLUTION

The European political and diplomatic situation of the 1820's was dominated by the legitimist system instituted at Vienna and by the Holy Alliance. This had become clear at the time of the Spanish and Italian insurrections of 1820–1. For the constitutional governments that were their expression found themselves totally isolated politically; and at

* His is a noble nature who dares to raise mortal eyes against the common fate, and with a free voice, detracting nothing from the truth, declares the evil state that has been given to us as our destiny. . . . He considers all men to be allies, and embraces all with true love, offering strong and ready help, and expecting the same, in the successive perils and anguishes of the common war.

the Troppau and Ljubljana meetings Austria did not find it very difficult to bend English and French uncertainties and resistance, to get their agreement to a project of united repression. As long as this legitimist solidarity prevailed among the great powers, the prospects of the national Italian movement were bound to remain extremely uncertain. But as soon as one of its links was broken then all would be possible again, and the boldest hopes could be entertained. So it is understandable that the news of the victory of the July revolution in Paris struck Italy with the force of a bomb. The triumphs of the French revolutionaries had hardly died down when the Italian patriotic movement revived and returned to the initiative.

This time the attempt was made in the Papal State and the duchies, territories that were the weakest link in the chain of legitimism. The insurrectional movement rapidly gained the upper hand. The first city to rebel was Bologna, where on 5 February 1831 the papal pro-legate was forced to hand over power to a provisional commission. A few days later, on 9 February, an assembly of citizens at Modena proclaimed the fall of Duke Francesco IV, who had already abandoned the state at the first signs of agitation. Within another few days it was the turn of Parma, where a provisional government was set up. Then the movement rapidly won all the Romagna, the Marche and Umbria; the territories effectively controlled by the papal government and troops were reduced to Lazio, while in the liberated parts a government of the 'united Italian provinces' had been constituted, with its seat at Bologna. But this government had a very short life, being swept away by Austrian intervention, to which Louis Philippe's diplomacy opposed no obstacle. At the end of March the status quo had been re-established in both the duchies and the Papal State.

Once again, the Austrian intervention and the lack of French help are not enough to explain the sudden collapse of a movement whose beginnings had seemed so promising. In this case too, as in that of the Neapolitan revolution of 1820, one must emphasize the limits and the internal weaknesses of the movement and, above all, its heterogeneity and its divisions. Within the movement there was opposition between the old generation of leaders of the Italian Kingdom, who were prepared to wait patiently for France, and who had little faith in the independent chances of the movement they led, though they had not begun it, and the younger generation of the *Carbonari*. Neither did the exiles, who had set up an Italian Junta of liberation in Paris, share a common point of view: some of them followed Buonarroti and shared his decidedly republican ideas, while others held more moderate views. Finally there were disagreements that arose from rivalry between the various cities, each of which, especially in the duchies, was jealous of its position as a capital. At Parma, early on, the rebels went to Maria Louisa to ask her to stay in the state. Besides, some rather ambiguous manoeuvres had taken place during the preparations for the uprising: some of its instigators, notably Enrico Misley and Ciro Menotti of Modena, had for some time been in contact not merely with secret political circles in Italy and Paris, but also with Duke Francesco IV, a true-blue reactionary. By playing on his desire to succeed Carlo Felice on the throne of Piedmont in place of the suspect Carlo Alberto, they hoped to involve him in the planned uprising. This was the so-called 'Estense conspiracy', an episode that remains obscure and which, had it not ended in the hanging of Ciro Menotti by Francesco IV, would have the character more of an operetta than a tragedy. In any case it is an example of the dilettantism and provincialism of the 1831 conspirators and revolutionaries.

But though the July revolution had no immediate impact on Italy, it still continued to exert a deep influence on Italian events. France's return to a fully independent and even brilliant foreign policy had radically altered the European political and diplomatic scene. The Whig victory in the English elections of 1832 was similarly important. For now the bloc of legitimist powers was counterbalanced by one of liberal and constitutional powers; and in this new situation, which was characterized by a renewal of quarrels between the great powers, the prospect of a territorial modification of Italy in the direction of greater independence in relation to Austria, and greater unity, was once more realistic, as it had been in the eighteenth century.

To this end the perennial French concern at Austrian interference and predominance in Italy could be exploited, as could the anxiety of England, now a Mediterranean power with the acquisition of Gibraltar and Malta, at Russia's threatening closeness to the Straits. Advantages could also be made out of the Mediterranean ambitions of France, which had extended support to Mehmet Ali, and returned to the old Napoleonic policy in Egypt. After Ferdinand's resounding *volte-face* at Ljubljana, and his unconditional surrender to the principles of legitimacy, the Italian state best qualified and best able to work in this direction seemed to be Piedmont, which had already, in the eighteenth century, been wonderfully able to turn to its own advantage the antagonisms of the great powers. By means of diplomacy and a dexterous insertion of itself into the European balance, it was still perhaps possible for Italy to make progress along the road of independence and unity, even without war with Austria. The idea that Austria might be compensated for the eventual cession of its Italian possessions and influence by territorial advantages in the Balkans, and that the Italian situation could thus be resolved together with that of the East, had already been expressed by Gioberti in a letter of 1840 to Mamiani, and was fully argued by Cesare Balbo, a Piedmontese patrician and patriot, in his book *Le speranze d'Italia*, published in 1844, and welcomed with very lively interest in all Italy. Two years later, writing in a Parisian review on the question of railways in Italy, the young Camillo di Cavour declared:

> *Si l'avenir réserve à l'Italie des destinées plus heureuses, si cette belle contrée, ainsi qu'il est permis de l'espérer, est destinée à reconquérir un jour sa nationalité, ce ne peut être que par suite d'un remaniement européen ou par l'effet d'un de ces grandes commotions, de ces événements en quelque sorte providentiels sur lesquels la facilité de faire mouvoir plus ou moins vite quelques régiments que procurent les chemins de fer, ne saurait exercer aucune influence.**

Expressed by the man who was to be the main builder of Italy's unity, the idea of the correlation of that unity with a territorial rearrangement of Europe, though balanced by the other less probable hypothesis of a revolutionary commotion, becomes particularly effective. Without the new political pattern that emerged in Europe in the 1830's and was consolidated in the following decades, the events of the Italian Risorgimento would have been unthinkable.

---

* 'If the future has in store for Italy a happier fate, if, as one may hope, this beautiful country is destined to win back its nationality one day, it can only be as the result of a rearrangement of Europe, or as the consequence of one of those great "commotions" or events which are to some extent providential, over which the power to move a few regiments more or less quickly which the railways may afford us could not exert any influence whatsoever.'

The defeats of the Risorgimento

GIUSEPPE MAZZINI AND 'LA GIOVINE ITALIA'

Giuseppe Mazzini was born in Genoa in 1805, and while still very young began to publish in the *Antologia* and other periodicals of the day. He was forced to emigrate to France after being involved in a *Carbonari* conspiracy, and from France he addressed a letter to the new King of Piedmont, the irresolute Carlo Alberto, who had succeeded Carlo Felice in 1831; Mazzini invited the King to put himself at the head of the movement for Italian liberty and independence. The letter's contents were ingenuous and peremptory, but its passionate and romantic tone gave the measure of its author's personality. For Mazzini brought a moral fervour and intransigence to the political struggle, which he viewed, essentially romantically, as a mission. He had a seriousness that the old generations of Italian Jacobins and revolutionaries had lost, if they had ever had it, and which the climate of the Restoration certainly did not encourage among younger men. In spite of all disappointments and bitter moments, Mazzini was able to conserve these typically youthful qualities throughout his long career as a conspirator and patriot: hence the fascination he exerted over generations of Italians. In a country where machiavellianism in politics is often debased to a mere form of scepticism, Mazzini's asceticism, his statement that 'thought and action' must be absolutely one, demanded respect from his opponents and excited enthusiasm among his followers, raising the general level of political life to a new tension and seriousness. In this sense the influence of Mazzini in the history of the Risorgimento can hardly be over-estimated, and goes well beyond the confines of the political movement he directly inspired and organized.

To begin with, this movement was identified with *La Giovine Italia*, the society Mazzini founded early in 1831, and whose general instructions were drawn up in June of the same year. In some respects *La Giovine Italia* followed the model of the earlier secret political organizations, in that its members fell into two distinct categories, corresponding to two different levels of initiation. But in other more obvious ways it was radically different. Insurrection, which was the association's final aim, preparations for which remained secret, was considered as the crowning result of a work of teaching, or 'apostolate' (such terms borrowed from religious language are frequent in the Mazzinian political vocabulary). Where circumstances permitted, this 'apostolate' was to be practised in a public form, through the press and by speaking. In this way the circle of followers widened well beyond those of the earlier political societies, and in many places and regions included fairly solid nuclei of workers and common people. In Milan for example, in about 1833–5, more than three thousand people were affiliated. In other words *La Giovine Italia* was an intermediary stage between the old organizational form of the political groups and secret societies, and that of a political party, which still lay in the future.

But what was the basis and the teaching of the Mazzinian 'apostolate'? What was *La Giovine Italia's* political programme? Reducing it to a formula, one could say that it consisted essentially in the definition of an aim, the united republic, and of the suitable instruments by which it might be achieved: popular insurrections.

The first point was not new. Already in the celebrated contest of 1796, it will be remembered, Melchiorre Gioia had won the palm by maintaining the necessity for a united republic. More recently, old Filippo Buonarroti, with whom Mazzini had been in close contact from the beginning of his exile, and whose moral and ideological leadership he unhesitatingly accepted, had declared himself for the unitary solution in his *Riflessioni sul governo federativo applicato all'Italia*. What was new in Mazzini's thought was the emphasis he placed on the fact that there were no alternatives to this solution, that it was the only one founded on Italian history and tradition. He conferred on it the seal of historical necessity and so transformed it from one hypothesis among many into an idea-force. A nation, he argued, if it really is a nation, if, that is, it has unity of religion, of language, of customs, a 'genius' of its own, can only be a unitary organization. Besides, he went on, developing an argument already employed by Buonarroti, federalism favours the conservation of the privileges of the aristocracy while national unity tends to bring about a greater degree of equality, and in consequence the moral and social raising of the people.

Here is the key term and concept of Mazzini's political vocabulary: 'the people', who must be the protagonist and creator of the new national unity. If previous attempts had failed – Mazzini was categorical on this point – this had happened only because they had involved limited intellectual aristocracies and had not had the character of popular risings, and because they had waited for a sign from beyond the frontiers, instead of trusting to the immense revolutionary possibilities within the country. The Italian revolution on the other hand would be the work of the people, and would break out from within Italian society. But would the prospect of national unity and the establishing of a republic be enough to draw the 'multitudes' along the way that the 'middle class' and the 'intelligences' were already following? On this point Mazzini was a good deal less dogmatic, and his thinking was in fact noticeably ambiguous. If on the one hand he argues that it is necessary to 'dig down into the guts of the social question' and propose concrete improvements to the people, on the other hand he rejects the possibility of any attempt on property or any project of 'agrarian law'. This is part of his general aversion for what he called 'the class war', and it was on this ground that in about 1833 he began to move away from Buonarroti. But they were also divided by Mazzini's idea of an Italian action independent of France, and by his hostility towards the Jacobin notion of an initial period of dictatorship as part of the revolutionary process. As the years passed this aversion of Mazzini's became more acute; he justified it with the statement that unlike France, where the social differences between Louis Philippe's opulent, pleasure-loving bourgeoisie and the starving weavers of Lyons, or England, which was in the throes of the industrial revolution, a relative equality reigned in Italy. There were no great concentrations of wealth in Italy, and in the last analysis all, even the aristocrats, belonged to the 'people'. Swollen and dilated in this way, the 'people' became a nebulous, generic notion: it was a loose mass in which the task of agglutination was of necessity left to the 'intelligences'.

It had been relatively easy to constitute *La Giovine Italia* on the basis of these political ideals, and to set in motion a movement considerably more solid and with more positive ideas than the previous secret societies, but it soon became clear that it was difficult to develop and strengthen it. The Mazzinian networks in the South and in Piedmont were soon discovered and decimated, and an attempt to send an expedition of Italian political exiles and foreigners by way of Savoy to support revolutionary uprisings that were to have broken out in Alessandria and Genoa in 1834 was abortive and inglorious. A new wave of political exiles were forced to cross the borders, and spread about Europe, to Spain, France, England and Malta. Others even went to Latin America and formed an Italian Legion that fought in Brazil and Uruguay. One of these men was a young sailor from Nice, Giuseppe Garibaldi. So *La Giovine Italia* was scattered, and Mazzini himself took shelter in London early in 1837. Later, in about 1839, he gave the word for *La Giovine Italia* to be reorganized on a new basis, addressing the order of recruitment especially towards the numerous colonies of emigrant workers, and so seeking to accentuate the popular nature of his apostolate. His experience of the Chartist movement in England certainly helped to move him in this direction. But Mazzini's inter-class ideas ('the word worker has for us no indication of class in the meaning commonly given to the word') took much of its impact away from the attempt, and it was to have no concrete developments of any consequence. The Mazzinian insurrections of 1830–40, like those of the previous decade, were to have the nature of actions promoted by a political and intellectual élite, and almost fatally destined to failure. This was the case of the *coup de main* (not in any case authorized by Mazzini) attempted by the Bandiera brothers in Calabria in 1844, which ended in the death of all of its few – nineteen – participants. This fresh failure marked a further loss of prestige for Mazzini's movement and for Mazzini himself, who was accused of pushing under fire the young men who followed him. But there were other deeper reasons for the declining popularity of Mazzinian radicalism: the hour of the moderates had arrived in Italy.

THE MODERATES

The foundation of a moderate party, which was to come into conflict with the Mazzinians and rob them of the sympathies they had won all over Italy during their early period, was a gradual process, taking a number of years. The foundation had already been laid by that group of intellectuals which had formed itself around *Il Conciliatore*, and after its suppression had centred on the Florentine review the *Antologia*, which was however also compelled to cease publication in 1833. But it was only after 1840 that the gathering and forming of a moderate current of opinion took on more definite forms and began to proceed more rapidly.

The shock that a certain sector of Italian public opinion needed in order to become more aware of the tendencies that had already been developing for several years, in various confused ways, was provided by the publication at Brussels in 1843 of a book, *Il Primato morale e civile degli Italiani*, by a Piedmontese abbot who had formerly been a sympathizer with the Mazzinian cause, and had for some time been in exile, Vincenzo Gioberti. His thesis, expounded with a great over-abundance of scarcely pertinent historical and philosophical digressions, was already contained in his title. He maintained that Italy, as the seat of the Papacy, had held a position of primacy among the nations, and would do so once more when the Church, reformed and freed from its abuses, had resumed its universal function. Consequently, the reform and revival of Italy was inseparable from that of the Papacy. In this declaration the two traditions of Italian Guelfism and the new French liberal Catholicism à la Lamennais were mingled and muddled together; but it represented no more than the frame and stage-set of Gioberti's thought. The real substance of this was, rather, the fairly concrete political proposal of a confederation of Italian princes under the chairmanship of the Pope, which would have Rome as its 'holy city' and Piedmont as its 'warrior province'. It was a prospect of 'union' rather than 'unity', but nevertheless represented a definite step ahead.

The *Primato*, then, was received with very lively interest by the Italian reading public. But among so much praise and enthusiasm there were also some reserves and uncertainties. In particular, many people asked themselves whether Gioberti's plan of a confederation of Italian princes was not as impracticable as any other, in the light of the opposition Austria would inevitably show to any solution that might subvert the status quo and prejudice its own ubiquitous influence over the affairs of Italy. Gioberti was fully aware of this objection, and the fact that in the *Primato* he had not mentioned his hope of seeing Italy one day released from the 'abhorred Austrian' had been mere expedience. But he did consider that the idea of a league of Italian princes against Austria would be one hard to realize, and so, as has previously been mentioned, he cherished the idea of a diplomatic negotiation by means of which Austria would be compensated for the loss of her Italian possessions by gains in the Balkans. It has also been described how this idea was developed by Cesare Balbo in his *Speranze d'Italia*, the year after the publication of the *Primato*. Balbo's book may be considered a reinforcement of Gioberti's successful work.

There was another point on which Gioberti had prudently and expediently remained silent, although, unlike the monarchist Savoyard Balbo, he was fully aware of it: the problem of the reforms that the confederated Italian princes, and above all the Pope, would have to introduce in their states if they really wished to win the support of public opinion. As far as the Church state in particular was concerned, it could not constitute the centre of attraction Gioberti wanted if it went on being the worst governed and most oppressed of all Italian states. Gioberti knew this, and in 1845 he broke his previous silence with the publication of the *Prolegomeni del Primato*, in which he explicitly took issue with papal misgovernment, attacked the Jesuits and clearly showed his sympathies for a policy of reform, going so far as to criticize the timidity and hesitation of the Piedmontese monarchy. So a further step had been taken towards the delineation of a moderate Italian programme. It only remained to make it more concrete and more practical.

This was the task assumed by Massimo d'Azeglio, a brilliant Piedmontese patrician, who in 1845 had won great popularity for his courage in denouncing papal misgovernment in the Romagna, even though he was a moderate, and a man trusted by Carlo Alberto. In 1847 he published his *Programma per l'opinione nazionale italiana*, which may be considered the manifesto of the moderate party on the eve of 1848. It had been d'Azeglio's intention to give it this character, for while writing it he had consulted other authoritative representatives of Italian moderate opinion. The *Programma* sought an agreement between the princes 'of the Italian part of Italy' on a concrete programme of reform, to be introduced to their states with their common agreement: reform of the laws, the introduction of juries, greater freedom of the press and, finally, the abolition of customs barriers and the creation of a sort of Italian *Zollverein*. As for the question of independence, d'Azeglio stressed in his conclusion that it was a principle to be kept in mind, while at the same time stating his aversion for hasty attempts, and preaching the virtue of patience. So Gioberti's political thesis was made more concrete, brought closer to the needs of a society that had set out along the road of middle-class progress, and won wider agreement and sympathy.

For d'Azeglio's proposals and the moderate party were followed by the group of Tuscan liberals, led by Gino Capponi, who had previously centred on the *Antologia*, by the group of patriots of Bologna and the papal territories, led by Marco Minghetti, and by many patriots in Sicily and on the southern mainland. But the core of the moderate party consisted of the Piedmontese group, to which belonged Balbo, d'Azeglio, Gioberti, and the young Cavour, who was beginning his political apprenticeship in those years: men who, though they harboured no sympathies for revolution, had decisively broken with the extreme legitimism of Carlo Felice. They retained the better qualities of the old Savoy ruling class, its keen sense of the state and of public service, its attitudes to command and to government. Only the Kingdom of Naples, whose historic development had been in some respects similar to that of Piedmont, could boast of political figures gifted with such qualities and such 'style'. These were lacking in the Lombard middle and patrician classes, who had for too long lost the habit of political responsibility, and in the Tuscan squirearchy, which was, in spite of everything, the heir of a particularist, local tradition, to which any military spirit or marked sense of the state were foreign.

By means of the moderate party and its core of leaders, Carlo Alberto's Piedmont put forward its serious candidature to head the movement of Italian revival.

THE ECONOMIC AND POLITICAL SITUATION IMMEDIATELY BEFORE 1848

In the mean time many things had changed in Italy since the Restoration, particularly from the economic point of view.

The symbol of the new capitalist economy and its extraordinary energy were those railways which, as we have seen, Cavour had praised in one of his first writings. Italy too had its railways: from Florence to Pisa, completed in 1848; from Turin to Moncalieri; the first stretch of the Turin–Genoa line, opened in 1845; the Milan–Venice line, which still lacked the stretch from Treviglio to Vicenza; and other smaller lines. Together with the railways, the other institution that supported the new industrialism was the bank; and in this sector too there had been major developments. In 1823 the Savings Bank of the Lombard provinces opened, in 1844 the Genoa Banca di sconto, and in 1847 that of Turin. A similar bank had been operating in Florence since 1817. But the banks and the railways both led, from opposite directions, to the factories, with their thunderous, revolutionary machines. Italy had made most industrial progress in the field of textiles. In Lombardy alone the production of silk had risen from 2,200,000 kilograms in 1815 to 3,500,000 in 1841, when there were 15,000 looms and 101,644 spindles active in cotton manufacture. These figures are scattered indications, but they are enough to convey the picture of a capitalist economic development that was well under way, even though it did not involve the whole country, but only its most advanced areas. The sustained nature of this development and of the general tone of economic life is most clearly revealed by the development of foreign trade, which grew from a total of 275 million lire in 1830 to one of 650 million in 1850.

It is true that Italy's economic development did not keep pace with that of other European countries: the railway network was still in its infancy, and the internal trade from one state to another was less highly developed than foreign trade; the remains of feudalism and its restrictions were still a heavy encumbrance, especially in the south. Even so, Italy's development towards a middle-class, trading economy had reached the point of no return: Italy saw its entry into the international market and into free trading Europe as inevitable.

But this also meant that Italy was exposed to the risks and cyclical fluctuations of the capitalist economy and its circumstances, and that the weakest and most backward sectors of her economy were subjected to the harsh competition of a market in which the arrival of Russian corn, silk from Bengal or Australian wool dealt sharp counterblows. This had most effect on agriculture, which during the whole period 1818–46 experienced a downward curve of prices, especially corn prices. The farming concerns that were organized on a capitalist basis, or rather the most up-to-date and best managed ones, tried to protect themselves against this tendency by moving over to more remunerative and more industrial forms of farming, and by using, increasingly, the wage-earning labour-force that the crisis among small landowners made widely available and cheap. This took place most of all in the fertile countryside of lower Lombardy, where large-scale livestock-raising and the industrial processing of its products were considerably developed, and in Emilia. In the countryside around Bologna in 1845 there were already forty-five thousand agricultural day-labourers, as many as there were *métayers* and landholders. But elsewhere, as had already happened during the later eighteenth century, there was an attempt to adapt farming to the new conditions of the international market by the traditional means of intensifying exploitation, and by making agriculture more of an attack on the land, as it still largely was in the poorer parts of Italy, particularly in the South. So there was an assault on common land, the conversion of pastureland to areas of extensive cereal-growing (such as the Apulia Tavoliere) and above all there was the indiscriminate deforestation that upset the water-cycle and caused immeasurable harm to the southern economy.

So on the verge of 1848 the fundamental characteristics of the Italian economic development had already emerged, at least in rough outline. It was a development characterized, if not conditioned, by wide disparities between the various sectors of economic life and between the various regions, and mined by profound contradictions and tensions. The character and development of the 1848 movement partly reflected these tensions.

It brought together not only the impatience and the progressive aspirations of the middle classes and the intellectuals but also the resentments of peasants reduced to the level of labourers, and the unease of a broad section of the people who were not yet a proletariat but no longer entirely plebeian either, who were goaded by famine and unemployment into occasional outbursts of rebellion, and who were beginning to see also the first glimmerings of an elementary revolutionary awareness. The 'fear of communism' that spread among the privileged Italian classes at that time arose more from their mental narrowness than from the real state of things, yet there had been signs of something like communism. In Lombardy in February and March of 1847 there had been riots for food among the peasants, in Tuscany socialist and communist ideas had taken hold, both in the excited, heated atmosphere of Leghorn and in some limited areas of the countryside. There had been outbreaks of Luddism in Rome, and in southern Italy the traditional insistence of the peasants on the sharing-out of common lands. In certain areas there had also been strikes among workers and day-labourers. Besides, why should the workers and people not agitate and come out into the streets, when the '*signori*' did not disdain to do so? The general political effervescence of the moment encouraged every kind of protest and every kind of hope, even among the humble and among those who had always been cheated of their hopes. Not only the unrest of the middle class and the intellectuals, but also the resentment and expectation of the people brought Italy into the European events of 1848.

Under the combined pressure of Mazzinian agitation and moderate action, Italy's political temperature rose to that particular point of general excitement, not uncommon in the history of revolutionary crowds, when there is a conviction that the time is ripe, and when every event, whether or not it goes or seems to go in the anticipated direction, is interpreted as a sign of the times. This was the atmosphere reigning in Rome when, in June 1846, the Cardinals met in conclave to elect Gregory xvi's successor. There were two favourite candidates: Cardinal Lambruschini, who would have continued Gregory's reactionary policy, and Cardinal Gizzi, who had the reputation of a liberal. Neither of them was able to prevail, and the conclave fell back on a compromise solution, Cardinal Mastai-Ferretti, Bishop of Imola, and a relatively second-rank figure. Disappointment at the defeat of the liberal candidate was heightened by the fact that at one point during the night of 16–17 June the news of his election had been spread and believed, and provoked irrepressible displays of enthusiasm. But this disappointment was not enough to destroy the general persuasion that something extraordinary was bound to happen. The new Pope's concession, a month after his election, of a sweeping amnesty to political prisoners – an action that was in itself predictable and normal – seemed to be that very event which everyone was waiting for. Pius ix was already pointed out as the personification of the liberal, Italian Pope invoked by Gioberti, and demonstrations in his favour spread across all Italy; there were scenes of indescribable enthusiasm.

This atmosphere of general expectation and collective euphoria soon affected the political action of the moderates, and even more that of the Mazzinians, who were determined to seize the moment and convinced that the hopes Pius IX had aroused would end in over-throwing him when it became clear that neither the Pope nor the other Italian rulers were able to fulfil them. Thus, demonstrations in favour of the new Pope took on a more organized and more political character. Faced with these pressures, the Pope had to make concessions: in March 1847 he relaxed press censorship, and a little later authorized the creation of a state council composed of laymen. In Florence too, at the same time, the Lorraine government abolished press censorship, allowing a combative political journalism to be born. Still in the spring of 1847, Milan gave Cobden, the apostle of free-trade, a tumultuous welcome, equal to what he had received in other Italian cities. In October, the government of Turin followed the example of Rome and Florence, announcing a series of adminis-trative reforms and considerably relaxing the rigours of press censor-ship. These measures were preceded by the dismissal of the Foreign Minister Solaro della Margarita, whose reactionary, pro-Austrian views were well-known. At the same time, the negotiations for a customs-alliance between the Papal State, Tuscany and Piedmont, which had been in progress since August, were concluded with the signing of a broad agreement, which did not however define the precise ways in which it was to be put into effect. So Gioberti's idea of a confederation of states under the auspices of a reformist, Italian Pope, seemed on the way to a triumphal realization. But in the mean time Austria, concerned at the turn Italian events were taking, had not remained idle, and in July 1847 had put on a warning demonstration of force by occupying the citadel of Ferrara with an Austrian garrison. The reply soon came: in September 1847 and January 1848 there were anti-Austrian demonstrations and angry incidents in Milan, while anti-Habsburg feelings mounted in all Italy, and people were already speaking openly of war. The Mazzinians above all were moving in this direction, and were active as they had never been before. Mazzini himself, who felt like 'a steed scenting the battle', was not at that time averse to lending his own support to Carlo Alberto, provided the latter openly declared himself against Austria and made the cause of unity and independence his own.

Events were, then, following one another so thick and fast that the breaking-point seemed near.

THE ITALIAN 1848

The only Italian state that remained impervious to the reformist current of 1846–7 was the Kingdom of Naples, whose ruler, Ferdinand II, soon had to pay the price of this intransigence. He had granted no reforms, and now found himself facing revolution. This started from Palermo, where an uprising of a fairly improvised, popular nature which had begun on 12 January, gathered more support on its way, involving the middle class and the aristocracy, whose interests and attitudes were opposed, yet who were united in a common autonomist urge and tradition. Early in February the whole island, except for the fortress of Messina, was in the hands of the rebels, a Sicilian government was set up and the downfall of the Bourbon dynasty proclaimed. Meanwhile the revolutionary agitation had crossed the straits and spread to the mainland southern provinces, particularly the Cilento peninsula. On 29 January Ferdinand II was forced to perform the task of granting a constitution, thus going well beyond the concessions previously made by other Italian rulers. Under the pressure of public opinion these others in turn very soon had to align themselves with the new situation that had taken shape in the Kingdom of Naples, and constitutions or statutes were conceded in Florence, Turin and in Rome itself. In all these cases it was a question of documents on the lines of the French constitution of 1830, which provided for a state based on the two-chamber system, suffrage according to taxation, and the formation of a national guard as a civilian militia. Only the later constitutions of Sicily and the Roman Republic, which will be described further on, had a more radical and democratic character.

The news of the Parisian revolution of February certainly helped to hasten the decisions of the Italian rulers. The news from Budapest and Vienna towards mid-March created a new situation and gave a further powerful impetus to the Italian revolution. Hungary was in rebellion, Vienna itself in a state of agitation, Metternich forced to resign: the great opportunity, the 'great commotion' that Cavour had spoken of, without much belief in it, seemed really to have arrived.

At Milan, revolutionary excitement that had been held back for a long time erupted on 18 March and soon overwhelmed the hesitations and prudence of the city's local government, taking on the character of a general uprising, whose co-ordinating body was a Council of War, to which Carlo Cattaneo belonged. The people's determination, the support of the peasants and the inhabitants of neighbouring cities, who were informed of the course of events in Milan by balloon-flights and had flowed towards the city in armed columns, were too much for the fourteen thousand strong Austrian garrison under the command of Radetzky. On 23 March, after five days of street-fighting, Milan was free. In the mean time Venice too had rebelled, and on 22 March the Austrian garrison capitulated and a provisional government led by Daniele Manin restored the old Venetian Republic.

On the very day of the entire victory of the Milan uprising, Piedmontese troops under the command of Carlo Alberto, with the tricolour at their head, crossed the Ticino, and in the following days were joined by contingents from Tuscany, the Papal State and Naples. The first war of independence had begun, and the boldest hopes of Italian Guelfism and moderate liberalism seemed near realization. But disappointments were not slow to follow, and difficulties to emerge. On 29 April Pius IX, who had made the patriots ecstatic two months before with his invocation of the divine benediction on Italy, made an allocution dissociating himself, as pastor of all peoples, from the present struggle; he thus destroyed the neo-Guelf myth of an Italian revival under the auspices of the Church. A few days later, on 15 May, after a confused day full of actions and reversals, Ferdinand II of Naples won back full control of the situation, inflicting a serious blow on the liberal movement.

So the burden of war now rested almost entirely on the shoulders of Piedmont and the provisional government set up in Milan: two partners who were far from being in perfect agreement. As Cattaneo and the Lombard democrats had feared, Carlo Alberto's intervention, which many people had thought slow, had been an action more in the spirit of the traditional dynastic policy of the house of Savoy than in that of the hoped-for common crusade for the liberation of Italy. This became clear from the movements of Piedmontese diplomacy at the court of Milan and the other courts of Italy, from May to July. Its double objective, which it reached in May, was to persuade the provisional governments that had emerged from the Milanese and Venetian insurrections to arrange, by plebiscites, the annexation of their various territories by the Kingdom of Sardinia, and in the second place, to defer until the war was won any decision on the political form of the new Italian state that would emerge.

This last point was supported with the argument that for the moment it would be necessary to subordinate everything to the conduct of the war, an argument that would have been irreproachable if the war had in fact been conducted resolutely by Piedmont. But it was not. On two occasions Carlo Alberto's troops let slip golden opportunities: first when, as soon as they had crossed the frontier, they failed to pursue

Radetzky's forces, who were engaged in a difficult retreat across an unreliable country, from Milan towards the forces of the Quadrilateral*. The second missed chance was the failure to follow up the victory of Goiti (30 May) and the Austrians' surrender of the fortress of Peschiera; Radetzky was allowed to recover himself, and to counter-attack, defeating Vicenza. This was in fact the turning-point of the war: from that moment the initiative was in the hands of the Austrians, who on 25 July won an important victory at Custoza. Carlo Alberto fell back to Milan, not so much to ensure the city's defence as to forestall a popular movement to do so. Immediately after his entry into the city he angered the Milanesi by negotiating a cease-fire with Radetzky, which was followed by an armistice signed by General Salasco on 9 August.

From the dynastic, Piedmontese point of view, Carlo Alberto's, the only solution now offering itself was a peace that would save Piedmont's face and allow her modest territorial gains in Lombardy and the duchies. Savoy diplomacy worked towards this aim during the following months, trying to bring about a Franco-English mediation, and all the time moving further away from Italian patriotism. In the light of these directions of policy it may be understood why the Duke of Genoa, Carlo Alberto's second son, refused the crown of Sicily, offered to him by the Sicilian parliament. But this Piedmontese ambition too proved illusory – Franco-English mediation achieved no result.

At this moment of defeat, of the recrudescence of Piedmontese and Savoy parochialism, and of the failure of neo-Guelfism, the demo-cratic alternative, already fleetingly suggested by Mazzini, of an Italian Assembly elected by universal suffrage, which would have the task of leading the struggle against Austria and of speeding the approach of Italian unity, was once more put forward. The movement for such an assembly won its first victory in Tuscany, where a new ministry was formed in October 1848, led by Guerrazzi, from Leghorn, and Montanelli, who was the leading theorist of the popular assembly idea. At Rome meanwhile democracy was on its way: the assassination of the government minister Pellegrino Rossi, by members of a political society, on 15 November, followed a few days later by Pius ix's flight to Gaeta (where he was soon joined by the Grand Duke of Tuscany, Leopold ii), left the field free for the extremist radicals of the capital, and, even more, the provinces. Elections were held, which produced an assembly composed largely of democrats. In February 1849 this assembly declared the end of Papal rule and proclaimed the Roman Republic. The democratic wave, which had swept over Florence and

* The system of fortifications whose bases were Mantua, Verona, Peschiera and Legnano.

Rome, also affected Turin, where, in December 1848, the task of forming a new government was entrusted to Gioberti, who, waging for some months an open battle against the *municipali* (supporters of a parish pump policy), allied himself with democratic elements. His governmental actions were however far from limpid. After negotiating with Florence and Rome for the convocation of an Italian elected assembly, he became involved in an attempt to restore the rule of the Grand Duke in Florence, by means of a Piedmontese armed intervention. But Gioberti came into conflict with Carlo Alberto, who tried to gain control of the army, and with the democrats; he was eventually forced to resign, in February 1849. A few days later Carlo Alberto broke the armistice with Austria signed in August, and resumed hostilities. This was an enterprise with small chance of success, taking place as it did at an unfavourable diplomatic moment, when the forces of reaction were triumphant in Vienna and in Paris, and the political atmosphere had lost its earlier excitement. It seemed to be undertaken almost as a point of honour. Military operations were once more conducted shakily, and immediately took an unfavourable turn for the Piedmontese army, which was irrevocably beaten at Novara on 23 March. In view of the extreme gravity of his political and military failure, Carlo Alberto chose to abdicate in favour of his son Vittorio Emanuele II, who immediately embarked on peace negotiations with Austria. These were concluded on 6 August, and sealed Piedmont's renunciation of any territorial gain and any support of the revolutionary Italian movement. But in the mean time the new King had had to suppress an uprising in firmly democratic Genoa, which had rebelled against the clauses of the treaty.

At the beginning of spring 1849, a year after March 1848, when the way to the most glowing aspirations had been opened, the Italian cause seemed irremediably compromised. Piedmont was defeated, Lombardy and the Venetian mainland were once more occupied by the Austrians, the Bourbons were restored in Sicily after a struggle lasting from May 1848 to March 1849, and in Florence, in May, an Austrian expeditionary force put the Grand Duke back on his throne. The only citadels of Italian freedom were now Rome and Venice. Napoleon III sent an expeditionary force against Rome and its republican government, under the specious pretext of attempting to reconcile the Roman liberals with the Pope. This force met with the firm resistance of a whole population, ranked firmly around Mazzini and the other *triumviri* and under Garibaldi's military leadership. Oudinot's troops were driven back to begin with, on 30 April, and were only able to enter Rome on 3 July, after facing fierce resistance. Two days before, the Assembly had approved the Constitution of the Republic, the most advanced of the Italian constitutions, and the only one to show any sensitivity towards social problems.

The last to fall was Venice, which Garibaldi had in vain tried to reach with a march that belongs to the legend of the Risorgimento. The surrender took place on 24 August, after a long, exhausting siege, borne worthily and courageously by the old republic.

This is the story of Italy's 1848. The account may have seemed confusing, but this is a confusion inherent in the events, so much that the Italian expression *fare un quarantotto* has become a synonym for disorder and disarray. For the revolutionary Italy of 1848 was like a mosaic whose pieces did not fit together: once again, belying the hopes of Gioberti's federalism, the various rulers, particularly Carlo Alberto, paid most attention to the interests of their respective states; once again the old regional rivalries had flourished: Lombards had been mistrustful of Piedmontese, and the people of the Veneto suspicious of Venice, the Sicilians had risen against Neapolitan rule, there had been antagonism between Turin and Genoa, between Florence and Leghorn. But above all, the ruling class had lacked the capacity (or the will) to utilize and canalize the discontent of the people at that moment.

Even so, there had been considerable popular participation in the risings of 1848, far more than in those of 1820 and 1831. In the towns, in Milan, Venice, Rome, Leghorn and Palermo, the people had taken an active part in insurrections, and had fought bravely. In the countryside of Lombardy, we have seen that peasants were also a part of the general movement, while in the South and in Sicily they had supported the movement by greatly accentuating their demands and agitations for the sharing-out of Common lands. Nor, on the other hand, even in the declining phase of the revolution, were there any movements like that of the Holy Faith, save in Tuscany. This was in spite of the fact that Austria, mindful of recent experience in Galicia, had done all it could to stir up such feelings. But this participation, or at least availability, of the masses had been met with indifference, and in many cases with fear. The elections held in various Italian states almost all took place on the basis of suffrage according to taxation, and where they did not, as in Sicily, the restriction of the vote to those who could read and write was alone enough to provide an insurmountable barrier for the great majority of the population. The National Guard, where it was formed, often behaved like a class militia. Little, very little was done to relieve the weight of the economic crisis and of famine: some public works, some alleviation of taxes, which were however largely outweighed by the fall in the value of money. Only the Roman Republic, in February 1849, issued a decree arranging for the considerable inheritance of confiscated church property to be re-distributed among the poorest peasants. But the pressure of too many interests prevented these Roman 'decrees of Ventosus' from being applied.

The defeat of the 1848 movement was certainly a grave blow to the cause of Italian independence and liberty; but this had by now gone too far on its way to be stopped.

The victories of the Risorgimento

ITALIAN DEMOCRACY FROM 1849 TO 1857

The experience of 1848 had no deep effect on the political attitudes and convictions of Giuseppe Mazzini. In spite of the defeat that had been suffered he remained convinced that the Italian situation would remain highly explosive, and that a recovery of the revolutionary movement was imminent – an illusion shared by the majority of Italian democrats. To avoid a repetition of the failure of 1848 it was necessary only that the insurrection of the various oppressed nations of Europe – Italy, Hungary and Poland – should be more general and more co-ordinated. In other words, against the Holy Alliance of the princes there should be a Holy Alliance of the people. To this end he set up a central European democratic committee, in July 1850, in London. Members of this included Ruge for Germany and Darasz for Poland; France was represented by Ledru-Rollin, whom Mazzini, to many people's surprise, had preferred to Blanc. For in Mazzini's eyes Blanc was the living incarnation of those socialist 'systems' which to his mind brought into national democracy an element of division and dogmatism that threatened its energies and weakened its impact. The cause of the people and of the emancipation of oppressed nationalities could permit no divisions: and in any case Mazzini's eyes were turned on Hungary, Poland, Germany and of course on Italy, more than on France.

But in taking this course was there not a risk of robbing the projected revolutionary movement of those popular forces that were its only hope of success, and which made the problem of the 'right to work', passed over in silence by Mazzini, the only really important one? Was it legitimate to sink the social problem in the national one, as Mazzini was, basically, doing? Those who asked themselves such questions as these were answered by a short work, the *Federazione repubblicana*, written by Giuseppe Ferrari, a Milanese, formerly a

professor at the University of Strasbourg, noted for his scathing polemics against the Jesuits and for the part he had played in the Lombard
insurrection of 1848, as well as for his occasionally bizarre and paradoxical, but always keen intelligence. In this pamphlet he maintained
that the revolution in individual states should precede the struggle for
independence, in contrast to what had happened in 1848, and that
this revolution would have to have a frankly social, or rather socialist,
emphasis, which must go as far as proclaiming the need for agrarian
law. The model was that of the Paris revolution of February to June
1848, and the signal for revolt and support for it would once more
come from Paris. In fact, Ferrari rejected as provincial and utopian
Mazzini's concept of an Italian initiative.

The attempt to regroup Italian democracy on this programmatic
basis, competing with the Mazzinian movement, was unsuccessful:
one way or another, Ferrari's ideas aroused confusion and uncertainty.
There were some, like his friend and fellow-Milanese Cattaneo, who
had taken a leading part in the provisional Milanese government of
1848, who rejected Ferrari's socialist aspirations, in accordance with
a completely and consistently bourgeois view of the development of
Italian society. Others, like Carlo Pisacane, a young and brilliant
ex-officer from Naples, who had distinguished himself in the defence
of the Roman Republic, were opposed to the leading rôle assigned to
the French revolution, since it condemned Italian revolutionaries to
wait for the French to act. But as far as socialism was concerned,
Pisacane was not only in agreement with Ferrari, but even strengthened the dose: the very fact that Italy was a backward country
compared with France, and that her peasant problem involved the
ancien régime, meant that Italy could more easily get over the bourgeois
phase of the revolution; for this reason the Italian revolution should
have a markedly indigenous character, and should develop independently. So Pisacane may have felt intellectually drawn towards Ferrari
in one sense, as far as his analysis of the motive forces of revolution
were concerned, but on the other hand his persuasion that it was
necessary to do something, and act from within Italian society, drew
him back towards Mazzini.

In spite of the 'formalism' of his programme, Mazzini's personal
magnetism, his tactical ability, and the prestige that he had won from
his part in the glorious Roman Republic made him still the only
Italian democrat with a following among *émigrés* and at home. Between
1850 and 1853 he succeeded in gathering together many of the threads
that had been scattered after 1849, and in building up an important
organizational network in the Papal State, in Tuscany, in Liguria,
where it was linked with the first workers' co-operative group, and in

Lombardy. In Milan especially the Mazzinians were able to establish a firm relationship with the Brotherhoods of workers and artisans and with the people of the city. Only in the South and in Sicily was the Mazzinian organization thinly represented. In February 1853, even though his conspiratorial network in Liguria had recently been uprooted and decimated by the police, Mazzini once more gave the word for an uprising. This was to have taken place on 6 February in Milan, and other Italian cities and regions were to have joined in. Once it was victorious, the revolution was to exert pressure on Turin to resume the war of independence. In fact, the only ones who came out into the streets on the prearranged day were groups of the Milanese lumpen-proletariat, whose attempted uprising was easily crushed.

Once again, in spite of defections and extremely harsh criticisms, Mazzini refused to give up. He took shelter in his native Genoa, where he lived secretly for three years and built up a new political body, the Action Party, whose task, as its name indicated, was to be an advance-guard guerrilla organization, formed of professional revolutionaries. Cut off from contact with the people, Mazzini once more fell back on the idea of a revolutionary élite, whose example and whose militia would attract the people back to their side. On this basis, the collaboration between Mazzini and Pisacane developed during this period.

As has been said, Pisacane's historico-political idea and vision of the Italian revolution were very different and a good deal more advanced than Mazzini's. But they agreed on the need for a military action, and in repudiating the idea of waiting for a French upheaval. Mazzinian political activism had only to be combined with a precise knowledge of the Italian problem for enough leverage to be produced to overthrow the whole edifice. The weakest link in the chain of reactionary rule was not, as Mazzini had thought, in the cities of northern Italy, among the lower and middle classes of Milan, Genoa and Leghorn, but in the South, among peasants starved of land and of justice. They were the motive forces of the Italian revolution, and this would occur not by means of a conquest of the poor South by the bourgeois North, but, on the contrary, by a revolutionary explosion in the South, which would then be communicated to the whole country: it was to be a revolution 'from below' in both the geographical and the social sense. Thus was born an idea that would be dear to Bakunin, and after him, to many representatives of Italian democracy. This meeting between Mazzini and Pisacane produced what may in a sense be considered the last Mazzinian revolutionary attempt, the Sapri expedition of June 1857. Pisacane set sail from Genoa at the head of a party of patriots, who were later joined by political prisoners freed from the island of

Ponza, and landed at Sapri on the evening of 28 June. But the peasant jacquerie Pisacane had hoped to arouse did not materialize; on the contrary, the peasants of the place gave strong support to the Bourbons, and Pisacane and almost all his companions were killed. A few months after his tragic end, Pisacane's political testament was printed in the newspapers: it displayed the revolutionary clarity of mind with which he had set off on his hazardous enterprise, fully aware of its risks and small chance of success, but deeply convinced that he still had to perform his duty as a revolutionary.

The immediate effect of the Sapri disaster was to create a void around Mazzini once again. Many people considered that he had been too often pardoned for his rashness. But this time, unlike what had happened in 1848, those who left Mazzini moved towards more moderate instead of more radical positions. This way had in any case been paved by Mazzini himself, who had in the last years, as in 1848, been defining a political line (the so-called 'neutral flag') that subordinated all problems, including that of the form of government, to the achievement of unity and independence. Though in the days of the vacillating Carlo Alberto it had been hard to imagine that Piedmont could give full guarantees and assurance of the victory of the Italian cause, things were now greatly changed. Something radically and profoundly new was emerging in old Piedmont.

CAVOUR AND PIEDMONT

One of the legends of Italian Risorgimento historiography is that in the discussions at Vignale between Radetzky and the new King, Vittorio Emanuele II, after the defeat of Novara, the King refused to commit himself to repealing the Statute, and gave up possible territorial gains for its sake. In fact this suggestion was never made to him, and it is known for certain that Vittorio Emanuele assured Austria he would oppose the democratic party, as he was in any case personally inclined to do. In November 1849, after crushing the revolt at Genoa, he did not hesitate to dissolve the Chamber, which had shown itself unwilling to approve the peace treaty. Vittorio Emanuele accompanied the decree of dissolution with a quite explicit proclamation (written by the Prime Minister, d'Azeglio), hinting at a possible repeal of the Statute, if the elections did not prove favourable to the moderates. But the moderates' victory, and d'Azeglio's firmness, were able to banish the danger of an absolutist restoration, and Piedmont, alone among Italian states, went on to be a constitutional monarchy. In fact, once the critical immediate post-war moment was past, its government, in spite of firm opposition from the '*municipali*' and conservatives, and the King's own uncertainty, resumed the reformist line that had characterized the various Italian governments in the years 1846–8. In February 1850, Siccardi, Lord Keeper of the Seals in d'Azeglio's government, presented to the Chamber a set of laws whose overall tendency was to limit the privileges of the clergy (by the abolition of ecclesiastical courts and of the remains of the right of sanctuary, and by reducing the number of religious holidays), and so to bring Piedmontese legislation into line with that of other Italian states, in a field in which it was particularly backward. Siccardi's laws were passed without meeting excessive resistance, but the civil marriage bill presented by d'Azeglio faced a different reaction, being so strongly opposed by the Chamber that d'Azeglio was forced to resign in October 1852. After a turbulent crisis, Count Camillo Benso di Cavour, who in the previous ministry had held the post of Minister of Agriculture, and had pledged himself not to make the civil marriage bill the subject of a vote of confidence, was called to form a new cabinet.

So the man to whose name is linked the achievement of Italian unity rose to power: one of the few figures of Italian history who has come down to posterity with the glamour of the conqueror rather than that of the defeated. He was the younger son of an old noble family, intended by his father for a military career, which he had soon given up for a life of travel, business, speculation, study and love, and, at a riper age, to devote himself to politics. In a society with many reduced aristocrats slinking into the middle class, and many middle-class people posing as aristocrats, he combined all the virtues of both classes: he had the intellectual restlessness and habit of command, the taste for earning and for spending money, the freshness of energy of a newer social class, and the style of an old one. His political opinions were moderate, far from any sympathy for the revolution or for the Mazzinians' political romanticism; yet he realized that it was impossible to govern against the widespread democratic longings that were fermenting among the middle and lower-middle classes, and even before he took the reins of government he made sure of a safe majority in Parliament by forming an alliance (called the *connubio*) with the more moderate left-wing elements and their leading representative, Urbano Rattazzi. Being in this way guaranteed against the impatience of the Mazzinians and the retrograde nostalgia of the court '*municipali*', he was able to proceed relatively calmly with the programme of liberalization and modernization of Piedmontese society which he had in mind.

This programme affected the economic field most of all. Having

read Adam Smith, and being an enlightened and enterprising agri-
culturalist, Cavour's conception of economic development was essentially that of a free-trader. In his opinion the way to the revival of
Piedmontese society passed by way of the victory of the mercantile
and capitalistic tendencies already at work in it, and this victory in
turn presupposed a radical, invigorating liberalization of the market,
and Piedmont's full entry into the great circuit of the European
economy. Cavour, profoundly convinced of the justice and the
fecundity of such a prospect of economic development, had already,
during the eighteen months when he had been Minister of Agriculture,
arranged a series of commercial agreements with France, England,
Belgium and Austria, all of which had been marked by a definite
liberalism. His vision of capitalist development was essentially based
on the possibility that it would germinate from below, through the
bold actions of individual producers and farmers, as had happened in
the advanced societies of western Europe, in England and in France.
But this would take a long time, and Cavour, who was no doctrinaire,
and had learned from the texts he had read the distinction between
theoretic economics and political economy, did not exclude the
possibility of short cuts and expedients that might allow the economy
of Piedmont, or of Italy, to make up for lost time. The action of the
state had to be directed towards this aim – the aim of hastening and
making easier the free development of the bourgeois economy. So
Cavour planned and promoted the construction of infra-structural
public works on a grand scale: the canal that took its name from him,
and which permitted the rational irrigation of the countryside around
Novara and around Vercelli, the Fréjus tunnel, railways. To this
picture belongs also the constituting of a great central state institute
of credit, the National Bank, embryo of the future Bank of Italy.

The fruits of this economic policy soon appeared: at the beginning
of 1859 Piedmont had 850 kilometres of railways, privately and
publicly owned, as against 986 kilometres in all the rest of Italy. Its
foreign trade was markedly better than that of the neighbouring,
flourishing Lombard-Venetian Kingdom; whereas in the rest of Italy
economic development marked time after its rise between 1830 and
1846, Piedmont was the one state able to keep up, to some extent, with
the dizzy rise of Europe's capitalist economy.

But economic freedom was inconceivable without political freedom,
and the freedom of the middle classes inconceivable without that of all
citizens. Cavour was fully aware of this, and so carried very resolutely
on with the work of freeing the state from the Church, begun by
d'Azeglio. In 1855, rather than give up a law suppressing a large
number of religious communities, he was ready to face a difficult

government crisis, the so-called Calabiana crisis, and to resist the King, who had promised Pius ix that he would do what he could to prevent this law from being passed. Under Cavour, Piedmont was not only the one Italian state in which political and parliamentary life followed the norms of constitutional monarchy and the Statute, but also the only one where there flourished an effective freedom of the press, of political groups, and of teaching. This eventually made the Kingdom a centre of attraction for many of the Italian political exiles, who came to settle in Turin in ever-increasing numbers, and were given important positions in teaching and administration. There were soon tens of thousands of them: so many that the problem of their living together with the Piedmontese population became a serious one. Among them were men of great reputation and authority, such as the Romagnolo Luigi Carlo Farini, the Lombard Cesare Correnti, the Modenese Manfredo Fanti, who became General of the Piedmontese army, the Sicilian Francesco Ferrara, an important economist, responsible for the *Biblioteca dell'economista* series, which introduced to Italy the classics of modern political economy, the Neapolitan Bertrando Spaventa, a philospher of the Hegelian school, and Francesco de Sanctis, also of Naples, the most learned critic and literary historian of nineteenth century Italy. The political émigrés in Piedmont were not only from various regions, but also held differing political views: some, like Mamiani, Bonghi and Bianchi were more or less close to the moderate attitudes of Piedmont and Cavour; others, like the close-knit group in Genoa whose leading members were Rosolino Pilo, Agostino Bertani and Pisacane himself, had been or still were Mazzinians. After the failure of the Sapri attempt, as has already been hinted, there was an increasing tendency among the *émigrés* to move closer to Cavour's attitudes. In this way, under the leadership of La Farina and Daniele Manin, there developed the National Society, whose intention was to gather around itself, under the flag of monarchic unitarism, all the elements of Italian patriotism. Giuseppe Garibaldi joined. So Mazzini's isolation was complete. To begin with, the Society was tacitly authorized, and later publicly and officially encouraged: we shall see in the next section that it was a major instrument in Cavour's foreign and national policy.

CAVOUR'S DIPLOMACY AND THE SECOND WAR OF INDEPENDENCE

The idea of Cavour as the diplomatic and patient weaver of the slowly-achieved unity of Italy is one of the most commonly accepted. But it would be wrong to suppose that the goal of unity, which he was in fact to achieve, was clear before his eyes from the beginning, or that all his diplomatic activity was directed towards this great end. For as we shall see, up to a quite late date Cavour considered the unity of Italy under the house of Savoy to be a practically unattainable objective, and his talent was not an inflexible ability to wait for situations to mature and the days of decision to arrive, but rather the empiricism of a statesman who knew how to draw the maximum advantage from situations and circumstances as they gradually arose. He was able to do this because he was fully aware of the fact that, as events were to show, the existence of an unclearly-defined European political situation was an indispensable condition for any Italian initiative.

From this point of view the situation during the 1850's was a good deal more favourable than that which had been opened up by the July revolution of 1830. Cavour was one of the first to realize that the rise of Bonapartism did not imply France's return to an isolationist or, worse, legitimist policy, in spite of the slogan '*l'empire c'est la paix*'. The dynamic and progressive rôle of English policy in Europe being firmly established, Piedmontese diplomacy won another trump card in the deterioration of Austro-Russian relations, which was a sequel of the events of 1848, and reached the point of open conflict with the re-raising of the Eastern problem, and the war in the Crimea (1853–6). Piedmont sent an expeditionary force to fight beside the French and English troops around Sebastopol, and so won the chance to join the great powers in the business of European politics, and to take part in the Congress of Paris in 1856. In fact it was Vittorio Emanuele II rather than Cavour who exerted most pressure for intervention in the Crimean War, but Cavour was certainly able to draw the greatest possible political advantage from Piedmont's military contribution. The Congress of Paris, at which Cavour represented Piedmont, did not provide the territorial gains Piedmont had hoped for (the annexations of the duchies of Parma and Modena); and the discussion of the Italian problem, raised by Cavour, only took place at the last session, and was confined to a speech by the English delegate, Lord Clarendon, condemning the misgovernment inflicted on the subjects of the Papal State and the Kingdom of Naples. No common document was arrived at. But if these were the limits of the Paris Congress as far as the Italian question was concerned, Cavour's feverish diplomatic activity, in particular his consolidation of his already good personal relations with Napoleon III, were very soon to show clear results. Besides, the very fact that the Congress of Paris produced no practical results strengthened Cavour's belief that the problem of Italy could not be solved by diplomatic means, and that it would be necessary to face bravely up to the possibility of further armed struggle against Austria. '*Le canon seul*', Cavour wrote to Emanuele d'Azeglio, '*peut nous tirer d'affaire*'.

But who was to be Piedmont's ally in the new war of independence? The hope that it might be France seemed to evaporate on 14 January 1858, when the news spread across Europe that the Emperor had had the luck to escape from an attempted assassination, and that the would-be assassin was an Italian, Felice Orsini, who had intended by his gesture to strike at the man of 2 December, and the destroyer of the Roman Republic. But the unforeseeable happened: Orsini's dignity in facing trial and death, and the letter he addressed to Napoleon from prison, exhorting him to free Italy – it was published, probably on the Emperor's own authorization – persuaded Napoleon that a solution to the Italian problem had to be found and could not be put off. Six months after the attempt Napoleon met Cavour at Plombières, and during their discussion they laid down the basis for a future alliance and for Italy's political form in the case of victory. Piedmont was to cede Nice and Savoy to France, and would gain all northern Italy above the Appenines: the territories of central Italy, except Rome and the surrounding region, would constitute a Kingdom of central Italy, under a sovereign still to be chosen, and southern Italy would conserve its unity and its frontiers, though the ruling dynasty would be changed. Napoleon perhaps had in mind the son of Joachim Murat. These three Italian states would form a confederation under the presidency of the Pope. These agreements (of which only the parts concerning the constitution of the Kingdom of northern Italy under the house of Savoy and the cession of Nice and Savoy featured in the treaty signed in January 1859) were strengthened by the marriage of the Princess Clotilde, Vittorio Emanuele's daughter, to Prince Jérome Bonaparte.

There followed for Cavour months of unnerving waiting, haunted by the fear that his plan's success would be prejudiced by England's intervention as a mediator. But the Austrian ultimatum of 19 April provided the *casus belli* foreseen in the treaty, and freed him from these uncertainties. Hostilities opened on 29 April, and military operations soon went favourably for the Franco-Piedmontese army: the French victory of Magenta opened the doors of Milan, and the victories of

Solferino and San Martino offered the chance of bringing the campaign to a swift victorious conclusion. But this chance was not taken, due to new and unforeseen circumstances – unforeseen by Napoleon, at any rate.

For in central Italy in the mean time the respective rulers had been overthrown by bloody insurrections and, encouraged by the National Society, the idea of annexation to Piedmont became more popular every day. These developments of the situation, added to the fear of a possible Prussian intervention, induced Napoleon to make hasty peace negotiations with Austria at Villafranca on 11 July, the terms being that Piedmont should only be ceded Lombardy, with the exception of the stronghold of Mantua; otherwise, save for the constitution of a hypothetical Italian federation, the status quo was to be preserved. Faced with this *fait accompli*, which left Austria still firmly entrenched in Italy, Cavour resigned, in great bitterness. The King gave the task of forming a new government to La Marmora. Though Cavour was no longer in power, his supporters, and the men of the National Society, were still active in Bologna, Florence and the Legations, and urged annexation with increasing insistence. Napoleon III, who at Villafranca had firmly opposed the restoration of the dethroned rulers by an Austrian intervention, was thus placed in a rather delicate and uneasy situation. He ran the risk of dissatisfying all parties: the Austrians, who wanted Italy to return to the status quo; the Italians, who had regarded the Villafranca agreement as a betrayal; and the French, who had had to abandon the idea of winning Nice and Savoy. The Emperor's own inclination was to escape from this impasse by a solution that favoured Italy's interests; but before any action materialized Cavour had returned to power in January 1860, and brought an end to the extremely delicate situation by negotiating what was by this stage the only realistic solution: Piedmont's annexation of Tuscany and Emilia, and France's of Nice and Savoy. Both were brought about by the typically Napoleonic method of a plebiscite, which took place on 11 and 12 March in Emilia and Tuscany and 15 and 22 April in Nice and Savoy; both produced an overwhelming majority in favour of annexation. Yet the *annus mirabilis* of the Italian Risorgimento was not yet over. Before its end it was to produce other portentous events, and the goal of Italian unity, still considered unreachable, was to be reached.

THE EXPEDITION OF THE THOUSAND
AND THE UNITY OF ITALY

Up to spring 1860, then, the political initiative had been firmly in the hands of Cavour and the moderate party. The democrats, particularly Mazzini, had found themselves confined to the position of begetters of events whose development was no longer in their hands. But the pause following the plebiscites, and the well-founded sensation that with them Piedmont and France considered that they had reached the pillars of Hercules, beyond which they could not go, gave new energy to the democrats' programme of complete unity. Italian unification could not be left half-finished, and if the King and the diplomats had not got the strength to complete it, the people would have to do so. The idea, originally formed by Pisacane and Mazzini, of an expedition to the South, and more particularly Sicily, which would then come up through the peninsula, to Rome, and perhaps even to Venice, began to take root in the minds of Sicilian émigrés such as Crispi and Pilo, especially since the anti-Bourbon revolt had been gathering ground in Sicily since early April. The Sicilians managed to persuade Garibaldi, whose relations with Cavour had recently worsened, to head the expedition. Neither Cavour nor Vittorio Emanuele, who refused Garibaldi a regiment he had asked for, were in favour of the enterprise; for some days it was uncertain whether it was to go ahead, and very few people believed it would be successful. However, on 6 May the expedition of the Thousand set sail, with arms that would not have been out of place in a military museum, and a fund of 94,000 lire. Cavour gave the order for it to be stopped if it landed at the port of Cagliari, but not if it passed wide. The two steamers laden with volunteers had to make a detour at Talamone to get further supplies of arms, and so passed a good distance away from the coast of Sardinia; so they went on undisturbed to Marsala, the Sicilian port where the *Garibaldini* landed on 11 May. They did so on the advice of some fishermen they had met at sea, who signalled to them that there were no Bourbon troops there. Italy's star was evidently in the ascendant.

The first clash with Bourbon troops was on 15 May at Calatafimi, and was a hard battle. In the end the *Garibaldini* won, and the victory had a galvanizing effect on them and on the bands of Sicilian '*picciotti*' (young men) who had joined them. On 30 May, after a brilliant manoeuvre of disengagement from the main body of the Bourbon forces and three days of fighting along the road, Garibaldi became master of Palermo. With mingled amazement and enthusiasm,

Europe watched the unusual spectacle of a handful of armed men getting the better of a powerful regular army and putting the fate of a kindom in doubt.

Cavour found himself, on his own admission, '*dans le plus cruel embarras*'. It was true that when Garibaldi had taken the title of dictator in Sicily he had done so in the name of Vittorio Emanuele, and he seemed firm in his loyalty to the monarchy. But on the other hand it appeared that he was determined to march to Rome, where a French garrison had been stationed since 1849. England gave clear signs of following Garibaldi's exploit with sympathy, but the possibility of diplomatic complications from other directions could not be excluded. Cavour's main perplexity however probably arose from the presentiment, or rather the sure knowledge, that the annexation of the southern territories would considerably alter the terms of the problem that future Italian governments would have to face. Southern Italy, with its *galantuomini*, its countrysides devastated by drought, its peasants hungry for justice, was a different matter from his own Piedmont and from Lombardy, with their farming-businessmen, their canals, their relative prosperity. Those predictions of a slow, gradual capitalist development, which applied to the Po area, could certainly not be applied to the South. This preoccupation frequently appears in Cavour's papers and those of his correspondents in the South during this period.

But Cavour was an expert player and accepted this game too, even if he no longer had the lead. He could certainly not oppose or hinder Garribaldi's enterprise, but he could try to take the control of it away from him and from the democrats. So there began a subterranean struggle between Garibaldi and Cavour, in which the Piedmontese statesman lost some battles and won others, but came out victorious in the end. Cavour was in fact unable to persuade Garibaldi to announce the immediate annexation of Sicily to Italy – the island continued to be ruled by a provisional government dominated by Crispi – or to persuade him to give up the idea of a landing on the mainland (though this is a disputed question). Further, Cavour was unable to spark off an uprising in Naples which would have produced a moderate government before Garibaldi made his triumphal entry on 7 September. On the other hand, Cavour managed to win Napoleon III's assent to a body of regular Piedmontese troops' moving south to occupy the Marche and Umbria.

In the first days of September, after the entry of the *Garibaldini* into Naples, the subtle conflict that had for some time existed between the fiery, glorious General and the shrewd Piedmontese politician reached its climax. On 11 September Garibaldi, knowing the impatience (or sense of inferiority) Vittorio Emanuele felt towards his Prime Minister, wrote asking the King to dismiss Cavour. But Cavour had foreseen this move, and in a discussion with the King, on 8 September, in the presence of Farini, had managed to get from the King a formal promise to support his policy. Strong in this assurance, he was able on 11 October to get the Parliament's assent to plebiscites for annexation to be held in Sicily and the South, similar to those that had been held in Emilia and Tuscany. So the hopes of Garibaldi and the democrats of using their military victories as a political bargaining-counter were dashed. The plebiscites were held on 21 October, and produced both in the South and in Sicily an almost unanimous vote in favour of annexation. The trial of strength had ended in Cavour's total victory. Garibaldi had already given up the idea of going on to Rome, and now there was nothing left for him but to hand over to Vittorio Emanuele, who had advanced south at the head of the Piedmontese army, overcoming resistance in the Papal State, to join up with Garibaldi's forces. Garibaldi had just inflicted the last decisive defeat on the Bourbons near the Volturno. The meeting with the man who was now King of Italy took place at Teano on 27 October, and was far from being as cordial or solemn as patriotic hagiography later presented it.

But the reasons for this fresh defeat of Garibaldi and the democrats are not only to be found in Cavour's diplomatic ability but also, perhaps principally, in the internal developments of the situation in Sicily and in southern Italy. At the moment of his landing at Marsala, and during his advance across Sicily and southern Italy, Garibaldi had appeared to the peasant masses as a mythical liberator and avenger of their sufferings, almost a messiah. Some of the first actions performed by the provisional government he established in Sicily, such as the abolition of the odious grist-tax and the decree of 2 June concerning common land, encouraged these hopes. But disappointment soon followed: on 4 August in the duchy of Bronte, Nino Bixio, the General's faithful lieutenant, suppressed with arrests and mass executions one of the many peasant agitations that had broken out in Sicily during those days of euphoria and hope. The disappointment of the mass of the people showed itself not only in the slackening flow of volunteers into the ranks of Garibaldi's forces, but also in cases of genuine revolt. In September a general peasant uprising, with the massacre of a hundred and forty liberals, broke out in Irpinia, and was quelled only by a column of Garibaldi's troops under the command of the Hungarian Türr. These were the first warnings of brigandage – the peasant guerrilla activity that was to stain with blood the countryside of a good deal of southern Italy during the first years of the new Italian state.

Besides, Garibaldi had not only failed to satisfy the southern peasant masses, but even to calm the fears of the landowning classes. It was their firm opinion that the return to normality and the re-establishment of order in the countryside would be better entrusted to a legitimate King and a regular army, such as those of Piedmont, than to a demagogue and improvised general, surrounded by a dangerous group of democratic agitators. The notabilities and aristocrats of Sicily were advocates of autonomy or unity according to the circumstances, but they were always conservatives; no less than their fellows on the mainland, they implored the Piedmontese to intervene, and joyfully welcomed Cavour's solution of annexation by means of plebiscite. Under the vigilant eyes of the local nobleman and his agent the southern peasants went to place in the urn their 'yes' to the unity of Italy. The scene of the plebiscite in a Sicilian village is vividly described in the novel *Il Gattopardo* (*The Leopard*). Together with these new citizens, however, Italy acquired their sufferings and their grudges: the nation inherited the heavy and difficult 'southern problem'.

ART AND CULTURE OF THE RISORGIMENTO

The existence of a definite Risorgimento culture has already been hinted at. It was in general Romantic, and its emphasis was national and historical. In the history of Italy and of Italian culture it was the moment for a systematic process of retrieval, with the aim of forming a national awareness.

The neo-Guelfs saw Italy as the nation whose free communes, supported by the Papacy, had been the first to raise the banner of revolt against Imperial universalism and the chivalric hierarchy of the feudal world. To those who opposed the Church's authority, and the so-called neo-Ghibellines, Italy was the land of Arnaldo da Brescia and the other mediaeval heretics, and which, in the person of Machiavelli, had pointed an accusing finger at the temporal power of the popes. It was not only a country of writers and merchants, but of soldiers, of men who had fought against foreign invaders: the Milanese Alberto da Giussano, who had defeated Barbarossa; Francesco Ferrucci, heroic defender of Florentine liberty, and the protagonist of a historical novel by Guerrazzi; Ettore Fieramosca, who also appeared in a historical novel by Massimo d'Azeglio, and had defeated the Frenchman La Motte at the *disfida di Barletta*. But setting aside these more obvious and naïve aspects, the action of cultural retrieval performed by Romantic culture during the Risorgimento period produced notable results. The most important, destined to leave a deep mark on generations of future Italians, was without a doubt the *Storia della letteratura italiana* by Francesco De Sanctis, the first history of literature not conceived, as eighteenth-century histories had been, as an anthology of fine passages and good authors, but as an account of the historical development of Italian writing and culture. In this it is not merely a literary history, but also represents the nearest approach to a general history of Italy that the nineteenth century was able to produce.

Beside the name of De Sanctis we should remember that of Ferrari, who, in the wake of Sismondi and Quinet, wrote very stimulatingly on the history of Italian towns and revolutions; Michele Amari, author of an exemplary historical study of Moslem Sicily; and Niccolò Tommaseo, to whom we owe an important dictionary of the Italian language. In the mass, the work achieved by Italian Romantic culture is impressive, and still provides the basis of the teaching of humanistic studies in Italian secondary schools. This of course does not mean that there were no gaps: the discovery of the Renaissance as an historical period, for example, was mainly the work of foreign scholars such as Michelet and Burckhardt.

So, although there certainly was a culture of the Risorgimento, it cannot be said with such confidence that there was a Risorgimento literature. This does not mean that no works were written with the aim of expressing the feelings and civic passions of the generations that lived through the Risorgimento; but only that these writings have no great literary value. There were for instance a large number of historical novels, in which one may look in vain for any trace of Manzoni's great example. The same is true of the patriotic lyric poetry of Berchet and his imitators. Poems such as that on the siege of Venice by Fustinato, or that on the expedition to Sapri by Mercantini, merely succeed in casting a falsely elegiac tone over episodes whose dramatic quality was quite different. Among Italian poets of the Risorgimento only Giusti, with his satiric and burlesque elements, has a personality of his own, if a minor one; of prose writers only Ippolito Nievo, a democrat of very advanced opinions who took part in the 1860 expedition, succeeded in producing anything artistically valid, in his *Confessioni di un italiano*. As for the theatre of the period – even though this is an eminently civic literary genre – it was practically non-existent. To an informed observer like Gogol, who travelled in Italy during the first decades of the century, the Italian scene appeared 'arid and empty', capable only of 'repeating the eternal old Goldoni'. The historico-patriotic tragedies of Niccolini or Silvio Pellico were certainly not such as could fill this gap.

In the last analysis the only artist of the time who succeeded in achieving original and genuine artistic expression on a widely comprehensible level, and who may therefore be considered an artist of the Risorgimento, was Giuseppe Verdi. The Hugo-esque libretti of his operas, his romanticism and popular musical spirit inflamed the audiences of the age. But an art like Verdi's, in which the native, traditional element of Italian temperament occupies such a large place, cannot suffice to represent an entire historic period.

13

A difficult take-off

THE PRICE OF UNIFICATION

If in spring 1859, at the moment when the French and Piedmontese troops were crossing the Ticino, anyone had forecast that in little more than a year the whole peninsula, with the exception of Venice and Lazio, would be unified, very few people, perhaps not even Cavour, would have believed it. Yet the great event had taken place, and on 4 March 1861, after the fall of Gaeta, the last Bourbon stronghold, the Parliament of the Kingdom of Sardinia, met again and solemnly proclaimed the unity of Italy. This had been made possible by a number of factors: an extremely fortunate diplomatic situation, and Cavour's great ability in exploiting it; Garibaldi's spirit of adventure and the '*stellone*'* that had shone over him; the blood of those who had fallen on the battlefields of Lombardy, and of the peasants massacred at Bronte – a series of events and an interplay of opposing forces such as rarely appear at any one historical moment. When such a combination does occur it must give later observers the impression that the normal rhythm of life has been forced.

All such forcing, all accelerations, have their price; and the unification of Italy was no exception. In the first place, there was a price to pay in the most literal and commonly accepted sense of the word: we shall see that the first presidents of the Council and the first finance ministers of the new Kingdom of Italy realized this. But the price of unification was above all a political one, and should be seen as a consequence of the way unification was brought about. As we have seen, it was achieved by a series of annexations to Piedmont of the various pre-existing Italian states. The desire to hasten matters and confront Europe with a *fait accompli*, and, above all, the firm resolve of Cavour

* '*Stellone*' ('big star') is the slightly jocular word applied to the star-shaped emblem placed above the female figure that symbolizes Italy; it represents the good fortune that has helped Italy at crucial historical moments (Trans.).

and the moderates to oppose and even silence the democrats and followers of Garibaldi, made the new state develop from the start more as an expansion of the old Piedmont than as a new, original political organism. Not only did the capital of the Kingdom stay at Turin until 1864 – a completely out-of-the-way position, to reach which the southern Italian deputies had to make a journey of several days, on the railways of the time – but the first King of Italy continued imperturbably to be called Vittorio Emanuele II. What was more serious was that projects for an administrative system based on the autonomy of the regions and on decentralization, prepared by Farini and Minghetti, were dropped. Instead a rigidly centralized system was adopted, with prefects more or less the rulers of local affairs, in a way that was more Napoleonic than French. The electoral law that was extended to the whole country, besides, was that which had been in force in Piedmont since 1848: given the lower level of economic development of most of the other regions, especially the South, the result was that the limited nature of the franchise inherent in the censorial system was accentuated, and in more than one region of Italy the vote became the privilege of a few notabilities. In the elections of 1861, the first in Italian history, there were 167,000 names on the electoral lists in northern Italy, 55,000 in central Italy, 129,000 in southern Italy, and 66,000 on the islands. Those who effectively exercised the right to vote were even fewer: in many cases deputies were elected with a few dozen votes. So the Italian state was born with a heavily bureaucratic and censorial stamp, and for the great majority of its citizens was personified by the tax-collector and by military conscription. Hence the state's rapid unpopularity, the more acute for the great hopes aroused by the general political upheaval that had taken place. It was this very unpopularity, this gap between government and governed, that was the heaviest price Italy had to pay for the way unification had been achieved. It is a price Italy has not yet finished paying today.

The divorce between government and governed, between the élite and the mass, which emerged during the unified state's first years of life, could perhaps have been reduced had there been an opposition movement able to channel existing discontent and suggest realistic alternatives. But Garibaldi had withdrawn to the little island of Caprera, and Mazzini was still an exile. In any case, both of them were by now old, tried and bitter in spirit: there is no trial harder for a revolutionary to overcome than that of seeing the essential part of his programme put into action by his adversaries. They could still, as we shall see, keep alive agitation for the joining of Rome and Venice to Italy. They could try to establish a more solid contact with the masses than they had made in the past, by joining the First International or by hymning the new rising star of socialism. But their strength, and that of their few followers, was, more than anything, the tenacity of survivors. And even if Mazzini's doctrines could still find some support among the lower middle class and the urban artisans, their impact on the common people of the towns and the countryside was weak or non-existent. The rural masses, abandoned to themselves, found themselves almost by necessity forced to express their protest and resentment in the most elementary and immediate ways.

In southern Italy, the most derelict part of the country, this occurred in the traditional, desperate form of brigandage. The bands that had formed in southern Italy since Garibaldi's invasion were formed mainly of peasants and draft-evaders; the support that Bourbon and papal agents had given them is not enough to explain the bitterness of the guerrilla warfare they waged for four years, against a contingent of 100,000 regular troops, on whom they inflicted losses considerably heavier than those of all the wars of the Risorgimento. By thus becoming bandits, the southern peasants did not mean to express any affection for the old order of things, as was recognized by the commission of inquiry set up by the Italian Parliament, and led with perceptive judgement by the deputy Massari. The peasants wished rather to express hostility towards the new order, and to give vent to their own disappointment and despair. Theirs was a pitiless rustic war, unsparing in its cruelty and savagery. But the suppression that was in the end imposed on it was equally so.

The people gave displays of their rage also in the cities of the South; there was the Palermo revolt in 1866, for instance, which had to be quelled by an expeditionary force. In the North, on the other hand, there were violent and widespread peasant uprisings in 1869, following the imposition of the much-hated grist-tax. In this case too military intervention became necessary, and there were thousands of arrests. Mass-protest thus became a constant social and political feature of the new Italy.

It is to this underlying discontent and frustration that one must refer if one is to understand how a first embryo of organized, revolutionary popular opposition took shape in Italy. The clearest thinker concerned with this development, and the man who did most to bring it about, was Michael Bakunin. After a life of tempestuous revolutionary activity, Bakunin landed in Italy in 1864, convinced that here was the weakest link in the chain of reactionary Europe, the country with the most promising prospects of revolution. Bakunin's influence was decisive in moving many of the workers' and people's societies towards more radical views of the revolutionary struggle, and in loosening the hold that Mazzini's ideas had over them. Bakunin's proselytizing was particularly successful in Naples and the South, where the idea that the peasant masses would be the motive force of the future Italian revolution had been current since the time of Pisacane. Mazzini's condemnatory attitude towards the Paris Commune helped to raise Bakunin's prestige even higher, and to make his revolutionary intransigence appear to many people as the symbol of that mysterious and powerful 'International', under whose flag the glorious Parisian *communards* had fought. In fact very little was known in Italy of the violent polemics that were raging in the ranks of the First International during those very years, between the followers of Marx and those of Bakunin, or of the uncertainty with which the General Council of the International itself had reacted towards the Paris Commune. In about 1871 anarchism, socialism and internationalism were equivalent if not synonymous in Italy, and the name of Bakunin was much better known than that of Marx. Under this influence the Italian sections of the International multiplied, and the activity of their members became more intense. In August 1874 there was an actual attempt at an insurrectional *putsch* (which swiftly collapsed). So the internationalist movement, which had almost broken up in the rest of Europe after the Paris Commune, was in contrast entering on its most active phase in Italy. What was more important was that the exhortations to the Italian opposition of proletariat and people were made in the name of an ideology – anarchism – that was already on the wane in other countries, with the exception of Spain.

This was of course related to the backwardness of Italian economic and social structures and, in particular, to the slowness with which modern industry and a working proletariat gradually took shape. The great majority of those who belonged to the Italian sections of the International were artisans and members of the middle class: those barristers without briefs and billiard-playing students of whom Friedrich Engels spoke with sarcasm. But we must also remember that in a country where the gap between government and governed and the unpopularity of the public authorities were, as we have seen, so deeply and firmly rooted, anarchism seemed a necessary stage on the road towards the forming of a popular opposition movement. The negation of the state was in the last analysis the first stirring of an awareness of the state and of the need to transform it.

THE 'HISTORICAL' RIGHT AND THE 'ROMAN QUESTION'

In June 1861, a few months after the proclamation of the Kingdom of Italy, Count Cavour unexpectedly died, aud Italy was suddenly deprived of her great leader. But he left the new state with a stamp and style which it would have been difficult for his successors to shake off. The men who inherited Cavour's heavy responsibilities belonged to the so-called 'historical Right'; they took pains not to wander far from the road he had indicated: moderation, a scrupulous regard for the Statute, and a keen sense of the state, were characteristics of their political activity. Many of them, like Rattazzi, who was twice Prime Minister, Lanza, who was Prime Minister from 1869 to 1873, and Sella, inflexible and scrupulous Finance Minister, were Piedmontese, and as such better able to assimilate the lesson of Cavour's moderation. Those who were not, such as the Tuscan Ricasoli and the Emilians Minghetti and Farini, had worked with Cavour in the delicate operation of annexation, and so their opponents considered them to be *piemontesizzati*, a word that enjoyed a certain popularity at the time. However, Piedmontese or Piedmont-ized, the men of the Right were a fairly homogeneous political class, in spite of the inevitable frictions that arose between various of them; they had more style than any of the teams that have followed them in power, up to the present day. Their integrity at times bordered on asceticism and they were too aristocratic to cultivate that attachment to power and that taste for cheap popularity that parvenus may fall into. But they lacked the capacity for initiative that Cavour had in the highest degree possessed; for this reason they succeeded in being capable administrators of their inheritance, but no more than that.

From the point of view of national politics, the main problems facing Italy's ruling class immediately after unification were those of the incorporation of the Veneto and of Rome into the new Italian state. The first of these objectives was achieved in 1866, with what is euphemistically termed 'the third war of independence'. On the military level this campaign was a disaster for the Italian forces, who were beaten on land at Custoza and on sea at Lissa; it was an unhappy début for the new army and for its High Command. The acquisition of the Veneto was made possible only by the victory won against Austria by Prussia, Italy's ally, at Sadowa.

The attainment of the second objective, the liberation of Rome, was a harder task, which met with more obstacles. For it was not merely a question of annexing a new province to the Italian state, but also, above all, of destroying the temporal power of the popes. While the fact that Italy might annexe one last stretch of territory of no strategic importance, in the very middle of the peninsula, could not have excited much opposition among the governments of Europe, the fact that the Supreme Pontiff was to suffer, after centuries, a repetition of the humiliation at Agnani, aroused the indignation and opposition of all European Catholic opinion, in particular that of the French, which Napoleon III had every reason to placate. And it must not be forgotten that there was still a French garrison in Rome, and that the Second Empire had contracted the moral obligation to defend the Papacy's temporal sovereignty. This was made clear in August 1862 when Garibaldi, at the head of the volunteers he was always able to raise, once more crossed the straits of Messina, having decided to repeat his march of liberation of 1860, but this time all the way to Rome. The government's attitude (Rattazzi was Prime Minister) appeared to be ambiguous, even co-operative, but French diplomatic pressure and the alarming prospect of a clash between Garibaldi's volunteers and French regulars soon persuaded them to modify this. Regular troops were dispatched against Garibaldi's forces, and gained a rapid victory over them at Aspromonte in Calabria. Garibaldi himself was wounded in the foot, and arrested.

After Rattazzi's resignation, and a short-lived government under Farini, the new Prime Minister, Marco Minghetti, tried to negotiate with France a solution of the Roman question. He wanted, amongst other things, to put a stop to Vittorio Emanuele II's personal political activity, which had played a leading part during the sad days of Aspromonte. So the so-called Convention of September 1864 was arrived at, on the basis of which France committed herself to withdrawing her troops from Rome within two years, and Italy to guaranteeing the papal territory against outside attack. An additional clause established that the capital of the Kingdom of Italy was to be transferred from Turin to Florence. In spite of appearances, this was a provisional solution: it was clear that the Italian government intended the shift of capital to Florence as an approach towards Rome, and that the 'Roman question' was far from closed, but merely put off. Only two months after the September Convention, the publication of the papal *Sillabo* did much to reopen the question and strip bare its most universal implications. The *Sillabo* was an out-and-out declaration of war on liberalism, and the prelude to the doctrine of papal infallibility, which was to be proclaimed by the Vatican Council of 1869. At this point the Italian government was forced to realize that besides a legitimist Europe there existed an anti-clerical one; besides Catholic public opinion there existed liberal opinion. In Italy especially, the wave of anti-clericalism was very powerful, and in 1866 a series of markedly anti-clerical proposals was brought before Parliament for its approval: the suppression of many religious orders and the confiscation of their property, compulsory civil marriage, and compulsory military service for seminarists. Then in 1867 Garibaldi repeated his Aspromonte attempt. On this occasion too the Prime Minister was Urbano Rattazzi, who, trusting in an uprising of the Roman people, permitted and even encouraged Garibaldi's preparations. But the enterprise came up, once more, against the firm opposition of France, which sent back to Rome the troops who had been withdrawn under the terms of the Convention. Left to look after themselves, Garibaldi's forces were scattered by the French troops at Mentana on 3 November. The 'Roman question' was thus back where it had been before, and the Italian government, urged on from one side by democratic public opinion, which reacted indignantly to the Mentana episode and forced Rattazzi to resign, and on the other side held back by France and by European legitimism, was in an impasse. It was freed from this however by an event that was not and could not have been foreseen: the Franco-Prussian War and the disaster of Sedan. Two weeks after the defeat of France, on 20 September 1870, Italian troops entered Rome by the breach of Porta Pia. Just as Sadowa had given Venice to Italy, so Sedan restored her capital.

In spite of the somewhat lucky way in which it was accomplished, and in spite of the uncertainties and errors committed, it is none the less certain that the men of the Right had tenaciously pursued the aim of re-uniting Rome with the nation; once again, Garibaldi and the democrats of the Action Party had to resign themselves to seeing their aims achieved by their adversaries. Not only had Rome become Italian but this had come about without any bargaining with the temporal power, by force. One year after the proclamation of the doctrine of papal infallibility, the breach of Porta Pia seemed to represent the revenge of liberalism and European democracy, and gave a character of universality to the events of the Risorgimento.

For Italy, a country whose Statute declared that the religion of the state was the Catholic faith, there now arose the difficult problem of relations with the Papacy. An attempt to deal with this was the so-called Law of Guarantees, approved by the Italian Parliament immediately after the taking of Rome; on the basis of this law the state promised to respect the Pope's inviolability and freedom and to allow him an indemnity of three million lire a year, and instituted a system of separation between Church and state. This was not accepted by Pius IX, who rejected any possiblity of conciliation or compromise, and closed himself within the Vatican. So Italian Catholics were faced with the problem of reconciling their duties as citizens with their duties as believers. Should they for example participate in elections, so supporting a usurping government? The Vatican answer was radical: neither as electors nor as candidates. In practice, from the 1874 elections onwards, this intransigence was softened. Besides, among the 500,000 Italian voters, mostly from the middle class, there were few intransigents or 'clericals', and we may therefore suppose that the papal *non expedit* was an ingenious way of not exposing Catholic candidates to a battle in which they would probably have been defeated. As for the peasant masses, the Church and clergy of the days of the *Sillabo* and the Vatican Council, with their political and social conservatism, were certainly not inclined to exploit their discontent. 'Communism' or 'socialism', condemned in the *Sillabo*, were not in their eyes errors any less grave than triumphant bourgeois liberalism, nor were they so exasperated and short-sighted as to fall into the theory of 'the worse, the better'. The most far-seeing of the militant Catholics even realized that one day the new bourgeois state would need them; then there could be negotiations on a basis of greater equality. For the moment it was most convenient to maintain an official attitude of absolute intransigence, and at the same time to profit from the freedom the Italian state had left the Church, to keep alive the Catholic conscience of the faithful.

ECONOMIC POLICY OF THE GOVERNMENT OF THE RIGHT

Though the government of the Right ended its fifteen years with obvious concrete achievements in terms of foreign policy and the completion of national unity, the question of its economic policies is less clear-cut.

The men who belonged to the government from 1861 to 1876 were obsessed with the task of making up the state's awesome deficit and balancing the budget. Italian finances were burdened with the arrears of the enormous expenses incurred by Piedmont during the final phase of the Risorgimento, and placed to the account of the new unified state. The small Crimean War alone had cost fifty millions. Later, the war for the liberation of Venice had devoured very considerable sums, and put Italy deeper in debt. In 1866 the budget deficit exceeded credits by more than 60 per cent, making necessary the issue of 'forced' paper currency by the National Bank, such was the discredit into which Italian state bonds had fallen. This was the lowest point reached by Italian finance; from 1869 onwards, thanks mainly to the latest harsh fiscal turn of the screw inflicted by Sella, – the introduction of the already mentioned grist-tax dates from January 1869 – conditions improved, and the eagerly sought balance was achieved in 1876.

In the mean time, even though the financial policies of the Right have gone down under the name of 'policy of meanness', the impulse given by Cavour to the construction of public works and infrastructures was not allowed to slacken. The effort made in the field of railway-building was the most impressive: Italy's railway network grew from 2175 kilometres in 1870 to 8713 kilometres in 1880. It is true that foreign capital preponderated in the building of the railways; but the state too had made a substantial contribution.

A policy of public works and of adjustment of the budget, of which more than half was absorbed by military expenses and by the interests on the National Debt, could only be achieved, in a country of limited economic resources, by means of extremely severe taxation, mainly in indirect form. In fact the Italians were soon the most heavily taxed people of Europe: between 1862 and 1880 the state's regular income was more than doubled. The effects of taxation were felt on the level of consumption, which was kept more or less stationary; hence, production too was affected. The very low buying-power of the great mass of consumers certainly did not favour the development of such manufacturing industries as existed, which were, in any case, quite unable to compete with the foreign products that the liberal policies of the Right allowed free entry to the country. In the South in particular, this combination of free-trade and taxation practically extinguished the scattered local industry. As for agriculture, it benefited from the general rise of prices for produce, and was thus able to make up for the heavy tax-demands it was called on to satisfy; but on the other hand there was no modernization, especially in southern and central Italy, and no reduction of the absolute burden of taxation. The large-scale sale by the state of property formerly owned by religious orders (about one million hectares were involved) did not profoundly alter the existing pattern of property-distribution, and the agricultural panorama of many regions was still marked by the presence side by side of small-holdings on a subsistence level, and large estates of a type that, if not feudal, was certainly pre-capitalist.

Some scholars have maintained that the type of economic policy described here corresponds to the initial phase of capitalism, preceding its true 'take-off', in which the fundamental problems are an 'original' accumulation of capital and the construction of the necessary infrastructures; in short, a pre-industrial phase. And that is precisely what the Right did, with their inflexible taxation on the one hand

and their public works on the other, particularly in the sector of the railways. The problem, runs this argument, was not to encourage the development of industrial production, which would have been premature, nor even to modify the pattern of land-ownership, since this, with the development of small, peasant landowners, could only have had negative repercussions on the rhythm of accumulation. The problem was to encourage this accumulation and prepare the conditions in which the 'take-off' could occur.

Others have replied to these arguments with the observation that on the basis of available figures, however one looks at them, beginning with that of the national *per capita* income, which remained more or less stationary from 1860 to 1880, one draws 'the general impression . . . that whatever the economic transformation begun during those "preparatory" decades, it was not great enough to have any really significant influence on the national economy as a whole' (Gerschenkron). In other words, the fact that the last decades of the century do in fact show the 'take-off' of Italian industrialization does not mean that all that preceded it was necessarily a preparation, unless one wished to fall into a kind of historical Panglossianism. Nor, at this point, can the slowness of Italy's economic development during the first twenty years of the unified state be excused by the steep population-rise. For this too is a largely historical element: the birth-rate often rises in those countries whose agricultural population (in Italy's case more than 60 per cent of the active population) is still for the most part tied to a way of life dominated by overwork and under-consumption, where two extra arms bring in more than one extra mouth consumes.

So where the economic policy of the Right is concerned too, we are brought back to the terms of the judgement on its general policy that has already been suggested. It limited itself to administering Cavour's legacy, and ruling Italy as he had ruled Piedmont. But Italy was not Piedmont; it was something a good deal more complex and contradictory. The men of the Right would soon have to realize this.

TOWARDS AN ARRANGEMENT

The decade 1861–70 may in some ways be considered almost as an appendix and coda to the Risorgimento. To a political class that had been formed in the struggles of that movement, the problem of the completion of national unity and its growing with the re-uniting of Rome to Italy was bound to appear as the most important one, and the test of any government. The fact that the Right had on the whole shown itself able to perform this task did much to lead public opinion and the electors to submit to the rule of statesmen of whom they had many other more or less valid reasons to complain. With the taking of Rome the heroic cycle of the Risorgimento was finally closed, and public attention was naturally drawn towards internal problems and to the economic situation.

So it was discovered that 78 per cent of the population were illiterate, and that the conditions of life in the country were often below subsistence level; above all, it was learned that one part of Italy, the South, was marked by extremely backward conditions of life. An investigation into the conditions of the southern peasants was conducted by Franchetti in 1874, and one into the peasants of Sicily, by Franchetti and Sonnino, in 1876. These were the first of a type of politico-social study that was to be known as *letteratura meridionalistica*, which was to have its famous exponents and devotees throughout contemporary Italian history. One of the most able of these students of the South was Giustino Fortunato, whose writings did much to dissipate the georgic, Virgilian myth of southern Italy as a mother of harvests, which, however incredible it may seem, was still current in some sectors of public opinion, and to unveil the bitter truth of a South without water and without civilization.

Little by little, as public opinion turned towards internal problems, the conviction grew that the heroic, spartan policy imposed on the country by the Right could no longer be borne, and that the country itself needed a breathing-space of fewer taxes and more freedom. So the old opposition inspired by Mazzini and Garibaldi, who died in 1872 and 1882 respectively, was gradually replaced by a new opposition, less intransigent in its principles but closer to the real state of things: the 'historical Left' was replaced by a 'young Left'. The elections of 1865, which saw a reduction of the number of ministerial candidates in the South, produced the first signs of this opposition group, which slackened off in about 1870, but came to its maturity in 1874.

It was a loosely-joined group: the 'young Left' brought together various tendencies and various levels of political awareness. In the first place there were the broad strata of the northern middle and lower-middle classes, who demanded not only a less vexatious taxation policy but also the extension of the vote to the upper fringes of the working class, greater decentralization and, in general, 'reforms' that would make the state more democratic. The manifesto of this section of public opinion was the speech made at Stradella in October 1875 by Agostino Depretis, a former deputy of the Left in the Subalpine Parliament, who had been with Garibaldi in Sicily. But the 'young Left' was not only the party of the Milanese and northern middle classes, but also of many men of property, and of a large part of the southern humanistic and professional middle class. These people did not much care for reforms, when they were not actually opposed to such things as compulsory elementary education and extensions of the vote. All that they demanded, and that with great insistence, was a lightening of taxation, and larger allocations of money for the South, which they identified, of course, with their own interests and privileges. They wanted a state that was less Piedmontese and more generous towards the southern provinces, but were far from thinking that the problems of those provinces could be resolved within the context of a general democratization of Italian public life. In fact, a blind regional pride often closed their eyes to the economic and social reality of their land, and led them to attribute all the ancient evils and deficiencies from which it suffered to the policies of the governments that had ruled since unification.

The Left affirmed itself in the elections of 1874, especially in the South, and though it did not win a majority of seats, it put forward its serious candidature as a possible government. The time was ripe for a change in the country's politics, and when on 18 March 1876 Minghetti's government was defeated on an everyday question of procedure, public opinion realized that something final had happened, and spoke of 'parliamentary revolution'. The subsequent general elections were a triumph for the Left, but a triumph that was aided by the threats and manipulations of the new Minister of the Interior, Giovanni Nicotera, who had been a companion of Pisacane on the expedition to Sapri, but had considerably watered down his democratic radicalism since that time.

The coming to power of the Left did not mark that radical change of direction that many had feared and some had hoped for. The set of reforms introduced during the first years of its government was not negligible, but neither was it outstanding: a law establishing free, compulsory education from six to nine years old was introduced, the previous Casati law of 1859 having only provided for two years of compulsory education (but the law was not at all systematically enforced); the grist-tax was abolished in 1879; the legal codes were reformed, and even incorporated a limited recognition of the right to strike; and there was, finally, the electoral reform of 1882, to which we shall return. But the most notable change, felt by everyone, was in the style of government and the tone of political and public life; it was the time of *trasformismo*. This term is usually applied to a parliamentary practice of which Depretis was a master: it consisted of assuring the government an adequate majority in Parliament, either by a preliminary deal with the more prominent members of the opposition, and by eventually absorbing them into the government, or by means of favouritism, and by corrupting those deputies who had previously been less marked by the stains of parliamentary life; or by a combination of these methods.

The result was a transformation of the traditional parties and the formation of a secure government majority, in some respects analogous to that secured by the Subalpine Parliament after Cavour's *connubio* with the constitutional left. We must not be misled by the frequency of government crises: in most cases these were provoked by Depretis, as a means of reshuffling and re-balancing government personnel, and in fact, from 1876 until 1887, the year of his death, Agostino Depretis was the master of Italian parliamentary and political life. Although *trasformismo* was execrated by writers like Carducci as a fount of corruption and the first cause of the decline of the tone of public life, it was tacitly accepted by all Italian politicians, of Left and Right, and continued to dominate politics even after the death of Depretis. Giolitti himself, the greatest Italian statesman after Cavour, was to employ it as a means of sustaining his long period of leadership.

The success of the new direction Italian politics had taken is not entirely to be explained by the changes that had been made in parliamentary practice, by the fact that a tacit process of evolution had established the principle of the responsibility of ministers to the Chambers and not simply to the King, as the Statute declared. The governments of the Right too had been parliamentary governments, subject in practice to the Chamber's vote of confidence. The reasons for the success of the Left must be sought deeper, particularly in the composition and the attitudes of the new political class which the Left's rise to power had put at the head of the country.

We have already seen that the opposition which emerged in 1874 and reached power in 1876 was a conglomeration of fairly varied social and political opinions, a coalition of sometimes conflicting interests. *Trasformismo* was the expedient and method that made it possible for this coalition to hold together, on the level of governmental activity too. To put it more briefly and explicitly, it was a contract between the middle classes of northern Italy and the *galantuomini* of the South, on the basis of a compromise, of which both groups reaped the advantages. The northern middle class had a free hand in a policy of reforming and democratizing the state, on the condition that the established interests of the dominant southern classes were not touched. The latter were assured adequate representation in the government; in fact, with the arrival in power of the Left the southern element in the government was considerably increased, and from that date on the growth of southern influence in public administration has been a characteristic of modern Italy.

The formal expression of this contract was the electoral reform of 1882, which was passed after years of debate in Parliament and in the country. Among the various solutions proposed, the suggestion of universal suffrage was rejected as being too radical and heavy with unknown quantities, even though it was pleaded by leading parliamentarians, not only of the left, like Crispi, but also of the right, like Sonnino. Instead, a law was passed lowering the level of wealth, age and education that qualified a man to have the vote, and introducing a system whereby the voters were checked against the electoral lists. The electorate thus increased from half a million to more than two million: from two to seven per cent of the population. But it must be noted that this reform was designed in such a way as to benefit the towns more than the countryside. So those who gained most from the extension of suffrage were the lower middle class and the upper levels of the working and artisan classes. It is no coincidence that during this period, at the same time as this reform, a part of the anarchist movement broke with its previous intransigence and detachment from parliamentary activity, moving towards more realistic positions, and towards socialism. The main representative figure of this new tendency of the popular Italian opposition was the Romagnolo Andrea Costa, who had been arrested after the internationalist disturbances of 1874, was elected in 1882 in the constituency of Imola, and was the first and for the moment the only Italian socialist deputy. The class-limitation of the 1882 electoral reform was of course more apparent in southern Italy, where the absolute increase in the number of voters was smaller and, even more markedly than in the North, confined to the towns, with their flocks of lawyers without causes, improvised careerist journalists and lifelong students. So southern politics remained dominated on the whole by deputies' cliques of supporters, and by the *galantuomini*.

The compromise achieved by *trasformismo* and sealed by the electoral reform of 1882 certainly resolved the social and regional conflicts that had arisen from the way in which Italy had been unified. From this time on, the northern middle class, in particular the entrepreneurs of Lombardy, would have a freer hand, and wider possibilities of developing their economic projects, while the sons of the southern men of property filled more and more posts in the administration, magistracy and government, and the South was to obtain an increasingly larger share of the budget for public works. But it was a solution that deferred rather than solved the country's great problems, and so helped to make them, in the long run, more acute. The acceptance of the premise that the rural areas and more backward regions of Italy were not ready for the democratic advancement that was achieved in the cities and more advanced areas created the conditions for an uneven development, and a heightening of the already existing conflict between town and country, between North and South. We shall be able to observe later how Italy's political and economic development from the 1880's on corresponded precisely to this pattern.

14

Origins and character of Italian capitalism

THE AGRICULTURAL CRISIS AND THE PEASANTRY

During the fifteen years of government by the Right, Italian agriculture, as had been suggested, had gone through a period of largely favourable circumstances, produced essentially by the continued rise of prices and the continued demand for produce. This situation changed radically during the years when the Left reached power. The arrival of American corn, made possible by a drastic reduction in sea-freight charges, had created a great agricultural crisis in all the European countries: in Italy it was the more serious in that an agricultural system as poor in capital as Italy's was weak and unprepared to face it.

The vast importations of American and Russian corn – the figure rose from one hundred and fifty thousand tons in 1880 to one million tons in 1887 – caused a sharp fall of almost 30 per cent in the price of corn, making it not worth growing on poorer land, and bringing about a clear decline in the overall figures for national production. But cereal-farming, which had long been the chief resource of Italian agriculture, was not the only thing to be disturbed by the crisis: the cultivation of olives and vegetables and stock-raising also suffered. The only sector that drew any advantage from the crisis was that of viticulture, whose production rose from twenty-seven million hecto-litres in 1879–80 to thirty-six million in 1886–7. But this was due to exceptional circumstances: the destruction of French vineyards by phylloxera; and the rise was destined to last only a few years, as we shall see. In general, the amount earned by agricultural production and by stockbreeding fell from 28,308 million lire (in 1938 lire) in 1880 to 25,916 in 1887.

Once again it was of course the poorest country people who had to pay the price. It is not necessary to point out that the figure of 1,837 lire, the lowest average *per capita* income of the history of the unified state, reached in 1881, was still an astronomic figure as far as the mass of Italian peasants were concerned. In the thick of the agricultural crisis, the eighteen volumes of the Parliamentary Inquiry into the conditions of life in rural areas, which had been undertaken under the direction of Stefano Jacini in 1877, threw a broad beam of light on the state in which the largest class of the Italian people existed. With the publication of the inquiry official Italy learned that in wide areas of the countryside undernourishment was the rule, that malaria raged in the southern countryside and pellagra, a deficiency disease caused by a diet based on maize, in that of the North, and that these diseases claimed thousands of victims each year. The inquiry described hovels, children forced to work at a very early age, illiteracy and degradation.

But, as one knows, parliamentary inquiries often end up forgotten before there has been time to apply tne remedies proposed by their diligent compilers. One may add that in Italy this had been the rule: Italian parliamentary history is rich in inquiries, conducted with great care and seriousness, from Jacini's and those of the Giolitti era into the conditions of southern Italy, to the most recent on unemployment and poverty; but the many volumes in which they have taken shape have perhaps been more read by scholars and historians than brought to fruition by the politicians of the day.

The victims of the great agricultural crisis could not wait, however; many of them were seized by the resolute and desperate desire to escape from the spiral of poverty and degradation in which they were imprisoned. So, at first unobtrusively, then with growing speed, there took shape the phenomenon of mass-emigration, which in the late nineteenth and early twentieth centuries was common to Italy and to the poorest countries and areas of central and eastern Europe. So in the mean villages of southern Italy the agencies of the great navigation companies opened, becoming the only signs of civilization in those places. Swarms of emigrants crammed themselves into the holds of transatlantic ships, and poured, as workers, into the vast melting-pot of North America, or else tried their chances as farmers in Latin America. Others, especially in northern Italy, preferred permanent or seasonal emigration to France, Belgium, Switzerland and above all Germany. They did not always acclimatize themselves easily in these countries and sometimes, as at Aigues-Mortes in 1892, there were clashes between the workers of the country and the Italian immigrants, who were accused of selling their labour at a lower rate than the normal one, and of being the Chinamen of Europe. But many of those who returned to Italy, especially from Germany, had learned what a union was, and how to make a strike; they would not neglect to apply at home this experience they had acquired beyond the mountains.

Italian emigration soon became impressive in its proportions. In the five year period 1886–90 the average annual number of emigrants was about 222,000. To realize the effects one has only to consider the difference between the natural and the effective increase in the population: from 1872 to 1882 the first was 36,000 greater than the second, while from 1882 to 1900 the gap was 114,000, which means that the population of Italy, discovered to be almost thirty-four million by the census of 1901, would, without emigration, have been thirty-six million.

But not everyone went away, of course, and not all those who stayed were resigned to accepting their living conditions as their fate. The great agricultural crisis of the '80's not only gave rise to the huge wave of emigration, but the Italian peasant movement too took its first steps: another characteristic thread in the history of modern Italy, and one with some highly original elements. It began in the country areas of Mantua – where in 1884 there were agitations and widespread agricultural strikes – of Ferrara, Ravenna and the Polesine, all provinces commanding the lower course of the Po, in a landscape of dams, of great works of improvement, of improvised villages that lacked even the normal, familiar presence of a church. The labourers who worked in these places, who had often emigrated from the neighbouring provinces, constituted a human and social aggregate to which there was no parallel in the agricultural proletariat of the other European countries. Unlike the serfs of the German countryside east of the Elbe, they did not have behind them a past of subjection and resignation. They were a newly-formed social class, and in some ways their attitude was closer to that of workers and wage-earners than that of peasants. The countryside where they lived and worked, a continually changing landscape, helped them to realize the futility of any effort to reconstruct the unity of the old peasant equilibrium. Hope was not to be placed in a return to the past, but in the future, in progress and in socialism. And socialist propaganda, which had up to that time been confined to limited circles of intellectuals and to the higher levels of the urban proletariat, made its first deep penetration among the labourers of the Po valley, by means of whom socialism began to spread through the countryside.

The name of Andrea Costa has already been remembered; we may add those of Camillo Prampolini in Reggio Emilia, Dr Nicola Badaloni in the Polesine, Egidio Bernaroli at Mantua, Nullo Baldini at Ravenna and Bissolati in the Cremona countryside. These were the men whose tenacious and indefatigable activity organized the first labourers' 'leagues', promoted the first co-operatives, spread the ideas of socialism in the country areas of Emilia and the lower Po valley, and who were at the head of the first strikes. Modestly and obscurely, they achieved a work the importance and consequences of which perhaps not even they themselves realized. Italy was the only European country in which in the following decades the development of socialism and the workers' movement was not to come up against the deafness and mistrust of the peasant masses: the country where the conquest of the countryside by the urban proletarian and intellectual advance-guard was to be least difficult. In certain cases, even (Emilia is a typical example), it was the 'red' countryside that besieged the 'white' town, and won it over.

CAPITALIST DEVELOPMENT, AND THE PRUSSIAN EXAMPLE

For men like Camillo Cavour, Carlo Cattaneo and Francesco Ferrara, who had grown up in the age of triumphant capitalism and free-trade, Italy's development into an independent bourgeois country pre-supposed her unreserved entry into the great circuit of European trade. Once exposed to the sharp but invigorating wind of competition, Italian agriculturalists and business-men would have to make a virtue of necessity, roll up their sleeves and transform their concerns into modern organizations able to compete on the international market. Naturally they would run up against the wall of privileges, dispro-portions and particularism that constituted the Italian *ancien régime*, and they would therefore be compelled to transfer their battle to the political level: so economic and social regeneration would both advance from below, from the free initiative of individual producers, as had in fact happened in the great bourgeois European countries. This would be a slow process, admittedly, but its gradualness would guarantee its seriousness and its success.

On the whole the governments of the first twenty years of the unified state remained faithful to this project, and, in particular, to its liberal assumptions. The commercial treaties arranged (the main one being that of 1863 with France) were, like those previously negotiated by Cavour, based uncompromisingly on the principles of free-trade. But, unimaginative executors of Cavour's legacy as they were, his successors did almost nothing to remove the obstacles that, in the broader, contradictory new Italy, obstructed the free development of bourgeois energies from below.

As the years passed and stagnation continued, the more alert sectors of public opinion began to suspect that such a prospect of a long development from below might not be best adapted to a country that, like Italy, had to make up for a great deal of lost time and was pressed by urgent problems demanding immediate attention. People began to wonder whether it was not possible for Italy too to take those short-cuts that had allowed the new Germany, a few years after its consti-tution as a nation, to become a great independent power whose products now reached the markets of the world, and whose technical ability aroused the envy of all its competitors. So, still confusedly, there took shape the prospect of a Prussian line of capitalist development: an economic transformation brought about from above, and with the state's contribution as a determining factor, under the banner of protectionism and the reinforcement of the country's international prestige.

In about 1874, during the years when the Left was preparing itself for power, 'economic Germanism' began to be discussed in Italy, and a group of economists, outstanding among whom was Luigi Luzzatti, had founded a review, the *Giornale degli economisti*, with the very aim of propounding the need to reconsider the free-trade bias traditionally part of Italian economic policy. Their ideas would not have met with such agreement among intellectuals and, what is more important, among entrepreneurs, if they had not echoed the truth of Italy's situation. That the state, the builder of railways and arsenals, should act as an accelerating force in the country's economic development was something not only admitted in theory but practised by all the governments that had ruled Italy, and even the governments of Piedmont under Cavour. Another premise for an economic develop-ment on the Prussian model, and one analogous with what was happening in Bismarck's Germany, with its *Junkers* and liberal indus-trialists, was the *modus vivendi* that had been established, as we have seen, between the social groups of highest standing and influence in Italy, the bourgeois manufacturers and businessmen of the North, and the southern landowners. Strong in this unity, the dominant Italian classes could face fairly calmly the inevitable upheavals and the foreseeable popular reactions to an economic development engineered from above and by forced marches. They had on the other hand the certainty that no-one would cheat: neither of the two parties stood to gain anything from fishing in troubled waters and using against the other the resentments and protests that came from the lower levels of society.

The first hints of this new economic course were given in about 1878, when pressure from the textile and machine industries of the North succeeded in winning a first protective customs tariff from the government. From that moment Italy's economic life became more sustained and the money market more animated. This development was assisted also by the introduction to Italy of new forms of credit specifically designed to finance investments, on the example of those already tried experimentally in France by the Péreire brothers. The new banks – the *Credito mobiliare* and the *Banca generale* – also moved in this direction. Some of the capital was invested speculatively: the 1880's saw the first rush towards speculative building. Rome was subjected to indiscriminate demolitions, and the centre of the capital emerged with a pretentious new face, forever marred by a number of eyesores, of which the most monumental is without doubt the so-called 'Altar of the nation' (the monument to Vittorio Emanuele II), for which a competition was held in 1884. In Florence the old and historic Calimala quarter was completely destroyed to give way to a piazza which is today the only jarring sight in a city of incomparable beauty and aesthetic unity. Demolition squads were active in Naples, too, but without more than partially solving the traditional problems of overcrowding and public hygiene, the gravity of which were tragically emphasized by the cholera epidemic of 1878.

But a considerable part of the capital on the market was employed in more productive, more long-term investments, in industry. From 1881 to 1887 the indices of production of the various branches of industry show a clear and constant rise. In the cotton industry the importation of raw cotton rose from 218,000 quintals in 1881 to 617,000 in 1887. The advance of the metal industry, considering the low level it started from, was spectacular; the chemical, machine and mineral industries all made steady progress. The electricity industry also took its first steps: Milan, with the building of the Santa Radegonda power-station in 1884, became one of the first cities in Europe to make experiments in electric lighting.

On the whole, following a calculation made by Gerschenkron, the production of Italian industry made a general increase of thirty-seven per cent from 1881 to 1887, with an annual growth-rate of 4·6 per cent. The state's encouragement and participation played a vital part in launching and accelerating this process of development: the Terni company, which began to build the first big Italian steel-works in 1884, and was run by the engineer Vincenzo Stefano Breda, enjoyed considerable state support from the time of its founding: the Navy was its main, if not only, customer. The ship-building industry too, in which the leading figure was the engineer Luigi Orlando, was heavily supported by the state, with a subsidy of fifty-three million lire conceded in 1885. The same was true of the chief shipping companies, the Florio and Rubattino lines, which merged in 1881 to form the *Navigazione generale italiana*. It is worth noticing how many of the new captains of Italian industry were men with a militant democratic or Mazzinian past: Luigi Orlando had been a member of *La Giovine Italia;* Giovanni Pirelli, founder of the Italian rubber industry, had fought with Garibaldi. Vincenzo Florio, the most prominent figure in the *Navigazione generale italiana,* had been active in the Sicilian patriotic movement, and as for the Genoese arms-manufacturer Raffaele Rubattino, his had been the two steamers that the Thousand had used for their exploit. Finally, Erasmo Piaggio, manufacturer of arms and machinery, was another ex-*Garibaldino*.

Italy's first modest industrial boom thus coincided with the beginning of the great agricultural crisis described in the previous section; so a typical 'scissors' situation was created. The rise of prices of the industrial products that were protected by customs barriers tallied with the fall in agricultural prices, and the draining of capital from the country to the town, from South to North, steadily increased. It was clear that if the country was to go on in the direction of the development that had been undertaken, the landowners had in some way to be compensated for the losses thay had suffered, and the relations between the country's dominant classes had in some way to be rearranged on a new basis. So the new tariff of 1887 was drawn up; it marked a very important step in the history of Italian capitalism, and may really be considered the birth-certificate of what Gramsci was to call the agricultural-industrial bloc of the Italian dominant classes. Its effects on the history of modern Italy were no smaller than the consequences to Germany of the protectionist, conservative course that Bismarck took in 1879.

Not only were the customs barriers that had been erected to protect infant Italian industry substantially raised by this new tariff, but protection was extended also to certain sectors of agriculture. Those that most benefited were sugar, hemp and rice, all almost entirely confined to the North, and the fundamental sector of corn, which received considerable protection. The vast importations of American corn were thus checked, and the laziness and absenteeism of the southern proprietors, who gained most of their profits from large-scale cereal-growing, were once again encouraged. So northern Italian products – the wool of Biella and Valdagno, Lombard cotton – finally conquered the national market, and Italy's industrial development entered firmly on its launching phase, while the South however remained locked more tightly than ever within its backwardness and its subordinate position. Far from involving a process of levelling and of regeneration from below, the development of capitalism in Italy represented a widening of the already immense social and regional gaps existing in the country. The result was a social fabric in which new and old were juxtaposed and interwoven, in which a capitalism with all the characteristics of imperialism in Lenin's analysis – a high degree of monopolistic concentration, a close interrelationship of banks and industry, state protection – co-existed with an agriculture that in some regions was still at a semi-feudal stage, and with omnipresent handicrafts at a cottage level.

'A modern state in an almost exclusively agricultural society creates a universal sense of unease; that is, it creates a general awareness of the incongruity of the whole, and of every part', wrote Antonio Labriola in 1896. Incongruity is a term that will often come to mind as we go on with our examination of contemporary Italy.

TRIPLE ALLIANCE AND COLONIAL AMBITIONS

The keystone first of Piedmontese and then of Italian foreign policy had been friendship with England and with France. Relations with the first of these powers have remained substantially unchanged, and marked by cordiality and understanding, throughout the course of Italian history, except for the Fascist period. But things went differently with France: the episode of Mentana heralded a progressive cooling that became increasingly marked, to the point of breaking out in the late 1880's, as we shall see, in open hostility. Parallel with this cooling towards France was the increasing friendliness Italian foreign policy showed first towards Germany – we must recall the alliance of 1866 – and later also towards Austria. In 1873 Vittorio Emanuele II made visits to Vienna and Berlin, two years after the Emperor Franz Josef had visited Venice. The central European empires, particularly in the person of Bismarck, spared no effort to aid this new Italian political course, and to deepen the gap that had opened between France and Italy. Several times in 1876 and 1877 the Germans and Austrians urged Italy to take the initiative of occupying Tunisia, where there had for some time existed a strong Italian minority; they hoped in this way to achieve the double aim of distracting Italian claims for the Trentino, made with insistence by the 'irredentists', and of creating a new source of friction with France.

To begin with, Italian diplomacy seemed unwilling to listen to these entreaties, and at the Congress of Berlin of 1878 Italy kept to a political line of disengagement that was described as a 'clean hands' policy. There were of course protests in Italy, and quite vociferous ones, from those who accused the government (Cairoli was Prime Minister) of having been unable to negotiate Italy's annexation of the Trentino in exchange for Austria's occupation of Bosnia-Herzegovina, and, more in general, of having followed a weak, renunciatory political line. These protests became stronger and more insistent when, in April-May 1881, France went on to occupy Tunisia and transform it into a protectorate. The idea of a final breaking of the French alliance and a closer relationship with the central empires became increasingly popular, save among the inflexible irredentists. So in May 1882 a treaty was signed by Italy, Germany and Austria; it has come down to history under the name of the Triple Alliance.

This treaty consisted essentially of a reciprocal guarantee between the signatory powers against possible French aggression, and an equally reciprocal promise of friendly neutrality in the case of a declaration of war against France by any of the three parties. On Italy's insistence there had in fact been added a clause stipulating that the alliance should in no case be understood as directed against England. In 1887, when the treaty was renewed, it was also specified, on the insistence of the Italian Foreign Minister, Count di Robilant, that Italy should be entitled to compensations any time the status quo in the Balkans should be altered in Austria's favour. This was a way of keeping open to some extent the question of Italian territories still under Austrian sovereignty.

Apart from these strictly diplomatic aspects, the Triple Alliance also had a political value and meaning, especially as far as internal politics were concerned. For there can be no doubt that Italy's adherence to the alliance should be seen as a display of elective affinity with Bismarckian Germany, a nation that was offering Europe the proof that respect for a nation's hierarchy at home and a policy of force and prestige abroad were the best bases for that nation's economic and cultural development. The new king, Umberto I (Vittorio Emanuele II had died in 1878) and his queen, Margherita, who had German blood in her veins, were particularly sensitive to this conservative, hierarchic interpretation of the treaty; but they were not alone: broad sectors of the political class and of public opinion also saw it in this light. In their eyes, furthermore, Italy had finally come of age with the Triple Alliance, ceasing to be a second-class power and winning back some of the prestige she had lost with the disastrous war of 1866. It may also be said that from this point of view the signing of the Triple Alliance played a considerable part in solidifying and making self-aware the nationalistic feelings that were breeding within the country. The struggle between nations, said the fashionable positivist philosophy, was as impossible to eliminate as were the struggle for existence and the process of natural selection among living beings. Could a nation like Italy escape from this iron necessity?

But nationalism is, by definition, always directed against someone, and this, for many Italians, could only be Austria, the 'eternal enemy' which still occupied the extremely Italian cities of Trento and Trieste. However, the treaty of the Triple Alliance allowed little hope in this direction, and when in 1882 the Triestine irredentist Guglielmo Oberdan was hanged by the Austrians, the Italian government that had signed the Triple Alliance a few months before found itself gravely embarrassed, and had to turn a deaf ear to vehement student demonstrations. But if the hope of reaching the frontiers of the Brenner and the Quarnaro had for the moment to be cultivated in moderation, there were plenty of other fields in which Italy could give proof of her rediscovered national pride. Why, for example, should not this eminently Mediterranean, colonizing nation share in the colonial expansion that all the other European powers were engaged in? At an early stage, this idea of Italy's Mediterranean, civilizing mission took hold of men and groups of the Left, and was actually advanced by the first Italian socialists, who thought that colonies would be able to gather some of the emigrants who were at the time pouring overseas, and could have provided a virgin land for enthusiastic experiments in collective land-management. And it was not entirely by chance that an ex-*Garibaldino*, General Baratieri, was chosen as commander of the first expeditionary force to Africa. But of course the prospect of a colonialist expansion was greeted most warmly by the reactionary groups, and those most impregnated with nationalistic spirit. However, whether democratic or reactionary, inspired by humanitarian motives or by futile jingoism, Italian colonialism was from the start marked by vague and impractical ambition; according to Lenin's definition, it was the 'imperialism of ragged wretches'. It was, one may say, a colonialism for domestic use, created for purposes of internal policy, to convince the Italians that Italy too was a great power, and so to surround with a halo of prestige a state that would otherwise have had little.

Its beginnings were as unhappy and discordant as its whole history. Italy had opposed a *fin de non-recevoir* to England in 1882 when it was suggested she should collaborate in the occupation of Egypt; but in 1885 England persuaded her to occupy Massaua in Eritrea, and after General Gordon's defeat by Sudanese Dervishes Italy found herself involved in military operations against Ethiopia. In January 1887 a contingent of five hundred men was attacked at Dogali by an overwhelming force under the command of Ras Alula, and completely wiped out. This made an enormous impression in Italy, and the Foreign Minister, di Robilant, the same man who had successfully and firmly negotiated the renewal of the Triple Alliance, was forced to resign. What could have remained a minor incident thus became a question of national honour, and Italy found herself morally committed to pursuing a colonial policy that would bring nothing but disappointment.

CULTURAL AND LITERARY LIFE

The Italian literary scene in and around the 1880's was certainly not lacking in animation: from the Milanese *scapigliati*, an Italian version of Parisian Bohemia and a typical example of an avant-garde for its own sake, to the realist admirers of Zola, the minor disciples of Manzoni and the continuing flow of dialectal poetry, there was a wide range of literary currents and experiments. Even so, most of the prose-writers and poets of the time were limited writers, whom no-one reads today, and whose names survive only in literary histories and on the name-plates of streets. The only name that is perhaps worth remembering is that of Edmondo De Amicis, and not for his literary qualities, but because he was, in his books and his journalism, a faithful and sincere witness of the feelings and the dignity of the Italian lower middle class, and for his *Cuore*, one of the few Italian children's books.

Two names alone have resisted the ravages of time: those of Giovanni Verga (1840–1922) and Giosuè Carducci (1835–1907). The first, who lived most of his life in Milan, after having tried his hand at the bourgeois novel, with mediocre results, found his true vocation in novels and short stories set in his native land, Sicily. Verga's South, with its haughty, penniless noblemen, its rapacious *nouveaux riches* of peasant origin, and its fatalistic common folk, has all the marks of authenticity, or rather of that internal truth of things that can be revealed only by a literary representation both authentic and truly felt. Such characters as Mastro-don Gesualdo, a self-made man who marries a noblewoman and ends in inertia and discouragement a life that had begun with the desperate will to succeed, or *padron* 'Ntoni, the fatalistic old patriarch of a combative family of fishermen destined for failure, are almost symbols of the true nature of the South.

But the rediscovery and reassessment of Verga are of relatively recent date. The author of *Mastro-don Gesualdo* and of *Malavoglia* lived until 1922 and passed his last days in his native Catania, without producing anything; and in his lifetime he had far fewer readers and admirers than he has today. His stories of fishermen and peasants did not greatly interest a bourgeois public which was soon to be enthralled by the Superman and by the aesthetes of D'Annunzio's novels.

Giosuè Carducci had a very different fate and fortune. In his lifetime he was universally saluted as the principal poet of the new Italy, or, as he himself put it 'prophet of Italy in the finest season', and crowned a life rich in honours with the Nobel prize, conferred on him in 1906. It is understandable: the evolution of Carducci's attitudes and of his poetry very faithfully mirrors that of Italian bourgeois public opinion from the end of the Risorgimento to the years of the first displays of nationalism. In his youth he was a Republican and Jacobin, exalting the French Revolution in the sonnets of *Ça ira*, and author of an *Inno a Satana* which, published in 1863, seven years before the breach of Porta Pia, appeared to many readers as the battle-cry of the new Italy that was opposed to clericalism and the temporal power of the popes. In middle age and old age his work assumed more elevated and official tones: he exalted Queen Margherita, the 'eternal regal feminine', wept over the fallen at Dogali, celebrated the myth of the Roman Empire and the glories of Savoy and Piedmont. In fact, both his Jacobinism and his official patriotism were those of a professor, of the great professor he was: they were artificial, manufactured at a desk. The only things of his that are still read with pleasure are those arising from his family life and personal affections.

Though, as we have seen, the Italian literary scene of the 1880's was fairly varied, the same cannot be said of intellectual tendencies. For the scene was dominated by the triumphant new positivist philosophy. While the realist writers piled up their novels about prostitutes and congenital diseases, sociologists applied themselves to studying the measurements of the skull, to obtain the proof of criminal proclivities. One of them, Niceforo, discovered that the disparity between southern and northern Italy was in fact to be traced to the differences between the shapes of the heads of their respective inhabitants. Philosophers, for their part, disputed on 'natural selection' and the struggle for existence, politicians theorized on the rôle of élites and the political class, literary criticism of the De Sanctis school gave way to historical philology. 'Science' and 'progress' were the watchwords of the moment, and the sympathy of the intellectuals turned increasingly towards those countries which seemed the receptacles and the demonstration of these new ideas. German books multiplied in the bookshops and in the libraries of Italian scholars, and the intellectual influence of the Germanic world had by now almost prevailed over the traditional influence of French culture. In the field of ideas, as in that of politics and economics, it was Germany's hour.

The single pathetic island of resistance to the spreading advance of positivism was the group of Hegelians in Naples, last spokesmen of the historical idealism that had set its mark on the Risorgimento period. They were isolated survivors, yet it was their circle that produced the one powerful thinker that late nineteenth-century Italy can boast of, Antonio Labriola.

Labriola was a pupil of Bernardo Spaventa, the most authoritative spokesman of Neapolitan Hegelianism; he then came under the influence of Herbart's philosophy, and finally arrived, when already in middle age, at the discovery of Marxism, the themes of which he expounded in a series of essays published between 1895 and 1900. 'Discovery' is perhaps a misleading term: in the 1880's Marx's name was no longer unknown in Italy, and certain of his works had already been translated. Carlo Cafiero, who had been Bakunin's companion at the time of the First International, had published a summary of *Capital*, and a socialist newspaper printed at Lodi, *La Plebe*, had done much to spread knowledge of Marx's thought in Italy. But Marxism too had been received within the context of positivism in Italy, and in consequence the most common opinion and notion of it was that of a sort of 'social Darwinianism' and 'economic determinism', almost as if Marxism were a calendar on which, with scientific and positive exactness, the stages of the decay of capitalism were marked, up to its inevitable arrival at socialism. Besides, this positivist version of Marxism was not only an Italian phenomenon; it belonged to all European socialism of the time of the Second International, and to theorists such as Kautsky, Lafargue and Plechanov.

Labriola was the only one of these Marxist theorists (if one may apply to him a definition that he himself did not welcome) to give historical materialism an interpretation radically different from that which was current. In his opinion Marxism was not a whole encyclopaedic philosophical system, but another historical ideology, a philosophy of praxis, the distillation of the political and intellectual experience accumulated by a given historical subject, the industrial proletariat in its struggle for freedom. The truth of Marxism ended where this experience ended. So the materialist view of history remained a system open to new integrations and developments, which explains why Labriola, unlike his young friend Benedetto Croce, held firmly to his socialist convictions in face of the wave of revisionism inspired by Bernstein and Sorel at the end of the century. The fact that social evolution had taken different paths from those hypothesized by Marxists of a positive stamp, if not by Marx himself, only proved the falsity of their schemata, and certainly not that the battle of the proletariat was in vain; Labriola was to go on fighting and thinking and accumulating new experiences, constructing – not waiting for – socialism.

Consistently with his view of Marxism as a 'philosophy of praxis', Labriola felt morally and intellectually committed to militant political action, and he took an active, intelligent part in the work of guiding and organizing the new Italian workers' and socialist movement. But we shall examine this in its place. For the moment let us only observe how new and original was Labriola's interpretation of Marxism, and emphasize how it was this very originality that left him isolated and misunderstood.

15

The end of century crisis

FRANCESCO CRISPI

In July of 1887, the year when the new customs tariff came into force and the Triple Alliance was renewed, and the year of the Dogali disaster, Agostino Depretis, the man who for ten years had been considered the master of Italian politics, died. On his death the post of Prime Minister was taken over by Francesco Crispi. During the Risorgimento Crispi had been a Republican and a Mazzinian, and Garibaldi's right hand man in Sicily. In his first parliamentary speeches he had spoken for universal suffrage and the abolition of royal nominations to the Senate; but he had inherited the verbal, platform violence of nineteenth-century radical democracy more than its substance. He remained a temperamental and easily swayed extremist when, after rallying to the monarchy, he approached even closer to the prevailing tendencies of the political class and of Italian public opinion, embracing his new convictions with as much ardour and as totally as he had embraced those of his youth. The philogermanism that triumphed in Italy in the '80's, improvised and optimistic colonialist ambitions, the unscrupulousness and spirit of initiative displayed by the new captains of industry, the traditional hatred felt by Sicilian landowners for rebellious peasants, in short all the ingredients of the new landowning-industrialist bloc were present in him, in an accentuated and at times frenzied form. It was no chance and no mistake that Fascism took him as one of its precursors.

Crispi's arrival in power immediately gave Italian politics a new course and an unusually animated rhythm. In the brief space of two years the commercial treaty with France, which had asked for a revision of the customs tariff of 1887, was broken off; a military agreement was made with Germany, which Crispi himself, who had taken over the Foreign Ministry too, negotiated with Bismarck; the colonial adventure in Africa was resumed, with Asmara occupied and Eritrea proclaimed an Italian colony; finally, there was the threat of a war with France. This last in fact existed more in Crispi's over-heated imagination than in reality: he claimed that the French navy was in the Gulf of Genoa, ready to attack Italy's coasts; the English fleet rushed to the scene, and was surprised to find no-one there. However, Italo-French relations did reach a high state of tension: the clash between Crispi's nationalism and the Boulangist wave in France gave Europe some anxious moments.

In domestic politics too Crispi sought to make affirmations of prestige: by means of Abbot Tosti he encouraged parleys with the Holy See, with possible conciliation in view. But the failure of this attempt led him back to his old anti-clerical fold; and it was he who had a statue put up to Giordano Bruno, in June 1889, in the very place where Bruno had been burned at the stake, in the Campo dei Fiori in Rome. Apart from these and similar outbursts of caprice, the political line he followed in domestic affairs was essentially directed towards a reinforcement of the executive power at the expense of the legislative, and towards an authoritarianism masked by efficiency and lack of prejudice. The posts of mayor and of president of the provincial administration became elective everywhere; but as a protection against the risks of decentralization, the administrative provincial committee was instituted, the long arm with which the prefects could reach local bodies; the machine of state was rationalized with the institution of the administrative legal department, but at the same time care was taken to bring out a new law of public safety which considerably extended the already wide discretionary powers of the police; Parliament worked harder, but this was partly because Crispi devoted himself to minimizing its rôle, strengthening the government on the other hand, and, within the government, the rôle of the Prime Minister. A decree of 1887 extended the competence of that office; and when it was held by someone like Crispi, who also held the posts of Foreign Minister and Minister of the Interior, the figure of Prime Minister came close to that of the Chancellor of Germany. Crispi fervently admired Bismarck.

So the turn towards authoritarianism and Prussianism, the origins and bases of which have been described in the preceding sections, became entirely explicit and operative with Crispi. But unfortunately for him, the circumstances in which it was brought about were not as favourable as they might have been, and his lack of moderation certainly did not help to overcome them. In an economic situation that was already showing hints of decline, the breaking of the commercial treaty with France and the tariff war that followed deprived Italian foreign trade of 40 per cent of its exports, and threw whole sectors of the national economy, such as the silk-manufacture of the North and the viticulture of the South, into the most fearful crises. So in 1890 Italy had to come round to a more moderate line of policy. At almost the same time the artificial, speculative building boom, which had involved almost all the towns of Italy during the preceding years, was burst, and there began the series of resounding banking scandals that were to go on for four years, uncovering a whole under-growth of favouritism and corruption. For the moment nothing much had leaked out to the general public: the report of the commission of inquiry appointed by the government minister Miceli at the end of 1889, which contained very serious revelations concerning the activity of a number of the main banking concerns, was not published. At the last moment interventions were made to save the concerns that were most in danger, such as the Banca Tiberina, which received a large loan, thanks to Crispi's own influence; his actions in this connection were not entirely above board. Only time was won in this way; a few years later the latent crisis exploded resoundingly. But by then Crispi was no longer in power: in February 1891 the turbulent Sicilian had resigned. The pretext for his fall had been provided by another of his rash outbursts in Parliament, when he had accused all the Italian governments which had held office up to 1876 of having followed a 'policy of servility towards the foreigner.' This was enough for the Chamber, which realized how much the new policy of national dignity and prestige that Crispi had brought in was costing the country; it took the chance offered by this gaffe to free itself of the inconvenient, authoritarian Prime Minister. But Crispi was not to remain away from power for long. In spite of his excesses and his lack of man-oeuvring ability, he was in the end the only Italian politician able to personify the basic tendencies of nascent capitalism. He may not have been a Bismarck, but then Italian capitalism was not German capitalism either.

THE ORIGINS OF THE SOCIALIST MOVEMENT

The turn Crispi had given to the course of Italian politics had among other effects that of accelerating the formation of a popular oppo-sition, which, as has been suggested, had been taking shape ever since the Left had come to power. In about 1885 this opposition still seemed extremely scattered and fragmented, but of the various regions of Italy there were two in which the opposition ideas and gathering forces were most solidly based: the Romagna and Lombardy. In the first, as we have seen, the formation of a labouring community had made it possible for socialist ideas to spread, and for a revolutionary socialist party of the Romagna to be formed in 1881. Under the guidance of Andrea Costa, this party had gradually extended its influence to neighbouring Emilia, as far as the province of Mantua, which in 1884 had been the scene of the first peasant agitations. In the Romagna the Republican opposition too was very strong, its most representative figure being Angelo Saffi, the old *triumvir* of the Roman Republic. As for Lombardy and its dynamic capital, the democratic traditions of the five days and of the uprising of 6 February 1853 were far from extinct: of the great cities of Italy Milan was certainly the one with the largest left-wing vote. Radicalism, whose organ was the *Secolo*, one of the most widely-read newspapers, and whose exuberant and romantic leader was Felice Cavallotti, had a following among the middle class and the higher levels of the working class. But gradually, as the city's industrial and economic development increased the presence of the industrial proletariat, the more politically active workers moved away from democratic tutelage, and set themselves up as an independent force. So in 1882 the Italian Workers' Party (Partito operaio italiano) was born; in a short time it became a considerable political force in Milan and in all Lombardy, so much that in 1886 Depretis agitatedly declared its dissolution. But the party was soon able to resume its activity, and went on with its work of organizing the workers. In 1891, inspired by Osvaldo Gnocchi-Viani, the first *Camera del Lavoro* was founded, a sort of workers' organization on a territorial basis, which, though it had points in common with the French *bourses du travail*, also had distinctive elements, to which we shall return. The men of the Italian Workers' Party proclaimed themselves 'manual workers', and so they were, with a few exceptions: stone-masons like Silvio Cattaneo, glove-makers like Croce, printers like Lazzari. Their profound mistrust for middle-class politicians, from whom they had freed themselves with great effort, often became a mistrust for politics. To organize a strike, form a league, obtain wage-improvements and reduced working-hours: these were the concrete and serious things workers should concern themselves with, instead of wasting their time with the high-sounding words democracy, republic, and even socialism, which was discussed, without much attempt at defining what was meant by it, by impenitent Anarchists, and by the reformed type on the Costa model, by Republicans, and sometimes even by the odd conservative who was particularly keen on all things German.

At the beginning of the last decade of the century the Lombard opposition and that of the Romagna were joined by the Sicilian opposition, with the movement known as the Fasci. The effects of the agricultural crisis and of the tariff war with France had been particularly sharp in Sicily; they had been felt by the sulphur industry and by the export trades in citrus fruits and wine, in other words by the most dynamic sectors of the Sicilian economy. The only ones to benefit were the big absentee landlords of the inland areas, whose political influence had done much to impose corn-protection. A situation of deep social unease had arisen, affecting the broad mass of the population, from the middle classes of the capital and of the east coast towns to the miserable sulphur miners and the inland peasants. Each of these social categories brought to the Fasci movement its own discontent and demands, and once again, as in 1820, 1848 and 1860, the various and sometimes contradictory complaints of different social groups were held together by the Sicilians' powerful autonomist sense. In May 1892, on the occasion of the 18th congress of the Italian workers' societies, which was held at Palermo, the Fasci gave the first sign of their strength by sending huge delegations from all over the island. But it was soon to give much more solid evidence of strength.

Lombard democracy and the workers' movement, the socialism and the republicanism of the Romagna, and, finally, the autonomism of the Fasci in Sicily, were political organizations and movements on a regional basis, with a limited political horizon, drawn around leaders with local prestige. The problem arose of amalgamating these various opposition impulses and currents, and of selecting a nucleus around which such an amalgamation could hold itself. This, as was shown by the experience of foreign countries, and above all that of Germany, in which social democracy had at last emerged victorious from its long battle against the special laws, could only be the industrial proletariat. But to achieve this it was necessary for 'manual labourers' and Italian wage-earners to pass beyond the corporative limits of the workers' organizations and to acquire a political, socialist awareness. The main credit for having understood this, and for having lent their energies to advancing a process that would certainly have been slower if left to the natural force of events, must go to two men: Antonio Labriola and Filippo Turati.

The first, whose work as a thinker and philosopher has already been described, felt more than anyone the need for the Italian popular opposition to break once and for all with the old, inconclusive and sometimes sentimentally traditionalist anarchism and with vague, declamatory radical democracy. In a land where love of the fine gesture and the fine phrase often condemned political life to the level of operetta and farce, he thought, the coming of the workers', socialist world with its unions, its severe logic of the class war, its proletarian common sense, would bring an infusion of seriousness and modernity.

For Labriola too the model was German social democracy, and he spared no effort in striving to bring the nascent Italian socialist movement as close as possible to that model. He not only kept up an extensive correspondence with the leaders of European socialism, Engels, Kautsky, Bernstein and Sorel, but did not hesitate, although he was a university professor and a man of mild manners, to take part in the activity of organization and agitation, even leading the demonstrations in Rome on 1 May 1891.

Filippo Turati, a Lombard lawyer who had gone through a long maturing process from democratic to socialist ideas, lacked Labriola's intellectual rigour, and his Marxism contained many positive elements and residues of radicalism. Even so, his rôle in the work of unifying the various branches of the Italian opposition was no smaller than Labriola's. The magazine he founded, the *Critica sociale*, which began publication in 1891, played a leading part in spreading and accrediting socialist teachings among the Italian intelligentsia, and it was largely thanks to his persistent and able work that it was possible to hold a congress at Genoa in August 1892, in which all the main tendencies and organizations of workers and the people participated. The Genoa congress marked the final break with anarchism, and gave life to a new political organization called the Italian Workers' Party (Partito dei lavoratori italiani) which was soon to turn into the Socialist Party of Italian Workers, and finally, in 1895, took the name it still retains of the Italian Socialist Party.

The concessions Turati made to the workers' organizations in order to reach agreement, and the electicism of the new party, at first brought a negative reaction from Antonio Labriola, who was a good deal more aware than Turati of the difficulties involved in founding a modern workers' movement in a country as backward and as socially stratified as Italy. Even so, he too soon agreed that the new party had to be put to the test, and showed it when he shortly afterwards tried to commit it to support of the Sicilian Fasci movement, which had in the meantime been growing stronger and assuming a more and more markedly aggressive attitude. He had Turati's backing in this; and so for the first time in Italy's history the industrial-agriculturalist bloc of the dominant classes was confronted by a worker-peasant opposition bloc. This was no more than a first incomplete embryo: the road that the Italian socialist movement born at Genoa would have to travel to become a nationally based opposition party was to be long and rough. But the dramatic, swift pace that events had taken in this last part of the century did much to make it shorter.

CRISPI AGAIN

After Crispi's fall the task of forming a new government fell to the Sicilian Marquis di Rudinì, who, aware of the sense of weariness that a large part of Italian public opinion felt for Crispi's policy of prestige, sought above all to establish harmonious relations with France and to impose a financial policy of retrenchment and thrift. But the instability of the majority that sustained him shortened the life of his government; in May 1892 di Rudinì had to give way to Giovanni Giolitti. So the man who was to be the master of the Italian political scene for nearly fifteen years, and the only political figure of modern Italy to stand comparison with Cavour, made his entry.

There are in fact some grounds for such a comparison: Giolitti was also a Piedmontese, and he too hoped for an Italy made in the image of his Piedmont, with its small landowners and savings banks, its honest and efficient administrators, its patriotism without ostentation. Intellectually, Giolitti still firmly envisaged a regeneration of Italian society from below, to be achieved by the diffusion of small-holdings and of education: an idea that, as we have seen, had also been dear to Cavour. However, as he had openly declared in an electoral speech of 1886, he was entirely opposed to an 'imperial' policy, which would involve heavy military expenses. His first experience of government was too short – eighteen months in all – and too hectic for him to achieve his political aims in any way. The dominant event of the moment was in fact the breaking of the bank crisis, which Crispi had managed to hold back provisionally. The Italian public stood by amazed at the resounding bankruptcies of the main credit organizations, each of which uncovered an unedifying spectacle of intrigue and political corruption. An enormous impression was made, and a commission of inquiry had to be appointed, which after eight months of work presented an account from which, in spite of ambiguities, it was clear that there existed not entirely innocent links between the world of finance and that of government. Giolitti had had dealings with the director of the Roman Bank, and had even nominated him a senator; he did not escape unscathed. His political position became increasingly precarious and finally untenable. He was the first to realize this, and rather than resisting to the bitter end he concerned himself with laying the foundation for his eventual return. He spoke out in October 1893 to his constituents of Dronero, denouncing the 'mad building speculations' of the years of economic euphoria, and as a remedy for the state's distressed finances proposed that a graded tax be introduced. One month later, he resigned.

In the mean time the movement of the Fasci grew visibly in Sicily, and social tension became extremely acute. Giolitti, who like Cavour disliked ruling by martial law, was not the best man to restore order, and his refusal to take a course of repression was one more reason for his departure from power. Francesco Crispi, though no less involved in the scandal of the Roman Bank than Giolitti was, gave stronger guarantees; and the country turned to him.

But the old Sicilian politician had not learned much from his previous experience of government and his previous failure; he was more than ever convinced that he was the only man able to restore to Italy her greatness. Although as a Sicilian and ex-*Garibaldino* he should have been better able than others to appreciate the social context of the Fasci movement, he took a strong line against it: he proclaimed martial law and sent a general at the head of an expeditionary force of fifteen thousand men to re-establish order in the island. A few days later martial law was also declared in Lunigiana, where there had been uprisings among the marble-workers of the Carrara quarries. There followed mass-arrests and trials, held by military tribunals, which inflicted severe sentences. The leaders of the Fasci, Barbato, Rosario Garibaldi Bosco and Bernardino Verro, a noble figure in the struggle against the Mafia and on behalf of the peasants, were each given twelve years. The Catanese De Felice, a deputy and personal enemy of Crispi's, received eighteen. Nor was the Socialist party as such spared: in October 1894 it was dissolved together with all the groups, associations and *Camere del lavoro* of which it was in a sense the leader. To protect himself against predictable reactions on the electoral level to this authoritarianism, Crispi put into effect a drastic purging of the electoral lists. His policy towards Parliament was scarcely more liberal than that towards the country: from January 1894 to May 1895 the Chamber met only for very short sessions, until in May of the same year conveniently manipulated elections provided the government with a comfortable majority.

In the sector of economic and financial policy, the most outstanding action of Crispi's second government, and the one with the greatest consequences, was without doubt the series of negotiations with financial circles and with the German government, which brought about the constitution of the Commercial Bank, a body consisting largely of Germans, and modelled on the lines of the German mixed banks. The recent failure of the *Credito mobiliare* and the *Banca generale*, and Giolitti's law limiting the number of previously existing banks of issue to three (the Bank of Italy, the Bank of Naples, the Bank of Sicily), and restricting their activity in the field of credit, encouraged the rapid development of the new banking organization, which soon took on a primary role in the country's general economic life. In this way industry became even more markedly dependent on finance than it already was, and links with German capital became closer.

After the 1895 elections Crispi felt sufficiently sure of himself to resume the policy of colonial expansion that he had been forced to leave in mid-stream when he had to resign in 1891. He knew that the African undertaking was unpopular, not only with the crowds that came out into the streets to cry 'Viva Menelik' but also with a large proportion of the productive middle class, especially of Milan, who saw it as a useless waste of money. On the other hand he was convinced that a success in Africa would enormously strengthen his prestige and his leadership. As far as he was concerned the best thing would have been a cheap military victory, obtained at the least possible cost. But the military, of course, did not share this point of view: hence the frictions between army and government that were partly responsible for the disastrous end to the African campaign. On 1 March 1896 a contingent of fifteen thousand Italians was almost entirely annihilated by overwhelming Abyssinian forces at Adowa. When he heard the news, Crispi was shattered: five days later he resigned, this time with no more chance of a return.

Crispi's fall was welcomed by many as a victory for democracy, and the Adowa defeat was widely regarded as a sort of historic nemesis for the man who had imposed the emergency laws. But very soon it was realized that there had only been a partial victory: Crispi may have finally disappeared from the political scene, but there remained the social forces that had twice placed their faith in him. The monarchy remained, with the intrigues of the ambitious Queen, and so did the army and the generals who had warmly supported the African venture, some of whom were not ready to resign themselves to defeat. Industry remained doubly tied to government orders and to the War Office. The southern landowners remained; in 1892 at a congress in Sicily they had asked for the abolition of compulsory education, and they fiercely defended the corn-duty. In short, that power-complex of a Prussian type that had gradually taken shape over the past decades still existed.

But another bloc of social and political forces in opposition to it was becoming increasingly clearly defined: it included those of the business middle class who were least linked to protectionist interests, the southern lower middle class, the proletariat, the radicals, the republicans and the socialists. The socialists had been significantly successful in the elections of 1895, managing to augment their meagre parliamentary number; they seemed to have shaken off the prejudices of the corporations and workers' organizations, and the mistrust of politics that many of them had felt until a few years before. They had needed no Jaurès to convince them that a middle-class democratic government was preferable to an authoritarian one, and no commentator on Marx to explain to them that the bourgeois classes did not in fact constitute a 'single reactionary mass'. Crispi had performed this task by dissolving their organizations and imprisoning their deputies.

So the most pressing problem seemed to be to bar the way to a return of Crispi's type of reaction. Faced with this prime objective the divergences between socialists and radicals, between those who believed in the 'class struggle' and those faithful to the Mazzinian principle of association between capital and labour, became secondary. Before facing one another in the decisive battles of the class-war, the enlightened middle class and the proletariat still had to travel a long way together. For the moment the socialists restricted their claims to a minimal programme, approved by the congress of Feggio Emilia in 1893, which combined typically proletarian demands (for social legislation and the eight hour day) with others that any radical or democrat would have subscribed to (universal suffrage, an armed nation, defence of constitutional liberty above all). This evolution of Italian socialism towards more realistic solutions fitted in with the pattern of all international socialism at the time of the revisionism of Bernstein and Millerand, with the difference that while in France, and even more in Germany, the new reformist line on the whole represented a withdrawal and an acceptance of the established order, in Italy it emerged as the most suitable way to combat and destroy a discredited régime, and it was marked by aggressiveness and enthusiasm.

After so many years of *trasformismo* and of skilful parliamentary manoeuvres and reshuffles, the political parties of Italy were finally arranged on two sides of a clear watershed: on one side the 'partisans of strong government', on the other the 'defenders of liberty'. The final reckoning was soon to come.

THE TURN OF THE CENTURY

The four years from March 1896 to December 1900 are among the most tumultuous and spectacular of all the history of united Italy. Street uprisings were bloodily repressed, parliamentarians overturned the voting-urns, there were anarchist acts of violence, duels between political leaders, and, finally, the assassination of a king. The picture of a century's end heavy with apocalyptic fears and great hopes is complete. Retracing these events, however summarily, it is hard to avoid the impression of a mass of knots that can hardly be untangled, of a society striving to extricate itself from the contradictions woven into it – those 'incongruities' that Labriola had spoken of.

After Crispi's fall no Italian Prime Minister, not even a man of such firm conservative convictions as the Marquis di Rudinì, could, without displaying complete political myopia, have withstood the pressure of public opinion, which acclaimed the end of a foreign policy of rash adventuring and a domestic policy of repression. And in fact one of the new government's first acts was to issue an amnesty freeing many of those who had been condemned in 1894, and allowing the leaders of the Fasci movement to make a triumphal return to their island, in time to present the extraordinary commission appointed by the government with a memorandum, expressing their point of view on the reforms and innovations that should be introduced to resolve the grave social problems of Sicily. Thus the government openly admitted that the 1893 revolt had causes quite different from the foreign instigation Crispi had ranted about. But the government did not go far beyond this recognition; there was talk of internal colonization, the sulphur-producers were joined together in a consortium, some taxes were reduced. But the basic element of the Sicilian problem, the corn-duty, remained untouched. It was precious to the landowners, and so presented an insurmountable obstacle to the reform of Sicilian agriculture and society.

In the field of foreign affairs, the di Rudinì government was quick to put an end to the African enterprise: in October 1896 a peace treaty with the Negus was signed, on the basis of which Italy finally gave up all claim to sovereignty in Ethiopia and kept possession of Eritrea alone. Di Rudinì also worked to restore friendship with France, as he had already done during his first period of government. He recalled to the Foreign Ministry the man who had controlled Italian foreign policy during the first fifteen years of Italy's unity, Visconti-Venosta. He negotiated with France a solution to the Tunisian question: both the French protectorate and the special interests of the Italian community were recognized.

But in the meantime the country's political temperature was rising steadily. A bad farming year and the reduction of American importations after the Cuba war sent the price of bread up, and this in turn provoked a series of agitations and strikes and rekindled among conservatives the temptation to impose an authoritarian solution: Crispi's government without Crispi, and without colonial adventures. An article called *Torniamo allo Statuto*, by Sidney Sonnino, which appeared in the *Nuova Antologia* on 1 January 1897, created a wide

stir. It proposed that the parliamentary system be reformed by returning to its origins, to the time when ministers were responsible to the
King and not the Chamber. But the elections of March 1897, which
brought twenty or so socialist deputies into the Chamber, and an
adequate representation of other 'extreme' parties, showed clearly that
the most active and vigilant sector of public opinion was not prepared
to accept the prospect of an illiberal solution. Far from decreasing,
tension continued to rise, and reached its highest point when in March
1898 Felice Cavallotti, the 'bard' of democracy and the idolized
tribune of Italian radicalism, was killed in a duel with a right-wing
deputy. The discord between government and opposition was under-
laid by a threatening ground-bass of murmuring among the common
people, which at moments, as in Apulia early in 1898, swelled into
open rebellion. In May, when the price of bread went even higher,
the peasants' rage erupted in a spontaneous, convulsive form, similar
to that of the revolutionary *giornate* of the *ancien régime*. In Milan,
the scene two months earlier of the memorable funeral of Cavallotti, in
Florence, and in many other places, the crowd came out into the
streets, protesting tumultuously. There was no danger of a revolution, and the socialists themselves were taken unawares; but the
government behaved as if there were such a danger, and repressed
the Milan disturbances with cannon fire. Fifty people were killed,
and General Bava Beccaris, who was responsible for the massacre,
was decorated by the King. Hundreds were arrested, including all the
major socialist figures such as Costa, Bissolati, Turati and his friend
Anna Kuliscioff, the Milanese Republican leader De Andreis, and the
editor of the *Secolo*, Romussi. Even a priest, don Albertario, was arrested;
in his Catholic 'integralism' he was ready to use any weapon, even that
of demagogy, against the hated Italian state.

By thus striking the 'black' as well as the 'red', by suppressing
Catholic newspapers as well as socialist and radical ones, the government wished to be seen by public opinion as the guardian of the
liberal tradition against all extremism, and also to use a semblance of
anticlericalism as a sop to those of its members who, like Zanardelli,
were reluctant to take the responsibility for the arrests and for the
attacks on the liberty of the press. But the game was too transparent
to succeed, and the end of di Rudinì's second government was signalled
by quarrels between ministers, and by the King's refusal to allow new
elections. The sense that the brutal repression at Milan had gone too
far probably had some bearing on the fact that the new cabinet was
chosen for the most part from parliamentarians of the old Left of
Depretis. But as a guarantee, a general, Pelloux, was put at the head
of the new team; he had besides a reputation for liberalism, since he

had refrained from proclaiming martial law when he had been sent to control the disorders in Apulia in February. The first months of the new government marked a pause in the bitter political struggle: martial law was ended and the political prisoners granted an amnesty. But this was only the lull before the worst storm.

On 4 February 1899 Pelloux presented to the Chamber a set of bills intended to prohibit strikes in the public services, and to restrict the freedom of the press and the right to hold meetings and form associations; if these had become law they would have meant the end of the liberal state. A memorable battle was waged by the extreme left, later joined by the constitutional left of Giolitti and Zanardelli; it culminated in the session of 29 June, at which certain socialist deputies overturned the voting-urns to protest against the Prime Minister's attempt to end the discussion, which they had drawn out by obstructionist methods. But Pelloux was equally tenacious: he had reshuffled his government, dismissing its more liberal members, he defended his proposals and showed that he was determined to have them made law, even without the approbation of Parliament, by transforming them into decrees, a method which the Court of Appeal however declared to be unconstitutional. This pronouncement from the country's supreme judiciary authority, and the hardening of the deputies of the constitutional left into an open opposition forced Pelloux to admit defeat and hold an election. This, the fourth in the short space of ten years, was bitterly fought, and marked a distinct advance for the extreme left and for the constitutional left led by Zanardelli and Giolitti. Pelloux thus had to resign, and a new cabinet, led by an old deputy, Saracco, was formed; it had all the marks of a transition government.

But there was to be no easy return to normality: one month after the forming of the Saracco government, on 29 July 1900, King Umberto was killed by an anarchist. This of course made an enormous public impression, and did something to nullify the impact on public opinion of the advance made by the left in the recent election. The atmosphere was once more one of uncertainty and unease. Decidedly, the country seemed unable to find its own way and its own balance. Now, after the opposition parties had waged a victorious battle under the banner of respect for constitutional legality, that legality itself was shaken by an outburst of the old anarchism that fermented at a deep level of Italian society. It was felt that any moment might bring a return of the reaction of 1898.

Yet tranquillity was nearer than it seemed to those who had taken part in the struggles of the 'nineties: they had not yet had time to realize what a deep mark those events and experiences had left on public opinion and the attitude of the people. The struggles against Crispi and Pelloux had been followed by many ordinary people who had perhaps never before felt any sense of participation in parliamentary conflicts, or any awareness of what was taking place; they had been given the impression that it was impossible to turn back; and that the twentieth century would bring a new Italy. Proof of this feeling was given in December 1900 when the Prefect of Genoa declared the local *Camera del lavoro* dissolved, and the dockers of the great port, Mazzini's city, did not come out into the streets to protest, as had happened in highly civilized Milan, but confined themselves to downing tools. It was the first 'general strike', even if only on a town scale, of the many that Italy was to experience during the decades to come; and it took place without the least disturbance, in impressive and almost ostentatious calm. The strikers knew that right was on their side, and they were determined to win redress. Faced with this new and unusual spectacle of a whole town resolutely and calmly rejecting its arbitary decision, Saracco's government, which had at first upheld the Prefect's decision, was cast into confusion, and forced to repeal the dissolution of the *Camera del lavoro*.

Saracco, criticized by the right for his tardy pliancy and by the left for his primitive abuse of power, resigned. As his successor, the new King, Vittorio Emanuele III, appointed Zanardelli, the leading member of the constitutional left, which had also waged its own campaign against Pelloux. The new Minister of the Interior was Giovanni Giolitti, who, in the debate that had ended in Saracco's resignation, had made the following declaration concerning the Genoa strike:

For a long time attempts have been made to obstruct the organization of workers. By this stage anyone who knows the conditions of our country, as in any other civilized country, must be convinced that this is absolutely impossible. . . . We are at the beginning of a new historical period—anyone who is not blind can see this. New popular tendencies enter everyday life, new problems arise every day, and new forces, with which every government must come to terms. . . . The rising movement of the ordinary people increases daily; it is an invincible movement, because it is based on the principle of equality between men. No one can delude himself that he is capable of preventing the common people from winning their share of economic and political influence. Friends of institutions have one duty above all: to persuade these classes, and persuade them with deeds, that they can hope for far more from existing institutions than from dreams of the future.

These were new ideas and new accents, expressed with a ponderousness and a hint of self-evidence, which reveal how deeply they must have been pondered. The long battle against reaction was indeed won, and the new century opened with good omens of progress.

16

The fifteen-year 'Belle Epoque'

SOCIALISM'S MOMENT

The victorious outcome of the Genoa strike, and the coming to power of the Zanardelli-Giolitti government seemed to the Italian working-classes the signal they had so long been waiting for. The unions and *Camere del lavoro* multiplied with unexpected rapidity, and the rate of strikes, which had been modest up to that time, suddenly soared. In 1901 there were 1034 strikes, involving 189,271 workers, and in 1902 801 strikes involving 196,699 workers: figures that bear no relation to those of the preceding years when there had rarely been more than a few thousand workers who had gone on strike. From the workers on the Simplon tunnel in the extreme North of Italy to the Sicilian sulphur-miners in the extreme South, from the dressmakers of Milan to the dock-workers of Genoa and Naples and the steelworkers of Terni, thousands upon thousands of workers learned the fundamental elements of modern syndicalism in these first heated years of the century. Sometimes a struggle that began in a place of work spread, to involve a whole city: general strikes like that of Genoa in 1900 occurred in Turin in February 1902, in Florence in August of the same year, and in Rome in April 1903.

It was no different in the countryside; on the contrary: the whole Po valley, from the rice plantations of the Lomellina and Vercelli area to the reclaimed lands of Ferrara and the Polesine became covered by a close network of leagues and co-operatives, and every centre, large or small, had its agricultural strike of farm-labourers, sharecroppers, *mezzadri* (*métayers*). In those provinces of the Po valley where, as we have seen, peasant organization had already been developed, in the years 1901–2 the peasant movement became a river in flood, irresistible and powerful. But the ferment of the time was not confined to the countryside of northern Italy: in Sicily the federations formed at the time of the Fasci regained vigour and courage, and there were considerable agricultural strikes in the districts of Corleone and Trapani, and later in the countryside around Syracuse. In Apulia, one of the regions of Italy where the peasant movement took on a more pronounced revolutionary character, the first leagues were formed and the first strikes took place. The progress made by peasant and *mezzadri* movements in central Italy was slower and met with more opposition: in this part of the country there were only sporadic, limited agitations. In all Italy there were 222,283 workers involved in agricultural strikes in 1901, and 189,271 in 1902: more than the already large number of industrial strikers. The Italy of the humble, of emigration and hunger, finally made its voice heard, and joined its weight to the political struggle that was taking place.

The greatest beneficiary of this sudden and general awakening of the political consciousness of the masses was of course the socialist party, the party that fought under the colours of the class-struggle. The obscure labours of socialist organizers and propagandists during the years of Crispi's reaction were amply repaid: the workers and peasants who now flocked in their thousands to join leagues and *Camere del lavoro* did not make over-subtle distinctions between union-awareness and political awareness, between union and party. For them the leagues and co-operatives were all one with socialism. But not only workers and peasants came to join the party: it and its leaders also exerted a strong attraction for wide sectors of the lower and mid-bourgeoisie: for the productive and hard-working classes of northern Italy and for the professionals and office-workers of the South, who were engaged in those years as never before in the struggle against the cliques and caucuses that dominated the lives of larger municipalities. The intelligentsia, besides, had largely been won over to the ideals of socialism: Edmondo De Amicis, the most widely-read author in Italy at the time, the poet Giovanni Pascoli, the criminologist Giuseppe Lombroso, and Enrico Ferri, whose dazzling oratory soon made him the speaker most acclaimed by socialist meetings, all proclaimed themselves socialists. The German 'comrades' asked in amazement how it was possible in Italy to be both a socialist and a university teacher.

This breadth and variety of the Italian socialist movement made it something quite different from German social democracy, with its harsh, severe proletarian face, and from the other European socialist movements; this constituted its strength at energetic moments of expansion, but was a weakness at times of withdrawal and waiting. At those times the various social forces and ideals that were bound together by the Italian Socialist Party tended to split up: the proletarian nucleus of the workers and the farm-labourers of the Po valley gave signs of retreating within their old corporative organizations, sometimes in the moderate form of reformism, sometimes in the more radical form of anarcho-syndicalism, while the wide fringe of peasants and lower and middle-class people turned back to their previous democratic or anarchist convictions, or, as more often happened, fell into political passivity and inertia. It must be realized that the industrial proletariat still represented only a fairly limited part of the total working population: according to the census figures of 1901 those working in industry were 3,989,816 out of a total population of twenty-five million over the age of nine; and of these only a minority were true wage-earning workers, the remainder being artisans and independent workers. Besides, a high proportion of wage-earners – about 60 per cent – were engaged in the building and textile industries, two branches of industry whose working-force was of peasant origin, and where work was often arranged on a seasonal basis. The more aggressive sections of the Italian workers' movement, the printers, railway and steel workers, were on the other hand rather few in number, and some of them, like the printers, jealously corporative. This explains why the typical form of modern union organization, trade unions, took hold quite late in Italy, and relatively superficially. In 1902 the various federations counted only 238,980 members. A slightly higher number – 270,376 – belonged to the *Camera del lavoro*, an organization on a territorial basis, which acted as a union and also generally represented the workers' interests on the local level, and in the broadest sense. It was, as was said at the time, a sort of 'workers' commune', with all the local feeling and pride of the communes of the Middle Ages. For this very reason the *Camera del lavoro* was felt by the Italian workers to be an organization more closely corresponding to their needs and their ideals. Solidarity between the different workers of a town, and between them and the artisans and lower middle class was a more accessible sentiment and concept than that of solidarity of a profession on the national scale. A metal-worker of Milan, to put it simply, felt closer to a carpenter or even to an office-worker of the same city than to a metal-worker of Naples or Leghorn. This strong local sense was at once an element of strength and of weakness: without it the Genoa strike of 1900 would have been impossible; but on other occasions it showed itself to be an obstacle on the road to the development of a working-class, socialist awareness. For the moment, in the hour of victory and of sweeping advance, these internal defects of the Italian socialist movement were not fully revealed; but they were soon to emerge.

The democratic advance that swept over all Italian society in the first years of the century also affected organized Catholicism. At its head was the *Opera dei congressi*, a body founded in 1874 and organized in various sections, one of which, the second, was concerned specifically with social work, and had its offices in Bergamo. Up to that time its most conspicuous activity had been in forming country banks on the model of the Raffeisen banks in Germany. This had been done with success: in 1897 there were 705 rural Catholic banks, most of them in areas of smallholdings, such as upper and mid-Lombardy, and the Veneto north of the Polesine. The work done by the Catholics in defence of small landowners in these regions in the years of the agricultural crisis did much to accentuate the 'white' character that they still preserve, and to develop in the clergy of the Veneto and Lombardy an attitude of realism and the habit of contact with the people. This was the background to the life and development of a simple priest who was to remain such even when he became Pope: Angelo Roncalli. The activity of the second section of the *Opera* did not go beyond forming rural banks and benefit societies: it was led by the 'intransigents', those Catholics who, unlike the clerico-moderates, were not prepared to have any dealings with the Italian state. They were not at all willing to encourage any associations whose declared aim was, in the language of the day, 'resistance', or as we should say, unionism. Workers and masters should work together, not against one another: this was also the teaching of Leo XIII in his famous encyclical *Rerum novarum*, of 1891. But others were prepared to interpret the Pope's message in other, more advanced terms: as an exhortation to more courageous social activity among Catholics, and a struggle towards socialism, not on the level of mere opposition, but on that of competition. In the red-hot atmosphere of the last years of the century one group of Catholics moved increasingly in this direction; their leader was a young priest from the Marche and now in Rome, Romolo Murri. In 1898 he founded a combative magazine, the *Cultura sociale*, modelled on the socialist *Critica sociale*. Murri's followers, who soon defined themselves as Christian democrats, conducted an intensive work of propaganda and organization in the years 1898–1902, and also managed to form numerous Catholic leagues. The stronghold of the rising Catholic unionism was in the northern regions, especially Lombardy, with its textile factories operated by female workers, and its peasants, traditionally bound to the clergy. But in Sicily too, where another young priest who was to be much spoken of, Luigi Sturzo, was acquiring his first experiences, Christian democracy and its organizations flourished. The Church's official attitude towards the movement led by Murri was however far from encouraging: its organizing activity was for the moment halted, first by papal instructions of February 1902 and then by the dissolution of the *Opera dei congressi* in July 1904. The entry of organized Catholicism into Italian political life was to come not from the left but from the right, not according to the expectations of the Christian democrats, but to those of the clerico-moderates. For the advance of the socialist movement was soon to persuade the new Pope, Pius x, first to modify and then finally to remove the order, in force since the breach of Porta Pia, prohibiting Catholics from taking part in elections. They would instead be asked to join their forces to those of the defenders of the established order against the assault of subversive forces. Even so, the seeds sown by the Christian democrats of the early twentieth century were not thrown away. The early years of the century thus saw the entry on the political scene not only of the socialists but also of the Catholics.

ECONOMIC AND INDUSTRIAL DEVELOPMENT

The last quarter of the nineteenth century had been a lean time for the economy of capitalist Europe. But from the last years of the century it entered, as is well known, on a new phase of more rapid development and of great expansion. Italy, which had felt the effects of the previous crisis perhaps more than any other country in Europe, gained from this general recovery the impetus for new growth, and for a true 'take-off'.

From about the year 1896 all economic graphs in fact show an upward curve. From 1896 to 1908 the annual growth rate of Italian industry on the whole was noticeably high: 6·7 per cent. Some experimental industries such as metallurgy, chemicals and machinery showed a growth rate of more than twelve per cent. The automobile industry made a spectacular leap ahead, almost foreshadowing its colossal development in more recent times. Motor car production companies multiplied rapidly, from seven in 1900 to the respectable figure of seventy in 1907. Their leader was already Fiat, founded in 1899, whose shares soared in a few years from an initial quote of twenty-five lire to 1,885 lire. Another almost entirely new industry was that of electricity, in whose rapid development many people then over-optimistically saw the chance of freeing Italy from her massive coal imports. Electrical production rose from a hundred million kilowatts in 1898 to 950 million in 1907, and continued to increase steadily over the following years, to reach 2,575 million kilowatts in 1914.

From the predominantly agricultural country she had still been at the end of the nineteenth century, Italy was thus quickly becoming an agricultural/industrial country. In 1900 agriculture represented 51·2 per cent of the gross national product and industry 20·2 per cent. By 1908 this gap was narrowed to 43·2 per cent and 26·1 per cent, and the tendency was not to be reversed. Yet it was not until 1930 that, for the first time in the history of Italy, the value of industrial production overtook that of agriculture. Because of this industrial development some of the main Italian towns were increasingly assuming the character of big industrial centres. This naturally happened above all in northern Italy, where Milan strengthened its claim to be the spiritual and economic capital of the Kingdom, and Turin, with its factories and famous motor companies, won back the prestige it had lost after ceasing to be the capital; it was transforming itself from a large provincial town, dominated by a municipal and church aristocracy, into a major industrial centre, the field of action of an enterprising and open-minded middle class. In the South, only Naples had a nearby industrial zone, at Bagnoli, where a large steel plant belonging to the Ilva company began production in 1905.

Italy's industrial development during the first decade of this century in no way altered the character of the machinery of production as it had developed in the last years of the nineteenth century; in fact, it was reinforced. The development of the mixed deposit-investment bank of the German type, operating both in the sector of industrial credit and in that of industrial investments, did more to subordinate industry to finance, with the result that the larger investments and the most solid financial support went to those investments that offered more immediate and spectacular profits. Such were the 'protected' industries, the main protagonists of the first Italian industrial boom. Most important of all was the steel industry, which, by means of a series of takeovers and agreements, soon took on the dimensions of a trust, to which belonged not only the old second-stage mills of Terni and Savona but also the new integrated works at Piombino and Bagnoli, which worked iron-ore from the island of Elba. The steel-trust, in which the Commercial Bank had a considerable interest, produced at prices notably higher than those of the international market, and therefore depended on state subsidies. The cotton industry was also strongly protected, and from 1900 to 1908 production rose from 118,602 tons of thread to 179,776, and invested capital trebled. The sugar industry, also protected, showed the same sharp rise, which went as far as a crisis of over-production. The reason for this was not that the market was saturated – Italian annual *per capita* sugar consumption was three kilograms in 1913: one of the lowest in Europe – but the high price of sugar. Rather than lower the price, Italian sugar producers preferred to cut production by a half after 1913. Ship-building also benefited from state protection, while the machine industry, which had a firmer foundation and was better able to stand on its own feet, would not have made the large increases it did without the massive state orders that came after the railways were nationalized.

But the protection that the major sectors of Italian industry enjoyed is not enough to explain their rapid development. There is another factor to be taken into account: the low cost of labour.

At the beginning of the century the Italian worker was not only one of the worst paid in Europe, but also worked the longest hours. There was no law limiting the working day, so that in the end this was decided by the power-relation of worker and boss. If some particularly aggressive and united groups of workers had managed, by means of strikes, to obtain a working day of about eight hours, other, weaker groups where there was a predominance of female and peasant labour, such as the textile workers, often worked twelve hours a day, or even longer. In some cases the working day, following the traditional system, lasted from sunrise to sunset. As for wages, in spite of the increases that had followed the agitations and strikes of the first years of the century, the wide use of female and juvenile labour did much to keep them low. Women and boy workers were paid respectively about half and a third of what an adult male worker was paid. Nor was there any law at the beginning of the century to control female and child labour, save a law of 1886 prohibiting the employment of children younger than nine. Only in 1902 was this limit raised to twelve, and were limitations on women's work also brought in. The 1902 law, which was the result of a compromise between a government motion and a socialist motion, was however far from universally applied in the following years.

Low wages, long working hours, customs-protection, state commissions and prizes were enough to persuade many people that industry – or at least certain types – was something artificial, a hothouse plant, in Italy, a country of 'craftsmen and peasants' according to Luigi Einaudi. Men like Einaudi, Antonio De Viti, De Marco and Gaetano Salvemini spent much of their careers as scholars and publicists in exposing to public opinion the disproportionate privileges of the steel, cotton and sugar industries, modern baronial estates which had built up their power at the expense of the consumer, and particularly at the expense of the southern peasant.

But the shape of Italian economic development had been laid out long before; the interests that had formed in the mean time had drawn around the Italian state a mesh from which no government was by this stage capable of escaping completely. And so the attacks of free-traders and democratic partisans of the South, however well-documented and convincing, sounded like lamentations for the good old days, nostalgia for a choice that could have been made in its time, but which was no longer practicable. Italy's industrial development, in whatever way it took shape, was a fact; the formation of an industrial proletariat and a consequent proletarian awareness, was another. This had to be used as a means, if progress was to be attained and the country reformed: so argued the socialists; and their opinions were received sympathetically by the man who was to be the central figure of Italian politics for more than a decade: Giovanni Giolitti.

THE GIOLITTIAN SYSTEM

From 1901 to 1909 Giovanni Giolitti was the master of Italian politics, as before him Agostino Depretis and Camillo Cavour had been. He had been the *éminence grise* and most active member of the Zanardelli government, and was appointed Prime Minister in November 1903, remaining in this position until December 1909, except for the period March 1905 to May 1906, when there was a short-lived government under Fortis, who was in any case one of Giolitti's lieutenants, and an even shorter-lived one under Sonnino, leader of the parliamentary opposition.

Experienced politician that he was, Giolitti was certainly not lacking in empiricism and even opportunism. The freedom with which he manipulated the parliamentary majority; bought, by legal or illegal means, the votes of those deputies (the so-called *'ascari'*) who were prepared to barter them in exchange for favours towards their constituencies; the support he received from southern groups; and his unscrupulous fixing of election results, especially in southern districts, earned him the accusation of *'trasformismo'*; Gaetano Salvemini, one of the most combative representatives of southern radicalism, coined for him the epithet of 'minister of the underworld'. In fact Giolitti did no more, and perhaps rather less, than his predecessors had done. And unlike many of them he held very firm general political beliefs, and never, in the tortuous business of everyday politics, lost his overall sense of direction, or confused tactics with strategy.

One of the fixed points of his political credo was, as we have seen, an aversion to any 'imperialist' foreign policy *à la* Crispi, and his firm conviction that to resolve her grave domestic problems Italy needed tranquillity and peace above all else. Under his guidance, and with the co-operation of the Foreign Ministers Prinetti and Tittoni, Italian foreign policy continued to free itself from the extreme adherence to the Triple Alliance that had been Crispi's line, and drew closer to the

major European powers. Relations with France, especially, improved;
in 1901 and 1902 two treaties with France were drawn up, which
respectively recognized French interests in Morocco and Italian
interests in Libya. Italy also strengthened her friendship with England,
with whom diplomatic relations had in any case always been good;
England too recognized Italy's claims in Libya. Finally, relations with
Russia were improved. In 1904 the French President, Loubert, was
warmly welcomed on his state visit to Rome; in 1903 the King of
England, Edward vii, had been the guest of Vittorio Emanuele. Also
in 1903 the Tzar was to have come to Italy; but the violent campaign
promoted by socialists and anarchists caused the visit to be put off
until 1909. So after the agitation of the Crispi period, Italian politics
passed into a phase of withdrawal and appeasement, which was favoured
by the political and diplomatic situation of the moment, free from
serious clouds or frictions. Even the Prussian Chancellor, Von Bülow,
found that it was not such a bad thing if Italy performed 'waltz-turns'
outside the Triple Alliance. As for colonial policy, once the project for
an invasion of Abyssinia had been abandoned, and with Italian claims
in Libya suspended for the moment, activity was confined to the
assumption of direct administration in Somalia (1905), where the
Italian protectorate had for some time been recognized.

Sheltered by this policy of reducing tension, Giolitti was able, during
the first decade of the century, to attend fairly calmly to the experiment
in liberal policies and reforms which, after the dark days of 1898, the
country expected from him. He too, as we have seen, was still attached
to the Risorgimento ideal of a renewal of Italian society from below,
first affecting the countryside. But he was too little of a doctrinaire and
too much of a politician not to realize that Italian industrial development,
in whatever forms it took shape, and the birth of the workers' movement, were by this time irreversible processes, and that the industry
and the unions were by now the most highly organized pressure groups
and the most dynamic forces of all Italian society. Hence his plan
designed to press for and encourage political co-operation between the
forces of the liberal middle class and those gravitating around the
Italian Socialist Party. If Italian industrialists could be convinced that
wage-increases conceded to their workers would in the long run be in
their own interests, and if the socialists were able to control the
impatience and subversiveness of the masses who followed them, there
would be some hope that the circle of poverty and backwardness that
imprisoned the less developed areas and sectors of Italy might gradually
be loosened. There would be some hope that the alliance formed
between workers and businessmen, socialists and advanced liberals,
would exercise its power of attraction and help to isolate selfishness and

reactionary attitudes at the top of the social pyramid, and the resentment of the oppressed at the bottom.

At first it seemed as if this courageous political plan had a good chance of success. The new Minister of the Interior did not lose his head when faced with the wave of strikes of 1901–2, and paid no heed to the insistence of those bosses, like Count Arrivabene of Mantua, who led their own oxen to work when there were strikes, goading them on with the names of the hated peasant leaders; Giolitti confined himself to ensuring that there were no other violations of the law on either side. This was something new in a country where strikers were often seen as malefactors; and it seems that there were agricultural strikers who rallied to the cry of '*Viva* Giolitti!' Not only the mass of peasants and workers engaged in the current movement of vindication, and who by their strikes were winning higher wages and improvements in their working conditions that had seemed impossible up to a few years before, felt that something had at last changed in Italy. The feeling was shared by all public opinion. Parliament concerned itself with social legislation, passing the laws on female and child labour and on the constitution of a national labour office, while in the country and in the press the great themes of the Italian question were argued with a fervent sense of participation: the southern problem, universal suffrage, the reduction of military expenditure.

But there was resistance to this new political course. The most intransigent and obtuse came from those landowners of the South and also of the Po valley, taken unawares by the wave of strikes, and unwilling to make any concession. But the industrialists were not entirely persuaded that it was a good moment to raise their employees' wages, and some of them went as far as to protest against the law on female and child labour. Finally there was the court. Although the new King was not so obviously reactionary as the old one and his exuberant consort, he was shy and withdrawn, and unable to resist the influence of the army. Military expenses remained an untouchable article of the budget, of which they took up a considerable part, and in labour clashes the forces of public order, sent to restore the peace, too often opened fire on the strikers. There was no year when Italy did not have its 'proletarian massacre', as people called them.

A dulling of the economic situation in the second half of 1902 was enough to put industrialists and agriculturalists on the counter-offensive. The organizing of blackleg labour from province to province, and the increasingly general use of agricultural machinery, permitted them to win back some of their lost positions. The workers' movement experienced its first hard defeats: the Po valley strikes of the spring and summer of 1902 ended with further defeats, as did the great strike of the Como textile workers in September of the same year. Then in the South, where the forces of law and order twice opened fire, at Candela in Apulia and at Giarratana in Sicily, the old Camorra and Mafia cliques gained the ascendancy almost everywhere. Faced with these first failures, the more bitter in that they interrupted a long series of victories, the alliance of forces that had taken shape around the socialist party began to split up into its various components. Though the more sophisticated groups of the urban proletariat, who were organized in trade-unions, and the stronger of the provincial peasant federations of the Po valley, under the influence of their reformist leaders, continued to place their faith in Giolitti and to support his policies, the less clearly defined masses of the people expressed their disappointment, once more revealing their old mistrust for the state, and urging the *Camera del lavoro* to resort to that decisive, threatening expedient, much spoken of at the time in France and Italy, the 'general strike'. As for the radical middle class of the South, it too was increasingly detaching itself from the socialist party, which it accused, with some reason, of lacking interest in the southern problem and concerning itself only with the corporative interests of the workers and peasants of the North.

Very soon the socialist party found itself internally split between various currents. There were the reformists, of whom Turati was the most authoritative and intelligent representative; they were prepared to go on collaborating indirectly with Giolitti, and even directly, with socialist participation in the government. Then there were the 'intransigents', or revolutionaries, who loudly demanded total opposition. The most conspicuous members of this group were Enrico Ferri and Arturo Labriola, a young Neapolitan publicist who had tried with little success to combat the cliques that controlled the administration of his city, and had then moved to Milan, where he had founded a newspaper, *L'Avanguardia socialista*, and developed his petit-bourgeois extremism in a working-class guise. During the later part of 1902 and 1903 this second current continued to gain ground, even though it had been defeated at the Socialist Party congress held at Imola in August 1902, and when in November 1903 Giolitti offered Turati a position in a new government he had to reject it, since he realized that acceptance would have lost him his popular following. A few months later his friend Bissolati had to give up the editorship of *Avanti*, which was taken over by Ferri, and in April 1904 at the Bologna congress the revolutionary group, led by Labriola and by Ferri himself, won the party majority. After a few months the deep discontent of the masses burst out in the first general strike of Italian history, declared by the Milan *Camera del lavoro*, which was dominated by men close to Labriola,

after a massive 'proletarian massacre' in Sardinia. By a singular coincidence the first day of the general strike was also the day of the birth of
the heir to the throne. But the displays of jubilation organized from
above were very soon reduced to silence by the demonstrations of the
strikers, whose 'proletarian mourning' contrasted with official Italy's
'happy event'.

On this occasion too, Giolitti, convinced that the current movement
would soon run its course, as in fact it did, kept to his rule of resisting
the temptations of martial law. Once the storm was over, he merely
dissolved the Chamber and proclaimed fresh elections. The keynote
of the electoral campaign was the indignation of reasonable men at the
excesses of the demonstrators and subversives; advances were made by
the government candidates, while the socialists lost a good deal of
ground. It was on this occasion that the new Pope, Pius x, agreed to
modify the severity of the *non expedit*, and a first group of Catholic
deputies entered the Chamber. The Vatican tried to minimize the
importance of the event by describing them as *'cattolici deputati'*, rather
than *'deputati cattolici'* (i.e. Catholics who were also MPs rather than
MPs who were Catholics).

Giolitti had not abandoned his political plan; and he did not allow
himself to be carried away by the backlash it had helped to provoke.
He resigned in March 1905 and allowed his opponents of the right
and the revolutionary leaders of the PSI to exhaust their energies for
about a year in the vain attempt to form a majority and a common
platform. During this period occurred Sonnino's short-lived government, in which men of the radical left participated, and for which
the socialists also voted on certain occasions. In May 1906, in a more
favourable and settled political atmosphere, Giolitti returned to
power. His new government was to last until December 1909, and in
this period the 'Giolittian system' worked better than at any other
time. Even though the socialists did not take any part in the government,
and could not have done so, since they had so clumsily compromised
themselves with Sonnino, they were no longer hostile to the government on principle, and occasionally they supported it. The reformist
ideas of Turati and Bissolati won back the party majority at the
Florence congress of 1908, and the formation of a General Confederation of Labour in 1906, promoted and run entirely by reformists,
permitted a firmer control of the syndicalist movement, and meant
that the independent initiative of individual *Camere del lavoro* could be
to some extent bridled. Once the hints of stagnation of the years
1903–5 had been overcome, the favourable economic situation allowed
labour disputes to be conducted in their normal terms. Parliament
meanwhile returned to problems of social legislation, approving

measures concerning work on holidays, work in the rice fields and other unhealthy occupations, night-work, and labour-contracts. As for the South, special laws were introduced for Sicily, Calabria and the Basilicata. Previously, in 1905, the project of the proposed aqueduct in Apulia had been approved. After the nationalization of the railways, brought about by the Fortis government in 1905, the private telephone lines were now taken over by the state. These were, in short, years of good work and profitable administration.

Because of the circumstances in which it took place, the end of Giolitti's long period of government was, as we shall see, an alarm-bell. Under the influence of opposing forces the waters of Italian political life were once more agitated, and the country entered a new and difficult phase of its history. But before going on to examine this new period, it is worth pausing to look back at the road which Italy had travelled under Giolitti's guidance.

ITALIETTA

On 29 June 1906 the Finance Minister, Luzzatti, presented a long report, discussing ways in which the financial situation could be improved, and taking note of the greater confidence now placed in government bonds. He ended by proposing that the interest on them be converted from 5 to 3·75 per cent. Benedetto Croce records in his *History of Italy* that this produced an ovation; deputies embraced one another in the half-circle of the Chamber. The nightmare of financial embarrassment, which had hung over the unified state's first years of life, and had re-emerged during the dark days of the chain of banking scandals, had finally been put to flight, and Italy became aware of her incipient prosperity.

During the first decade of the century a considerable part of the population had in fact experienced a rise in their standard of living. The entrepreneurial middle class had taken advantage of the good economic circumstances, skilled workers had won wage increases and a shorter working day, the salaries of low-grade civil servants had risen, the agricultural labourers of the more highly-developed areas of the Po valley had seen their co-operatives develop and occasionally prosper: Giolitti had allowed them a share in contracts for public commissions. So many Italians enjoyed, if not prosperity, at least a thrifty middle-class decorum, and with it, the possibility of a life in which there was room for the amusements that *Belle Epoque* Italy provided: holidays by the sea or in the mountains, the theatre, conversation. In music, Puccini's operas triumphed, with the tenuous and delicate sentiments of their bourgeois characters (*La Bohème*), with fashionably oriental exoticism (*Madame Butterfly*, 1904), with their facile, tuneful manner. In poetry it was the time of the 'crepuscular school', who sang the sweetness and the melancholy of middle-class life. For anyone in search of stronger emotions, there were the Futurists, the *enfants terribles* of the day, who declared war on spaghetti and exalted the beauty of the motorcar in contrast to that of the Nike of Samothrace. The scene was dominated by the inimitable Gabriele D'Annunzio and his no longer young friend the 'divine' Eleonora Duse; and a new, modern and disturbing art, the cinema, was taking its first steps. Italy was the country where the possibilities of this new means of expression were first grasped, and where the film industry took shape considerably earlier than in other European countries. The studios of Rome, Milan and Turin produced the first historical epics, such as *Cabiria, The Last Days of Pompeii, Quo Vadis?*, and the first 'vamps' of the cinema, Francesca Bertini and Lyda Borelli. Another fashion of the day was for sport, and in particular motor-racing: Italian cars, Fiats, Maseratis, Alfa Romeos, reaped victory upon victory, and the scions of the most illustrious families tried their skill. For the mass public there was football, which swiftly became extremely popular, and cycling, with its arduous Tour of Italy.

Many, as we shall see more clearly in the next section, felt irritated and unsatisfied by this *Italietta*, finding it mean and lacking in energy. The upheavals of the Great War, the post-war period, and the beginnings of fascist dictatorship would be necessary to make many Italians, looking back on their recent past, regard *Italietta* and the Giolittian era with nostalgic regret, almost as a modest, domestic golden age, the time when the lira was at a premium, feelings more temperate and mild, and officials more honest.

No-one has managed to evoke the modesty and the glory of this Italy before the flood better than Benedetto Croce, in his *History of Italy* (first published in 1927); in any case, no-one could have performed the task better than Croce, who had grown up and developed during that period, and had absorbed and mastered its most vital elements. For his mental attitude and even his philosophy are characterized by a fundamental eclecticism, though at a very high level. His concept of historiography and the reform of the Hegelian philosophy he effected by introducing the criterion of distinct ideas allowed room for a happy blending of the austere idealism of that generation of intellectuals who had lived through the Risorgimento with the new materialistic demands of Marxism, which he had studied in his youth. His reading and literary tastes, as they are reflected in his abundant critical work, were of a traditional type, but his aesthetic views, with the theory of art as intuition, provided against his will, a justification of the fragmentary and most restless tendencies of modern Italian literature. His very battle against positivist Italian culture was at once a vanguard and a rearguard action, in that by exposing its dilettantism and superficiality he ended in rejecting the demands for renewal from which it had started. For no-one knew better than Croce the art of conservative innovation, and no-one did more than he to make Italian culture aware of its own roots and continuity, and to confer on it some self-sufficiency, which with his followers faded into provincialism. It is no wonder, therefore, that when he came to write a history of Italy he gave a picture whose dominant note was continuity and the praise of moderation, within the context of a non-polemical view of the historical process.

In fact, the new Italy that was taking shape in those years was also a screen hiding the permanent Italy of the peasants and the humble. The great circle of darkness and poverty that surrounded the islands of progress within the country had only been repulsed a short distance. Between the census of 1901 and that of 1911 the social composition of the population had not undergone any significant variations: 34 per cent of the active population were still engaged in agriculture, against 16·94 per cent in industry, in the broader and more generic sense of the word, including crafts. In 1901 15·17 per cent had been in industry: so the development of production had gone ahead more rapidly than the formation of an industrial proletariat. Italy was still fundamentally a country of peasants, of illiterates (the percentage was particularly high: 38 per cent) and of emigrants. In the first decade of the century the annual departure-rate rose continually, reaching the peak figure of 873,000 in 1913. By this time the number of Italians who had left their country since the years of the great crisis amounted to between five and six million, and the great majority of them came from the South. The southern question, as was shown by the inquiry into the condition of southern peasants appointed by Giolitti, was still more than ever open; for even the economic-industrial development of the southern regions had helped to make it more bitter, and to make the South a semi-colony of the northern capital. And all Italy's other great problems remained as open as that of the South, which summarized the rest.

If the new political course embarked on by Giolitti could have continued, further progress and changes might have been achieved, and it might even have been possible to break the crust of backwardness that still weighed on most of the country. But by now the domestic political horizon was darkening, and there were signs that the Italian economy was moving out of its prosperous phase. The forces that had never ceased blindly to oppose the experiment now began to glimpse the possibility of a revenge.

ANTI-GIOLITTISM OF THE LEFT AND OF THE RIGHT

1908, the year of the terrible earthquake that destroyed the towns of Reggio and Messina, is in many ways a crucial year in the history of modern Italy. The Austrian annexation of Bosnia-Herzegovina, its diplomatic sequels, and the resentment it aroused in irredentist circles, had shown public opinion clearly that international relations were once more entering on a critical phase, and that Italian foreign policy would soon have to face the problem of adapting itself to the new international pattern of Europe in the age of imperialism.

The deterioration of relations between states was reflected internally by the economic situation. The crisis that had hit the steel and auto-mobile industries in 1907, provoking spectacular falls on the stock market and hasty bank interventions, in 1908 affected the textile, cotton and sugar industries too. The salvage operations performed by the banks, and the understandings between the various industrial and banking groups, with the forming of trusts and cartels (the Steel Trust, Italian Cotton Institute, and Sulphur Consortium) allowed them to weather the worst of the crisis. Even so the annual growth-rate in the manufacturing industries was markedly lower than it had been in the previous decade: it has been calculated that for the five years 1908–13 the average annual growth was 2·4 per cent. Besides – a fact whose importance cannot be overestimated – the difficulties of the years 1907–8 did much to accelerate the already well-advanced process of the monopolistic concentration of the productive and in-dustrial apparatus, and thus to expose the state increasingly to the pressure of the great trusts and protected industries.

Such a situation, dominated by uncertainty and dissatisfaction, was of course fertile ground for the opposition to Giolitti.

In the first place, there was a left-wing opposition. 1908 was the year of one of the bitterest battles of the Italian socialist movement, the agricultural strike that afflicted the countryside around Parma for long months, and was a kind of general test for a new group that was gradually gaining a footing in Italian socialism: that of the revolution-ary syndicalists. The standard bearers of this group were Arturo Labriola, guiding spirit of the 1904 strike, and Alceste De Ambris, who, as secretary of the Parma *Camera del lavoro*, was the central figure of the 1908 strike; they harked back to the theories of Pelloutier and Sorel, whose *Reflections on Violence* had been made known in Italy by Benedetto Croce. From the assertion that the mass of the 'producers' should be more closely identified with the socialist movement, the union with the party, they drew ammunition for a deep criticism of the reformist 'bureaucracy' that dominated the Italian Socialist Party and the General Confederation of Labour. Between 1906 and 1908 the syndicalist movement had managed to win support among the masses, the workers of Turin, the peasants of the Mantua district and the Apulia *braccianti*. The total collapse of the Parma strike was indeed a very serious blow to the syndicalists, in as much as it consolidated the reformist leadership within the party and the syndical organization. Yet syndical incitements to 'direct action' had left some mark, less on the proletariat than on the common people of Italy, who were still alert to the old appeal of anarchism, and on restless intellectuals, ready for all kinds of experiment. Among the contributors to syndicalist newspapers was a young elementary-school teacher from Forlì, author of an inflammatory poem on John Huss, who had experienced more the Bohemian side of exile than its reality – Benito Mussolini. In four years' time this impetuous person was to be the editor of *Avanti*, the official organ of the Italian Socialist Party. Everyone knows what he was later to become; but perhaps not everyone realizes that in his vertiginous rush from the extreme left to the extreme right he drew with him many of the most ardent anarcho-syndicalists.

This interchangeability of opposing positions, of the anti-Giolittism of the maximalist left with that of the nationalist right, was a typical phenomenon of Italian public life in the years preceding intervention in war. At the first nationalist congress at Florence in 1910 there were many who had sympathized if not with socialism at least with the theories of national regeneration expressed in their liveliest form in the periodical *La Voce*, edited by Giuseppe Prezzolini. For nationalism too had emerged in the context of irritated impatience with Giolitti's *Italietta*, and was only later to develop into explicitly authoritarian and imperialistic positions. For the moment the nationalists too were content to oppose the official *Italietta* of scheming politicians and free-masonry with the energies of labour and production. In practice these last were identified with the steel industrialists, who lavishly financed the movement. Even so, it was a convincing-sounding argument that there was an affinity of interests between the producer-workers and the producer-industrialists, and that they should fight side by side against the meanness and pusillanimity of the rulers and the triumphant lower middle class. The first pronouncements of the corporativism that was to become the official doctrine of fascism thus provided common ground for the opposition of the right and that of the left. Naturally there were also divergences, and no revolutionary socialists were prepared, at least for the moment, to accept the programme of colonial expansion and power politics that the nationalists demanded. But the differences of policy and programme counted for less than the common feeling of dissatisfaction and the common rage against prosaic, reformist, Giolittian *Italietta*; the *Italia vile* that was the target for the glittering darts of the poet par excellence of the 'new Italy', Gabriele D'Annunzio.

Today, D'Annunzio's aristocrat-parvenu attitudes, the preciosity of his language, his cult of the superman and the aesthete, make him appear the personification of a decadent and reactionary intellectual viewpoint. But in the eyes of many of his contemporaries his exhibitionism seemed freedom from prejudice, his cult of fashion modernity, his age youth (*'giovinezza'*, as the fascists were to sing). Not only the nationalists, who invoked a greater Italy, and were aroused by the rhythms of *Canzone d'oltremare*, but also men of different and even opposed political attitudes, republicans, radicals, socialists even, were followers of D'Annunzio. One may say that D'Annunzio dominated a good part of the generation of Italian bourgeois and intellectuals who demanded Italy's intervention in 1915, in the war that the Futurist manifesto had described as the 'world's hygiene'. Some interventionists hoped that the war would lead to a full restoration of traditional values and hierarchies, others hoped for total subversion and revolution; but all wanted an end to inglorious Giolittian *Italietta*.

THE LIBYAN WAR AND UNIVERSAL SUFFRAGE

But Giovanni Giolitti had for some time scented a hostile wind, from the time when resistance from economic and financial circles had forced him to withdraw his attempt to break the monopoly exerted over Italian shipping by the *Navigazione Generale Italiana*, and form a new competing company, subsidized by the state. He also realized that he had to go down with all colours flying: to this end he repeated the manoeuvre he had already performed during his first Prime-Ministership, once more presenting the project for a graded income-tax, which he had kept all this time in the drawer of his own desk, and close to his heart. The chamber, and the industrialists and financiers, of course rose in arms against the proposal, and Giolitti was quick to resign. This time his absence from power was slightly longer than it had been in 1905–6, but his return caused correspondingly more of a stir. He came back in March 1911, after a second Sonnino government, as short as the first, and a government led by Luzzatti, an able and intelligent expert on economical and financial problems. On his return to power, the old Piedmontese statesman soon realized that the atmosphere had changed and was once again troubled – to remain in charge of Italy's destinies he had to play for high stakes.

Giolitti did so. As he had done in November 1903, when he had for the first time assumed the post of Prime Minister, he returned to the socialists, in the person of Bissolati, now editor of *Avanti* once again, and a man whose reformist sympathies were universally known, and invited him to join the government. The answer was once more a refusal; but this did not prevent Giolitti from giving his government a decidedly reformist programme. He took over from the previous Luzzatti government and got Parliament to approve a bill drawn up by the Minister of Public Instruction, Credaro, increasing the State's contribution to elementary education, and raising teachers' salaries. Giolitti himself added a bill nationalizing life insurance, and had it approved by the Chamber in April 1912, in spite of strong opposition from liberals and conservatives. But far the most important reform introduced by Giolitti in this new period of rule was the electoral reform. There already existed a proposed law, drawn up by the Luzzatti government, which would grant the right to vote to all men who could read and write. Giolitti went further and proposed to extend the vote to illiterates of over thirty years of age, provided they had done military service. Part of Giolitti's intention was certainly to counterbalance the predictable increase of socialist votes in northern Italy and in the towns, with the votes of the peasants, who came – in the South – to the polling booths under the watchful eye of their masters' right-hand men, the *mazzieri* and – in the country areas of the Veneto and Lombardy – under the watchful eye of the priest. Even so, the electoral reform, passed by Parliament on 25 May 1912, amounted to the introduction of universal manhood suffrage, and so satisfied an old demand made by Italian democrats and socialists.

But this veering to the left had to be counterbalanced by something that would satisfy the nationalistic aspirations of right-wing anti-Giolittians. At the Florence nationalist congress Luigi Federzoni had asked the Italian government to claim the rights of pre-emption held for some time over Libya. Pressure in the same direction was also exerted by leading financial interests such as the Bank of Rome, a body closely linked with Vatican circles which had interests in Libya, and the chairman of which was Ernesto Pacelli, a member of the same family as the future Pope Pius XII.

In close agreement with his Foreign Minister, di San Giuliano, an old-style conservative, and motivated partly by the fear that, after the French occupation of Morocco, some other European power might advance claims on Libya, Giolitti decided to prepare the way for the undertaking, and in September 1911 war was declared on Turkey. It ended a year later, with the treaty of Ouchy, recognizing Italian sovereignty over Libya and the Dodecanese.

Unlike previous colonial exploits, the Libyan War was popular among broad sectors of public opinion. Nationalists saluted it as Italy's return to the Mediterranean policy of ancient Rome; Catholics saw it as a new crusade against the Moslems, and many people, especially in the South, saw the new colony as a land that would absorb thousands upon thousands of peasants, and so put an end to emigration. Among non-socialists only a few isolated figures like Gaetano Salvemini warned that Libya was not that promised land which many had imagined and as interested propaganda had allowed people to believe it to be, but an enormous 'sand-pit' which would cost Italy far more than it would earn her. The socialist party was opposed to the war, and the young Benito Mussolini organized demonstrations against the departure of soldiers, the demonstrators going as far as to stretch themselves out on the railway tracks. But there were also some socialists who supported the project, especially in the South. On the whole, the war was popular, and it was not until the return of the soldiers that many people were persuaded that Libya was indeed a poor land, without water but with a great deal of sand.

Then the euphoria began to die down, and it began to be realized that the war, which had lasted far longer than had been anticipated, had cost the state a sum that it would be difficult to extract from her new conquests (the cost was officially put at 512 million lire). Besides, the Arab tribes of the interior continued to wage guerrilla war, which meant that Italy had to maintain an adequate expeditionary force, and was involved in fresh expenses. In the meantime, the peasants who had been dazzled by the mirage of cheap land had to wait.

The revolutionary socialists were soon to become aware of this disillusionment. At the Reggio Emilia congress of July 1912 the reformist group, which had held the party majority since 1908, was defeated. Those members who, like Bissolati and Bonomi, had declared themselves in favour of the war, were expelled; the editorship of *Avanti* was entrusted to Mussolini. He devoted all his considerable demagogic ability to this new occupation, and managed to treble the newspaper's sale.

The upsurge of radicalism and intolerance from the bottom of Italy worried Giolitti, and the unpredictable nature of the coming elections, the first held on a basis of universal suffrage in Italian history, led him to place no obstacle in the way of the many agreements that the liberal candidates made with the Catholics. In constituencies where a socialist, republican or radical victory was possible, the Catholics promised to vote for a liberal, having first won the promise that once in the Chamber he would not vote in favour of such things as divorce, or the abolition of religious instruction in schools. After the elections the Catholics were able to claim that they had supported as many as 228 successful candidates. In the northern provinces, where the socialists had their strongest positions and the clergy still exerted a strong influence over the people, Catholic votes had in fact had a considerable effect. In the South, on the other hand, more summary and traditional methods were applied, and it was proved that the system of cliques and intimidation still worked in a régime of universal suffrage.

However, Giolitti survived the difficult test with a fairly reassuring majority: 300 deputies, against 160 of the left, of whom 78 were socialists. The nationalists had succeeded in winning only three seats, and the Catholics about thirty. But Giolitti's majority was more apparent than real, patched together, not homogeneous, composed as it was of deputies who had arranged their election with Catholic electors, of intransigent veteran anti-clericals, of Giolittian liberals in favour of compromise with the socialists, and of 'young liberals', a recently-formed political group that showed marked sympathy for nationalism and its authoritarian tendencies. Finally, there was the usual shoal of members of any government, followers of Giolitti today, of his successor tomorrow. Giolitti was forced to realize as much when the terms of the Gentiloni Pact, till then kept secret, were divulged, and he had to face a rebellion of the radicals and a return of militant anti-clericalism. Once again, rather than face the fire of his enemies, he chose to resign, convinced that he would in the end be recalled to office, as had happened more than once before. But this time things happened differently: Giolitti returned to power for a last brief and dramatic spell only after another seven years, in an Italy shaken by war and by political conflict, and in a radically changed situation that he would have difficulty in understanding. Giolitti was however already beginning to lose contact with reality, and to place too much reliance on his own tactical ability. He had hoped to win the sympathies of the socialists with his concession of universal suffrage, but in fact he had only succeeded in losing once and for all the support of the nationalists and conservatives, while on the other hand the Libyan War was far from conciliating the right-wing, and had made an irreparable break with the socialists. So on his right and on his left mounted dislike and resentment of the *Italietta* he represented, and the old wizard was no longer able to dominate the forces he had conjured up. The 'Giolittian system' was finally broken. The fact that its supreme controller did not realize the fact is further proof that the breaking was irreversible.

17

From the war to fascism

THE INTERVENTION

The first difficult test that the new government, led by Antonio Salandra, had to face, was the 'red week' of June 1914. This is the rather exaggerated name usually applied to a piazza uprising of an improvised, spontaneous nature that disturbed the country for a week, and had its epicentre in the Romagna and the Marche, a zone where the republican, socialist and anarchist opposition had deep roots. It was a provincial revolution, led by two provincials, the Romagnoli Benito Mussolini and Pietro Nenni, and the anarchist Errico Malatesta, and fired by provincial and local passions – almost a popular, proletarian version of the uprisings of 1830–1 in the same regions, against the papal government. The large industrial and working centres of the country, called on to show solidarity with the rebels of Ancona and the Romagna by a general strike, only partially responded to the appeal from the socialist party and the General Confederation of Labour.

The 'red week' had not been a revolution, and had in some episodes been, rather, a caricature of a revolution; but this did not prevent it from appearing as a threatening symptom of revolution to those conservatives whose mental picture of revolution was as vague as that of many revolutionaries of the day. So it seemed to Salandra, who had a hundred thousand men sent to the Romagna, and so it seemed to the King, on whom a strong impression was made by the revolutionary pronouncements to which 'red week' gave rise. Both the Prime Minister and the Sovereign were of the opinion that the critical moment Italy was going through demanded far more energetic methods than those adopted by Giolitti in his day, and that it would be extremely dangerous to allow the revolutionry wave to recede on its own, as Giolitti had done on several occasions. Hannibal was at the gates and his attack had to be repelled with vigour. The never-forgotten temptations of an 1898-style solution became increasingly attractive.

This was the internal Italian situation when in July 1914 came the ominous news of the assassination at Sarajevo, and Austria's ultimatum to Serbia. Italy was still a member of the Triple Alliance, which had been renewed recently, in December 1912, and there were some, like the nationalists, who argued that she should join the battle at the side of her allies, to win those compensations in the Balkans that the treaty recognized in the case in question. But Giolitti quickly telephoned from Paris that the Austrian ultimatum to Serbia did not constitute a *casus foederis* in the terms of the treaty, and the government welcomed the suggestion, proclaiming Italy's neutrality in the world conflict that had meanwhile burst out.

This took place in July 1914. Nine months later, in April 1915, the Italian government, represented by its Foreign Minister, Sidney Sonnino, signed a treaty with the Entente powers, unknown to the Italian Parliament, promising to enter the war within one month, on condition that when the war was won Italy should receive Trento, with the southern Tyrol, Trieste and Dalmatia, excluding the city of Fiume. One month later, on 24 May 1915, Italy went to war against Austria.

The Austrians called it, plainly, treason. Though this accusation does not stand up, and though Giolitti's interpretation of the Triple Alliance was correct, it is still difficult in considering the history of Italy in the months from July 1914 to May 1915 to escape the impression of a sudden change of direction. One is bound to wonder how a country which had for fifteen years followed a policy of appeasement and was completely unprepared for war could suddenly have taken the decision to enter the struggle. The question is all the more legitimate in that the country as a whole, without question, did not want war. The masses influenced by the socialists and by the Catholics, the majority in Parliament, Giolitti, who was still the most highly respected political figure, were all opposed to war. Nor should we overestimate the part in the decision to intervene that may have been played by certain industrial interests, such as the steel trust, whose links with the Italian nationalist movement were well known. Not only is it simplistic to attribute the war to the interests of dealers in cannon, but it is clear that equally powerful interests were working in the opposing direction: one of the accusations impetuously flung at Giolitti by the interventionists was that of being in the pay of the Commercial Bank and its German money.

The interventionists, it is true, could boast of some prominent names, such as Luigi Albertini, editor of the extremely authoritative *Corriere Della Sera*, Cesare Battisti, a Trento socialist who had taken refuge in Italy, Bissolati, Salvemini, Gabriele D'Annunzio, who had returned from France, free for once from the pursuit of his creditors, to make inflammatory, warmongering speeches on the Quarto rock and in the Campidoglio. There was, finally, Benito Mussolini, the youngest and noisiest recruit to the interventionist cause; he had abandoned the socialist party in 1914 and founded, with, apparently, French funds, a newspaper of his own, the *Popolo d'Italia*, in whose columns, with the zeal of a convert, he preached the regenerative and revolutionary virtues of war. But the crowds of students and members of the lower middle class who came out in the streets in the 'radiant' days of May 1915 to denounce Giolitti and hymn the war could easily have been scattered by the police, as were the workers and peasants who in many places staged demonstrations against intervention. The interventionist crowds were not broken up, and were indeed encouraged in their action: this was because the government and the court had already decided to make use of them, to give some colour of popular choice to the decision they had taken by signing the Treaty of London, unknown to Parliament and to the country.

But what then was the reason for this decision? The French resistance on the Marne certainly played a part in hastening Italy's decision, and an even greater part was played by the belief, in spite of the experience of the first year of war, that the conflict would be of brief duration. Giolitti himself, who was more pessimistic than anyone on this score, said that it would last longer than three months, but not as long as three years. Even so, these arguments do not in themselves constitute an explanation, and the deciding factor was probably the conviction that a short victorious war would, by imposing stricter discipline on the country, make it easier for the state to move towards a more authoritarian, 1898-style position, would give new life to the forces of conservation and the established order and remove the threat of subversion. So intervention was also, and perhaps above all, a domestic political action, a kind of small *coup d'état* thinly dressed in the forms of legality. Parliament in fact gave the government full powers by a wide majority; but it was a Parliament that, squeezed between the pressures of the executive and those of the piazza, had already lost its freedom. It was probably in view of the internal effect of intervention that in May 1915 Giolitti refrained from carrying his battle for neutrality through to the end, even though he could have done. Probably, though he may have denied this in his memoirs, he had learned of the terms of the Treaty of London, and realized that its repudiation would have resulted in the abdication of the King who had signed it. As an old Piedmontese and faithful servant of his King, he was not prepared to press to that point.

So Italy entered the war psychologically and militarily unprepared.

The clamour of interventionist demonstrations and of D'Annunzian rhetoric were soon to disappear as the first hospital-trains returned from the front.

ITALY AT WAR

From the military point of view, the war that dragged on for three years against Austria and two against Germany, against whom war had been declared later, in August 1916, was above all a static war of attrition. For up to October 1917, in spite of efforts at an offensive by both sides, by the Italians on the Isonzo and by the Austrians along the valley of the Adige and the Asiago tableland, the front line hardly changed. The only notable advance had been Italy's winning of the town of Gorizia in August 1916. But in October 1917, after the collapse of the Russian front, the Austrian and German troops succeeded in breaking the Italian front at Caporetto and penetrating into the Venetian plain. The Italians only succeeded in halting their advance on the Piave, where the Italian armies put up a brave resistance until in November 1918 the collapse of the Austro-Hungarian Empire and the disarray of its army allowed them to return to the offensive and victoriously enter Trento and Trieste. On the whole the Italian army, which had lost 600,000 men, had fought well, and the peasants flung into the trenches had done their duty with the same resigned determination that they applied to their daily tasks as civilians. If one considers that, at least in the first two years of war, the Italian army was one of the least-prepared and worst-armed that fought on the various fronts of Europe, one cannot but feel respect for the tenacity and self-abnegation of the Italian soldier. At the outbreak of hostilities the Italian forces lacked artillery, machine-guns, trucks and officers. Officers had to be improvised with all haste, with results that may easily be imagined. As for the general staff and its commander until the defeat of Caporetto, General Cadorna, they were often unequal to the tasks they had to perform, and the incompatibilities of character between some of its main members certainly did not improve its efficiency. The defeat of Caporetto, which Cadorna blamed on the 'defeatism' that had wormed its way into the army, fostered by the 'reds' and the 'blacks', was, rather, largely the result of lack of co-ordination between the various armies.

The domestic effects of this war, which had lasted beyond the most pessimistic estimates, were enormous, and their importance can hardly be calculated. We must not forget that in 1914 the Italian state was still young and delicate: only three years past its fiftieth anniversary; it was therefore bound to be seriously disturbed by the sort of tests it was required to face. In the first place the war effort demanded a corresponding effort from the industrial productive apparatus. The army had to be provided with the artillery, arms and means of transport which it lacked; the millions of men who wintered in the trenches had to be clothed and shod. All the main sectors of Italian industry worked at full speed: production of automobiles was 9,200 per annum in 1914 and 20,000 in 1920, while the production of electrical energy was almost doubled. The steel industry also made very considerable increases. In a war-economy in which the notions of market and market-price were almost abolished, profits, naturally, were not lacking, and there were spectacular increases of capital: to cite a single example, Fiat increased its capital from 17 million lire in 1914 to 200 in 1919, an enormous increase, even taking into account the powerful inflationary process that was taking place. As a result, the typical traits of Italian capitalism – its high degree of concentration, the close interrelationship of banks and industry, dependence on state orders, agreements between different sectors as to the regulation of the market – were greatly magnified. The great trusts of the Ilva and Ansaldo companies and the banks that controlled them, the *Banca Commerciale, Credito italiano, Banco di Roma, Banca di Sconto*, had taken over entire departments of the Italian economy, to the point where a liberal economist, Riccardo Bachi, was able to write in 1919 that the Italian economy was dominated by 'a small brigade of a few great financiers and a few great industrialists'. They were by now powerful 'baronies', with whom the state had constantly to make treaties.

The state too went through a process of profound change. In the first place, it became a more authoritarian state, in which the executive power systematically prevailed over the legislative. True, Parliament still met, though more rarely, and there were also debates on votes of confidence and government crises: in June 1916, after the Austrian assault on the Asiago tableland, the Salandra government had to give way to a government of coalition and national union, presided over by Boselli, and in October 1917, under Vittorio Emanuele Orlando. Even so, save for these solemn occasions on which Parliament was called on to give proof of its own solidarity and patriotism, it worked little during the war, and almost all power of control was removed from it. Giolitti gives evidence of this: in his memoirs he did not hesitate to write that 'the governing powers had in fact suppressed the action of the Italian Parliament in a way that had no parallel in the other allied countries', that 'all discussion of the budget, all control over state expenses, had been suppressed', and 'Parliament was kept in the dark as to financial commitments'. The press, especially the socialist press and that of the opposition, fared no better, and newspapers often appeared with entire columns blank, owing to the censor's severity. For those considered subversive and defeatist there was also the threat of police-arrest and prison.

But though the Italian state in wartime was authoritarian, it was not strong in the generally accepted sense of 'stern but efficient'. The many demands of the war had meant that its previously existing structure, divided into a few ministries according to the classic form of the liberal state, had had to be extended and substantially modified. New ministries were formed, and a proliferation of departments and commissariats, and the complex machinery of the committee for industrial mobilization was set up. The task of this body, which was directed by a general, was to supervise the production of all factories (1,996 in all) engaged in war-supplies. The haste with which this transformation of the state machinery was effected gave rise to a web of jurisdictions and offices, and encouraged the fragmentation of the state apparatus into a series of fiefs and watertight compartments in which, as Antonio Gramsci was to write, 'the autocrats multiply by spontaneous generation' and each of them 'does, undoes, knits, destroys'. The managing personnel brought to the forefront by the war was extremely mixed, being formed of men of the old ministerial bureaucracy, soldiers, leaders of industry promoted from one day to the next to positions of great public responsibility. From all these contacts and relationships there also emerged a new attitude among the dominant classes: industrialists learned from soldiers how to use an iron fist in their factories, soldiers learned from industrialists the taste for initiative, politicians learned from both. One must appreciate this complex transformation of the state, which made it at the same time more authoritarian and more inefficient, more 'collectivist' and more exposed to the pressures of powerful private interests, if one hopes to understand how there came about the protection, the complicity and the lapses of public authority that made possible episodes like D'Annunzio's exploit in Fiume or the immunity of fascist violence. The war, in other words, had literally unhinged the structures of the liberal state, and had undermined its remaining authority; and this took place at the very moment when huge strata of the population, whose world had up to then been circumscribed by a provincial horizon, were forced by the pressure of events to become aware of their common destiny and of the existence of a national community.

Humble, provincial Italy, the Italy of those whose main problem was to survive, and who left their village and parish pump only to go to America, was hurled into war, and its poor sons learned that they were citizens only when they found themselves in military uniform and were sent to fight in the trenches. One may go so far as to say that a national Italian public opinion, in the widest sense of the term, emerged only with the First World War. Which is to say that this public opinion was born in the shadow of a great torment and trial: from this time on, when a peasant had to consider the 'nation' his mind would naturally turn to the only one he had known, that of shoulder-stars and trenches, of sacrifices and humiliation. Correspondingly, in the mind of the petit-bourgeois, the wartime officer, the concept of the nation, though seen the other way round, was also associated with that of war: for him Italy was to be the Italy of Vittorio Veneto, which was celebrated with all the tinsel of D'Annunzian rhetoric. Thus, two types of psychological block were formed: the first led Italians to think that being Italians and patriots meant being D'Annunzians and interventionists, the second that being democrats, revolutionaries or republicans meant also being to a greater or lesser extent, defeatists and *Caporettisti*. The bitter results of this scarring of public opinion would soon appear, in the full post-war light.

The victory had solved none of the perennial problems of Italian society; it had, rather, aggravated and magnified them. There was an extremely concentrated, unbalanced apparatus of production; a state machinery that had grown too hastily, improvised, split into watertight compartments, and so largely taken over by the strongest economic groups; a managing personnel who were largely new and heterogeneous, held together only by a common inclination towards authoritarian methods; a public opinion which had taken shape under the shadow of war and suffering; Italy's old incongruity reproduced itself again, at a higher level – that of tragedy.

A MISSED OPPORTUNITY FOR REVOLUTION?

The euphoria of victory soon faded. When in April 1919 the Prime Minister, Orlando, and the Foreign Minister, Sonnino, abandoned the Paris conference as a display of protest at the slight consideration of Italy's interests by the other victorious powers, the sense of disappointment that had for some time been insinuating itself through the country spread rapidly, and the government was forced to resign.

So the myth of the mutilated victory was born. In reality the peace negotiations which were later signed by the new government allowed Italy not only the Trento area and the city of Trieste, the traditional demands of the interventionists, but also the Alto Adige, with its strong German minority, and Istria, with its strong Slav minority. The question of Dalmatia, which the Treaty of London had assigned to Italy, remained to be settled with the new Jugoslav state, as did that of the city of Fiume, which on the other hand, according to the terms of the treaty and the point of view of the Allies and of Wilson, was to be left a free town. Italy's insistence in pursuing these two objectives certainly did not predispose the Allies in her favour, which must explain the final failure of Italian diplomacy on this point. Besides, many Italian politicians, including Bissolati, shared the opinion that in deference to the principle of nationhood it would be convenient to renounce Dalmatia. So the whole picture is not one of a diplomatic Caporetto, even if the peace treaty could probably have been more favourable to Italy, had the Italian government followed a straighter line, and displayed less ambition. However, the sense of disappointment that spread through the country from April to June 1919 – there was not even any commemoration of the date of Italy's entry into the war – and the myth of the mutilated victory itself had deeper origins than the recent diplomatic failures. These were no more than the last straw.

Once the storm was over Italy realized that she remained a poor country and, what was more, heavily in debt to her allies. The peasants who came back from the war found the same poverty that they had left behind, fields that were more badly worked and stables more empty; and the glittering wartime officers faced the prospect of uncertain salaries of inflated money: a far from exciting or attractive reward for men who had fought for three years in the trenches. Was this then what they had fought for? Was this what six hundred thousand Italians had sacrificed their lives for?

From this question to the answer that the war, with its losses, its waste, and its speculations, had been a folly, was a short step, which many Italians took. Had not the Pope reigning in the terrible year 1917 put out a pressing appeal to the governments to put an end to the 'useless slaughter'? And now that the accounts were drawn up, that was exactly how the war appeared. A profound surge of popular feeling rose against the Italian state and its ruling class, and those who had hoped that intervention in the war would prevent a revolution were terrified to witness this growth of a revolutionary restlessness that seemed more threatening and disruptive every day.

Few years in the history of modern Italy, and perhaps none save 1943, were years of such deep and general social and political crisis and revolutionary ferment as 1919. Labour was greatly agitated: the membership of the unions, a matter of hundreds of thousands before the war, was now to be counted in millions, and the figures for strikes and strikers went far beyond the highest point reached in the years

1901–2. Factory-workers went on strike and managed to win substantial wage-increases and an eight-hour day. There were strikes among employees of public services such as railwaymen and post-office workers, among the *braccianti* – unskilled agricultural labourers – of the Po valley and the central Italian *mezzadri*, and even among the faithful government clerks. In the countrysides of Lazio and southern Italy the peasants, now war-veterans, organized and encouraged by the associations that had been formed among ex-combatants, occupied the big estates, and forced the government to give the *fait accompli* some kind of legality. In June a number of cities experienced violent demonstrations against the cost of living, which in some cases had an openly insurrectional character; and in July a general strike, though one that had limited success, was put into effect, as a display of solidarity with revolutionary Russia. Then in September came D'Annunzio's invasion of Fiume, achieved with the connivance of the military authorities. This was, as we shall see, the first of a series of subversive acts from the right that was to culminate in Mussolini's march on Rome. But this did not prevent many people from greeting it, at that moment, as a further symptom of the existing revolutionary situation, and a proof that the germ of insubordination had also penetrated within the ranks of the army. There were even some who went so far as to moot the project of a union between D'Annunzio's nationalist subversion and the revolutionary ferment of the people; to this end there were contacts between the soldier-poet and certain representatives of Italian socialism and anarchism. The feeling that the days of the liberal state were by now numbered and that it was fast breaking up was by now general, and when in November 1919 elections were held – the first in Italian history on a proportional basis – some of those electors who traditionally voted for the candidates of order and for the government preferred to stay at home, convinced that by this stage every effort was useless, and paralysed by fear of the imminent inevitable defeat. The elections did, at least in part, confirm those fears: the socialist party was victorious, with 1,756,344 votes and 156 deputies, followed at a distance by the recently formed Popular party, which obtained 1,121,658 votes and had more than a hundred deputies, reaping the reward of the attitude the Church had taken towards the war. If the South, with its cliques and aristocracy, had not provided the government candidates with a large number of votes, the defeat of the old dominant class would have been catastrophic. But on the other hand, in the great industrial centres of the North and in the fertile countryside of the lower Po valley, the country's nerve-centres, the socialist party scored a resounding triumph.

But the socialist party was quite without any clear view of the situation or the way in which it could have been developed. It has often been stated that the Italian Socialist Party's main handicap in the immediate post-war period was its internal division between the 'maximalist' group, which held the majority, and openly proclaimed its revolutionary aims, and the reformists, who were on the other hand inclined, as always, towards a policy of reform and of co-operation with the most advanced sectors of the bourgeois parties. Starting from this assumption, it has been stated that if the reformists had not 'betrayed' the party the revolution would have been achieved in Italy, or conversely, if it had not been for the impatience and demagogy of the maximalists, a serious policy of reform could have been pursued, and the victory of fascism prevented.

In fact it was not the quarrel between two political possibilities that paralysed the Italian Socialist Party so much as its lack of any political line. The maximalists were not seriously revolutionary, nor the reformists seriously reformist. The vague ambition of Bombacci, Lazzari and even Serrati, who continually put off until the next day the revolution which they proclaimed to be inevitable, was balanced, on the other side, by the reluctance of the reformists, Turati in particular, to assume precise responsibilities, and their fear that by joining the government the socialists would find themselves involved in the bankruptcy of the bourgeois state. And the whole party shared a lack of sensitivity towards the new post-war situation that had taken shape in the countryside, where a general rush for land was taking place on the part of peasants now finally able to satisfy their age-long hunger for land, after the freezing of ground rents and the rise in prices of farm-produce. Between the census of 1911 and that of 1921 the number of small proprietors rose from 21 per cent to 35·6 per cent of the total population. By proclaiming their intentions of land-socialization and general expropriation, the socialists alienated large numbers of the peasant class. None of them knew, probably, that Lenin, for whom they professed such great admiration, had not hesitated, in the cause of revolution, to take over the agricultural programme of the social-revolutionaries, based on the multiplication of smallholdings. This failure of the socialist leaders to understand the peasant problem was accompanied by a preconceived hostility towards the Popular party and its syndical organization, whose basis and strength was in the countryside. Instead of trying to attract to the revolutionary camp the most advanced Catholic organizations and individuals, and so break the religious bond that held together socially and politically heterogeneous forces within the Popular party, the socialist party, with its traditional anti-clericalism, helped to strengthem this bond and to make more difficult any collaboration between socialist and Catholic syndicalists and workers.

The only group that applied itself seriously to the problems of the Italian revolution, which others confined themselves to prophesying as imminent and inevitable, was that gathered around the Turin weekly *L'Ordine nuovo;* it included Antonio Gramsci, Angelo Tasca and Palmiro Togliatti. Turin was without doubt the most proletarian of Italian cities, and its workers the most advanced section of the Italian proletariat. In April 1917 they had met with the cry '*Viva* Lenin!' the Menshevik delegates who had come to preach the necessity of continuing the war, and in August of the same year they had staged a rebellion against the cost of living and against the war which had had to be put down with troops and the use of force. In some of the main factories of Turin – that of Fiat in particular – they had gone on to constitute factory councils, modelled on the soviets. The men of the *Ordine nuovo* soon discovered in these councils the most suitable weapons of the revolutionary struggle, and an example of workers' self-government that could be held out to all the Italian proletariat when victory had been won. The Turin movement of factory councils was certainly the vanguard of the Italian revolutionary movement, its most advanced and most highly aware section, but like all vanguards, it could easily be isolated and defeated. During late 1919 and early 1920 the industrialists recovered from their defeats and formed a General Confederation of Industry, which became a counter-revolutionary general staff. They realized the weakness of the Turin movement and for this reason chose Turin as the battlefield for their final counter-offensive. The metal-workers of Turin were forced and provoked by the actions of their bosses into a general strike in April 1920; they were defeated, and Gramsci had to admit that the hope of making Turin the Italian Petrograd had shown itself to be without foundation, and that the rhythm of Italian life in general was far from keeping time with that of its advance guard. This was the first step in that long and difficult political meditation that was to lead him, in the fascist prisons, to define in his *Quaderni* the project for an Italian revolution that would be better adapted to the varied and contradictory reality of a country full of contrasts and disturbances of balance.

The defeat of the Turin metal-workers' strike marked the first receding of the revolutionary wave that had disturbed Italian society. Revolutionary energies were still powerful, but the forces of conservatism were already reorganizing themselves and already gave hints of passing decisively to the counter-attack. Things were entering on a period of uncertainty and precarious balance, a period which, as Gramsci was one of the few to realize, would only be ended by a final solution: either with a revolution or with an equally radical and violent reaction.

ECONOMIC CRISIS AND ORIGINS OF FASCISM

During the tormented year 1919 and the first months of 1920 the government was led by Francesco Saverio Nitti, a southern politician of notable open-mindedness and knowledge, with an understanding of economic matters rare in an Italian Prime Minister, but lacking the vigour and energy that the times demanded. A man of deep demo-cratic convictions, Nitti tried to obtain the support and co-operation of the left, but succeeded only in arousing the hostility of the right and of military circles, who execrated him for having granted an amnesty to deserters. His weakness was shown clearly at the moment of D'Annunzio's invasion of Fiume, towards which his attitude was indecisive and equivocal. When in June 1920 Nitti's government was forced to resign, the only politician with enough prestige to rule the country at such a difficult time was old Giolitti, who had never hidden his hostility to Italy's intervention in war, and who had kept himself apart for five years until he should be called for again. Giolitti's return, after so many accidents and misadventures, seemed a return to common sense and normality and to the old pre-war Italy; and for a short while it really seemed as if the veteran Piedmontese statesman could perform the miracle of reviving the past.

Consistent in his hostility towards any imperialist, adventurous foreign policy, Giolitti applied himself in the first place to settling the still open question of the Adriatic, signing a treaty with Jugoslavia in November 1920, according to which Italy renounced her claims to Dalmatia in exchange for recognition of her sovereignty over all Italy and the city of Zara, while Fiume was made an independent state. D'Annunzio, whether he liked it or not, had to accept the *fait accompli*, and in December he and his 'legionaries' left Fiume. So a dangerous furnace of nationalism, which had done much to overheat and poison public opinion, was extinguished. This success in foreign affairs had been preceded by another, far more ostentatious, in domestic policy. In September 1920 the metal-workers, who had for some time been involved in a union dispute with their respective employers, had occupied the factories, putting up the red flag, and guarding the factories with arms. For a few days it seemed as though the hour of revolution had finally struck. As on the previous occasion of the general strike of 1904, Giolitti immediately realized, rightly, that neither the socialist leaders nor the General Confederation of Labour would dare to push through to its final consequences a movement that did not in any case have real revolutionary possibilities; he temporized until both parties to the dispute agreed to accept his mediation and to reach an agreement by which both saved face.

It really seemed as if the convulsions of the post-war period were over and that Italy, under the guidance of her wisest statesman, would return to the road she had successfully followed during the first decade of the century.

But it was not to be so. After the tumultuous, exuberant development of the wartime period, and the subsequent downward curve of the years immediately after the war, the Italian economy was in fact entering on a period of acute and general crisis. Production stagnated, and the difficulties of some of the larger industries soon involved the loan-banks. In December 1921 the *Banca di Sconto* closed down, involving thousands of small savers in its collapse and creating the feeling of a return to the time of the banking scandals of the 1890's. In the mean time the unemployment figures rose continually, while at the same time the number of strikes diminished. The main victim of the crisis was the union movement, which saw its effectiveness and its margins of manoeuvre and success enormously reduced. The stagnation to which it was confined naturally aggravated the differences and frictions in the socialist camp, which had already previously emerged on the occasion of the occupation of the factories and the strike at Turin in April. In this climate there was a series of splits within the party. The first, and the one that was to have most consequences, was the break-away of the left wing, which in January 1921 seceded to form the Italian Communist Party, a small group whose radical extremism did not bode well for its future fortunes. The communist secession was followed in October 1922 by that of the reformists, so that when fascism came to power the old and glorious Italian Socialist Party was split into three parts.

The economic crisis weakened the Italian workers' movement, but had a galvanizing and fortifying effect on 'Italian reaction', a term that may be taken to include all the sects and groups – soldiers, industrialists, landowners – which had been helpless in the face of the wave of subversion of 1919, and dreamed of a return to the discipline and order of the state in wartime. The crisis of the unions and of the socialist movement, the disillusionment and bewilderment that were by now rife among the masses, allowed them to glimpse the possibility of an authoritarian and final solution. Giolitti, with his traditional policy of balance, seemed out-of-date. What was wanted was a man of greater strength and energy and bolder views, who would be able to replace a precarious and uncertain balance, providing the country with something stronger and more final.

As is well known, this man was found in the person of Benito

Mussolini. After his clamorous departure from the socialist party and his crossing to the interventionist camp, the exuberant Romagnolo had enlisted in the army, and stayed there long enough to adorn himself later with the title of ex-combatant and war-wounded, even though it seems certain that he never went into the front line, and was wounded during training. He then returned to the editorship of the *Popolo d'Italia*, and founded the fascist movement in 1919. This new political body, composed of demobilized soldiers and adventurers, and based on an extremely heterogeneous and demagogic programme, was a typical by-product of post-war disorientation, and such small prestige as it enjoyed derived, by reflection, from D'Annunzio's exploit in Fiume, of which Mussolini had made himself one of the noisiest advocates and publicists. In the elections of November 1919 the fascists succeeded in mounting a campaign only in Milan, where they polled a derisive vote of little more than four thousand. On this occasion Mussolini contemplated giving up the political struggle and devoting himself to some other of the many activities, from aviation to the theatre, in which he believed himself gifted. During the first half of 1920 the new fascist movement remained a circumscribed phenomenon of little importance. The only Italian city it succeeded in penetrating was Trieste, whose atmosphere was in many ways exceptional: the closeness of Fiume, the military administration to which the city was subjected, and above all the existence of a state of chronic tension between the Slav and Italian populations, which had been greatly aggravated by the end of Austrian rule, made Trieste a good breeding-ground for an intensely nationalistic movement such as fascism. With the smug complicity of the local authorities, the first fascist *squadre** were able to devastate Slav clubs and centres, attack the *Camere del lavoro* and besiege the poor quarters, as they waited for the time when they would be able to apply these methods to the rest of the country.

But this wait would certainly have been in vain if the economic crisis had not created in the country a situation ideally suited to the development of the fascist movement. The workers' movement's weakened capacity for resistance, the growing and encouraged authoritarian tendencies of the dominant groups and privileged classes, demobilization and the availability of large masses of unemployed men, the ebbing of the lower middle class away from the working class and the socialist movement: all these things combined to facilitate the first steps and self-assertions of fascism. Mussolini's unquestionable tactical and political ability and the grave crisis of the state and of the liberal ruling class did the rest. The economic crisis, far from generating

---

* The *squadre d'azione*, embryo of the fascist militia, were organized gangs consisting mainly of aggressive youths. Members of the *squadre* were *squadristi*. (Trans.)

the revolution, as some had hoped or feared, brought reaction: Italy's situation in 1921 and 1922 thus in many ways anticipates that of Germany in the years immediately preceding the rise of nazism.

FASCISM'S RISE TO POWER

Fascist *squadrismo* made its large-scale *début* at Bologna, a stronghold of socialism, on 21 November 1920; when a new socialist local administration was taking office, the fascists of Bologna managed to provoke serious incidents and a climate of civil war within the city. From that moment there began a pitiless guerrilla war in the countryside of Emilia and Tuscany between the fascist *squadre* and the socialist organizations and the workers; it gradually spread to the other regions of the country. In the first months of 1921 hardly a day passed without reports in the newspapers of a *Camera del lavoro* set on fire, a co-operative sacked, socialist or even republican and Popular party leaders forced to drink castor oil and 'banned' from their towns. It was a provincial war, with all the bitterness and passion of provincial wars, but it was above all a class-war without quarter. The hatred that the landlords of Emilia, financiers of the *squadre*, felt for their peasants, was no less than that which the nationalists of Trieste felt for the Slav population: it was an instinctive, almost racial hatred.

But the success of fascist punitive expeditions and raids would not have been possible without the silence and at times complicity of the army and the executive power. Many prefects and generals competed in their blindness to fascist violence and aggression, but later raged with particular severity against the eventual reaction of the fascists' adversaries. A particularly heavy responsibility for the protection of *squadrismo* must be laid on the shoulders of Giolitti's War Minister, the ex-socialist Ivanoe Bonomi, who in July 1921 became Prime Minister. Even so, the fact that soldiers, prefects, ministers and Giolitti himself favoured or at least permitted the actions of the fascists should not be taken as a sign and proof that the Italian political class was by now prepared to accept the fascist take-over of the state, or was resigned to this course of events. For many politicians of the time were convinced that because of its heterogeneous programme and social composition, and because it was more an emotional than a political phenomenon, fascism would have a brief life, and would dissolve from within. In the meantime it could be made useful, then discarded at the right moment.

Mussolini himself was fully aware of the inner weaknesses and contradictions of the fascist movement. Unlike D'Annunzio, he did not believe in his own rhetoric, and was far from confusing his own desires and ambitions with reality. He soon realized that unless fascism made some concrete achievement it would suffer a crisis and dissolve, as soon as the short-lived political circumstances of its beginnings had passed. This achievement could only be power, and the identification of fascism with the state. But to achieve this aim fascism had to make itself more 'respectable' and purge itself of its more extreme elements. So between summer and November 1921 Mussolini conducted a victorious battle within his party against the fascist 'left wing' led by Dino Grandi, an ex-republican from the Romagna; Mussolini reassured the monarchy, first muting and then explicitly denying previous republican pronouncements; he won the trust of industrialists by declarations of total economic liberalism; finally, he abandoned his old anti-clericalism, and discoursed on the Catholic and universal mission of Rome. The Vatican was not entirely insensitive to these blandishments: the new Pope, Pius XI, elected in February 1922, contributed to the final victory of fascism by withdrawing the Church's support from the Italian Popular Party and its combative leader, Don Sturzo.

As fascism gradually became more respectable in the eyes of right-thinking people, the hindrances and barriers that had been raised against it fell. One by one, the men of the old liberal ruling class surrendered or actually moved over to the fascist side. First to do so was Salandra, the Prime Minister responsible for intervention. Some, like Giolitti, retained up to the last minute the illusion that they were able to dominate the situation, and involved themselves in a difficult game of battles, treaties and bargaining, which Mussolini ably controlled: at every 'victory' of the *squadre*, every successful blow, he raised the price of his demands. So passed several months of agitated political activity, disturbed in the way typical of periods preceding a final settlement. To superficial observers the situation might still have seemed fluid and open to several solutions, but in fact the game was over, and it was now only a question of tidying up its conclusion. In October 1922 this comedy of equivocations at last came to an end. When the Vatican was increasing its distance from the Popular party, and the socialist party broke its unity of action agreement with the General Confederation of Labour, in other words, when his last opponents were divided and defeated, Mussolini openly blackmailed the King and the state with the threat of insurrection. On 24 October, after a fascist meeting in Naples, the fascist *quadrumvirs* decided, with Mussolini's agreement, to march on Rome. The Prime Minister at that moment, Luigi Facta, a trusted Giolittian, advised the King to sign a declaration of martial law, but the King, after some hesitation, refused to sign. Mussolini was awaiting events at Milan, and was ready if they took a turn for the worse, to take refuge in Switzerland. But now he was able to board a sleeping-car and come to Rome to receive from the King the invitation to form a new government, and to present himself in front of Parliament, to declare that it had been entirely thanks to his own will that he had not transformed it into a camp for his men. In spite of this bragging declaration, the Chamber gave a vote of confidence to Mussolini's new government, which included Popular and liberal ministers, by 306 votes to 116. Among the former were Bonomi, Giolitti, Orlando, Salandra and Alcide De Gasperi.

The 'fascist revolution' was thus accomplished with the assent and authorization of the established powers, and Italy, after four years of upheavals and hesitations, finally settled down. For in spite of everything the rise to power of fascism was, like all restorations, in some way a solution, in that it made possible the rediscovery of an equilibrium and the reconstitution of an 'order'. But it was the easiest and so the worst of the historically possible solutions. The forces of the Italian revolution had paid for their immaturity and their errors with a defeat which had very grave consequences. Their last rearguard fighters – in Parma, in the poor quarters of Rome, in old Bari, in Turin, where there were big strikes in August 1922, doomed to defeat from the start – saved proletarian honour, and laid down the basis for a long anti-fascist struggle.

18

From fascism to the war

FASCISM: FROM GOVERNMENT TO RÉGIME

Just as fascism's way to power had been smoothed by the economic crisis, the favourable state of the European and American economy on the whole from 1922 to 1929 did much to aid its process of consolidation. The new fascist government thus had to do no more than assist the current tendency, allowing those forces and men who controlled the country's economic life to have their own way. As early as his Udine speech on the eve of the march on Rome, Mussolini had railed against 'the railwayman state, the postman state, and the insurance-agent state', and once he had reached power he was not slow to put these anti-state aims of his into action, entrusting the Ministry of Finance to an economic liberal, Alberto De Stefani. The registering of bonds in the owner's name, introduced by Giolitti, was abolished, death duties reduced, the telephones denationalized, wages cut down. This extreme liberalism in domestic matters did not however prevent fascism from continuing the traditional Italian policy of customs protection, to which Giolitti had already made important concessions in 1921 by accepting the imposition of a new and stricter protective tariff. In this context we must also mention the policy of revaluing and stabilizing the lira launched in 1925 and taken to its end by Count Giuseppe Volpi, a man in the confidence of the industrialists, who succeeded De Stefani in the Finance Ministry; and the so-called 'corn battle', accompanied by the re-imposition of the protection duty on corn. Both these measures were intended to narrow the balance of payments gap and to permit the building-up of large supplies of hard currencies.

In short, this policy, combined with the favourable economic situation, yielded its fruit. In 1929 industrial production was 50 per cent higher than it had been in 1922. Particularly spectacular progress was made by the chemical industry, dominated by the Montecatini combine, which became easily the leading producer of fertilizers. Connected with the chemical industry was the new and promising one of artificial silk and rayon, the principal producer of which was the Snia Viscosa company. As for the automobile industry, its rhythm of production was well sustained: in 1926 60,500 automobiles were produced in Italy, the majority by Fiat. Because of this increased industrial production, unemployment diminished: at the time of the crisis it had reached a fairly high level, which had helped to prevent the discontent and spirit of absolute hostility to fascist government that existed among the working classes from being expressed by an extended and organized struggle. Agricultural production too showed a general increase, however much this may have been due to the new impulse fascism gave to cereal-growing with the corn battle. The plan inherited from previous governments for the splitting up of the Sicilian *latifondo* was deliberately dropped.

The improved economic situation and the government's support of the social groups who were its greatest beneficiaries undoubtedly made it easier for fascism to liquidate the surviving structures of the liberal state and construct an authoritarian state. The forming of the voluntary militia for national security, which gathered together and gave paid employment to all the ex-members of the *squadre d'azione*, in January 1923, and the promotion of the Grand Council of fascism into an organ of state, paved the way. There was now a fascist army beside the regular army, and a fascist consultative body appointed by Mussolini beside the elective Parliament. In April 1923 the Popular ministers were expelled from Parliament, and in July a new electoral law elaborated, of a type that would permit an absolute majority, deliberately designed to assure a large majority for the list of government and fascist candidates, known as the *listone*, or 'big list'. The elections were held in April 1924, in an atmosphere of intimidation and violence towards the adversaries of fascism, and with a return of militia arson. In spite of this, the results did not come up to Mussolini's hopes: though the fascist *listone* won a majority of votes and seats, thanks to the mechanism of the law, it received fewer votes than the opposition list in the northern regions of Italy and in the big industrial towns.

The climate of illegality and oppression in which the elections had been held was denounced in the Chamber with great passion and courage by the socialist deputy Giacomo Matteotti, on 30 May 1924. A few days later, on 10 June, this brave parliamentarian was kidnapped, and on 16 August his body was found in a thicket in the countryside near Rome. It seemed for a moment as if the government was alone, for few people doubted its complicity in the murder. Many fascist badges vanished from buttonholes, and Mussolini himself was aware of his own isolation. But he soon recovered his boldness, for on the one hand the parliamentary opposition, led by Giovanni Amendola, left the Chamber in what was called the Aventine secession, and was unable to appeal to the country and propose a real alternative, being once again paralysed by the fear of revolution; and on the other hand, Mussolini could count on the support of the King and the neutrality of the Vatican. On 3 January 1925 Mussolini confronted the Chamber, taking on himself all responsibility for the Matteotti crime, and provocatively challenging the Chamber to avail itself of its right to impeach him. By rejecting this flung gauntlet the Chamber in effect signed its own death-warrant, and the liberal state finally ceased to exist.

As Mussolini had threatened in his arrogant speech of 3 January, words were quickly followed by deeds. The following months saw the 'fascistization' of the state, effected by decrees and 'very fascist' laws, as they were described. The activity of other parties was checked by a law on associations, the liberty of the press was crushed, the Aventine dissidents expelled from the Chamber, the administration purged of officials suspected of anti-fascism, the autonomy of local administrations restricted, with elected mayors replaced by the *podestà* appointed from above, and the codes of law reformed. The Italian state increasingly took on a totalitarian character; it was led by the *Duce*, whom a special law accorded pre-eminence over other ministers. Opponents had to face the snares of the *Ovra*, the régime's political police, and the rigours of the Special Tribunal, set up in 1925 after Zaniboni's attempt on Mussolini's life; this court was soon busy doling out years of prison or exile, and even death-sentences. For the first time since unification there were again Italian political emigrants, or, as the fascists said, reviving an old term of the days of the communes, *fuorusciti* ('exile-outlaws'). The fascist monopoly of union organization, imposed in July 1925, and the subsequent Vidoni pact between the unions and the representatives of the industrialists (by which, in exchange for a guarantee of collective contracts, workers committed themselves not to strike or form committees within the factories), more or less silenced workers' opposition. In the mean time the General Confederation of Labour, last stronghold of free unionism, had been dissolved, and a number of its leading members seduced by fascist corporativism, the theory of which was expressed in a Charter of Labour solemnly published on 21 April 1927, Rome's birthday. This fascist-devised celebration had some time before replaced the 1st May.

Fascism was thus transforming itself from a government into a régime: a régime in which the Duce, who 'was always right', was the god, and the radio his prophet. In a country where the circulation of newspapers was still fairly limited, this new, powerful means of communication was in fact a deciding factor in forming and fixing public opinion. It was not for nothing that the fascist government had hurried to place it under its special control by forming a state corporation for radio transmissions in 1927. By means of the radio the Italians were daily informed of the successes of fascist Italy, however little Mussolini himself liked to speak directly to the microphones. He preferred, as he said, to address the crowd directly, at the great gatherings in the Piazza Venezia, where he harangued the people from the 'historic balcony'.

But Mussolini, as has already been emphasized, was too much of a politician to believe in the rhetoric of his régime. He realized clearly that even leaving aside the most evidently proletarian classes, broad sectors of public opinion were, if not declared opponents, at least unsure and mistrustful of fascism: it was therefore necessary to broaden the basis of common agreement. To this end the first approaches to the Vatican began, from 1925 onwards; Mussolini well understood that recognition from that quarter would, in a Catholic country, considerably strengthen the régime's prestige. The negotiations were long and difficult: they were greatly hindered by the fascist decision to ensure the monopoly of youth organizations with the creation of the *Balilla;* all others were dissolved, including the Catholic Boy Scouts. But although the régime was not prepared to make concessions as far as the fascist indoctrination of youth was concerned, it was ready to make some substantial ones in other fields. The Lateran Treaty of 11 February 1929 was reached: the Italian state recognized papal sovereignty over the territory of what was named the Vatican City, committed itself to a heavy indemnity, and revived and strengthened the article of Carlo Alberto's *statuto*, which declared the Catholic faith to be the national religion. The Holy See, for its part, declared that the Roman question was closed, and agreed to regulate its relations with the Italian state with a concordat, which, amongst other things, recognized that the Church marriage service had civil effect, and introduced the teaching of religion in state schools. This was the 'Conciliation', without doubt one of the actions of the fascist government which did most to strengthen its position, and one which had most effect on modern Italian history. For the validity of the Lateran Treaty is still explicitly recognized in the constitution of the Italian Republic.

Strong in this success, Mussolini was able to hold fresh elections, in March 1929. These followed the single list system, and were, from the point of view of democratic correctness, a farce. Yet it is probable that of the 8,506,576 ayes won by the single list (there were only 136,198 nays), many were a genuine expression of support.

The prestige of the fascist government was at its zenith: at home the re-establishment of order, the improvement of the economic situation and the conciliation with the Vatican seemed to right-minded people to represent so many good marks, while on the international level, in spite of its nationalism and its restlessness, fascism seemed a solid bastion against communism. Mussolini's début in foreign affairs – he held this portfolio too – had not indeed been such as to inspire confidence. In August 1923, following the killing of an Italian military envoy at Janina, Mussolini sent an ultimatum to Greece and occupied Corfu. But England's firm attitude soon forced him to withdraw from the island, and from then on fascist policy, partly because of the moderating influence exercised by career diplomats, was on the whole faithful to the traditional line of friendship with England. Indeed the most weighty recognition of Mussolini came from England: on 20 June 1927 the Conservative Chancellor of the Exchequer, Winston Churchill, declared that if he had been an Italian he would not have hesitated to be a fascist from the start. Questioned by the Labour Opposition, the Prime Minister, Baldwin, in his turn found nothing reprehensible in Churchill's statements. The conviction that fascism was what Italy needed and Mussolini, as Pius XI had said on the eve of the Conciliation, the man sent by Providence, had gained some footing in foreign public opinion. Rebounding to Italy, it helped to strengthen the régime's foundations further.

FASCIST ITALY AND REAL ITALY

Every totalitarian régime tends necessarily to try to create an ideology of its own. The attempt to provide fascism with one was made by the philosopher Giovanni Gentile, without doubt the most authoritative and brilliant of the fascist intellectuals. As Minister of Public Instruction he had been among other things the author of a reform of the schools with which he had tried to introduce to teaching the criteria of idealistic pedagogy, but which had in practice amounted only to a reaffirmation of the leading place of the humanities and of the class-oriented delimitation of Italian schools. In the article on fascism in the *Enciclopedia italiana*, another of the most substantial and serious cultural achievements of the régime, he defined fascism as a 'style' more than a body of doctrine, or, to adopt his idealist philosopher's terminology, an act rather than a deed. This amounted to an implicit recognition of the heterogeneity and contradictions of the fascist movement, a movement in which some – a few – insisted on seeing an uncompleted revolution in progress, and others – many – a completed and crystallized restoration. In fact this second and more real aspect of fascism was that which did most to form the régime's face. Gentile himself, who was replaced as Minister of Public Instruction by Cesare De Vecchi, a living example of reactionary obtuseness, perhaps realized this, and his dissertations on the voluntarist, actualist nature of fascism have a somewhat wishful and apologist ring.

In architecture the monumental 'archaeological' style of Piacentini, which was celebrated by demolitions and grandiose rebuilding in the historic centre of Rome, certainly represented the time and fascist taste more closely than did the experiments inspired by the rationalism of the *Bauhaus* that certain more alert and more accomplished architects sometimes managed to achieve, as, for example, in the fine station at Florence. In literature, D'Annunzio, however inimitable, remained the official poet. He never tolerated the obscuring of his fame by that of the Duce, and withdrew to the sumptuous villa assigned him by the state, where he spent a rancorous and idle old age, writing almost nothing. The official face of fascist Italy was, then, martial; in fascist language *littorio* (of the lictor). Its heroes were the transatlantic flyers and aces of aviation like Balbo and De Pinedo, its pride the great transatlantic liners that won the Blue Ribbon, its favourite motto one of the Duce's many 'lapidary' phrases that made a fine show of themselves inscribed on the régime's new public buildings. The one to be seen most often went: 'better to live one day as a lion than a hundred years as a sheep'.

This was the façade. The reality was a good deal more prosaic, and consisted in the euphoria of a rediscovered middle-class prosperity. None of the things that usually mark a period of prosperity in Italy were lacking: building speculation, the first modest automobile boom that came with the production of the first popular model, the *Balilla*, the general passion for sport, for the entertainment-oriented spectacles provided by the theatre and the cinema, and for popular songs. The beaches and mountain resorts were populated by middle-class families in the summer, while for those who could not afford the luxury of a complete holiday there were the popular trains organized by the national after-work organization, thanks to which it was possible to spend an enjoyable weekend, or rather 'fascist Saturday'. Nationalist pride, aroused by fascist propaganda, was no more than a pleasant added spice to this rediscovered well-being. Another spice of a different nature was provided by the jokes about the régime that were told with a knowing air, without being too seriously believed.

There was in this new wave of modest, circumscribed prosperity something profoundly different from the happy years of the *Belle*

Epoque and *Italietta*: there was more vulgarity, less sensitivity towards the very serious problems that still remained, and, above all, more corruption: a corruption that gradually increased as the régime consolidated itself, to the point of becoming almost an institution. The new men whom fascism brought to power, the so-called *gerarchi* (ie 'hierarchs'), were for the most part parvenus and provincials, of coarse tastes and little culture, completely without the habit of power and of detachment from it that are characteristic of seasoned and tested ruling classes. Such were Farinacci, *ras** of Cremona, who became party secretary, a vulgar and villainous man, Augusto Turati, another party secretary and provincial *ras*, and, finally, Achille Starace, worthy object of the most scurrilous and successful stories against the régime.

The pretentiousness of the façade made a singular contrast with the squalor and emptiness within, the clamour of big words with the poverty of feelings. It is no wonder that the best literature and art of the fascist period seem dominated by a sense of disgust at this contrast and this emptiness. Pirandello, whose adherence to fascism was made much of by the régime, had already populated his plays, which did not much please the public of the 1920's, with a disillusioned and hallucinated bourgeoisie. But Moravia's novel *Gli Indifferenti*, of 1929, gave a direct and unequivocal picture of the middle class of the fascist era, of its cynicism and intellectual poverty. Montale, perhaps the greatest Italian poet of our century, wrote of life's sadness, to which he opposed the 'prodigy of divine indifference'. Morandi, with his still-lifes and bottles, set an example of rigour and chasteness that was implicitly a protest against the rhetoric and noise of officialdom. Petrolini, an actor gifted with an instinctive and genuine comic force, created the character of Gastone, the inept and spoiled *figlio di papà*.

So the years of prosperity passed rapidly, amid the vulgarity and clamour of official rhetoric. The euphoria of a temporary, limited and artificial well-being was soon to pass, and the old Italian reality would return to beat at the door, as it had after the first decade of the century, but this time with a more tragic urgency.

ECONOMIC CRISIS AND CORPORATIVE ECONOMY

The great economic crisis of 1929 had less acute and spectacular repercussions on the economy and society of Italy than in America

---

* I.e. 'boss', nabob; the word comes from Ethiopia, where a 'ras' is second only to the negus. (Trans.)

or Germany, but its effects were perhaps deeper and more lasting in Italy. For the healing of the wounds of the crisis was a long and difficult process that effected fundamental changes not only in the country's economic structures but also in its political ones.

From 1930 the classic symptoms of the crisis emerged clearly in Italy too: the fall in prices and the consequent collapse of shares provoked drastic falls in production. Between 1929 and 1932 automobile production was halved, while production of steel fell from 2,122,194 tons per annum to 1,396,180, and that of cotton thread from 220,000 tons to 169,000. The average national income fell from 3,079 lire in 1929 to 2,868 in 1933, while unemployment rose from 300,000 in 1929 to 1,019,000 in 1933. In consequence consumption also went down, and the number of calories consumed *per capita* fell sharply. Frustration, and hunger, once more became widespread. The fascist policy of population-increase, followed for reasons of national prestige, did nothing to improve the situation.

To begin with, the fascist government considered reacting by intensifying, above all, the already-launched policy of public works. The large-scale demolitions in the centre of Rome, with the opening of the via dell'Impero and the via della Conciliazione, and the big project of land-reclamation in the Pontine marshes, begun in 1928, all belong to the years of crisis. The last-mentioned project was a truly impressive one, which fascism, however, did not fail to propagandize beyond its practical effect. But far more was needed to overcome the crisis and restore energy and future prospects to the national economy; what was needed was an overall revision and re-organization of the economic policy followed up to that date. This, save for the brief interlude when Count Volpi had occupied the Ministry of Finance, had followed a liberal line; but those same industrialists who at a time of prosperity had requested the government not to concern itself with their affairs now insistently demanded support and help. And once again the state flew to their side. The founding first of the *Istituto immobiliare italiano* (IMI) and then of the *Istituto per la ricostruzione industriale* (IRI) made it possible for state financing to salvage many industries that had been sorely tried by the crisis.

So there began a policy of increasing public spending and restricting private consumption, which first alleviated the effects of the crisis, and then made it possible to overcome it. While workers' wages remained low and indirect taxation reached record levels, state financing and industrial commissions increased continually. In many cases the industries financed and commissioned were those engaged in war production, which was to have grave consequences on the later developments of Italy's history. It became a patriotic duty, which the state was the first to perform, to prefer the national product, even when its price was a good deal higher than that of a similar product on the international market. Certain products of the Italian steel industry, for example, were 50 or even 100 per cent more expensive than those of other countries. So the so-called 'autarchic' policy took shape: a new edition, on a larger scale and with a patriotic mask, of protectionism, under whose aegis Italian capitalism had been born and had developed. The founding of a whole series of public corporations, such as ANIC (*Azienda nazionale idrogenerazione combustibili*) and AGIP, and the development of electricity production, in the attempt to adjust Italy's negative balance in the raw materials of power, should all be seen in the context of the autarchic policy, as should the renewed impulse given to the 'corn battle', with the founding of the *Federazione dei consorzi agrari*, and of compulsory stores of grain. Finally, measures had to be introduced to prevent the overflow of population from the land to the towns, and the growth of urbanization; and fascist propaganda turned to exalting the beauty of the rural life: the song *Campagnola bella* became one of the most popular tunes.

The organization of the economy was thus in many ways reminiscent of that of the wartime period, and like the latter it gave to superficial observers the impression of containing elements of collectivism and of state planning. In fact the state, by means of the IRI, controlled many firms and whole sectors of production: so much so that the public sector of the economy was larger in Italy than in any other capitalist country. Besides, by means of the corporations, whose organization was perfected and made operative in 1934, the state itself declared that it wished to assume the functions of a mediator between the complaints and interests of employees and workers, and to harmonize the demands of public and private interests. Mussolini and his propaganda even proclaimed that the fascist corporative state represented a stage beyond capitalism with its extreme free enterprise, and beyond socialism, with its suffocating state domination. Some, like Giuseppe Bottai, who was for a time Minister of Corporations, believed in these theorizings, but then had to admit that things went very differently in practice. For although it was true that the state sector of the economy was larger and more solid, it was also true that the state was, owing to the way it had taken shape and developed, largely a 'private' state, exposed to, and to a large extent dominated by, the pressures of the strongest and most influential groups and economic concentrations. The corporations were far from being the instruments of mediation between capital and labour, and of placing private initiative within the context of the national economy, that the 'left wing' fascists would have wished them to be: they were, on the contrary, dominated as they were by the main industries, the means by which the major monopolistic groups and concentrations such as Fiat, Montecatini, Snia Viscosa, managed to silence every remnant of working-class protest and demands, and to put pressure on the state to strengthen their position. Any surviving resistance they met with from state bureaucracy and administration could easily be got round, in the atmosphere of spreading corruption that such an interpenetration of state, party and corporation increased and encouraged.

So the price of overcoming the crisis of the '30's was an increase in the authoritarian and totalitarian character of the fascist régime. Now the fascist anthem *Giovinezza* accompanied and sometimes preceded the Royal March on official occasions. By this time party membership was increasingly becoming an indispensable passport to public offices, and every solemnity was employed to persuade Italians to put on black shirts and participate in the *adunate*.* In 1931, university professors were forced to swear loyalty to fascism: only eleven of them refused to do so. The régime's motto was now 'Believe, obey, fight.' So far, the last of these imperatives had had merely rhetorical force. But it was soon to have real meaning.

FROM THE ATTACK ON ETHIOPIA
TO ENTRY IN WAR

The economic crisis had also shaken the régime's political prestige, especially among the lower class who were its main victims. Mussolini's high-sounding words in his speech to the workers of Milan in 1934 on the overcoming of capitalism, were certainly not enough to cover the reality of lower wages, lasting unemployment, reduced consumption among the common people. So the régime was faced with an uphill climb also in terms of its own popularity and public support.

The classic means was to seek for an assertion of prestige on the level of foreign policy; besides, war supplies would, and in fact did, help some sectors of industry to escape finally from the crisis. The chosen object was Ethiopia, the last independent African state, whose admission to the League of Nations had been under Italy's own patronage. The pretext for a quarrel was found in the usual border incident. That Mussolini's main motives were of internal policy and prestige is borne out of the fact that, in the feverish diplomatic consultations preceding the invasion, the Duce rejected every compromise solution,

* The standard word used by fascist rhetoric to describe the vast public gatherings of the time; it was usually accompanied by the adjective 'oceanic'. (Trans.)

even very advantageous ones, for he was firmly decided to take things to a trial of strength and prestige. On 3 October 1935 the call to arms went out, and Italy became engaged in what was to be the last colonialist enterprise of modern history.

Military operations, after a few initial failures, went fairly quickly, and in May 1936 they ended in the capture of the capital, Addis Ababa; there remained only a sequel of insistent and obstinate guerrilla warfare. The course of the war was no doubt hastened by lack of humanitarian scruples on the part of the Italian general staff, who did not hesitate to use poison-gas. On the other hand the shaky way in which the great powers applied the economic sanctions that the League of Nations had imposed on Italy did the rest. In spite of the economic blockade, petrol continued to reach Italy, and the Suez canal remained open to Italian shipping.

The brevity of the campaign made it more popular. The old nineteenth-century myth of the fertile land of Africa waiting to fall into the arms of enterprising Italian planters still had a strong hold on the peasants, especially in the South, while the nationalists' motive of revenge for the humiliation of Adowa had its hold on the lower middle-class. At that time the song *Faccetta nera* aroused much enthusiasm: it celebrated the civil and amatory virtues of the Italian legionary who, after freeing a beautiful Abyssinian girl from slavery, gives her further causes for satisfaction. When on 5 May 1936 Mussolini, in one of his speeches from the balcony of the Palazzo Venezia, proclaimed that the Italian Empire was founded, the popularity of the fascist régime had once again reached a notably high point.

But the downward curve was not slow to begin, and once it had, it was rapid. The Ethiopian campaign, by provoking a serious deterioration in Italy's relations with England and France, had placed her in diplomatic isolation, and led her to draw closer to nazi Germany, relations with whom had gone through a period of tension as recently as June 1934, at the time of the nazi *putsch* in Austria and the threat of an *Anschluss*. The first overtures to Germany took a fairly prudent and muted form; the word used was not alliance but 'axis'. But later relations between the two countries became more and more an ideological and political alliance between two régimes inspired by the same principles. This alliance was sealed in 1936 by the common intervention of both Italy and Germany in the Spanish Civil War, in support of General Franco. This helped to win fascism the sympathy of the Church, but contributed to the further deterioration of relations with the western powers, who were committed to a policy of non-intervention, and to binding Italy closer to Germany. In fact, the more Germany became involved in the Spanish conflict, the more care she took to involve Italy as deeply as possible. In 1937 came the Anti-Comintern pact between Italy, Germany and Japan, and in 1938 the transplanting to Italy of German racist legislation and persecution of the Jews. This was without doubt the most unjustifiable and lunatic act of the régime; one of the Italian citizens forced to leave the country was the great physicist Enrico Fermi, who went to America, where he was to play a leading part in the research that led to the first atomic bomb. But by now the chips were down: each day the régime slid further down the slope it was on, and each day it took another step towards the irreparable.

There was indeed one moment when it seemed that the downward slide could be stopped: this was when in September 1938 Mussolini actively strove for the success of the Monaco meeting. But in fact, aware of Italy's military unpreparedness, he had merely wished to win time: the idea of war at Germany's side had already won him over, even though he intended to keep an autonomy of initiative for fascist Italy, as he showed in April 1939 by occupying Albania. One month later, on the eve of the outbreak of the Second World War, the 'Pact of Steel' was signed by Germany and Italy: Italy promised to intervene in support of Germany. It seems that when the pact was signed Hitler and his colleagues hid from Mussolini their intention of attacking Poland straight away, and gave him to understand that war would only break out in two or three years' time. It was only at the Salzburg meeting in August that Ciano, fascist Foreign Minister, was informed of the imminent attack. This explains how Mussolini, aware of Italy's lack of military preparation, consented to the declaration of Italian non-belligerence. But one year later, when it seemed that the collapse of France had decided the outcome of the conflict, he cut short all delay and hesitation: on 10 June 1940 Italy went to war.

Gradually, as the international situation worsened, and the shadow of war crept over Italy, there were further turns of the screw within the country, and the régime crossed the limits beyond which dictatorship becomes grotesque. Racial legislation, a true insult to the kindness of the Italian character, was accompanied and justified by an anti-Semitic campaign in which intellectuals of meagre stature and servile scientists distinguished themselves, and which was all the more repellent in that it was absurd and artificial. The use of the second person plural *voi* was imposed in place of the traditional polite form *lei*, and war was declared on the handshake, which was to be replaced by the fascist salute. These were unrealistic and gratuitous measures that clearly revealed the weakness and insecurity that lay concealed behind the régime's display of self-certainty and omnipotence.

So Italy went to war not merely militarily unprepared but in a state of latent political crisis: the public consensus that had formed around the régime at the time of the Ethiopian exploit had rapidly dissolved. The increasingly near prospect of war and the unpopularity of the German alliance had quickly caused people to forget the régime's colonial successes, which had in any case yielded little fruit, after so many promises. When in September 1938 Mussolini returned to Italy from the Monaco conference, he was welcomed by huge popular demonstrations: it was a good moment to display loyalty to the Duce and hostility to the war at the same time. But the latter sentiment was in many cases stronger than attachment to the régime, when it did not generate actual aversion. The opposition consisted not only of the working class, who had never been fascists, and the great majority of intellectuals, who were disgusted by the régime's vulgarity and corruption; at the moment of entry into war there was an opposition current within fascist organizations themselves, especially youth and student bodies. This was a 'left-wing' opposition, but there was also a 'right-wing' opposition of industrialists anxious at the infiltration of German capital, soldiers concerned at Italy's lack of preparation for war, and high-ranking bureaucrats afraid that entry into war would disturb the social balance so laboriously established, and expose the country to dangerous upheavals. The main member of this group was the Foreign Minister, Ciano, who, after Monaco, adopted an ever-colder attitude towards the inconvenient German ally and had tried, with the timidity of a creature of the régime, to delay Italy's entry into war. Among the fascist *gerarchi*, Ciano's attitude was shared by Giuseppe Bottai, Dino Grandi, formerly Ambassador to London, and Italo Balbo, who was soon to meet his death in the sky above Tobruk, in circumstances that immediately attracted reasoned suspicions. Among the soldiers, the doubts of Marshal Badoglio, chief of the general staff, were well known, and among the bureaucrats, those of Arturo Bocchini, chief of police. In July 1943 these men, with the support of the King, who was also mistrustful and hostile towards Germany, took part in a palace conspiracy that put an end to the fascist régime. But before describing that event it is necessary to take a retrospective look at the anti-fascist movement, and at those men and political forces which were preparing themselves, after years of defeats and humiliations, to raise a prostrate and disorientated Italy up from fascism.

ANTI-FASCISM

The most internationally known figure of Italian anti-fascism is that of Benedetto Croce. To begin with, in the period immediately preceding and immediately following the march on Rome, his attitude towards fascism had not been without uncertainties and even some positive approval. But after the murder of Matteotti and the speech of 3 January, he moved to a position of definite opposition. In June 1925 he edited and promoted a manifesto that was signed by forty intellectuals, and represented the answer made by the best part of Italian culture to a corresponding fascist manifesto written by Gentile, which celebrated the funeral rites of the liberal state. Croce then withdrew to his study in Naples, in dignified and significant detachment, to concern himself with his studies. One of the first works he published was the already mentioned *History of Italy*, a eulogy and passionate evocation of liberal Giolittian Italy. After some years followed the *Storia d'Europa*, whose anti-fascist inspiration was evident in the reduction of European history to a 'history of liberty'. As long as the régime lasted, Croce and his review *La Critica* continued to be a lesson in dignity and a point of reference for all anti-fascist Italian intellectuals.

But they sought in vain in the pages of Croce's works the historic reasons for fascism's victory: there was no analysis of the fascist phenomenon and its place in Italian history. His *History of Italy* ends in 1915, almost as if he wished to emphasize that what had come later was irrational madness, and that the country's salvation consisted simply in a return to the values and behaviour of the pre-fascist liberal state. With some slight divergences such was also the point of view of the older of the political expatriates, Treves, Nitti, Modigliani, Turati, who had formed a *Concentrazione antifascista* in France in 1927, and began the publication of an Italian-language paper *La Libertà*. Gaetano Salvenimi, too, who had been one of Giolitti's hardiest opponents, made a revaluation of pre-fascist Italy in the writings of his period of exile. But for young men like Piero Gobetti, who was removed by death from the anti-fascist struggle while still very young, or Carlo Roselli, who, together with Ferruccio Parri and others, had managed Turati's escape, and who himself made an adventurous escape from Lipari in 1929, the answer to the question of why fascism had won seemed to be the indispensable premise for the success of the anti-fascist struggle. The conclusion they reached was that the victory of fascism had been made much easier by the weakness and complicity of the liberal ruling class, and that post-fascist Italy should therefore be radically different from pre-fascist Italy. The political movement founded by Rosselli in France – 'Justice and Liberty' – was inspired by these principles, its programme was clearly revolutionary, and its ideology that of a libertarian socialism. Another reason for the break that soon emerged between the expatriates of an older generation and of the *Concentrazione* on the one hand, and the young men and 'Justice and Liberty' on the other, concerned the method of the anti-fascist struggle. The second group reproached the first for their delays and their rumination on platonic congressional resolutions; they maintained the need for a more radical type of struggle. In July 1930 the men of 'Justice and Liberty' organized Bassanesi's flight over Milan to drop anti-fascist leaflets, and other similar enterprises, and they applauded the attempt to assassinate the Prince of Piedmont, made by a very young man, Ferdinando De Rosa, at Brussels in 1929.

These were methods that the communists considered the expression of an amateurish activism, and an indication of lack of seriousness. They argued that the struggle against fascism was a struggle that had to go on every day, conducted by means of propaganda, syndicalist agitations and strikes; and it should be waged by the Italian workers and peasants, and by those militants who were prepared to stay in Italy in contact with the people. This was the road they had chosen. The party formed at Leghorn in 1921 had overcome, not without toil and internal struggles, the faction spirit of its early days, and had learned to its cost in terms of the blood of its own militants that it was untrue that all bourgeois governments, including fascist ones, were the same. It had flung itself into the anti-fascist fight with all its strength. After participating in the Aventine secession, but then realizing its uncertainty and weakness and returning to Parliament, the communist party had managed to keep up an organizational network, even after being declared illegal. Its press organ, *L'Unità*, printed clandestinely, managed to come out fairly regularly, and its activists stayed in the factories, in some cases even succeeding in organizing strikes and anti-fascist demonstrations. In Turin, Tuscany and Venezia Giulia some sort of communist organization continued to function throughout the fascist twenty years, and the communists, in spite of their rapid assimilation of clandestine methods, were by far the majority of the Special Tribunal's victims.

This was not all: of all the anti-fascists the communists were those who took the analysis of Italy's political and social reality in the light of fascist victory deepest, and produced a new and articulate programme of the forces and directions of the Italian revolution. This was contained in the propositions Antonio Gramsci presented to and had

approved by the party congress held at Lyons in 1926. They very clearly
affirmed the need to oppose the industrial-agrarian bloc that had
always dominated the Italian state, and of which fascism was the
latest and most brutal expression, with a worker-peasant bloc, linking
the workers of the North and the peasants of the South. The southern
question, to which Gramsci had devoted another study, was thus
indicated to be a national problem, not peculiar to the South. Peasants
and workers could achieve victory only together, and should go ahead
united, just as the bloc of Italian reaction was united: the experience of
1920, when the Turin workers and the *Ordine nuovo* group had wrongly
thought that they could be the Petrograd of Italy, had been a salutary
warning, and the Italian Communist Party was firmly resolved not to
repeat the mistake of the socialists, who in the post-war period had,
as we have seen, let the peasant movement advance on its own. Gramsci's plan for the Italian revolution certainly followed Lenin's plan for
an alliance between workers and peasants, and also Stalin's formula for
worker-peasant government. Even so, in giving body and substance
to this general idea, Gramsci was naturally led to take into account
Italy's history, and to give his own thought a pronounced national
slant, or, to use a term that recurs often in his writings, 'national-
popular'. He thus accentuated the historic peculiarities of the Italian
revolution and, in consequence, the autonomy of the party at its head.
Hence the perplexity he showed writing to Togliatti in 1926 about the
developments of the political struggle and the process of bureau-
cratization in progress in the Soviet Union. Hence also his decision
to return to Italy, which he took with full awareness of the risks it
implied. For in 1926 he was arrested and condemned by the Special
Tribunal to twenty years' imprisonment. Prison, the illness that undermined his weak constitution, the incomprehension occasionally
shown by his party comrades who were his companions in prison, were
not enough to prevent his brain from continuing to work, as Mussolini
had ordered. The *Quaderni* he drew up in prison, and which were published after the liberation, bear witness that he never for a moment
ceased to think and to work, and his letters to his wife and sons show
that his rich and passionate humanity were never extinguished.

The subjects dealt with and touched on in Gramsci's prison writings
are quite varied: from the philosophy of Benedetto Croce to the history
of the Risorgimento, the character of the modern party, literature and
its position in society. It would be a wasted effort to attempt to give
here a résumé of his thought. It must suffice to say that the thread
running all the way through it is the idea of Marxism which had also
been Labriola's: the idea of Marxism as an open system. He argues
on the other hand against mechanistic, systematic, interpretations.

A relevant example is his criticism of the textbook *On the theory of historic materialism*, by Bukharin. Antonio Gramsci died on 27 April 1937, in a Rome hospital, to which he had been moved from prison. No-one attended his funeral.

The man who had in the mean time succeeded to the party leadership, Palmiro Togliatti, had been at Gramsci's side since the days of *Ordine nuovo*, and they shared a common cultural background and sense of the peculiarity and individuality of the Italian revolutionary tradition. But the awareness that this tradition had partly been formed by anarchism and by a vulgar, inconclusive maximalism made him more sceptical and helped to give him a pedagogic attitude towards the party he led, and to plant firmly in him the belief that Italian communists had everything to learn from the Russian communists, who had achieved a revolution and been able to defend it against storms and high seas. Besides, for Togliatti, the outcome of political and social struggles, in the situation shaped by the reinforcement of reaction on a national and European scale, depended on unconditional class-solidarity with the Soviet Union. Hence his loyalty to the Comintern and the USSR, and the fact that he and Gramsci disagreed in their respective attitudes to the internal developments of Soviet policy. For Togliatti – as he was to declare later, in a speech of 1956 – there had to be 'a bond of steel' between the Italian Communist Party and the Soviet Union, and in the years 1926–45 he did not hesitate to follow all the wishes of Soviet policy and of the International. It seems that at the 6th International congress in 1928 he showed sympathy with Bukharin's ideas, but when, a little later, in the agitation provoked among communists by the 1929 crisis, the call went out for a struggle to the bitter end against the bourgeoisie and its social-democratic lackeys, he did not hesitate to expel from the party its right-wing members, including Angelo Tasca, formerly his colleague on *Ordine nuovo*, and a man of brilliant ability. Later, when the policy of the Communist International, of which he was a distinguished member, moved towards the idea of popular fronts, he was finally able to reconcile his most obstinate and mature convictions with his loyalty to the International itself.

This development of the Italian Communist Party did much to make the anti-fascist struggle more vigorous and more unified. In 1934 a treaty of unity of action was formed between the communist party and the socialist, which had in the mean time reunified itself. Later, all Italian anti-fascists took part in the Spanish Civil War. One of the first to reach the battlefields of Spain was Carlo Rosselli. This was the finest hour of Italian anti-fascism: five thousand Italian volunteers of the Garibaldi and International brigades fought for

Spain's freedom. In March 1937, at Guadalajara, these true volunteers found themselves face to face with false volunteers sent by fascism to support Franco, and defeated them: so the first military defeat of fascism was at the hands of Italians.

But after Guadalajara came sadder days and bitter experiences: the murder of the Rosselli brothers at Bagnoles-sur-Orne on 11 June 1937, by French assassins in the pay of the fascists, the fall of the Spanish Republic, the re-emergence of quarrels between the anti-fascist parties, the German-Soviet pact. But the bonds and sense of solidarity that had been forged during the Spanish Civil War were not entirely lost, and they would soon show their strength in the resistance.

19

The last decades

ITALY IN THE SECOND WORLD WAR

Italy's unpreparedness for the First World War was as nothing in comparison with her unpreparedness for the Second. Mussolini had exalted the power of the eight million bayonets that formed the Italian army. Setting aside the exaggeration of this figure (at the outbreak of hostilities about one million Italians were mobilized), modern war was not fought with bayonets, nor even with the 1891 rifle issued to the army since the first African war. Tanks were needed – and there were in all four hundred pocket-sized ones; aeroplanes were needed – there were fourteen hundred, most of them antiquated and unable to fly long distances without re-fuelling; ammunition was needed – there was enough for sixty days of war.

Mussolini himself was aware of Italy's lack of military readiness; but he was equally convinced that the war was by now drawing to its end, and that England would soon suffer the same fate as France. What he most urgently wanted was a place at the peace conference table, with some partial military success to raise his stocks with the powerful German ally. His Germanophilia was in fact compounded of opportunism: in his heart not even Mussolini felt much love for the Germans or for their Führer, who aroused in him an acute inferiority-complex. The meetings between the two were often reduced to a monologue from Hitler with rare and timid interruptions from the Duce. Things were complicated by the fact that Mussolini was proud of his knowledge of German; but apparently Hitler's was particularly harsh and hard on the ear. However, since German victory seemed inevitable, it was necessary to rise above sympathies and resentments, and at the same time to preserve military autonomy, so as to arrive at the peace negotiations in a good bargaining position. In other words, Italy's war was to be 'parallel' to Germany's, with its own forces and its own aims. Considerations of this sort induced Mussolini, a hundred hours before the French surrender, to order a futile and inglorious offensive on the western Alpine front, which resulted in a first resounding demonstration of the Italian army's lack of preparation.

The parallel war was later carried to Africa, where Italian troops managed to win British Somaliland, and carry out an offensive thrust in Libya, under the command of General Graziani, as far as the occupation of Sidi el Barani. At sea, there were a number of battles in the Mediterranean, resulting in the success of one side or the other alternately. The Italian navy, that branch of the forces which had been best able to maintain its independence of fascism, emerged honourably. But in the face of German prestige and omnipotence far more than this was needed to emphasize Italy's presence and autonomy. The German occupation of Romania in October 1940 irritated Mussolini and led him to cut short delay and put into action a political-military initiative that had been in his mind for some time, and towards which the German ally had earlier reacted with perplexity: the attack on Greece. Rarely has a military enterprise been prepared – or rather, improvised – with such amateurism and lack of reflection. The results were not slow to confirm as much: what Mussolini had been sure would be a military walk-over turned into a resounding defeat, and Italian troops were lucky to keep possession of Albania in face of the Greek counter-offensive. The soldiers of the Italian Alpine regiments, shod in cardboard-soled shoes, and sometimes without winter clothing, froze to death in their thousands in the mountains of Greece. A dolorous wartime song was born; like the German *Lili Marlene*, it seemed a foreboding of the inevitable defeat.

Meanwhile things went badly on the other fronts too. On 11 November 1940 English torpedo-craft had inflicted very grave losses on the Italian fleet while it was still at anchor in the bay of Taranto, while on the Libyan front the English had come to the counter-attack, and on 16 February 1941 they reached Bengazi. In East Africa too things took a decisive turn for the worst: it was now clear that the loss of Ethiopia was imminent.

On the home front the situation was no better. Rationing of foodstuffs and essential goods was strict, but this did not prevent those in privileged positions, including the fascist *gerarchi*, from evading the regulations and resorting to the black market. While the sons of the poor went to be massacred in Libya and Greece, the *figli di papà* found ways of evading conscription. Italy's economic dependence on Germany for basic materials was more marked every day; combined with military defeats, this soon scattered the illusion of parallel war. Italy was by now at the mercy of her ally, and her rôle that of a lowly second fiddle.

With the first months of 1941 began a new phase of the war that saw Italy in a position of complete political and military subordination. The German intervention and victorious campaign in Greece and Jugoslavia put an end to Italy's old aspirations of dominating the Balkans. The annexation to Italy of the town of Ljubljana and the creation of a Kingdom of Croatia, under a member of the house of Savoy who in any case never set foot there, was a meagre recompense. Next, the arrival of a German expeditionary force in Libya, under General Rommel, and its victorious offensive as far as Sollum, seemed a recognition of the definite subordination of Italian command to German. The last act of servility towards the Germans was the despatch of an Italian force to Russia.

With the attack on the Soviet Union and the intervention of the USA in December 1941 the war, as is well known, took an increasing turn for the worse for the Axis powers. By autumn 1942 the sense of defeat was general: the English victory of El Alamein in October and the American landing in North Africa made it clear that the alternating war in Libya and Egypt was near its end. The process of sending supplies to the troops fighting in North Africa became more difficult all the time, and the long convoy war that had dragged on as well with alternating fortunes was also being settled in favour of the English fleet, which possessed a notable advantage in radar, and had Malta, a base which the Italians had in vain tried to overcome. The tragedy was sealed by the news from Russia: in December 1942 and January 1943 the Italian army of 110,000 men had been defeated, and more than half its men died under enemy fire or from the cold. The few survivors were to recount how their 'German comrades' had refused them the means of transport they needed to save themselves.

The discontent that had for some time been building up in the country was gradually developing into anger and organized opposition. Contacts between opposition groups were increased and in December 1942 it was possible to set up an anti-fascist committee in Turin, in which, beside the socialists, liberals and communists, two new parties were represented, the Action Party, and heir of the 'Justice and Liberty' movement, to which most of the intellectuals belonged, and the very recently formed Christian democrat party. The Vatican was in fact withdrawing from the régime. Also in Turin, the most anti-fascist and the most working-class of Italian towns, the workers of Fiat and of other large factories went on strike in March 1943, and were successfully followed by their comrades in Milan. The political significance of the event escaped no-one, especially not the fascist leaders, who still remembered how after the march on Rome the Turin working class had had to be subdued by force. Many of them at this point began to think that a lost war was always better than a revolution.

This belief was naturally strengthened as the military situation moved steadily towards disaster. In May the last troops in Tunisia were pushed into the sea, and in June the English and American forces landed in Sicily. In the mean time Italian towns had been subjected to murderous air-raids. So behind the scenes of the régime there began a desperate search for a way out that would allow Italy to detach herself from the Germans and end the war with the Allies. The court became the common ground of the fascist opposition – Bottai, Grandi, Ciano, who had left the Foreign Ministry in February 1943 and become Ambassador to the Vatican, members of the old ruling class and of the army, including the new chief of staff, General Ambrosio – who were all convinced that it was useless to continue any longer a war that was already lost. When in July 1943 Mussolini came back from yet another inconclusive meeting with Hitler without having even tried to persuade him to leave Italy free to decide her own destiny, it became clear that the first thing to do was to remove him from power. At the Grand Council session that began on 24 July Mussolini's opponents confronted him and, after a dramatic night-long sitting, were able to pass, by nineteen votes to seven, a motion that invited the King 'to assume command of the armed forces and the fulness of his constitutional powers', and so amounted to a disowning of Mussolini and of the régime he had founded. But Mussolini did not realize the implication of such a *pronunciamento*, and when on the afternoon of 25 July he went to see the King, who had in the meantime been informed by Grandi of the outcome of the Grand Council meeting, he was surprised to be told that his resignation had been accepted and a new government formed; he was surprised again when on leaving the palace he found himself at the door of an ambulance, which he was made to get into, to be taken first to a Roman barracks and later to Ponza.

The Italians learned of the event from the radio late that night, and the following morning there were scenes of indescribable enthusiasm in the piazzas of Italy. Everyone was certain that the end of the fascist dictatorship would be followed, after a brief interval, by the end of the war. But it was not so.

THE FORTY-FIVE DAYS AND THE ARMISTICE

The forty-five days from 25 July to the announcement of the armistice of 8 September are one of those historic moments in which farce is mingled with tragedy. There is no more signal instance of the foolishness of the Italian ruling class in all its history.

At the head of the new government appointed by the King was Marshal Pietro Badoglio, a Piedmontese soldier who had led the military action against Ethiopia, and after the failure of the aggression against Greece had resigned as chief of staff, wishing to indicate by this action that he dissociated himself from Mussolini's military enterprises. He was hemmed in on one side by the conservative pre-occupations of the King and certain of his ministers, and on the other by the anti-fascist parties, who loudly clamoured for the liquidation of the régime and for peace. He did not wish to upset either party, and embarked on a policy of temporization and small acts of cunning, which was precisely the opposite of the great decisions that the gravity of the moment demanded. His first acts were to issue a proclamation announcing that the war was to continue, and to prohibit assemblies and meetings. The fascist party was dissolved, but the reconstitution of other parties was impeded; political prisoners were set free, but certain pro-German soldiers and officials were kept at their posts. Political life, Badoglio promised, would be resumed at the end of the war, with free elections; for the moment the Italians were asked only to have faith in the government.

But the government showed itself scarcely worthy of the trust it demanded. During August 1943, while Allied air-raids rained tons of bombs on Italy's towns every day, the government wasted precious time in the vain and futile quest for impossible solutions. When on 7 August the Foreign Minister, Guariglia, declared to his German opposite number von Ribbentrop that Italian foreign policy would undergo no change, approaches to the Allies, with an armistice in view, had already begun. The preliminary negotiations were drawn out by the Italian government's vain hope of persuading the Allies to withdraw their demand for unconditional surrender, and so to restore to some extent the prestige of a monarchy compromised by twenty years' collaboration with fascism. But in the mean time the Germans were not wasting time: they were pouring into Italy the divisions they had refused Mussolini when he had asked for them in his last meeting with Hitler. By its temporizings and hesitations Badoglio's government lost the trust of everyone: of the Germans, who scented the change of wind; of the Allies, who mistrusted the tergi-versations and machiavellianism of the plenipotentiaries from Rome; and finally, of the Italians, who, as the strikes at Turin and Milan in August showed, were increasingly determined to express their desire for peace. Badoglio and the King would have liked to extricate Italy from the conflict with the Germans' consent, and after having won favourable armistice terms from the Allies. To this end they held up before both Germans and Allies the spectre of a communist revolution, and chanted *après nous le déluge*. Even though the Allies were not impervious to this argument, military considerations were for the moment more urgent, and only formal agreements had been made with the USSR concerning the unconditional surrender.

In the end the unconditional surrender had to be accepted. The armistice was signed at Cassibile, a captured Sicilian village, on 3 September, by General Castellano. The Badoglio government was able to have the announcement of the armistice delayed until the Allied troops, who had already crossed the straits, were able to make a landing in southern Italy, which was to have been followed up by a paratroop landing in Rome. But on 7 September General Taylor, whom Allied High Command had put in charge of the Rome mission, declared that the planned paratroop landing was impossible, since the Germans were already in control of the capital's airports; so it was eliminated from the plan of operations. Meanwhile the fleet was already at sea, heading for Salerno, with its load of troops, and according to the terms of the Cassibile agreement the announcement of the armistice was now due. Badoglio tried in vain to persuade Eisenhower to delay the announcement or actually to divert the fleet's route. Naturally, the Allied Supreme Commander was adamant, and on the evening of 8 September, two hours after Radio London had already broken the news, he transmitted Badoglio's declaration announcing the armistice and ordering the troops to cease all resistance to the Allies but instead to resist 'possible attacks from other quarters'. Meanwhile, together with a group of generals and officials, Badoglio joined the King in his flight to Pescara, where a motor-boat awaited the unhappy refugees to carry them to territory already in Allied hands.

So, overnight, Italy found herself without a government, with a foreign army threateningly encamped on her soil, agitated by a whirl of contradictory reports. For some days there was chaos, and each person was left alone to make the right choices according to his own conscience. While some military commanders surrendered to the Germans and abandoned their units, others, like General Carboni in Rome, tried to organize resistance. The fleet, most anti-fascist of the forces, unhesitatingly complied with the terms of the armistice and sailed for Malta, where it arrived after losing one of its best ships on the way, the battleship *Roma*, sunk by the Germans. The soldiers of the Cefalonia garrison had no hesitations either, and 8,400 of them were massacred by the Germans. Many soldiers stationed in the Balkans joined the Jugoslav partisans. But the great majority of disbanded troops, who had suddenly found themselves without commanders and without orders, made the more elementary choice of the right road to get them home. Taking the wrong one meant falling into the hands of the Germans and ending up in a sealed railway carriage heading for the German concentration camps. During these days of disbandment and chaos the Italian people's profound modest virtues of kindness and tolerance shone brightly. No soldier was refused civilian clothes, no Allied prisoner who found himself unexpectedly at liberty was refused shelter and help, no Jew was without a hiding-place. In misfortune the Italian people began to rediscover their old civilized qualities.

THE RESISTANCE

In the days following 8 September things became clearer: it was soon tragically evident to everyone that Italy was split in two. In the South were the Allied armies, who had reached Naples on 1 October, and so had established themselves along a line from the Adriatic to Pescara, by way of Montecassino; and there was the Badoglio government. In the North were the Germans and a fascist government led by Mussolini, who had been set free on 12 September by a detachment of German paratroops. Indeed, both Italian governments were puppets. Mussolini's, the Italian Social Republic, did not exercise even its nominal sovereignty over all the territory unoccupied by the Allies: a good part of the Veneto was directly under German administration, and in a half-way condition between occupied and annexed territory. But the southern government too had direct sovereignty only over Apulia initially, and not until February 1944 did the other provinces, formerly under Allied control, pass under its jurisdiction. In its details the pictures was even more disturbing and chaotic: in Sicily the old resentment of fascism and of Rome had found expression in a separatist movement; in Naples, which had rebelled against the Germans before the arrival of the Allied troops, squalor and degradation reigned. In the North the people experienced the terror of German manhunts, and the vindictive, desperate arrogance of the reconstituted fascist units, who seemed to have revived the original spirit of *squadrismo*. Everywhere there was hunger, the black market, disorientation. And there were no firm hopes of a quick solution: every day it became clearer that the Italian front was a secondary one for the Allies, and as Stalin among others demanded, after the Teheran meeting their forces were mainly concerned with preparing the second front and the Normandy landing. To this end some divisions were even withdrawn from the Italian front. So the war stood still south of Rome, and Italy waited, stagnant. The idea that she might be able to exert any pressure on the course of events or make her own voice heard in some way seemed to most people utopian.

There was a first gleam of light in October, when the Badoglio government, after many hesitations, decided to declare war on Germany, thus showing that they attached a literal value to the Allies' promise to modify the conditions of peace according to the Italian contribution to the anti-fascist struggle. All those for whom the oath of loyalty to the King still had any value found themselves from this moment on authorized to disobey the government of the Italian Social Republic; and the first partisan units, organized by the communists and by the Action party, ranked themselves beside units commanded and formed by officers of the regular army. In the face of this upsurge of the resistance the Germans coined the strange epithet 'Badoglian communists', probably not realizing that their success in uniting the communists and monarchists in agreement could certainly not be put forward as a proof of their popularity in Italy.

In fact – to begin with at least – the communists and other anti-fascist parties were not at all in agreement with the King, whom they reproached for having made it easier for fascism to reach power and keep it until the catastrophe. At the congress of anti-fascist parties held at Bari in January 1944 the left-wing parties, led by the Committee of National Liberation, were unanimous in demanding the King's immediate abdication. But the old and wise Benedetto Croce had no difficulty in showing them that such a demand was completely unrealistic. For it was no secret to anyone that the Allies, and particularly England under Winston Churchill, supported the monarchy and were annoyed by the agitation of the anti-fascists. So there seemed no way out of the situation, and it was difficult to establish an anti-fascist and anti-German front.

The situation was resolved by an entirely unexpected person: the leader of the Italian communist party, Palmiro Togliatti, who landed in Italy in March 1944 after eighteen years of exile and of militant work for the International. Togliatti was in touch with the political attitude of the Soviet Union, which had a few days before been the first country to recognize the Badoglio government. He knew of Russia's eventual aim of dividing Europe into spheres of influence. But as before, in 1935, at the time of the popular fronts, he was profoundly convinced that this coincided with Italy's interests. Togliatti knew well what blood and tears had been spent in the attempt to build a socialist state, and he had no illusions about the possibilities of revolution in a country emerging from twenty years of fascism, quite apart from the presence of the Allied troops on Italian soil. So he thought that the 'Italian road' to socialism, as he called it, should pass by way of a gradual process of democratization of the state, and by the collaboration of the communists with the other parties, in order to achieve a series of intermediate aims. The first of these was to drive out the Germans and free Italian territory; so Togliatti did not hesitate to accept the compromise formula worked out by Croce and De Nicola, according to which the King agreed to hand over his powers to his son, who took the title of Lieutenant, at the moment of the liberation of Rome, and to put off a final decision about the monarchy until after the end of the war. Immediately afterwards a new government was formed, again led by Badoglio, but including members of all the parties belonging to the Committee of National Liberation, except the Action party.

This took place in March/April 1944. Also at this time there took place the partisan action of via Rasella, perhaps the most famous episode of the Italian resistance, which cost the lives of thirty-two German soldiers, and was followed by the murder of three hundred and thirty-five Italian patriots in the Fosse Ardeatine. Also at this time were the big strikes of the northern industrial towns, which irrevocably tore apart the fascist republic's smokescreen of social demagogy. Every day the fascist republic had more the air of a body foreign to the country, a *revenant* from a past that was by now buried. Its only action to make an impression on public opinion – and far from favourably – was the murky trial of Verona, a settling of scores between fascist *gerarchi* which ended in the execution of Ciano and of other protagonists of the 25 July *coup*.

So the resistance got into its full stride, and soon won itself the right to be considered a valid partner by the Allies. When in June 1944 the Allied troops entered Rome, General Badoglio handed over to a new cabinet led by Bonomi, in which the leaders of the anti-fascist parties were included, and which declared itself the expression of the Committee of National Liberation. This was a bitter pill for Churchill, who wrote to Stalin about it; Stalin wrote in reply that he was amazed the Allies should have allowed any action not to their liking to be taken in a territory under their occupation. In fact England and the US had not acted together on this point, and Roosevelt had, on the contrary, supported the forming of a government that would express anti-fascism and the resistance.

The liberation of Rome and of Florence, in June and August 1944 respectively, and the imminent prospect of a final Allied victory certainly did much to intensify the activity of partisan formations organized by the various parties in the North; *coups de main* and acts of sabotage multiplied, and various 'free zones' were constituted, entirely occupied and administered by the partisans, such as the Val d'Ossola,

Carnia, the republic of Torriglia in Liguria, and others besides. The subsequent course of events showed moreover that the Italian resistance was not an ephemeral phenomenon, and that it in no way intended to confine itself to the position of a body of snipers and saboteurs supplementary to the Allied armies, as the Allies, worried by the political implications of the resistance, would have liked it to be.

The ten months from September 1944, when the Allied troops were held on the Gothic line, to April 1945, when northern Italy was liberated, were very hard months for the partisan movement. To this period belong the most massive German manhunts and the most pitiless reprisals against the civilian population. The most terrible of all these was probably that inflicted on the commune of Marzabotto in Emilia, where 1,830 people were killed. The Germans reoccupied many free zones; and it was during this period that most of the 46,000 dead of the war of liberation lost their lives. The combatants' morale was lowered even further by the proclamation from the English General Alexander on 10 November 1944 inviting them to cease their operations, and by the news of the disagreements that had emerged in the Bonomi government, between anti-fascists and conservatives who had been out of Italy for many years. In spite of all this, and in spite of the heavy losses they had suffered, the partisan forces overcame the crisis of autumn 1944 and carried on their struggle. At the end of April 1945, when on the other fronts hostilities were almost over, the Allied troops broke through to the Po plain, and found the main cities already in the hands of the army of liberation, and the main industrial establishments saved from German vandalism.

Strong in these successes, the Committee of National Liberation of upper Italy, which had organized the insurrection, was able to negotiate and act with the Allies, with the authority of their support. It took the initiative of ordering the execution of Mussolini, who had been captured while trying to reach the Swiss border, wearing a German uniform, and of the other fascist leaders with him, on the afternoon of 28 April. Later the corpses were hung on show in a piazza of Milan where partisans had been shot. It was a gesture that meant, above all, a break with the past and a warning to those, in and outside Italy, who thought they could evade the demands for regeneration expressed in the resistance. For the latter was not merely a military event, considerable though its military contribution to the Allied victory had been; it was above all a very wide political movement. It had been the achievement not only of the workers who had sabotaged and the men of the military formations who had fought, but also of the peasants who had fed them and the priests who had hidden them. All these people were now convinced that things had to change in Italy, that the time of privileges and corruption was over; they wanted a clean and honest nation and were determined to fight for it and not let themselves slip into the quicksands of Italy's old political transformism. But the task was harder than the men of the resistance thought, in the enthusiastic days of the resistance.

POST-WAR HOPES AND FRUSTRATIONS

Anyone who wants to understand the spirit of the Italian resistance should consider the films of Roberto Rossellini, from *Roma città aperta* to *Paisà*, which inaugurated the Italian neo-realist school. They represent that spirit not only because many of their characters are men and women of the resistance – the Roman *popolana* superbly personified by Anna Magnani, the communist militant and the priest joined in martyrdom, the hungry and dogged partisans of the Polesine – but above all because of their completely successful attempt to provide a true and living image of Italy and its people, and because of their rejection of all consoling rhetoric and of all recrimination, because of the seriousness of their commitment and because of their rough emotion. But these films were considerably less successful in Italy than they would have been abroad. Why, many Italians asked themselves, display our miseries, the prostitution spreading through the towns, unemployment, the black market? Why probe and sound a past that was too near and too bitter? Was it not better to bury all that under a tombstone and begin to live and breathe again?

This refusal to realize what had happened, and to take a straight look at the reality of Italy, with its old evils, its inadequacies and injustices, was in the end an alibi, masking fear of innovation and a withdrawal from the effort to change things. Later it was to have a name, *qualunquismo*, and was to become a political movement with markedly reactionary characteristics. But in the wake of the liberation, many of the people who reasoned in this way were unaware of the political implications of their attitude. They merely wished to come out from the nightmare they had been in, and to start living again. Like every post-war period, this one had, besides its miseries, its pleasures and its euphoria: dance-halls multiplied visibly, American films, with their larger-than-life beauties, returned to the screens after many years' absence, the cyclist Bartali was back in action and winning again.

It was this second, *qualunquista* Italy, fond of peace and quiet, which prevailed in the end and, as after the First World War, the forces of conservatism and privilege, which had seemed isolated in the immediate wake of liberation, managed to find the consensus and mass basis that allowed then to retain their dominance. The instrument of this process of involution and abandonment of the struggle was the Christian democrat party, led by Alcide De Gasperi, a pugnacious Trentino, formerly a deputy in the Austrian parliament, and a leading member of the Italian Popular Party, who had worked as a librarian in the Vatican during the fascist years. In spite of the pronouncements of its left wing, and the advanced statements in its programme, the forces of conservatism were not slow in identifying Christian democracy, with its mass base among the rural population and its support from the Vatican, as the safest bastion of the established order. Besides, fear of communism led many agnostics or unbelievers too to vote for Christian democracy, even if unwillingly.

The story of this defeat of the resistance and its demands for reform is dramatic and full of vicissitudes – here we must confine ourselves to a mention of its main stages. Italy's political balance made a first shift to the right in December 1945 when the government, led by Ferruccio Parri, of the Action party, had to give way to one led by De Gasperi. Under this government, in June 1946, was held the first post-war election, which was combined with a referendum concerning the form of the state. There was a majority of 12,717,923 votes to 10,717,284 in favour of a republic, and in the Constituent Assembly the Christian democrats won 35·2 per cent of the votes, the socialists 20·7 per cent and the communists 19 per cent. As one can see, the three major parties took 75 per cent of the total: the rest was dispersed among various minor left-wing groups such as the Action party and the Republican party, and the parties of the extreme right.

So the political balance was once again steady. Though the Christian democrat party was easily the strongest, the socialists and the communists, who had recently renewed the 1934 unity of action pact, had as many and more votes when combined, and retained almost absolute control of the General Confederation of Labour, the general union organization to which the Catholic unions, a distinct minority, also belonged. So there was no choice possible other than a government led by De Gasperi, with the participation of Christian democrats, socialists and communists; but it was soon clear that its life would not be long.

Quite apart from the internal dissidence that already began to flourish, there were too many obstacles along the way, from the Allies' punitive attitude at the Paris peace conference to the question of Trieste, urged by Jugoslavia (which the right-wing parties exploited as a divisive element), and the enormous difficulties of an economic policy split between the need for reconstruction and the need to satisfy workers' claims. But the factor that did most to disrupt the coalition of the various parties represented in the government was the development of the international situation. As the Cold War gradually came to be the dominant element there were increasingly insistent political pressures from the Americans urging an end to the co-operation with the communists and their allies. Togliatti, with his acute responsiveness to international affairs, was more aware of this than anyone, and was generous in compromises and concessions, made in order to save the political plan he had promised himself to follow when he had landed in Italy in March 1944. The most conspicuous of these concessions, and the one with the heaviest consequences, was the communist vote in favour of Article Seven of the Constitution, which recognized and confirmed the Lateran agreements signed by Mussolini in 1929. It was probably not only a sense of what the moment required that induced the communist leader to take this decision, which was heavily criticized by other parties of the left; he was probably also conscious of breaking with the old, sterile anti-clericalism of the pre-fascist workers' movement.

However, if it was no more than a tactical move to suit the circumstances of the moment, it was no use. A little more than a month after the vote for Article Seven, De Gasperi, on his return home from a voyage to the US, provoked a new crisis in the government, taking as pretext the split that had appeared in the Italian Socialist Party, with the departure of its right-wing under Giuseppe Saragat. The crisis ended in the forming of a government consisting entirely of Christian democrats, with a few technical advisers. The most outstanding of the latter was Luigi Einaudi, who took over the Exchequer. His assumption of control of the country's economic affairs marked a drastic change from the direction previously followed in this field. The coalition government, pressed by the constant demands of unions and by the need for reconstruction, had in fact followed a distinctly inflationary policy, and in the space of a few years the cost of living had soared to fifty times what it had been in 1938. The concession to workers of a sliding scale had to some extent preserved the purchasing power of their earnings, however. The economic policy introduced and rigorously followed by Einaudi was on the other hand dedicated to the defence of the lira: the flow of credit was cut down, circulation reduced, production – which was still at a lower level than before the war – stood still, and unemployment rose to the terrifying figure of two million. But the lira was safe, and the continuance of the Italian state assured, also from the economic point of view.

Meanwhile the Constituent Assembly had almost finished its work, and it was time for the Italians to be allowed to elect the two elective chambers provided for in the new Constitution. No electoral battle in Italy has ever been fought so bitterly or with less restraint. The Popular Front, which gathered together communists and socialists, and whose electoral symbol was the head of Garibaldi, tried to make capital out of the economic difficulties brought on by Einaudi's credit-squeeze, and to summon the masses to the struggle against the 'black government' of capitalist restoration; but their success was limited. For its part, the Christian democrat party put the electoral campaign in terms of a dramatic either/or between freedom and communism, America and Russia. In all the piazzas and streets of Italy there appeared a poster showing a loaf of bread cut in half, with the warning that one of the halves was made of American corn, while another poster showed a soldier who, from behind the wires of a Russian concentration camp, begged his mother to vote against his gaolers. Who could hesitate in choosing between the Americans, who gave bread and made the promises of the Marshall Plan, and Russia, who had not sent back Italian prisoners, and who held Czechoslovakia in subjection? It must also be remembered that pro-American feeling had deep historical roots in Italy: there were few families in the South without some relative in America, and many who had had the chance to greet him when he had come to fight in Italy with General Clark's army. And the Americans sent parcels of food and clothing which were something more than a welcome gift in those hard times. On the eve of the elections of 18 April 1948 a letter arrived together with the parcel: it asked the recipient to vote against the communists and for the party trusted by America, the Christian democrats. The clergy too were deeply involved in the electoral struggle: votes came even from the nuns of closed orders, from hospital patients and from those in mental asylums. In fact, following a Christian democrat suggestion, the vote had been declared obligatory.

The result of the election went beyond the expectations even of those who had seen the turn events had taken: 12,708,263 votes, equal to 48·5 per cent, almost an absolute majority, for Christian democracy; 8,137,467, 35 per cent, for the Popular Front; the rest – bits and pieces – scattered among the smaller parties. It was an unchallengeable victory for the Christian democrat party and for the forces that had upheld it.

Meanwhile the Constitution elaborated by the Constituent Assembly had taken effect; but its plan of a republic 'based on labour', as its first article declared, and with wide possibilities for social demands, seemed already to have been left behind by the course of events. The unity of the resistance, which had found expression in that Constitution, had been swept away by the Cold War, and would certainly not be rebuilt until its end. In 1949 Italy joined NATO, and so made her final choice in foreign politics too.

The elections of 18 April 1948 ended the second post-war period. Italy emerged from it happily on the whole; much better, certainly, than from the first post-war years. Whereas in 1919 it had been possible to speak of a 'mutilated victory', in 1948 it could be said that though she had lost the war, Italy had won the peace. The territorial concessions made to France (Briga and Tenda) were insignificant, while the Alto Adige, claimed by the new Austria, had stayed Italian, thanks partly to De Gasperi's able diplomacy. Only on the eastern border had Italy had to cede to Jugoslavia those territories whose population was predominantly Slav, but she had kept the city of Trieste, which, after having been made a free territory under Allied control, finally returned to Italy in 1954. The colonies were lost, including Somalia, which remained under Italian mandate until 1960. But not many people lamented these losses in a world where the process of decolonization was gaining impetus all the time. On the domestic level, democracy had been restored, elections were held regularly, and the economic situation, thanks partly to American aid, was already showing signs of improvement. The industrialists were once more optimistic and enterprising, the senior civil servants and police officials were once more respected. Rossellini married Ingrid Bergman and made a film about St Francis; in short, order was restored. Those who had fought for a new and different order, the workers, the intellectuals, the peasants, could choose between a blind, unrewarding, hard struggle, and resignation, portrayed in the face of the out-of-work Roman protagonist of Vittorio De Sica's film *Bicycle Thieves*.

ECONOMIC MIRACLE AND COMMUNIST PARTY

To give an account, however summary, of the developments of the Italian political situation from 1948 until the present day seems to me not only difficult, in view of the distortion of such a near view, but futile. From the political point of view the situation has remained dominated by the Christian democrat party and its moderation, and in foreign policy by constant alignment with the positions of the pro-American policies of NATO. Intransigently anti-communist in the time of Truman and Pius XII, more relaxed in that of Kennedy and John XXIII, indulgent towards American barbarism in Vietnam, Christian democracy has made various readjustments of its political line, but this has undergone no real, substantial changes. The recent entry into the government of the socialists, who broke away from the communist party after the events in Hungary, has brought scarcely any change in the general Italian political situation.

This does not of course mean that nothing has changed in Italy in these last twenty years: political stability itself shows that the country has on the whole worked quietly and made progress. The years 1948–53 were still difficult years from the economic point of view, but from 1954 onwards recovery has been rapid, and since 1956 and Italy's entry into the European Common Market, overwhelming. This was the so-called 'economic miracle': production figures, the national income, consumption, all began to rise dizzily. No sector of industry was excluded from the general growth. The steel industry, with the new integrated plants of Cornigliano and Taranto, tripled its production over a few years, while the chemical and petrol industries, both private and state-owned, expanded explosively. Italian clothes and shoes made their mark on the main European markets; building, and the related industries of cement and bricks, did excellent business. But the most spectacular development was in the automobile industry, in which Fiat by now had a near-monopoly. The years 1956–67 were the period when the mass of Italians became motorized, and the great Turin factory, one of the 'big boys' of international industry, now produces more than a million vehicles a year. Following this sudden industrial expansion, millions of peasants left the countryside to look for work in the cities of the industrial North. This has without doubt been the greatest mixing of population that has ever taken place in united Italy: not the least consequence of it is that the country's double face has become even more marked. Another migration of peoples, of a seasonal and pleasure-seeking nature, on the other hand, is that of the twenty or more million foreign tourists who descend on Italy's beaches and towns every year.

Finally, after years of stinting and privation, the Italians discovered a certain well-being: consumption of meat and sugar, formerly very low, rose, and the rooftops became crowded with television aerials, which brought to everyone, together with the popular songs of innumerable festivals that took place the length of Italy, the paternal and persuasive voices of preachers and Christian democrat ministers.

The economic miracle also had its heroes. One of these, in a sense, was Enrico Mattei, a valiant partisan who, like an ex-*Garibaldino* of the late nineteenth century, became a leader of industry. To his name is linked the development of ENI and the attempt, made with a boldness and enterprise worthy of the old Italian merchants, to release Italy from the monopoly of the great international petroleum companies. With this intention, he made a series of contacts with colonial and newly independent peoples, and is also said to have financed the Algerian National Liberation Front. He died in 1962, in an air-crash, and sabotage was immediately suspected. The economic miracle had its artist too, Federico Fellini, whose exceptional talent sublimates the exuberance and vulgarity of the new parvenus, the Catholicism and atavistic clericalism, heavy with complexes, of the new Christian democrat Italy, its sense of and taste for sin, its progressive and traditionalist attitudes.

But like all the other miracles we have encountered during Italy's history, the economic miracle has its reverse side. The building-boom, which took the form of the most frenzied speculation, has damaged, probably beyond repair, the quality of Italy's main towns, and has irreparably scarred landscapes that are unique in the world. Mass-motorization has been artificially swollen beyond the country's economic capacities, both by the cunning use of techniques of persuasion and by the state's deliberately neglecting to improve means of transport. While thousands of kilometres of motorways are being built, the closing of 500 kilometres of railway line is contemplated, and public transport in towns, forced to move at walking-pace in the chaos of town traffic, runs at a frightening loss. The exodus from the countryside has made more acute the crisis of an agriculture that is still, in large areas of the country, regulated by outdated and anachronistic relations and contracts, which have only partially been chipped away by the government's agrarian reform.

Yet – it may reasonably be objected – these are the inconveniences and the price of progress; it certainly cannot be denied that in the last decade Italy has managed finally to break the chains of backwardness in which she was held for centuries, and has joined the small number of industrially advanced countries. But what leaves many Italians perplexed and sceptical when they consider the economic miracle is that there has been no parallel social progress. The condition of Italian workers remains precarious and hard; unemployment, in spite of the safety-valve of emigration, which has involved about three million people, still remains at a disturbing level. Social services such as schools and hospitals are absolutely inadequate; compulsory schooling up to the age of fourteen has only recently been introduced, and is in any case widely evaded, even today. Public administration remains inadequate and unwieldy, justice is slow, the universities mediaeval, the taxation system vexatious for the poor and powerless against tax-evaders; corruption is widespread. The old Italian incongruity of which Labriola spoke has by no means disappeared, but merely been reproduced at a higher level. Italy is still the country in which the death-penalty has been abolished and where many 'crimes of honour' are still committed, where there are a few dozen fabulously rich industrialists patronizing the arts and still several million illiterates, where hundreds of thousands of couples who no longer live together are unable to obtain a divorce, since divorce does not exist, the country where the rich are really rich and the poor really poor, where children are idolized and old age is hard and bitter, where intellectual progressiveness coexists with clericalism, alienation with superstition. This incongruity – as Labriola said, again – generates a universal unease, and one could say that these same Italians who have benefited from the economic miracle do not believe in their prosperity, but confine themselves to enjoying it as noisily and unthinkingly as they can, while it lasts.

The activity of the Italian communist party may be related to this unease. After the defeat of 1948 it seemed to many people that the star of Italian communism was by now on the wane; but this was not so. From election to election the communist party steadily increased its share of the poll, reaching almost nine million in the 1968 election. Neither the economic miracle nor the crisis following the 20th Congress of the Soviet Communist Party and the events of Hungary was able to halt this progress.

The secret, if that is the word, of this success, may be found in Togliatti's exhortation to his comrades to 'follow all the turns' of Italian society, a suggestion they were able to understand and apply. From 1947, the year when workers who had gathered to celebrate the 1st May at Portella della Ginestra were massacred by the bandit Giuliano, who was in the pay of the big landowners, the communist party has put itself at the head of peasant struggles in the South, and it was largely due to its efforts that the government had to decide to effect a partial agricultural reform. This did not weaken the positions and the popular support the communists had succeeded in winning in the southern regions; historically the communist party must take credit for having been able to arouse a political awareness in broad sectors of the southern peasant class, on whom the earlier democratic and socialist movements had been unable to make a deep impression. The communists thereby showed that they had not forgotten Gramsci's lessons. This general penetration among the peasant masses certainly represents the most conspicuous but not the only success won by the communist party to date. Avoiding the extremes of Stalinism, it has also been able to win a wide following among the intellectuals. Even among those who left the party in 1956, many have remained 'fellow travellers'. The majority of workers and many of the lower middle class of the country and the towns follow the communist party, or at least vote for it. The party takes every opportunity of making contact with the lower middle class, upholding the cause of small shopkeepers against the supermarkets, or that of small landowners overburdened with taxes, or that of artisans crushed by the competition of big business. Particularly important in the Italian communist party's most recent activity has been the trend towards 'dialogue with the Catholics', on the basis of common hostility towards bourgeois and capitalist individualism, and a common sensitivity to the problem of peace. Things progressed to the point that when Pope John XXIII died, some communist organizations hung the red flag at half-mast.

Like the socialist party at the beginning of the century, the communist party has become the force gathering together all the various and sometimes divergent impulses and currents of opposition that ferment in Italy's varied and contradictory society. This constitutes its great strength, but also its weakness, in that it places it continually before the dilemma of whether to keep faith with its own old revolutionary, proletariat vocation, or to transform itself into an opposition party 'within the system' and become a kind of Italian Labour Party. Palmiro Togliatti was fully aware of the difficulties of reconciling these two spirits of Italian communism, and of the need to succeed in the task, just as he was aware of the other problem of accentuating its national characteristics while still holding firm to the principle of connection with the Soviet Union's international policies. Togliatti's political testament, the famous Yalta memorandum, which he wrote a few days before his death, is evidence of how he remained committed to this very hard political and intellectual task right up to the end.

When his body was brought back to Italy, the bier was followed by a million people. Alive, he had been compared with Cavour, for his political lucidity and firmness. But Cavour died at the height of his glory, while Togliatti died in a vulgar, pleasure-seeking Italy. The sadness of the crowd that accompanied him for the last time contained the awareness of a goal that had not been reached, and the premonition of a long and weary road ahead.

Index

Abyssinia, 316
Acciaioli, Niccolò, 64
Abelard, Peter, 32
Adowa defeat, 302
Adrian VI, Pope, 104
Africa, 289, 294, 302, 304, 366
Agnadello, battle of, 94–7, 132
Albania, 358, 366
Albertario, Davide, 305
Alberti family, 57
Alberti, Leon Battista, 59, 75, 77, 87
Albertini, Luigi, 331
Alberto da Giussano, 262
Albinoni, Tomaso, 198
Albizi Family, 57
Albornoz, Gil d', 69–70, 97
Alderotti, Taddeo, 37
Alembert, Jean-Baptiste, d' 178
Alexander, General, 374
Alexander VI, Pope, 93–4, 97
Alexius, Emperor, 6
Alfieri, Vittorio, 182, 203–4
Alfonso V of Aragon, 46, 66, 75
Algarotti, Francesco, 180
Alula, Ras, 289
Amalfi, 4–5
Amari, Michele, 263
Ambrosio, Vittorio, General, 368
Amendola, Giovanni, 349
Ammirato, Scipione, 152
Andrea, Francesco d', 168
Andryane, Alessandro Filippo, 223
Angeloni, Luigi, 227
Angevins of Naples see Naples
Annese, Gennaro, 163
Antalemi, Benedetto, 25
Anthony of Padua, 34
Anti-Comintern pact, 358

Anti-Semitism, 358
Antonino, Bishop, 90
Aquisgrana, treaty of, 172
Argenson, Marquis d', 201
Ariosto, Ludovico, 99
Aristotelianism, 36–7
Aristotle, 71
Arnaldo da Brescia, 32, 262
Arrivabene, Count, 317
Artavelde Family, 83
Augustine, St, 71
Averroism, 36, 86, 88
Avignon, Papacy at, 24, 68–9, 71
Azeglio, Emanuele d', 257
Azeglio, Massimo d', 238, 252–4, 262

Bachi, Riccardo, 334
Badaloni, Nicola, 282
Badoer, Piero, 135
Badoglio, Pietro, Marshal, 359, 369–73
Bakunin, Michael, 267–8, 292
Balbo, Cesare, 232, 237
Balbo, Italo, 352, 359
Baldini, Nullo, 282
Baldwin, Stanley, 351
Banco di S. Giorgio, 54, 82, 139–40, 197
Bandiera brothers, 236
Bandini, Sallustio Antonio, 180
Baratieri, Oreste, General, 289
Barbarossa see Frederick I
Barbato, Nicola, 301
Barbiano, Alberico da, 70
Bardi company, 55, 58
Baretti, Giuseppe, 178
Baronio, Cesare, 148
Baroque, 146, 159
Bartali, Gino, 375
Bartolomeo, Fra, 92

Bassanesi, Giovanni, 361
Battista, Cesare, 331
Bava Beccaris, Fiorenzo, 305
Beatrice Portinari, 40
Beauharnais, Eugène, 211, 217–18
Beccadelli, Antonio, 75
Beccaria, Cesare, 179–80, 185, 189, 226
'Belle Epoque', 308–12
Belli, Gioacchino, 227
Bembo, Pietro, 99
Benivieni, Antonio, 92
Bentinck, Lord William, 215
Beolco, Angelo, 96
Berchet, Giovanni, 224, 263
Bergman, Ingrid, 379
Bernardino da Feltre, 87
Bernaroli, Egidio, 282
Bernini, Gian Lorenzo, 146, 159
Bernstein, Edward, 292, 299
Bertani, Agostino, 255
Bertini, Francesca, 321
Bessarione, Giovanne, Cardinal, 76
Bianchi, Nicomede, 255
Biandrata, 113
Bismarck, Otto von, 294–5
Bissolati, Leonida, 305, 318–19, 326, 331, 337
Bixio, Nino, 261
Black Death, 43–4, 71–2
Black Sea, 52
Boccaccio, Giovanni, 55, 65, 72–3, 76
Boccalini, Trajano, 153
Boccanegro, Simone, 53
Bocchini, Artur, 359
Bohemond of Taranto, Prince, 6
Boiardo, Matteo Maria, 86
Bologna, 36–8, 44
Bombacci, Nicola, 339
Bonaparte, Jerome, 257
Bonaparte, Joseph, 214
Bonaparte, Napoleon *see* Napoleon Bonaparte
Bonaventura of Bagnorea, 35
Bonghi, Ruggero, 255
Boniface VIII, Pope, 23–4, 40, 67
Bonomi, Ivanhoe, 344, 346, 373
Bonvesin de la Riva, 28
Borelli, Giovanni Alfonso, 168
Borelli, Lyda, 321
Borghini, Vicenzo, 128
Borgia, Cesare, 94

Borromeo, Carlo, Archbishop of Milan, 123–4
Borromeo, Federico, 124
Borromini, Francesco, 159
Borsieri, Pietro, 223
Bosco, Rosario Garibaldi, 301
Boselli, Paolo, 334
Botero, Giovanni, 129–30, 144, 147–8, 157
Botta, Carlo, 207
Bottai, Giuseppe, 355, 359, 368
Botticelli, Sandro, 84, 86, 92
Bourbons, the, 192–7, 214–15, 218
Bouvines, battle of, 2, 18
Braccio da Montone, 70
Bracciolini, Poggio, 76, 80
Brahe, Tycho, 148
Bramante, 141
Breda, Vincenzo Stefano, 285
Brenner Pass, 52, 173
Brunelleschi, Filippo, 58, 77–8
Brunetto Latini, 41
Bruni, Leonardo, 25, 79, 87–8
Bruno, Giordano, 147, 149–51, 165–6, 295
Bukharin, Nicolai, 363
Bülow, B. H. K. von, 316
Buonarroti, Filippo, 206–7, 217, 234–5
Buragna, Carlo, 168
Burlamacchi, Francesco, 112
Byzantine culture, 76

Cadorna, Luigi, General, 333
Cafiero, Carlo, 292
Caloprese, Gregorio, 168
Caltabellotta, peace of, 63
Calvin, Jean, 109, 110–11, 114
Cambrai, League of, 94–5
Campailla, Tommaso, 168
Campaldino, 55
Campanella, Tommaso, 89, 121, 147, 149–51, 153, 165
Campoformio, treaty of, 208
Canaletto, 198
Canosa, Prince of, 224
Caporetto, battle of, 333
Capponi, Gino, 238
Caracciolo, Francesco, 211
Caracciolo, Marchese Gian Galeazzo, 109, 113, 196
Carafa, Giampiero *see* Paul IV, Pope

Caramanico, Prince of, 196
Caravaggio, 148
Carducci, Giosuè, 277, 290–1
Carli, Gian Rinaldo, 185
Carlo Alberto, King of Piedmont, 231,
   233, 238–9, 242, 244–7, 252
Carlo Emanuele I of Savoy, 130–1, 152,
   154
Carlo Emanuele, III, 201
Carlo Felice, 223, 231, 233, 238
Carlos of Bourbon *see* Charles of Bourbon
Carnesecchi, Piero, 108, 114
Casanova, 178
Castellano, Giuseppe, General, 370
Castellione, Sebastian, 114
Castelvetro, Ludovico, 109, 113
Casti, Gian Battista, 180, 216
Castiglione, Baldassare, 89, 99–100
Castracani, Castruccio, 56, 65
Cateau-Cambrésis, treaty of, 111–12,
   130, 137, 171
Catherine, Empress of Russia, 181
Catholicism:
   Liberal, 228, 237
   and unionism, 310–12
Cattaneo, Carlo, 243–4, 250, 283
Cattaneo, Silvio, 297
Cavalcanti, Guido, 38
Cavallini, 34
Cavallotti, Felice, 297, 305
Cavour, Camillo di, 129, 201, 232,
   238–9, 253–62, 265–9, 273, 283–4, 300,
   383
Celestine V, Pope, 23, 35, 89
Cellini, Benvenuto, 146
Cesi, Federico, 166
Championnet, Jean-Etienne, 210
Charlemagne, Emperor, 1, 3
Charles of Anjou, Duke of Calabria, 56
Charles I of Anjou, King of Sicily, 21–2,
   30, 64–5
Charles of Bourbon, King of Naples, 173,
   194–5
Charles IV, Emperor, 69
Charles V, Holy Roman Emperor, 54,
   104–8, 110–13, 122, 137–8, 141
Charles VI of Habsburg, Emperor, 186
Charles VIII, King of France, 82, 89–93
Cherasco, treaty of, 171, 206–7
Chioggia War, 50, 54
Christopher Columbus, 28

Churchill, Winston, 351, 372–3
Ciano, Galeazzo, 358–9, 368, 373
Cino da Pistoia, 37–8
Ciompi risings, 46, 57, 73, 80, 90
Cirillo, Domenico, 211
Cisalpine Republic, 208–9
Clark, Mark, 378
Clement IV, Pope, 21, 23
Clement V, Pope, 24
Clement VII, Pope, 105–7
Clement VIII, Pope, 152
Clement XVI, Pope, 199
Clotilde of Savoy, 257
Cobden, Richard, 242
Cola di Rienzo, 48, 67–71
Colbert, Jean-Baptiste, 201–2
Colletta, Pietro, General, 222
Colonna Family, 67
Colonna, Vittoria, 109
Commines, Philippe de, 62
Communes, 11–14, 17–21, 26–31
Communism, 240–1, 342, 362–3, 376–7,
   382–3
Compagni, Dino, 55
Conciliation, 350–1
Condellac, Etienne-Bonnot de, 196
Confalonieri, Federico, 223
Conforti, Francesco, 211
Conradin, 21
Consalvi, Ettore, Cardinal, 221, 224
Consalvo, Grand Captain, 93
Constance of Hauteville, 18
Constantine the African, 17
Constantinople, 52, 81–2
Contarini, Gaspare, 109
Contarini, Giuseppe, Cardinal, 136
Conversano, Count of, 164
Cornaro, Caterina, 52
Cornelio, Tommaso, 167
Correnti, Cesare, 255
Corsica, 206
Costa, Andrea, 278, 282, 297, 305
Counter-Reformation, 111–14, 120, 123,
   126, 136, 140, 142, 145–9, 153–4, 167
Credaro, Luigi, 326
Crispi, Francesco, 259–60, 278, 294–6,
   300–3, 307
Croce, Benedetto, 292, 297, 320–2, 360,
   362, 372–3
Crusades:
   First, 6

Crusades—*continued*
Fourth, 7–8, 18, 26, 49
Albigensian, 32
Cuoco, Vincenzo, 216–226
Curione, Celio, 110
Custodi, Pietro, 187
Cybo, Caterina, Duchess of Camerino, 109
Cybo Family, 125
Cyprus, 82

D'Annunzio, Gabriele, 291, 321, 325, 331, 335, 338, 341, 343, 352
D'Aquino, Bartolomeo, 161–2
Dante Alighieri, 23–5, 37–42, 71, 99, 113
De Ambris, Alceste, 323
De Amicis, Edmondo, 290, 309
De Andreis, Felice, 305
De Deo, Emanuele, 206
De Dominis, Marc' Antonio, 148
De Felice, Giuseppe, 301
De Gasperi, Alcide, 346, 376, 379
De Marco, 314
De Nicola, Enrico, 373
De Ponedi, Francesco, 352
De Rosa, Ferdinando, 361
De Santis, Francesco, 255, 263
De Sica, Vittorio, 379
De Stefani, Alberto, 347
De Vecchi, Cesare, 352
De Viti, Antonio, 314
Della Porta, Giambattista, 146
Della Robbia, Giovanni, 92
Denina, Carlo, 204
Depretis, Agostino, 275–7, 294, 297, 315
Descartes, René, 166, 168–9
Di Costanzo, Angelo, 145
Diderot, Denis, 178
Diodati, Giovanni, of Lucca, 113
Divine Comedy, 40–2
dolce stil novo, 38–9
Domingo de Guzman, 33
Dona, Leonardo, Doge, 153
Donatello, 77, 84
Donizone de Canossa, Bishop, 8
Doria, Andrea, 106, 120, 138–9
Doria, Paola Matteo, 168
Dovizi, Bernardo, 99
Drengot, Rainolf, 15
Du Bellay, Guillaume, 109, 131
Du Tillot, Guglielmo, 196–7
Duse, Eleonora, 321

Edward VII, King of England, 316
Egidian Constitutions, 69
Eight Saints, War of, 48, 57
Einaudi, Luigi, 314, 377–8
Eisenhower, Dwight, 370
Elia de Cortona, 35
Engels, Friedrich, 268, 299
Enlightenment, 167, 171–83
Entente powers, 331
Enzo, King of Sardinia, 38
Equals, Conspiracy of, 206
Erasmus of Rotterdam, 77, 80, 111
Eritrea, 294, 304
Este, Duke Leonello d', 75
Este, Errole II d', 109
Este, Francesco III d', 173, 191
Este, Francesco IV d', 219
Estensi of Ferrara, 23
Ethiopia, 289, 304, 356–7, 366, 369
Evangelism, Italian, 108–9, 111–13
Expedition of the Thousand, 259–60
Ezelino da Romano, 19

Facta, Luigi, 345
Falconieri, 216
Fanti, Manfredo, 255
Fantoni, Giovanni, 207
Fantuzzi, 207
Farinacci, Roberto, 353
Farinata degli Uberti, 41
Farini, Luigi Carlo, 255, 261, 266, 269–70
Farnese, Elisabetta, 196
Farnese, Peir Luigi, 111–12
Fasci, movement, 297–9, 301, 304
Fascism, 294, 325, 342–68
Federzoni, Luigi, 326
Fellini, Federico, 381
Ferdinand II of Habsburg, Emperor, 154
Ferdinand of Spain the Catholic, II of Aragon, 94, 120, 122, 128
Ferdinando I of Bourbon, IV King of Naples, King of Two Sicilies, 194, 222, 231
Ferdinand II of Bourbon, King of Naples, 243–4
Fermi, Enrico, 358
Ferrante, King of Sicily, 66, 118
Ferrara, Duke of, 82
Ferrara, Francesco, 255, 283
Ferrari, Giuseppe, 249–50
Ferri, Enrico, 309, 318

Ferrucci, Francesco, 262
Fibonacci, Leonardo, 7
Ficino, Marsilio, 88
Fieramosca, Ettore, 262
Fieschi Family, 112, 139
Filangieri, Gaetano, 195
Filarete, 83, 87
Filelfo, Francesco, 75, 87
Filiberto, Emanuele, Duke, 129–32
Filippo of Bourbon, Duke of Parma, 196
Filippo Argenti, 41
First World War, 333–6
Flaminio, Marc' Antonio, 108
Flanders war, 48
Florence, 29–30, 38, 55–9, 84, 106, 125–8
    in Renaissance, 85–9
    see also Tuscany
Florio, Vincenzo, 286
Fonseca de Pimentel, Eleonora, 211
Forese Donati, 41
Formosus, Pope, 2
Fortis, Alessandro, 315
Fortunato, Giustino, 275
Foscari, Francesco, 51–2
Foscolo, Ugo, 216
Fossombroni, Vittorio, 221
Fra Angelico, 84, 90
Fra Diavolo, 210
Francesco III d'Este, 173, 191
Francesco IV d'Este, Duke of Modena, 230–1
Francesco, Gian, 92
Franchetti, Leopoldo, 275
Francis of Assisi, St, 33–41
Francis II of Lorraine, 188
Franciscans, 33–5
Franco, General Francisco, 357
François I, King of France, 98, 105–7, 110, 129, 138
Franconian emperors, 3
Franz Josef, Emperor of Austria, 287
Frederick I Barbarossa, 3, 17–18, 32
Frederick II of Hohenstaufen, 17–21, 36–8
Frederick III, King of Sicily, 66
French Revolution, 205–19
Frisi, Paolo, 173
Fugger Family, 83, 104, 138
Fustinato, Arnaldo, 263

Galanti, Giuseppe Maria, 180, 195
Galdi, Matteo Angelo, 207

Galiani, Ferdinando, 178, 180
Galilei, Vincenzo, 127
Galileo Galilei, 36, 127, 153, 164–7
Gallipoli (1416), 51
Gallo, Agostino, 123
Grand, Juste de, 84
Garibaldi, Giuseppe, 235, 246–7, 255, 259–61, 265–71, 275
Gastelli, Benedetto, 166
Gattemelata, Erasmo, 70
Gattilusio Family, 52
Gattinara, Marcurino da, 104–5
Gavalieri, Bonaventura, 166
Genoa, 5–6, 8, 27–8, 50, 52–4, 115–16, 137–40, 197
Genoino, Giulio, 121, 163
Genovesi, Antonio, 176, 180, 195–6
Gentile, Giovanni, 351–2, 360
George of Antioch, 16
Germany, 298–9
Ghibellines *see* Guelfs and Ghibellines
Ghibellines, neo-, 262
Ghiberti, Lorenzo, 58
Giambologna, 146
Gianni, Francesco, 188, 190–1
Giannone, Pietro, 181–2, 194–5, 203
Giberti, Bishop of Verona, 109
Gioacchino da Fiore, 23
Gioberti, Vincenzo, 232, 236–7, 241–2, 246–7
Gioia, Melchiorre, 207, 234
Giolitti, Giovanni, 277, 281, 300–1, 306–8, 315–20, 325–8, 334, 340–1, 345–6
Giotto, 24, 34, 56, 65
Giovanna, Queen of Naples, 65
Giovanna II, Queen of Naples, 66
Giovianni di Vicenza, 34
Girardi Cinzio, Giambattista, 146
Giuliano, Salvatore, 382
Giusti, Giuseppe, 263
Gizzi, Cardinal Pasquale Tommaso, 241
Gnocchi-Viani, Osvaldo, 297
Gobetti, Piero, 360
Godfrey of Bouillon, 7
Goldoni, Carlo, 178–9, 182, 198
Gondi Family, 126
Gothic style, 35, 50
Gozzoli, Benozzo, 86
Gramsci, Antonio, 335, 340, 361–3, 382
Grandi, Dino, 359, 368

Graziani, General Rodolfo, 366
Great Schism, 47, 69–70, 81–2
Gregory the Great, Pope, 1
Gregory VII, Pope, 5, 15
Gregory IX, Pope, 20, 35
Gregory X, Pope, 23
Gregory XI, Pope, 69
Gregory XIII, Pope, 147
Gregory XVI, Pope, 241
Guardi, Francesco, 198
Guariglia, Raffaele, 369
Guelf party, 56–7, 65
Guelfs and Ghibellines, 18–25, 29, 39, 181
Guelfism, neo-, 244–5, 262
Guerrazzi, Francesco Domenica, 245, 262
Guicciardini, Francesco, 83, 107
Guinizelli, Guido, 37–8
Guiscard, Robert, 15, 17
Gutenberg, Johann, 87

Habsburgs, the, 184–92
Hawkwood, Sir John, 48
Henry IV, King of France, 126, 130, 152, 154
Henry I, King of England, 16
Henry IV, Holy Roman Emperor, 15
Henry VII, King of England, 81
Henry VII of Luxembourg, 21, 65
Henry of Guise, Duke, 163
Hitler, Adolf, 358, 365, 368
Holy Alliance, 229
Holy League, 94–5, 133, 155
Honorius III, Pope, 18
Hugh Grandmesnil, 15
Humanism, 73–80, 88, 100, 147
Humanists, Florentine, 78, 88–9, 107
Hundred Years War, 44, 47–9, 81–2
Hus, Jan, 79–80

Iacopo da Lentin, 38
Ibn Jbair, 17
Idris, 17
Innocent III, Pope, 2, 18, 32, 69
Innocent X, Pope, 155
Inquisition, Spanish, 112–13, 118, 147, 149, 187, 194
Interdict, 136–7, 153–5
Italietta, 320–3

Jacini, Stefano, 281
Jacobinism, 205–8
Jacopone da Todi, 34–5
Jansenism, 189
Jean de Montreal, 48
Jerome of Prague, 80
Jesuits, 124, 147
Joachim, of Fiore, Abbot, 32
John of Austria, 163
John XXIII, Pope, 311, 379, 383
Joseph II, Emperor, 185, 187, 189, 199, 205
Julius II, Pope, 83, 94, 97–8, 140
Julius III, Pope, 113
Juvara, Filippo, 202

Kautsky, Karl Johann, 292, 299
Kepler, Giovanni, 148
Koyré, Alexandre, 164
Kuliscioff, Anna, 305

La Farina, Giuseppe, 255
La Marmora, Marchese di, 258
La Motte, Comte de, 262
Labriola, Antonio, 287, 292–3, 298–9, 304
Labriola, Arturo, 318, 323
Ladislas, King of Naples, 66
Lafargue, Paul, 292
Lagrange, Giuseppe Luigi, 204
Lamartine, Alphonse de, 224
Lambruschini, Luigi, Cardinal, 241
Lanza, Giovanni, 269
Lanzi, Luigi, 181
Lateran Synod (1059), 2
Lattanzi, Giuseppe, 207
Laurana, Luciano, 66
Lautrec de Foix, Viscount Odet, 118, 120
Lazzari, Constantino, 297, 339
League of Nations, 356–7
Leghorn, 127
Lenzoni, Carlo, 128
Leo III, Pope, 1, 3
Leo X, Pope, 97–100, 113, 140, 145, 147
Leo XII, Pope, 224
Leo XIII, Pope, 311
Leonardo da Capua, 168
Leonardo da Vinci, 62, 78
Leopardi, Giacomo, 225–9
Leopold II, Grand Duke of Tuscany, 245
Lepanto, battle of, 133, 152

Leto, Pomponio, 79
Libya, 316, 326–8, 366–7
Lodi, peace of, 48, 82, 84
Lodovico il Moro, 91
Lombardy, 45, 50, 122–3, 184–8
Lombroso, Giuseppe, 309
Longano, Francesco, 180
Lorenzo the Magnificent *see* Medici,
    Lorenzo dei
Loschi, Antonio, 86
Louber, Emile, President, 316
Louis IX, King of France, 21
Lousi XI, King of France, 81—2
Louis XII, King of France, 94–7
Louis XIV, King of France, 155, 171,
    200–2
Louis XV, King of France, 196
Louis Philippe, 230, 235
Lucretius, 76
Ludovisi, Ignazio Boncompagni, 200
Ludwig IV the Bavarian, 21, 65
Lusco of Vicenza, Antonio, 79
Luther, Martin, 80, 100, 111
Luzzatti, Luigi, 284, 320, 326

Machiavelli, Niccolò, 40, 54, 58, 85, 93–5,
    101–4, 107, 113, 147, 167, 181–2, 262
Mafia, 301, 318
Magnani, Anna, 375
Maiano, Giuliano da, 66, 87
Malatesta, Enrico, 330
Malocello, Lanzarotto, 52
Malpighi, Marcello, 166, 168
Mamiani, Terenzio, 255
Manfred, King of Sicily, 21–3, 38, 41
Manin, Daniele, 244, 255
Mannerism, 146
Mantegna, Andrea, 83, 86
Manzoni, Alessandro, 157, 159, 225–9,
    290
Marchese, Enrico, 28
Marco Polo, 24, 26, 28
Marengo, battle of, 211
Margherita, Queen of Italy, 288, 291
Maria Amalia, Duchess, 197
Maria Carolina of Habsburg, Queen of
    Naples, 195
Maria Louisa of Habsburg, 219, 231
Maria Theresa, Empress, 185–8, 201
Marilio, 36
Marino, Giovanni Battista, 167

Marseilles, 52
Marsillio of Padua, 24
Martin IV, Pope, 23
Marx, Karl, 268, 292
Mary Tudor, Queen of England, 109,
    113
Masaccio, 77
Massari, Giuseppe, 267
Mastai-Ferretti, Cardinal
    see Pius IX, Pope
Mattei, Enrico, 380
Matteotti, Giacomo, 348, 360
Maurice of Orange, 138
Maximilian, Emperor, 95
Mazzei, Filippo, 180
Mazzini, Giuseppe, 220, 233–6, 245–52,
    255, 259, 266, 275
Medici, Alessandro dei, 125
Medici, Catherine dei, 126
Medici, Cosimo the Elder, 59
Medici, Cosimo I dei, 124–6, 128
Medici Family, 47, 57–8, 83–4, 88, 93, 98
Medici, Ferdinando dei, 125–6, 152
Medici, Giuliano dei, 84
Medici, Lorenzo dei (the Magnificent),
    84–6, 90, 98, 125
Medici, Luigi dei, 221
Medici, Maria, 126, 152
Mehmet Ali, 231
Melanchthon, 110
Menotti, Ciro, 231
Mercantini, Luigi, 263
Metastasio, Pietro, 168
Metella, Cecilia, 143
Micelu, Luigi, 296
Michelangelo, 84, 93, 98
Michele di Lando, 57
Michelet, Jules, 170
Michelozzo, 59
Milan, 28–9, 59–63, 122–4
Milsey, Enrico, 231
Minghetti, Marco, 238, 266, 269, 270,
    276
Mocenigo, Giovanni, 149
Mocenigo, Tomaso, Doge, 49–51
Modena, 188–92
Modigliani, Giuseppe Emmanuele, 360
Molza, Francesco Maria, 109
Monaldo, Count, 228
Moncada, Guglielmo Raimondo, 122
Montale, Eugenio, 353

Montanelli, Giuseppe, 245
Montano, Cola, 79, 84–5
Montaperti, 55
Montecatini, 56
Montesquieu, 199
Morandi, Giorgio, 353
Morata, Olimpia, 113
Moravia, Alberto, 353
Moretti, Silvio, 223
Mori, Lorenzo, 210
Morone, Giovanni, Cardinal, 113
Murat, Joachim, 214, 217–18
Muratori, Ludovico Antonio, 168,180–2, 216
Murri, Romolo, 311
Mussolini, Benito, 324, 327, 330, 332, 342–51, 355–9, 368–9, 373, 374

Naples, 119–21, 163–4, 192–7, 243
Naples, Angevins of, 56, 63–7, 120
Napoleon I Bonaparte, 198, 206–8, 211–18
Napoleon III, 201, 246, 257–8, 260, 270
Natale, Michele, Bishop, 216
Nazism, 357
Nelson, Horatio, 210
Nenni, Pietro, 230
Neoplatonism, 86, 88–9
Neri, Pompeo, 185, 188, 190
Niccoli, Niccolò, 76
Niccolini, Giovanni Battista, 263
Niceforo, Alfredo, 291
Nicholas III, Pope, 23
Nicholas IV, Pope, 23
Nicholas V, Pope, 76, 79, 84
Nicoterra, Giovanni, 276
Nievo, Ippolito, 263
Nitti, Francesco Saverio, 341, 360
Normans, 14–17

Oberdan, Guglielmo, 289
Ochino, Bernardino, 109–10
Olivares, Duke of, 122, 158, 160
Orlando, Luigi, 285–8
Orlando, Vittorio Emmanuele, 334, 336 346
Orsini Family, 67
Orsini, Felice, 257
Ortes, Gian Maria, 180
Ossuna, Duke of, 121, 163
Otto I, Emperor, 1

Otto III, Emperor, 2
Otto of Frisinga, Bishop, 13
Oudinot, Nicolas-Charles, 246

Pacelli, Ernesto, 327
Pacifico, Nicola, 216
Pacioli, Luca, 87
Padua, 36
Pagano, Francesco Mario, 180, 195, 211
Paleario, Aonio, 108
Palermo, 38, 64
Palestrina, Pier Luigi di, 148
Palladio, Andrea, 136
Palmieri, Giuseppe, 180, 195
Palmieri, Mattoe, 77–8
Panizzi, Antonio, 224
Panormita, 75
Pantaleoni, Mauro, 5
Paoletti, Ferdinando, 190
Paoli, Pasquale, 197, 206
Papacy at Avignon *see* Avignon
Papal State, 67–70, 97–100, 140–4, 155, 198–9, 269–72
Parini, Giuseppe, 182, 185, 216
Parma, 192–7
Parri, Ferruccio, 360, 376
Paruta, Paolo, 137
Pascoli, Giovanni, 309
Paul III, Pope, 109–11, 113, 145
Paul IV, Pope, 109, 113, 142, 145
Paul V, Pope, 153
Pazzi family, 84, 86
Pecchio, Giuseppe, 224
Pedro of Toledo, Don, 118, 120–1
Pegoletti, Francesco, 26
Pellico, Silvio, 223, 263
Pelloutier, Fernand, 324
Pelloux, Luigi Girolamo, 305–7
Pepe, Guglielmo, 224
Pepin, 68
Péreire brothers, 285
Pessagno, Manuele, 28
Peter III, of Aragon, 22
Peter Leopold, Grand Duke of Tuscany, 188–9, 191
Petrarch, Francesco, 39, 68, 70–3, 75–6, 100
Petrolini, Ettore, 353
Philip II, King of Spain, 54, 112, 122, 134, 138, 152
Philippe Le Bel, King of France, 23, 28

Piacentini, Marcello, 352
Piaggio, Erasmo, 286
Piccinino, Nicola, 70
Piccolomini, Alfonso, 143
Piccolomini, Enea *see* Pius II, Pope
Pico della Mirandola, Giovanni, 86, 88, 92
Piedmont, 128–32, 200–4
Pienza, 84, 87
Pier delle Vigne, 37–8, 41
Piero della Francesca, 84
Pietro Aretino, 137
Pignatelli conspiracy, 162
Pilo, Rosolino, 255, 259
Pirandello, Luigi, 353
Pirelli, Giovanni, 286
Pisacane, Carlo, 250–2, 255, 259, 268, 276
Pisano, Nicola, 25
Pius II, Pope, 63, 80, 84
Pius IV, Pope, 113, 123
Pius VI, Pope, 199–200
Pius VII, Pope, 198–9
Pius IX, Pope, 241–2, 244–5, 255, 271
Pius X, Pope, 312, 319
Pius XI, 345, 351
Pius XII, Pope, 327, 379
Platina, Bartolomeo, 79
Plato, 71, 76, 88
Platonism *see* Neoplatonism
Plechanov, G. V., 292
Plotinus, 88
Pole, Reginald, 109–10, 113, 145
Poliziano, il, 86–7
Pollaiolo, Antonio, 84
Pomponazzi, Pietro, 36, 86, 100
Pontano, Giovanni, 66
Porcari, Stefano, 79
Porcari conspiracy, 84
Porta, Carlo, 227
Possevino, Antonio, 148
Prampolini, Camillo, 282
Prezzolini, Giuseppe, 324
Price-revolution, 116–17, 120, 135, 139, 142
Prina, Giuseppe, 218
Prinetti, Giulio, 315
Priuli, 96
Pucci, Francesco, 148
Puccini, Giacomo, 321
Pisa, 5–8, 46

Querini, Angelo, 198

Rabelais, François, 109, 141
Radetzky, J. J., 244–5, 252
Radicalism, 297
Radicati di Passerano, Alberto, 203
Ranza, Giovanni Antonio, 207
Raphael, 98–100, 141
Rattazzi, Urbano, 253, 269, 270–1
Ravenna, battle of, 94
Redi, Francesco, 166
Reformation, 113
Renaissance, in Florence, 85–9
    end of 11
Renata of France, Duchess, 109
Restoration, 219–32
Retz, Cardinal de, 126
Ribbentrop, Joachim von, 369
Ricasoli, Bettino, 268
Ricci Family, 57
Ricci, Scipione de', 189
Risorgimento, 216, 233–64
Ristori, 207
Robert, abbot of Santa Eufemia, 16
Robert of Anjou, King of Naples, 64–5, 71
Robilant, Count Carlo di, 288, 290
Roger II, King of Sicily, 16–17
Romano, Giulio, 146
Romanticism, 225–6
Rome:
    rebuilding of, 83–4
    in Counter-Reformation, 140–4
    sack of, 104–7
    liberation of, 269–70
    Mussolini's march on, 345–7, 360, 367
Rommel, General Erwin, 367
Romussi, Carlo, 305
Roncalli, Angelo *see* John XXIII
Roosevelt, Franklin D., 373
Rosselli, Carlo, 360–1, 363
Rossellini, Roberto, 375, 379
Rossellino, Bernardo, 84, 87
Rossetti, Raffaele, 224
Rossi, Pellegrini, 245
Rouher, Eugène, 207
Rousseau, Jean-Jacques, 178
Rubattino, Raffaele, 286
Rudini, Marquis de, 300, 304
Ruffo, Fabrizio, Cardinal, 200, 210
Russo, Vincenzio, 211

Sacchetti, Franco, 55
Sadoleto, Contarini, 109–10, 145
Saffi, Angelo, 297
Salandra, Antonio, 330, 345–6
Salasco, General, 245
Salutati, Coluccio, 78, 86, 88
Salvemini, Gaetano, 314–15, 327, 331, 360
Salviati, Leonardo, 128
San Giuliano, Antonio di, 327
Sannazzaro, Jacopo, 66
Sansovino, Francesco, 137
Sansovino, Jacopo, 135, 137
Santore di Santarosa, Annibale, 224
Saracco, Giuseppe, 306–7
Saragat, Giuseppe, 377
Sarpi, Paolo, 137, 148, 153
Savonarola, Geralamo, 80, 88–93, 100
Savoy, House of, 128–32
Scaligeri Family, 23, 51
Scamozzi, Vincenzo, 135
Sciarra, Marco, 121, 143
Second World War, 358, 365–8
Sella, Quintino, 269, 273
Seripando, Bishop of Salerno, 109
Serra, Antonio, 121, 157
Serrao, Bishop Andrea, 216
Serrati, Giacinto Menotti, 339
Serveto, Miguel, 114
Seyssel, Claude de, 131
Sforza Family, 59–63
Sforza, Francesco, 60–2, 70
Sforza, Francesco II, 106
Sforza, Galeazzo Maria, 79
Siccardi, Giuseppe, 253
Sicilian Vespers, 22–3, 65
Sicily, American landings in, 368
Sicily, Kingdom of, 63–7
Sicily, province of, 121–2, 192–7, 297–8
Siena, 111–12
Sigismund, Emperor, 50
Signorelli, Luca, 92
Sillabo, 270, 272
Sirleto, Guglielmo, 148
Sixtus, IV, Pope, 79, 83–4
Sixtus V, Pope, 142–4
Smalkaldic League, 108, 110
Sobieski, Janos, 155
Socinianism, 114
Solaro Della Margarita, Clemente, 242
Somalia, 316, 379

Sonnino, Sidney, 275, 278, 304, 315, 319 326, 331, 336
Sorel, Georges, 292, 299, 324
Soviet Russia, 362–3
Sozzini, Fausto, 113–14
Sozzini, Lelio, 113
Spain, 52
Spallanzani, Lazzaro, 187
Spanish rule, 111–14, 118–24, 152–5, 160–4, 171
Spanish Succession, War of, 171, 200
Spaventa, Bertrando, 255, 292
Spellanzani, Lazzaro, 180
Spinola, Ambrogio, 138
Spinola, Cornelio, 161
Spinoza, Baruch, 168
Staël, Madame de, 225
Stalin, 733
Starace, Achille, 353
Stendhal (Henri Beyle), 221, 224
Sturzo, Luigi, 311, 345
Suleiman, the Magnificent, 107
Suvorov, A. V., 210

Tanucci, Bernardo, 194
Tarello, Camillo, 123
Tasca, Angelo, 340, 363
Tasso, Torquato, 147
Tassoni, Alessandro, 131, 153
Taylor, General M. C., 370
Telesio, Bernardino, 151
Thirty Years War, 118, 122, 154, 157, 160, 163
Thou, Jacques de, 153
Tiepolo, Baiamonte, 27
Tino da Camaino, 65
Tintoretto, 146
Tiraboschi, Geralamo, 181
Tittoni, Tommaso, 315
Togliatti, Palmiro, 340, 362–3, 372–3, 377, 382
Tommaseo, Niccolò, 263
Tommaso di Savoia, 11
Torricelli, Evangelista, 166
Toscanelli, Paolo Del Pozzo, 78
Tosti, Abbot Luigi, 295
Treves, Claudio, 360
Tridentine Catholicism, 113–14, 123, 131, 145, 148
Trinci, Cosimo, 176
Triple Alliance, 288–90, 294, 315, 331

Trissino, Gian Giorgio, 99
Truman, Harry, 379
Tunisia, 368
Turati, Augusto, 353
Turati, Filippo, 298–9, 305, 318–19, 339, 360
Turkey, 50–1, 107, 133
Türr, Stefano, 261
Tuscany, Grand Duchy of, 58, 124–8, 188–92

Ugolino, Count, 23
Uguccione della Faggiuola, 56
Umberto I, King of Italy, 288, 306

Valdès, Juan de, 108, 114
Valla, Lorenzo, 75–6
Vanini, Guilio Cesare, 148
Vasari, Giorgio, 125, 128
Vasco, Dalmazzo Francesco, 204
Vasco, Giambattista, 180
Vatican:
    Library, 76
    City, 350
    see also Papal State
Venice, 6–8, 26–7, 49–52, 94–5, 132–7, 153–4, 197–8
Verdi, Giuseppe, 264
Verdun partition, 1
Verga, Giovanni, 290
Vergerio, Pier Paolo, Bishop of Capodistria, 109, 113
Vermigli, Pier Martire, 109
Veronese, Paolo, 135–6, 147
Verri, Pietro, 179–82, 185–7, 205
Verro, Bernardino, 301
Vespasiano da Bisticci, 76
Vico, Giovambattista, 169–70
Vienna, Congress of, 219
Villani, Giovanni, 55
Villani, Matteo, 45

Visconti Family, 50, 53, 57, 59–63, 75, 79
Visconti, Filippo Maria, 60–2
Visconti, Gian Galeazzo, 47–8, 51, 59–61
Visconti, Giovanni, Archbishop, 53, 59, 61
Visconti, Valentina, 94
Visconti-Venosta, Emilio, 304
Vitruvius, 78
Vittorio, Amedeo II, 200–3
Vittorio Amedeo III, 203
Vittorio Emanuele I, King of Sardinia, 223
Vittorio Emanuele II, King of Italy, 129, 201, 246, 252, 256, 259–61, 266, 270, 287
Vittorio Emanuele III, King of Italy, 307
Vittorino da Feltre, 74
Viviani, Vincenzo, 166
Volpi, Giuseppe, 347, 354
Volta, Alessandro, 187
Voltaire, 155, 178

Waldo, Peter, of Lyons, 33
Walter of Brienne, Duke of Athens, 56
Walter of Urselingen, 48
Watton, Sir Henry, 153
Waugham, 210
Wenceslas, Emperor, 59
Westphalia, treaty of, 154–5
William of Hauterville, 15
William of Ockham, 35
William the Conqueror, 15
William II, 17
Woodhouse, John, 174
Wyclif, John, 79–80

Young, Arthur, 184

Zamboni, Luigi, 206
Zanardelli, Giuseppe, 305–8
Zaniboni, Tito, 349
Zollverein, 220

Procacci, Giuliano.
History of the Italian people. Translated from the
Italian by Anthony Paul. [1st U. S. ed.] New York, Har-
per & Row [1971, °1970]

394 p. 25 cm. $10.00

Translation of Storia degli Italiani.

1. Italy—History. I. Title.

237080 DG467.P7513 1971   945   78–127832
ISBN 0–06–013433–X   MARC

Library of Congress   71 [30–2]